JIHAD & CO.

Black Markets
and Islamist Power

AISHA AHMAD

OXFORD
UNIVERSITY PRESS

Oxford University Press is a department of the University of Oxford. It furthers
the University's objective of excellence in research, scholarship, and education
by publishing worldwide. Oxford is a registered trade mark of Oxford University
Press in the UK and certain other countries.

Published in the United States of America by Oxford University Press
198 Madison Avenue, New York, NY 10016, United States of America.

CIP data is on file at the Library of Congress
ISBN 978–0–19–065677–5

3 5 7 9 8 6 4 2
Printed by Sheridan Books, Inc., United States of America

For Baba

Contents

Acknowledgments

IN THE MANY years devoted to making this book, I have incurred an enormous debt of gratitude. This manuscript is the end result of a collective global effort: from the fieldwork to the final revisions, I was blessed to inherit the experiences and insights of countless people who invested in the telling of this story. They are the heart of this book and its most beautiful features. Its flaws and failings are mine alone.

At its core, this work would not have been possible without my extraordinary colleagues overseas. In Afghanistan, I received immense support from Gul Mohammad Gulzai, Ahmad Jan Nawzadi, and Nasir Ahmad Nawidy. I was also fortunate to learn from several former members of the original Taliban movement. I am especially grateful to Mullah Abdul Salam Zaeef, who not only kindly shared his experiences with me but also critically reviewed my argument for accuracy. I am deeply touched that Mullah Wakil Ahmed Mutawakkil made the time, while recovering from illness, to clarify the empirical details of important historical events of the Taliban era. I am also greatly indebted to Sayed Rahmatullah Hashemi for making line-by-line scholarly comments on my Afghanistan chapters, based on his incredible insider's knowledge of the early Taliban government. I am honored by their generosity.

In Pakistan, I give special thanks to the former commissioners of Afghan refugees Abdullah Sahib and Rustam Shah Mohmand, as well as Khalid Rahman and his outstanding team at the Institute for Policy Studies in Islamabad, who organized workshops, focus groups, and seminars in support of my research. I also thank Professor Adnan Sarwar Khan and Professor Qibla Ayaz of the University of Peshawar; Professor Khan Bahadar Marwat of the Agricultural University, Peshawar; Professor Rasul Bakhsh Rais of the Lahore University of Management Sciences; and Asif Gul and Sohail Ahmad for their research assistance. I am grateful to several members of the Pakistani military and intelligence communities, including Lieutenant General Asad Durrani and General Ali Jan Aurakzai for their candid accounts of Pakistan's involvement in Afghanistan, and to the late Director-General Hamid Gul for his unparalleled insights. My prayers and thanks also go to the late Colonel Imam, who spent countless hours telling me his stories of the Afghan jihad and the Taliban.

For my Somalia research, I was fortunate to have equally outstanding colleagues. I am deeply indebted to Professor Yahya H. Ibrahim of Mogadishu University, who provided me with a no-holds-barred education on the economics of state failure. I am grateful to Dr. Ibrahim Farah of the University of Nairobi, who trained me in field methods, traveled with me to the unruly Somali border regions, and led the survey team in Eastleigh, composed of three outstanding research assistants: Jabril Warsame, Sagal Jama, and Abdikadir Mohamoud. I thank Jabril Abdulle from the Center for Research and Dialogue–Somalia for his support of the survey work and for many hours of constructive discussions on Somali politics. I extend my gratitude to Matt Bryden for his invaluable insights on clan networks and insurgency, Sahal Abdulle for his support of my field research in southern Somalia, and Liban Cashuur for facilitating my meetings in Somaliland. My dear friend Shelley Saywell generously shared her raw documentary film footage with me so that I could better bring my reader into remote Somali communities. I also express my deepest appreciation to Dr. Hawa Abdi and Dr. Deqo Mohamed for taking time away from their extraordinary, life-saving humanitarian work in the Afgooye corridor to assist with this academic research.

My excellent colleagues also facilitated my meetings in both Lebanon and Mali. I thank Gry Synnevåg and Soumaila Guindo for their tremendous assistance in Bamako, and thanks also to Amir Abdul Reda for his energetic work in arranging my meetings in Beirut and the Beqaa Valley. To those colleagues around the world who assisted me in the field but requested anonymity, thank you for your kindness and hospitality.

In making this book, I gratefully acknowledge the generous financial support from the Norwegian Research Council, which supported both my fieldwork and writing process. Furthermore, because I began this work as a doctoral candidate, I also acknowledge the support I received for my dissertation from the Canadian Social Sciences and Humanities Research Council, the Security and Defence Forum of the Canadian Department of National Defence, the Canadian International Development Research Centre, the Center on International Cooperation at New York University, and the Horowitz Foundation for Social Policy.

Throughout the writing stage, I benefited from the sharp insights of Steve Saideman, David Welch, and Stuart Soroka. I wrote the first draft as a fellow at the Belfer Center for Science and International Affairs at the Harvard Kennedy School, where I received helpful feedback from Steven Miller, Sean Lynn-Jones, Monica Duffy Toft, Kelly Greenhill, Annie Tracy Samuel, Joshua Shifrinson, Peter Krause, Sarah Bush, Michael Beckley, Ahsan Butt, and Melissa Willard-Foster. My colleagues Daniel Douek, Theodore McLauchlin, and Christopher Anzalone also offered very useful comments. My department at the University of Toronto then generously funded a book manuscript workshop for me, where I received helpful advice from Ed Schatz, Lucan Ahmad Way, Louis Pauly, Antoinette Handley, Jacques Bertrand, Matthew Hoffmann, Paul Kingston, and Stathis Kalyvas. Roger Hayden provided wonderful comments on an earlier draft, which made the writing significantly better.

In revising the penultimate version, I was fortunate to receive razor-sharp critical feedback from Barnett Rubin, Peter Andreas, Will Reno, and Stig Jarle Hansen. My research assistants were essential at this stage: Ajmal Burhanzoi blessed the final draft with his phenomenal insights from Afghanistan; Swilai Burhan and Sahra Togone assisted with translation of documents in multiple languages; Fazan Baig and Zabikhulla Yari reviewed the text and footnotes for clarity; and Christopher David LaRoche and Lucas Ria proofread the final draft. In bringing the project to completion, I am profoundly grateful to my editor David McBride and the fantastic production team at Oxford University Press for their meticulous line-by-line comments, enthusiasm for my research, and commitment to sharing these stories with the world.

Throughout this long process, I received an abundance of personal support that made it possible for me to produce this work. My primary care physician, Dr. Raymond Rupert, helped me to manage the plethora of health challenges that accompanied my fieldwork. I extend a special thank you to Ann Olson, Troy Goodfellow, and Faisal Ahmad for supporting me throughout this journey and reading multiple drafts of my chapters. I was well loved by Emily Agard, Mary Ann West, Kelly Rico, Jai Jayaraman, and the Petta family. I could not have asked for better and more stalwart friends.

Finally, this book is dedicated to my father, the only person I know who truly understands the rigors of academic research and the intrigues of the black market. Long ago, he forsook my grandfather's smuggling business and chose a life of books, science, and penury. As I embarked on this project, my father accompanied me on my field research in Afghanistan and Pakistan, as my *mahram*, cultural interlocutor, and colleague. He used his immense professional, personal, and family networks to ensure that I had access to every institution and interview subject that was necessary for the completion of the work. He coached me ahead of challenging interviews and events, debriefed me after major successes and setbacks in the field, and ensured my security in insecure places. In remote and rough regions, he took care of me when I was hungry, angry, lonely, tired, and sick. We fought constantly. The truth is, however, that I could never have known this much about either smuggling or jihad without my father. We are thus bound, not just by blood, but by these painfully bittersweet pages that have defined our journey together.

The book is a tribute to our love. All is forgiven.

Introduction

THE FASHION CHOICES on display in Hamar Weyne market in downtown Mogadishu were painfully retrograde. Strolling through the colorful clothing shops, I ran my fingers through rows of monochrome nylon and polyester blend fabrics, sewn in the same uniform style worn since the outbreak of the civil war. In each of these stores, the only available options of *khimar*—the long hijab worn by most Somali women—were cut from heavy and unbreathable cloths. The 2013 spring collection was disappointingly dull.

As the noonday sun grew hot, I turned to my friend and said, "Here, feel my hijab." As she drew near, I handed her the end of my soft headscarf, a thin weave of black cotton with embroidered pink roses. She rubbed the cloth between her thumb and index finger, carefully studying its texture and weight.

"Wow, this is nice. Where did you get it?"

"It's from Pakistan," I replied. "Very light and cool."

"You can't find anything like this in Mogadishu," she mused, fanning herself in the sweltering heat. Her thick polyester headscarf weighed heavily in the midday sun. "There are some Chinese cottons on sale in Bakara, but yours is much better. A lot of women would prefer this one."

"Well, if you think there is demand, I can arrange to ship a container from Karachi," I offered. "Besides, Pakistani markets are weak right now, and business in Somalia is booming. So, we could buy low and sell high. If you can hustle the shipment from Mogadishu Port, we might get a good profit."

"I can handle Mogadishu Port," she said confidently. As a Somali humanitarian doctor, my friend had decades of experience navigating emergency medical supplies through the seaports and checkpoints. "But can this style be worn in al-Shabaab territory?" she prudently asked. "Remember, the Islamists still have a lot of power, so it has to be an Islamic dress."

"Not to worry, this is one hundred percent sharia-compliant," I quipped with a wink. "I've worn this style across Taliban-held areas with no problems.

IMAGE 1.1 Shopping with Dr. Deqo Mohamed in the fabric district of Hamar Weyne market in downtown Mogadishu, Somalia.

Besides, you didn't even notice that mine was a different cloth until you studied the fabric."

"Good point. Let's check out the other markets to see what the competition looks like, and do an assessment." She paused, and then looked at me with a smile. "If this works, we could make a lot of money."

"Sounds like fun," I laughed, putting my hand on my friend's shoulder as we wove through the winding streets. "We can be the hijab queens of Mogadishu."

MY BREEZY PAKISTANI fabrics never did make it into Mogadishu's markets. As the insurgency flared, my doctor friend had patients to heal, and my academic research kept me too busy to keep up with the latest hijab trends from the runways of Istanbul and Jakarta. Somalia's bazaars thus remain flooded with monotonous polyesters, leaving the opportunity ripe for a bold entrepreneur with a keen fashion sense. For us, however, the moment has passed.

The truth is, despite the thrills and temptations of the bazaar, I have always chosen to be an observer and researcher, not a businesswoman. This book began as a search for understanding in the most volatile and war-torn parts of the Muslim world. Across vast geographic, linguistic, and cultural distances, I watched as jihadist groups rose in seemingly ungovernable spaces, building powerful proto-state polities out of the rubble of civil war, fueled by moneys secretly channeled from the bazaar. My research took me on a decade-long journey, from sunny seaports to rowdy arms bazaars, to uncover exactly how the war economy fueled these conflict processes. Throughout my studies, I was compelled by a key puzzle: Why are Islamists able to build such wealth and power, when so many other armed groups try and fail?

In searching for answers, I prayed behind Islamists in the mosque and then sipped chai with their financiers in the market. I discovered that the local war economy plays an instrumental role in the success of militant Islamist groups; but how could the practical, nonideological business interests of the bazaar possibly end up supporting hyperideological jihadists? Why did these seemingly opposing interests end up as symbiotic? By looking beyond the obvious ideological and identity-based explanations, my research uncovered a powerful, hidden economic logic behind this business-Islamist alliance. It turns out that the reason the bazaar chose to support jihad was surprisingly simple: the Islamists had lowered their costs.

This book tells the story of why and how business and political interests collude in civil wars across the Muslim world, leading to an unexpected rise in Islamist power. The characters in this story are a sundry lot. Some of them are rich business tycoons sitting poolside at five-star hotels, negotiating multimillion-dollar deals on their cell phones. Others are hustlers, drug dealers, and gunrunners, all trying to make a quick buck in the middle of a war zone. The story tells of doped-up militiamen arguing over their makeshift checkpoints with AK-47s and women and children fleeing their abuse. There are egotistical warlords, rugged field commanders, and masterfully cunning intelligence officials who carry forward the plot. And of course, there are the Islamists, preaching religious revivalism as the solution to the world's problems. This book brings together these seemingly disparate characters to tell the story of how business interests have fueled the rise of Islamist groups in civil wars across the Muslim world.

The only way to tell this story is to enter these worlds at the ground level. Understanding the financial origins of this Islamist power necessarily requires a journey into these volatile civil war economies. From afar, chronic civil wars look desperately poor and politically hopeless, trapped in repetitive cycles of violence and futility. From the inside, however, these are dynamic environments, full of both peril and potential. Even in the direst circumstances, human beings find ways to build friendships, tell jokes, solve problems, and trade goods. To survive under these conditions, one must be creative and adaptive, responding to strife and lack with resourcefulness and resilience. There is hardship, but also hope.

Nowhere is this energy more evident than at the local bazaar. Amid deadly violence, the instinct to buy and sell permeates human affairs. The marketplace in a war zone is an incredibly lively space, where people from all walks of life congregate in pursuit of their individual fortunes. These streets are raucous with noisy haggling, honking traffic, and stereos blasting pop music. There are arms depots, confectioneries, and clothing shops. Even when the state dies, these markets live on.

"If you want to test it, fire in that direction," offered the gunmaker in a Pakistani tribal area. "These are the best replicas, even better than the Chinese models."

"Come try my halvah!" called the owner of a local sweet shop, offering a sample of his treats. "It's the sweetest in all of Mogadishu."

"You want Byzantine artifacts?" asked the antiquities smuggler, hustling stolen treasures out of Iraq and Syria. "If you're interested, we have bigger ones off-site."

"That color is very popular with young ladies these days," coaxed the dress tailor in Peshawar. "It is so lovely on you that I will give you a special price."

This electricity of the bazaar can be felt in conflict zones around the world. The buzz of commerce transcends culture, language, and geography and connects street merchants to large conglomerates. The bazaar is much more than just a place of exchange, however; it is a window into the very heart of these conflict zones. On every price tag, whether on a bazooka or a sack of sugar, are the embedded costs of war.

As the stories in this book reveal, the arms dealer, confectioner, antiquities smuggler, and dress tailor all have a unique ability to transform their security environment in surprising and unexpected ways. Within these seemingly unruly markets, there is a powerful economic logic that shapes the preferences and choices of the local business class. As these economic actors respond to the conditions of civil war, they also act as agents of social and political change. In the Muslim world, the business class can even drive the creation of a new Islamist political order out of enduring chaos.

This book is the culmination of a long and intimate journey through these conflict-affected markets, which began years before I became an academic. In many ways, I was born to tell this story. From playing in rowdy arms bazaars to trekking through rugged mountain passes in the Pakistan-Afghanistan border region, some of my earliest childhood memories are of smuggling and violent conflict. Many of my extended family members were prominent actors in the secret cross-border trading business throughout the Soviet-Afghan War (1979–1989), the Afghan civil war (1992–1996), and the early Taliban era (1994–1998). The relationship between private business and political conflict was part of our everyday life experience and shaped our physical and emotional reality.

My grandfather was the toughest, shrewdest businessman I have ever met. A veritable godfather of the smuggling industry in the Pashtun border region, he hosted powerful local mafias, Afghan commanders, and elite Pakistani officials at his opulent mansion in suburban Peshawar. These family networks afforded me with unadulterated access to the private dinner table conversations of these elites in my youth. I learned the details of the secret deals between these powerful players and overheard far too many of their shouting matches. Their outrageous escapades, both the hilarious and the terrifying, add color to the pages of this book and give a rare, intimate look at the intersection between business and civil war. There were kidnappings, gunfights, suitcases full of cash, and absolutely shocking levels of domestic violence. Woven into the analysis are vivid descriptions of family homes, interpersonal relationships, and volatile emotional worlds. These stories are my sole inheritance.

Understanding the relationship between violent conflict and illicit trade therefore came naturally to me. As a young researcher interested in political conflict in the Muslim world, my first job took me to East Africa in 2004 to work with a local peacebuilding research center. Landing in Nairobi, I instinctively gravitated to the bustling Somali refugee community in the congested Eastleigh neighborhood. I felt comfortable in the noisy smugglers' bazaars and made fast friends with hustling entrepreneurs from Mogadishu. Thousands of miles across the Indian Ocean, my conversations with Somali traders were remarkably reminiscent of my grandfather's dinner table. Sometimes our exchanges would digress from the research and turn to fanciful business ideas that could potentially make us all rich. From the logic to the laughter, the smuggling world was familiar territory. But despite these gregarious moments, like the prospect of selling Pakistani hijabs in Hamar Weyne market, I chose to observe the business community rather than to practice. My experiences in Peshawar were sobering enough for a lifetime.

Nonetheless, it was somewhat befitting that the first research project I conducted in East Africa focused on regional arms smuggling networks. To learn the ropes, I teamed up with two ambitious young Somali scholars who knew the field well. The arms trade in Somalia was an obvious nexus between business and conflict—a relationship I had already witnessed in Peshawar during the 1980s' Soviet-Afghan War. My teammates helped me identify similar patterns in Somalia, and together we traced illicit gunrunning networks in East Africa from Mogadishu, through the Somali badlands, and across the Ethiopian and Kenyan borders to local criminal organizations.

"We sell [these guns] for about USD$350," explained a young gun salesman in Bula Hawa, a remote Somali border town next to Kenya and Ethiopia. "[The net profit is] about USD$150, or USD$200 for the best ones. [We get them from] the center, Hamar [Mogadishu] the capital city, and also Baidoa. We sell them openly at houses, like you see now," he said, showcasing his collection of assault rifles. "But there is also the option of black-market purchases. [But] I'm an entrepreneur, a businessman," he smiled widely. "I can sell cars . . . there are many options. I can sell anything; Somalis can break apart a rock and sell it."[1]

The economic rationale behind the arms trade was easy to understand, but the human costs were also unavoidable. "I would actually like to leave this business," said an older Somali dealer, who had been in the business since the start of the civil war. "But under the circumstances, we are left with no choice but to pursue this business to support our children and families. Why would we sell these things that kill people if we had other jobs we could do? I would definitely leave [the arms trade] if there were better ways to make a living."[2]

Even though their livelihoods depended on the conflict, most Somali gunrunners hoped for a political solution that would put an end to the cycle of violence. Their stories reminded me of the arms dealers in the Pakistani border region, many of whom felt the same way. "My family [was] famous for manufacturing ammunition, and my uncle was as much an expert as anyone," explained a young Afghan man. "I used to help him by polishing this or that. But he didn't see a future in it, so he didn't reveal a lot of his skills to us. He didn't want any of his kids to get into [the arms business]."[3]

The truth was that everyone, including these gunrunners, had suffered a personal tragedy: a mother, a child, a friend. They all had loved ones who had disappeared or been raped or killed. The psychological and emotional consequences of living under conditions of prolonged civil strife were grave. The scars of war were everywhere.

After nearly four decades of war in Afghanistan, every family has a story of terrible personal loss. "There were about 12 of them all carrying Kalashnikov rifles with their faces covered," recalled a father from Kabul. "They asked us to give them our daughter. We refused. One of them then lifted his Kalashnikov and shot my daughter dead in front of our eyes. She was only 20 and was just about to finish her high school. We buried her body."[4]

The emotional devastation is similar across war-torn Somalia. "We left after several bombs were dropped near my house," explained a mother who fled from Mogadishu to the Gedo region. "Four of my children are with me now, but two of my children are still missing. I still have no idea where they are. Now we are facing diseases. . . . We have no food. We are just waiting for God and the Muslim umma [to help us]."[5]

Faced with these miserable conditions, finding a resolution to the political crisis becomes the popular obsession of everyone living in a civil war. To make sense of their own tragedies, people naturally seek out an explanation for their grief. Understanding the origins of the conflict is part of that mental process, as individuals try to reconcile their personal horrors with their worldviews. *Why did this happen? Who is responsible? How will it ever end?* These questions are all very human.

People in the midst of crisis often turn to prayer. When faced with calamity and loss, a person's spiritual beliefs can provide a vital source of succor and hope. In the Muslim world, however, religion also offers a powerful metanarrative to explain human tragedies, both on an intimate level and on the global stage. For many believers, Islamic histories and prophecies not only provide a framework for understanding personal suffering but also suggest a solution to modern political failures. Faced with the darkness of enduring civil war, many pray that Islam may light the path to peace.

Beyond this emotional and spiritual rhetoric, however, there is much debate among Islamists on exactly *how* religion can help solve specific security crises. My conversations with political Islamists and their supporters on these issues were deeply thoughtful and detailed. Across the Muslim world, I spoke with scholars, activists, and religious leaders of many different stripes. Referring back to a classical approach to the Sunni Islamic sciences, including *Tawheed* (monotheism), *Aqidah* (creed), and *Fiqh* (jurisprudence), we discussed the authenticity and interpretation of various Hadith (prophetic statements) and debated the merits of competing approaches on historical and juridical grounds.[6] There is both an art and a science of conversation within these religio-cultural communities; knowledge of both is necessary to participate in these closed-door discussions.

At first blush, these Islamists seem to have very little in common with the hustlers in the bazaar. A closer investigation, however, reveals an indisputable connection. By engaging with both smugglers and Islamists, I observed the hidden nexus of business and Islamist interests that emerges in contemporary civil wars. What we are witnessing in the modern Muslim world is an unexpected mechanism through which Islamist and business elites come together to create a new form of political order out of disorder. Indeed, the emergence of new Islamist proto-state polities constitutes an unusual but powerful type of contemporary state formation taking place across the Muslim world.[7]

My research identified a two-staged dynamic that explains this business-Islamist relationship: first, the business community adopts an Islamist identity to mitigate uncertainty and improve access to markets; second, the business community collectively shifts its material support to a new Islamist faction, based on the belief that this will lower costs. This two-staged dynamic produces a powerful business-Islamist alliance, which gives birth to a new Islamist proto-state. By exploring this strategic relationship between the mosque and the market through an extended journey into the field, this book promises to shed much-needed light on the financial origins of Islamist power.

A Note on Concepts

In putting forward this analysis, there are a number of contentious concepts that first require clarification. To start, I define the Islamist proto-state narrowly as a nascent political entity that features a primitive near-monopolization of force, consolidation of territorial control within or across state borders, a hierarchical religio-political leadership with repressive capabilities over its populations, and rudimentary governing institutions to enforce its rule of law.[8] The proto-state is more than just another warlord fiefdom, however; it is an emergent polity that can perform many but not all of the normal functions of a sovereign state.[9]

Of course, many critical observers have argued that there is nothing especially "Islamic" about many of these self-declared Islamists. To clarify, the term "Islamist" includes a diverse range of groups and movements, with a wide array of social objectives, organizational structures, and ideological contents, and does not refer to a single coherent set of beliefs or identities.[10] Across the Middle East, North and West Africa, and South Asia, Sunni Islamist groups have hailed from a wide range of traditions, from Deobandi to Ikhwani to Salafi-Jihadism.[11] These theological and ideological differences are substantive and meaningful, and they affect group membership, goals, and behavior.[12] This book is concerned with Islamist groups across this range of complex ideological differences.

Acknowledging this diversity, I begin by defining Islamist groups inclusively as substate political movements that utilize Islamic ideas, identity, symbols, and rhetoric and that espouse the re-creation of order on the basis of Islamic laws and institutions.[13] This initial definition, however, requires further refinement. Indeed, many political actors in the Muslim world utilize some degree of religious symbolism, including those that have no substantive religious agenda. A cursory or careless view could cause researchers to incorrectly categorize these other actors as Islamists. To distinguish Islamists from other groups, I therefore examine their internal identity structure, with a particular focus on their primary political objectives and membership criteria. In my analysis, I consider an Islamist group to be one that is principally defined by membership in the Muslim umma, the imagined conception of a universal Islamic nation that supersedes other substate identities, such as ethnicity, clan, and other categories of kinship.[14]

Because this book focuses specifically on civil wars, the Islamist groups in my analysis are actively involved in military and political competition, and I therefore also use the terms "jihad" and "jihadist" to describe these groups and their actions. Notably, there is an active debate within academic circles and among Muslim scholars about the meaning and scope of jihad.[15] To focus my analysis, I define "jihad" very narrowly as the use of military force for the purposes of advancing social or political causes that have an Islamist character, motivation, or mandate.[16] A jihadist group is thus an Islamist organization that uses organized, politicized violence to achieve goals, including but not limited to the creation of an Islamist political order.

To understand Islamist success, I compare these groups to the other leading factions that are primarily defined by ethnic, tribal, and clan identities. Although ethnicity, tribe, and clan are distinct categories, these terms have valuable conceptual overlap. In each category, membership is determined through collective ancestry and includes an element of nested identity.[17] Much of the ethnic conflict literature works across these subclassifications.[18] Building on this literature, I define an ethnic, tribal, or clan group inclusively as one that determines membership on the basis of lineage within a select kin group. I examine these kin groups with an understanding that these categories are multilayered and that subgroup identities, such as local subclan networks, are often more salient in political and military competition than in the larger group sets.[19]

Using these conceptual definitions, my research then compares the relative success of Islamists versus ethnic and clan warlords. Importantly, I use the term "warlord" without any intended pejorative connotations.[20] Acknowledging the spirited debate over this term, I employ a narrow definition of a warlord as a leader of a substate armed group that exercises control over a territory and patronage over a constituency within the boundaries of a sovereign state.[21] Accordingly, Islamist leaders that meet these criteria can also be conceptually categorized as warlords. I define ethnic or tribal warlords in this analysis, however, as exercising control over their own claimed ethnic or tribal territories and constituencies.

Notably, while some warlords do engage in business activities, I categorize them as political actors because they are primarily concerned with accruing political or military power. By contrast, businesspeople, including those engaged in criminal enterprises, are individuals concerned with economic, rather than political or military, gain.[22] I define "business" as for-profit commercial activity, so that traders, industrialists, telecommunications giants, and service providers alike may be included in this study. Of course, these businesspeople often have extensive regional ties and even global connections; nonetheless, I refer to these indigenous business actors as "local" in order to differentiate them from larger multinational corporations that work in conflict zones.

I consider a business community to be the collective body of individuals involved in these for-profit activities within a particular geographic space. Although it is not a definitional requirement that the business community be formally organized, I note that these elites do often create local business organizations and associations to facilitate and coordinate economic activities within their respective war economies and create order in these markets. I use the term "market" to connote both an actual space and an abstract conception: the bazaar is a physical marketplace where buyers and sellers congregate for the purposes of exchange; the prices of goods in the bazaar, however, are set by the invisible market forces created by supply and demand.

Finally, I also use the term "mafia" to describe some of these local business elites, which requires clarification. This word, which originally referred to specific Sicilian criminal organizations, has been used to describe criminal business networks in many other contexts. These business actors have been labeled "mafias" exactly because they have built organized, hierarchical enterprises that are rooted in family and other personal social networks and that engage in both licit and illicit activities.[23] From Somalia to Lebanon to Mali to Islamabad, virtually everyone I spoke to described the organized business networks operating in their areas as a "mafia." I use this term in that same spirit.

It is worth noting that business activities in conflict zones often involve a combination of licit and illicit types of industry, including smuggling, racketeering, narcotics sales, arms trading, and human trafficking. However, smuggling, by definition, is the movement of goods that evades the laws and borders of a state; so, in the absence of functioning state institutions, it is hard to distinguish this activity from normal trade.

In civil wars the conceptual boundaries between criminal and noncriminal categories are highly blurred, and it makes little sense to talk of illegality in lawless societies. Opium farmers in Kandahar also complained to me about lousy wheat crops, and arms traders in Bula Hawa expressed interest in possibly selling cars. The same businessman who imported life-saving medicine to hospitals also dominated the deadly counterfeit drug market out of Dubai. One of the biggest heroin smugglers in Pakistan once allegedly tried to build a blanket factory. And the head of a large Somali cigarette company made his first fortune by embezzling food aid during a famine crisis.

I found no clear evidence that involvement in criminality made businesspeople any more or less inclined to support Islamists over other factions. Quite a few were surprised and vexed later on, once these zealous jihadists banned their illicit activities on religious grounds. But before these unexpected outcomes were known, at the critical moment when these Islamists needed the business community to rally behind them to win the war, both the tea seller and the drug smuggler answered the call.

Preview of the Book

Looking ahead, this story brings the reader directly into the nexus of business and Islamist interests in order to explain the origins of the proto-state. Chapter 1 presents my two-staged argument and explains the rationale of the case studies. In the second chapter, I build my theoretical argument more substantively, delving deeply into how the two-staged dynamic works: first, how the business community strategically adopts an Islamist identity as a practical mechanism for building trust and reducing costs in the context of civil war; and second, why Islamists have the unique ability to court the valuable financial support of the local business elite at a critical juncture by offering better security at a lower price. I posit that these two mechanisms—the long-term Islamicization of the business class and the short-term strategic support for Islamists from the business elite—explain the rise of Islamist power in civil wars across the modern Muslim world.

The empirical chapters then explore this dynamic with detailed evidence from the Afghan and Somali cases. The third chapter examines the first process: the long-term Islamic identity construction within the smuggling industry in the Pakistan-Afghanistan border region. It chronicles why and how the Pakistan-Afghanistan trading community adopted an increasingly Islamist identity, starting from the Soviet-Afghan War (1979–1989), in order to increase trust, lower uncertainty, and advance its business interests. In chapter 4, I examine the second mechanism by evaluating how security costs affected the short-term strategic choices of these traders during the Afghan civil war period (1992–1996). Comparing every major armed faction in the Afghan civil war, I show that these cost calculations prompted the business class to shift its support at a critical juncture, pulling back its support from the ethnic warlords and investing in the new Taliban movement.

Next, I explore the same two processes in Somalia. In chapter 5, I unpack the reasons why Somali businesspeople turned to Islamist identity to lower their costs during the Somali civil war (1991–2007), leading to a long-term Islamicization of this business class. The evidence shows that Islam provided the Somali business elite with an effective way to increase trust across clan lines and also build relations with wealthy partners in Gulf States. In chapter 6, I investigate the second process; I evaluate how the Somali business community grew frustrated with the high security costs it was forced to pay to clan warlords during the civil war, driving its members to seek out an alternative. Measuring these costs, I show how the business class made the strategic choice to shift its support away from the clan warlords and invest in the new Islamic Courts Union movement.

After unpacking the financial drivers behind the rise of these Islamist proto-states, chapter 7 then addresses the colossal downfall of the Taliban and Islamic Courts Union, which in both cases resulted from large-scale international interventions. Reviewing the legacies of these interventions, I examine the rise of militant insurgencies that have emerged in the aftermath of the destruction of these proto-states and the struggles of the new internationally backed governments that took their place. Despite abundant international support, the chapter shows how these externally funded states have failed to create a level of order comparable to that created by their locally funded Islamist predecessors. Indeed, the evidence suggests that it was much easier for the international community to break these Islamist governments than it was for them to fund effective alternative governments in their place.

Looking beyond Afghanistan and Somalia, I then extend my analysis in chapter 8 to three other critical contemporary cases: the Middle East, North and West Africa, and South Asia. I investigate how business and Islamist interests colluded to help finance the rise of the so-called Islamic State (or Daesh) in Iraq and Syria, al-Qaeda in the Islamic Maghrib in northern Mali, and neo-Taliban factions in the Pakistan-Afghanistan border region. These mini case studies provide preliminary evidence on the financial origins of these jihadist groups, most especially their ties to the local business class. In the final chapter, I discuss the broader theoretical and political implications of the research. The conclusion highlights the important and underexplored connections between civil war and state formation, which point to new ways that the international community can best deal with these complex security threats in the future.

In the pages ahead, we follow the money from the bazaar to the battle-field to explain why Islamists are able to gain power in a political vacuum. As these jihadists raise their flags and declare their holy wars, it may appear as though zealotry has vanquished all rationality. Do not be fooled. Underneath the fiery religious rhetoric is the cold, hard cash of the underground economy. Amid the anarchy, the logic of the market prevails.

I

Mosques and Markets

The Prophet Muhammad (peace be upon him) said: "The most beloved places on Earth to Allah are its mosques, and the most despised places on Earth to Allah are its markets."

SAHIH HADITH, narrated by Muslim

BY THE SUMMER of 1993, Afghanistan's civil war had spilled over into neighboring Pakistan. The winding bazaars in the border city of Peshawar were stocked with assault rifles, rocket-propelled grenades, and antitank weapons left over from the Soviet campaign. In the alleyways of nearby Darra Adam Khel, customers could find a spectacular assortment of ordnance in the mud-brick workshops that specialized in locally manufactured replicas. The streets teemed with militiamen and peddlers in a clamorous racket of haggling, gunfire, and traffic. Peshawar was the main entrepôt servicing the underground Afghan war economy. During the day, wealthy Pakistani smugglers and rugged Afghan commanders cut deals, using suitcases of cash to hustle weapons, drugs, and ammunition. At night, the city was raucous and alit.

Poverty was rampant in the refugee camps, but business was booming in the bazaars. In the noisy streets, small players sold everything from bullets and radios to suture kits; the biggest contracts, however, were negotiated privately in the suburban courtyard mansions of Peshawar's most powerful tycoons. Battle-weathered Afghan militiamen would arrive at the doors of these private estates in heavily armed trucks and jeeps, but only the lead commander and a handful of aides could enter. Seated on plush Persian rugs beneath glittering chandeliers, AK-47s politely resting off to the side, traders and commanders would sip tea, smoke cigarettes, and negotiate for much-needed supplies. These meetings were usually quiet and polite, interrupted only by the call to prayer. Once a deal was struck, the trucks drove back across the unruly border.

Back in Afghanistan, Burhanuddin Rabanni's largely Tajik Jamiat-i-Islami Party and Gulbuddin Hekmatyar's predominantly Pashtun Hizb-i-Islami faction had shelled the capital city of Kabul nearly to ruins. After the decade-long Soviet-Afghan War, the anticommunist guerrillas of the mujahideen had turned against each other in a brutal civil war. Seven major factions fought over the countryside, each representing a distinct ethnic or tribal group. These rival factions ravaged entire villages with systematic campaigns of ethnic cleansing and rape aimed at civilian populations. Millions of Afghan refugees languished in crowded, underserviced camps. Pakistan and other neighboring states chose favorites among the seven leading commanders, using the refugee and smuggling networks to pump money and guns back across the border.

Multiple internationally sponsored ceasefire initiatives were attempted to put an end to ethnogenocidal campaigns, but to no avail. The warlords all made lofty promises of peace while standing before the holiest Islamic sites in Mecca, swearing to work together for a brighter future. They broke their oaths almost immediately upon returning to Afghanistan. The result was an enduring civil war stalemate between deeply entrenched ethnic factions, with no end in sight.

Out of this seemingly endless cycle of violence, however, Afghanistan's future took a striking and unexpected turn. In the spring of 1994, a ragtag group of Islamist militiamen calling themselves the Taliban emerged out of a remote village in Kandahar Province and demanded an end to the violent excesses of the ethnic warlords. Within a span of mere months, these puritanical Islamist newcomers seized power in the southern and eastern provinces of Afghanistan before turning their gaze toward the west and north of the country. They were organized, disciplined, and surprisingly well-resourced. Within two years they had captured the majority of the countryside and routed their rivals. By 1998, the Taliban had consolidated their reign over every major city in the Afghan state, enforcing a new, ultraconservative Islamist political agenda. Music, sports, and female education were all banned as the heavy silence of Taliban rule covered the countryside.

Meanwhile, four thousand kilometers away, a similar story was unfolding in another Muslim country. After the Somali government collapsed in 1991, scores of clan-based militias raided abandoned weapons depots in downtown Mogadishu for Soviet and American armaments left over from the Cold War. Gunrunning ships, covertly moored near Somalia's sandy white beaches, steadily pumped more munitions into the infamous Bakara arms market in the unruly capital city. Hawkers in the bazaars sold everything from antitank weapons to stolen food aid, shouting "*Harash*! *Harash*! [Sale! Sale!]," in a desperate effort to sell at any auctioned price.[1] Gunfire could be heard in the streets day and night.

By the mid-1990s, this boon of weapons and aid had given birth to a new Somali business elite, and Mogadishu became the primary smuggling conduit servicing the entire Horn of Africa.[2] While millions of refugees fled the violence and famine, Somalia's industry titans and tribal commanders could be found meeting at five-star luxury hotels in neighboring Nairobi and Dubai. The most powerful business magnates often struck deals sitting poolside, sipping mango juice and cappuccinos, far from the frontlines of conflict and without a weapon in sight. Over time, Mogadishu's millionaires built a powerful regional smuggling network based on a web of reciprocal agreements with competing warlords.

Inside Somalia, however, communities were torn apart by the tribal violence. Militias based on two dominant rival subclans from the Hawiye family, the Abgal and the Habr-Gidir, fought for control over the capital city, while Darod, Isaaq, and other clan communities either fled or were killed. As the conflict dragged on, the number of subclan factions proliferated, and tribal warlords carved the country into a motley assortment of privately held fiefdoms. Armed gangs roamed the streets in pickup trucks with mounted machine guns, high on khat, a local narcotic.

Somalia's famously exquisite coral stone architecture was shelled to rubble by the firefights. From afar, Mogadishu's devastation created the picturesque illusion of ancient Roman ruins; but on the ground, women and children desperately huddled together in the crumbling coliseums and arches. Along the Kenyan border, hundreds of thousands languished in cramped, scorching-hot refugee camps. Millions more were displaced inside the country, too poor or weak to flee. Over a dozen internationally sponsored peace processes were initiated. All failed.

For over a decade, Somalia appeared to be trapped in a hopeless stalemate. Yet much like the Afghan story, the Somali conflict also experienced a dramatic and unprecedented Islamist shift. In early 2006, a group of seemingly benign local Islamic courts in Mogadishu banded together to challenge the power of heavily entrenched clan warlords. Once again, the new Islamist movement proved surprisingly successful. By June of that year, the Islamic courts consolidated Mogadishu under one political authority for the first time since the collapse of the Somali state. Six months later, they had captured over 90 percent of the countryside. After fifteen years of continuous state collapse, the new Islamic Courts Union established the rule of law and created a functioning government in Somalia, almost overnight.

Despite originating in two of the most deeply divided parts of the world, both the Taliban and the Islamic Courts Union movements successfully created a striking degree of centralized, statelike power over their fragmented societies. In both cases, these Islamists broke an enduring stalemate and established a significant degree of control over the majority of their populations, a feat that none of their respective rivals could accomplish. Out of the rubble of civil war, they built surprisingly robust proto-states that were neither traditional tribal systems nor conventional authoritarian regimes. These new polities quickly filled the political vacuum, and re-created order from anarchy.

As a plethora of new jihadist groups raise their banners from the Pakistani mountains to the Malian desert, understanding this global phenomenon could not be more urgent. Why and how are Islamists able to create these relatively robust new polities out of the chaos of civil war? What explains the rise of these Islamist proto-states? To answer these questions, I explore the early genesis of the original Taliban movement in Afghanistan from 1994 to 1996 and the Islamic Courts Union in Somalia from 2004 to 2006, and then extend my analysis to explain the rise of more contemporary jihadist proto-states in Pakistan, Mali, Iraq, and Syria. In tracing the financial origins of these polities, my research uncovers the hidden economic logic that explains why traders, truckers, and tycoons strategically chose to support Islamists.

The Economic Logics of the Proto-State

Through my journey to the field, I discovered that the emergence of these modern Islamist proto-states is rooted in an interactive dynamic between business and Islamist interests, which evolves over time into a powerful relationship. My research uncovered two specific economic logics that explain this business-Islamist cooperation: the need for higher trust and lower costs. First, in the long term, the business community adopts an Islamist identity to increase social trust and access to markets, which sets the stage for an Islamist takeover; second, in the short term, business elites make the strategic calculation to shift support to Islamist groups that provide them with better protection at a lower price, thus funding the Islamists to seize control of the state. These two rational, economic motivations lay the foundation of the business-Islamist alliance on which the Islamist proto-state can be built.

First, all business relies on trust, and civil wars are low-trust environments of an extreme variety. Although civil wars create lucrative new opportunities in illicit business, ethnic and tribal conflict also results in worsened unpredictability, increased protection payments, and lost prospects. Social divisions also hike up transaction costs, limit access to markets, and prevent expansion of industry. In the Muslim world, however, Islam can provide a valuable source of social capital that cuts across these frustrating local divisions. To keep the wheels of industry turning, members of the business community can assert their Islamic identity as a practical way to build trust-based relationships with prospective partners and clients. Showcasing their Islamic identity effectively helps businesspeople to increase cooperation, reduce transaction costs, and gain access to markets across factional lines.

In states with high levels of ethnic and tribal fragmentation, this common Islamic identity can, over time, provide a mechanism that symbolically unites a divided population. This identity reconstruction takes the place of modern nationalism, which has weak roots in many postcolonial states. Although members of the business class may embrace their religious identity for instrumental purposes, over time these interactions cultivate a powerful relationship between business and Islam. In the long term, this Islamic identity creates an alternative framework for connecting nationhood to statehood in these contentious spaces.

Second, Islamists have a unique ability to lower the business community's security costs, which is akin to lowering taxes. In a civil war, security must be purchased from an array of substate armed groups, which can get very expensive for businesses. Within this competitive security environment, however, Islamists are able to offer lower overall costs to the business class. Consider that while ethnic and tribal warlords can only plausibly sell security to businesses from their own kin groups, Islamists can often offer protection across these divisions. Accordingly, because Islamists are able to sell their protection services to the entire business class, rather than to just a narrow kin group, they can lower security prices for a wider pool of consumers. Incentivized by these lower costs, the business class pulls out of its expensive and suboptimal relationships with ethnic warlords, and opts into the cheaper Islamist alternative. In order to keep up with the Islamist's surging revenues and balance against other rivals, the ethnic or tribal warlord is then compelled to more heavily extort his kin base, which only expedites his being inevitably priced out of the security market. In contrast, the Islamist appears to be offering a better-quality product at a lower cost. For the profit-minded CEO, funding the Islamists thus looks like a good strategy.

It is through this calculation of security costs that the material interests of the business community align with those of ideologically driven Islamists, leading to a powerful collective mobilization of the business class. The more business elites buy into the Islamist option, the further the Islamists can lower their security prices; much like the big-box chain that drives out the mom-and-pop shop, the Islamists begin to dominate the security market. Once this collective action reaches a tipping point, the momentum of the Islamists is virtually unstoppable.[3] This influx of support allows the Islamists to begin to monopolize the market for security provision and to bankrupt rival groups.[4] By courting the business community with these lower security prices, the Islamists win the security competition through an economy of scale. On the battlefield, this threshold effect produces a dramatic shift in the balance of power. With the widespread support of the business class, the Islamists break the civil war stalemate and reconstruct political power out of enduring fragmentation.

Though many factors affect success and failure in a civil war, these two economic logics underlie the business-Islamist alliance that gives birth to the proto-state. Turning to empirics, my research finds that this marriage between profit-driven business elites and ideologically motivated Islamists has repeatedly occurred in civil wars across the modern Muslim world, and consistently resulted in a dramatic rise in Islamist power. In present-day Syria and Iraq, extremist groups built strong ties with smuggling and criminal net-works, dominating trade routes, arms trafficking, and the black-market sale of oil and antiquities in their region.[5] In North and West Africa, al-Qaeda-affiliated networks dominated the multibillion-dollar illicit tobacco and narcotics industry. In Pakistan, local Taliban commanders extorted the local smuggling business and also participated in lucrative criminal activities of their own.

Despite evidence from these and other important cases, however, there has been no systematic academic research on the complex, nuanced interactions between the business world and militant Islamist groups. Security research-ers have recently discovered evidence that terrorist groups and transnational criminal organizations often rely on the same networks for their operations.[6] Some scholars have even asserted that crime and terror are indistinguishable, and thus treat these distinct categories as one and the same.[7] The view from the ground, however, shows that business and jihadist interests are highly dis-tinct. While the businessman accumulates earthly riches and pleasures in the here and now, the jihadist sacrifices both wealth and body to attain a glorious afterlife. These are strange bedfellows indeed. What explains their friendship? My conversations with both Islamists and business elites in these conflict zones offer a nuanced look at this crime-terror nexus and explain why and in what ways these two disparate sets of actors come together to forge a powerful symbiotic relationship.

This new business-Islamist story is consistent with what we already know about the logic of civil war economies. The existing literature shows that violent conflicts create and empower new mafias and industry titans.[8] We know that these types of economic actors matter. The Muslim world also has a very long history of using Islam for trade and commerce. Yet oddly, save for a small handful of scholars, most researchers have completely overlooked the local business class in jihadist conflicts.[9] To date, the relationship between Islamist groups and moneyed elites remains undertheorized in the civil war literature.

This oversight is peculiar because the existing scholarship on civil war economies teaches us that resources are critical to understanding insurgent group behavior and success. From Paul Collier and Anke Hoeffler, we know that natural resource endowments, especially of lootable resources, can prolong civil war.[10] The prolific resource curse literature also shows that a reliance on resource rents affects long-term state capacity[11] and can make the state more vulnerable to armed rebellion.[12] William Reno explains why contemporary warlord economics have serious state-destroying effects.[13] Peter Andreas uncovers how even well-meaning international interventions can inadvertently fund illicit war economies and sustain conflict.[14] Some scholars have argued that rebels are motivated by greed, while others contend that they are driven by grievance; however, virtually all of them agree that resources affect the duration, severity, and outcomes of violent conflicts.

In this book, we move beyond these older scholarly debates and engage with the political and economic actors on the ground. As their stories reveal, both the grievances of the jihadists and the greed of the business class shape the conflict environment in a reciprocal manner. Grievance is not a mask for greed, nor do economic interests drive all grievances. Rather, the jihadist and the CEO serve each other's distinct interests. These material and ideational interests are part of a symbiotic, interactive relationship, which fuels the rise of the Islamist proto-state.

An intimate understanding of the economic power players inside these conflict zones is essential for this work. Surprisingly, most existing civil war research overlooks the role and agency of local business actors and focuses instead on natural resource endowments.[15] Yet a civil war economy is much more than the measurement of available material resources; rather, it is an elaborate social world made up of living, breathing human beings, each of whom makes calculated choices amid chaotic violence. The participants in these civil war economies are sentient agents who make conscious and strategic choices to protect and advance their interests. From the commercial towers of Wall Street to the street merchants of Mogadishu, markets reflect the human instinct to "truck, barter, and trade."[16] All economic activity in conflict zones—whether aid distribution, arms trafficking, heroin smuggling, or precious gemstones mining—is managed by local economic actors. These business elites are not just a channel for material resources but are political players in their own right. These moneyed elites use their wealth to finance armed groups and transform conflict dynamics behind the scenes, thus determining the future and the fate of the political contenders who seemingly rule over them.

If money is all that matters, however, why then can't international interventions create political order in these unruly places? Indeed, the international community has spent hundreds of billions of dollars on complex, multidimensional state-building projects across the modern Muslim world, much more than anything the local business class could ever mobilize. Yet these multilateral efforts have largely failed to produce anything like self-sustaining sovereign states or even proto-states.[17] Rather, these costly initiatives have, at best, created fragile and corrupt governments or, in the worst cases, have provoked additional violent insurgencies. Why then have comparatively cash-strapped Islamist groups more often succeeded in capturing and creating statelike power, while these large-scale foreign interventions have failed?

The answer is that different sources of revenue produce different political outcomes. Previous research has already shown that states with an abundance of oil or other natural resources often remain weak and authoritarian. Looking at the Afghan case intently, Barnett Rubin finds that high levels of aid dependency in a government can produce similar rentier-state effects by alienating the state from its tax base.[18] Resource abundance also affects how armed groups treat their populations; Jeremy Weinstein finds that where an insurgent group gets its money shapes how violently it behaves.[19] Money does matter, but not simply in terms of the raw dollar amount. Foreign aid, natural resources, and extortion revenues all impact political relationships in different ways. International funding and natural resource endowments cannot replicate the relationship between citizen and state created when a population pays for its own protection through taxation. That process of state formation is fundamentally endogenous and cannot be created from the outside-in or the top-down.

In this book, I argue that Islamists are uniquely positioned to catalyze this endogenous process of order creation. From North Africa to the Middle East to South Asia, a plethora of Islamist groups have successfully constructed new polities to fill the void of state failure. Out of enduring civil war stalemates, Islamist newcomers around the world have bested their rivals on the battlefield and established their rule of law over seemingly ungovernable spaces. These proto-states reflect a new form of order-making taking place in the most troubled and fragmented parts of the Muslim world.

To understand these theoretical processes, I followed the money behind these Islamist proto-states. Afghanistan and Somalia provided a particularly useful lens to explore this contemporary phenomenon, because most modern jihadist groups are rapidly evolving cases. As complete stories, the original Taliban and Islamic Courts Union movements provided a valuable historical window into the financial origins of modern Islamist power.

Journey to the Field

My research for this book took me from crowded smugglers' bazaars to rugged mountain passes in search of these hidden connections between the mosque and the market. The poverty I witnessed in these places was devastating. A woman in Kandahar begged me to save her dying infant, imagining that I could somehow keep her near-skeletal baby alive. In Mazar-e-Sharif, I watched barefoot kids play in a blown-out tank like it was a jungle gym. At a refugee camp in Hargeisa, a father wept in front of me over children he lost to the famine, starved to death in his arms. Undocumented Syrian refugees shared their traumas with me in crowded camps, weak and exhausted by years of war and hunger. Most people living in these broken societies are desperately poor and have no power to change their circumstances.

Journeying into these conflict zones, however, I show how these civil wars are remarkably dynamic business environments. Behind the horrifying images of hunger and desolation, war zones also have an unexpected opulence. In fact, the absence of the rule of law creates lucrative opportunities in tax- and regulation-free trade and a plethora of new criminal activities. The business classes that emerge out of these environments not only profit from the violence but also play a critical role in how it unfolds. The suffering in the refugee camps is inextricably linked to the secret intrigues of the business tycoon in his gated and guarded estate.

To understand their stories of both fortune and failure, I met with powerful CEOs and smugglers in Peshawar, Kabul, Nairobi, Mogadishu, Hargeisa, and Dubai, and learned how these elites do business in the high-risk context of civil war. The research that went into this book required many years of intensive field study. I spent months in the smugglers' bazaars in northwest Pakistan, and interviewed traders and smugglers about their experiences during various stages of the war. While stationed at Peshawar University,

I traveled across the winding and historic Khyber Pass through the mountainous tribal belt, the key transit conduit connecting Pakistani and Afghan markets. In Kandahar, I interviewed traders, farmers, and ex-combatants involved in smuggling and the opium industries about their economic and political conditions. In Islamabad, I sat down with the highest-ranking Pakistani intelligence agents, including those who were directly responsible for supplying armed groups in Afghanistan, and with members of the original Taliban movement involved in fundraising and financial management.

In Nairobi and Mogadishu, I talked to leaders of the early Islamic Courts Union movement, as well as the clan warlords who fought against them. I met with scores of business elites, militia commanders, and political power players who shaped Somalia's destiny for over two decades. I slept under the stars in the Dadaab refugee camp when tracking covert arms-smuggling routes into the Horn of Africa and then flew to Dubai to meet with trading tycoons at posh hotels. To understand their stories, I also surveyed over a thousand members of the Somali business community across clan divisions about their interests, identities, and political preferences. For details on my research process, I provide a comprehensive discussion of my methodology, case selection, field research, survey design, and the security and ethical challenges of the work in the appendix of this book.[20]

My analysis is based on both cross-case and within-case comparisons. I use the substate armed faction as the unit of analysis to uncover why Islamists were able to seize political power in these civil war competitions while other groups with similar characteristics and endowments failed to do so. In Afghanistan, I compared the dominant armed political groups in Afghanistan during the 1992–1996 civil war period: Burhanuddin Rabbani's Jamiat-i-Islami (Islamic Society of Afghanistan), Gulbuddin Hekmatyar's Hizb-i-Islami-Gulbuddin (HIG, Islamic Party–Gulbuddin), Maulvi Khalis's Hizb-i-Islami-Khalis (HIK, Islamic Party–Khalis), Abdul Rasool Sayyaf's Ittehad al-Islami (Islamic Union), Mohammad Nabi Mohammadi's Harakat-i-Inqilab-i-Islami (Islamic Revolutionary Party), Abdul Ali Mazari's Hizb-i-Wahdat-i-Islam-i-Afghanistan (Islamic Unity Party of Afghanistan), General Rashid Dostum's Junbesh-i-Milli (National Movement), Pir Sayed Ahmed Gailani's Mahaz-i-Milli-i-Islami-i-Afghanistan (National Islamic Front of Afghanistan), Sighbatullah Mojaddedi's Jebhe-i-Nejat-i-Milli (National Liberation Front), and Mullah Muhammad Omar's Taliban.

For Somalia, I investigated the leading armed groups throughout the 1991 to 2007 Somali civil war period, with special attention to the dominant warlord–led political alliances and Islamist-led opposition movements.

Specifically, I compare the late 1990s coalition of Islamic courts, the 2000–2004 clan-based Transitional National Government (TNG), the 2004–2007 warlord-run Transitional Federal Government (TFG), and the 2004–2006 Islamic Courts Union (ICU) movement. I also consider three other notable Somali Islamist groups: Hassan Dahir Aweys' militant Salafi group al-Ittihaad al-Islamiyya, the Islamist Sufi faction Ahle Sunna Waljama', and the nonviolent, Muslim Brotherhood–affiliated group Harakat al-Islah.[21]

Of all these groups, only the Taliban and ICU managed to create statelike power out of their respective civil war stalemates. The conventional wisdom in the existing literature suggests that the success of these Islamists must be due to religious convictions, tribal sympathies, or foreign ties. In both the Afghan and Somali theaters, however, all of these competitive armed factions were ideologically motivated, tribally organized, and externally backed. It was therefore possible for me to compare each of these armed groups based on each of these dimensions, and thus evaluate the prevailing wisdoms. By tracking these armed factions over time, I was able to examine my business-Islamist explanation against these competing arguments, using detailed evidence from the field. For this reason, the Afghan and Somali cases provided me with a fruitful opportunity for comparison.

It is worth noting that as two of the most fragmented societies in the modern world, Afghanistan and Somalia were particularly hard cases for testing my economic argument. Considering how poor and violent these countries are, these were difficult cases in which to apply a rational, economic model. Furthermore, given the intensity of ethnic and tribal hostilities in these war zones, Afghanistan and Somalia should have been especially tough cases for Islamist success. The bar for success was also incredibly high; in spaces where lawlessness abounds, it is a tremendous feat for any group to create a semblance of centralized political order.

Yet as my analysis shows, in both conflicts the intersection of business and Islamist interests created a striking shift on the battlefield that led to the creation of centralized, statelike power, in ways that other well-funded interventions simply could not. The Afghan and Somali cases are hardly outliers; rather, they are paradigmatic cases that have broad relevance for civil war–affected Muslim countries. Because the Taliban and Islamic Courts Union are modern historical cases, however, I was able to conduct an in-depth investigation on a decidedly contemporary phenomenon, without the frustration of chasing current events. By closely comparing these substate armed groups, the empirical evidence thus shows that local business support is a critical missing variable that helps explain why Islamists succeed in creating order when other comparable groups fail.

I then extend my analysis to three other cases: the Middle East, North and West Africa, and South Asia. To understand these conflicts, I traveled from the smugglers' bazaars in Beirut to the grand mosque in Bamako, speaking with scholars and practitioners who are tracking these war economies at the ground level. In doing so, I specifically examined the economic foundations of the dominant jihadist group in each conflict theater. I discovered that the rise of jihadist power was intrinsically related to the interests of the local business class. The evidence from these cases shows that the intersection between secular business elites and ideological Islamists produces the same effects across vastly different linguistic, ethnic, and cultural spaces throughout the Muslim world.

Demystifying the Proto-State

As Islamist groups stake their claims in war zones around the Muslim world, the need for new research on the origins of the proto-state is urgent. In northwest Pakistan, Tehrik-i-Taliban (TTP) factions have established radical jihadist fiefdoms throughout the restive tribal areas. Al-Shabaab continues to hold territory across southern Somalia and has extended its reach into northern Kenya. In North and West Africa, al-Qaeda in the Islamic Maghreb has embedded itself in local tribal networks and expanded its reach across the Sahel region. In the Middle East, the so-called Islamic State claims to have established a Sunni caliphate across Iraq and Syria and has extended its ideological reach as far as Libya and Afghanistan. The extremist group Boko Haram, which controls large swaths of territory in northern Nigeria, has also pledged allegiance to the purported caliphate and declared itself a new province of this radical jihadist movement.

Time and again these militant Islamist groups have bested their rivals on the battlefield and established their reign over seemingly ungovernable spaces, inventing a radically new type of Islamist proto-state, often with no regard to preexisting borders. Out of anarchy, they have demonstrated a remarkable ability to create social and political order. Despite their strikingly different cultural, linguistic, and geographic origins, these groups have proven to be ideologically uncompromising, purposefully violent, and surprisingly wealthy.

The rise of these new Islamist polities is a serious international security issue for both policymakers and academics alike. In policy circles, the question is how to contain the groundswell of Islamist power in these contentious spaces. As jihadist groups overtake their rivals on the battlefield, the Pentagon has increasingly relied on unmanned drones to target insurgent commanders across the Muslim world. Intelligence officials and military strategists in the United States have hoped that these leadership decapitation strategies will slow down the militants.[22] But without knowing why these groups have risen to power in the first place, decision makers are too often flying blind. In some cases, these counterterrorism strategies have stalled the advance of militant groups, but in others they have inadvertently expedited the radicalization and proliferation of jihadists. This book presents a rational, economic framework for understanding these proto-state polities, offering the policy world creative new strategies for engagement that may help limit the bloodshed.

From a scholarly perspective, the book also contributes to the academic literatures on international security, state formation, and civil war. By taking seriously the domestic economic origins of this new, globalized proto-state polity, this book is situated on the fault lines of debate within these literatures, at the nexus of international relations (IR) and comparative politics. By engaging with civil war economies at the ground level, it provides a new theoretical framework to help explain the rise of modern jihadist-created polities across the world in such a way that engages contemporary security scholars across these subfields.

For IR scholars, the rise of these proto-state polities constitutes a fundamental challenge to the principles of sovereignty and territorial integrity that govern the contemporary international system. Indeed, these types of modern jihadist groups constitute one of the gravest international security concerns of the post–Cold War era. Traditional IR theorists understandably have a difficult time making sense of the plethora of new, nonstate armed Islamist groups, which reject the state and its borders, the system, and the institutions and norms that govern international relations. But if constructivists are right that both the actors and the system are constructed through social interactions, then these modern jihadists are signaling to the world a fundamental shift in international affairs. By taking the symbiotic role of local identities and economic structures seriously, this book helps to explain this Islamist proto-state as a new social construct on the world stage, situated within a culturally complex, evolving international system.

Exploring the internal origins of this new socially constructed polity, this research therefore also engages with the ongoing debate about the role of war in modern state formation in comparative politics. It builds on the traditional state-building literature, which posits that war helps create the extractive and coercive capabilities of the state, and that violence is an ordinary feature of the primitive accumulation of power.[23] The conventional wisdom holds that the threat of war compels rulers to engage in a competition for power and resources; over time, this competitive "extraction and struggle over the means of war created the central organizational structures of the state."[24] These economic drivers of state formation are also well established in the literature, as Hendrik Spruyt reveals in his analysis of how the need for lower transaction costs and a stable business environment played a key role in the success of early European states.[25] We also know there is a relationship between criminality and state formation; as Charles Tilly aptly states, "Banditry, piracy, gangland rivalry, policing, and war making all belong on the same continuum."[26]

Yet contemporary intrastate conflicts have been nothing like the wars of territorial acquisition that gave birth to the early European state. Rather, civil wars have been hugely destructive, more often resulting in state failure than state formation.[27] Reno and other civil war scholars heartily agree that shelling your cities to rubble is not a steppingstone to long-term state formation; it is the path to enduring failure.[28] This futile type of violence has sparked much debate about whether political order can be created in such war-torn countries. Robert Jackson and Carl Rosberg argue that arbitrarily created colonial borders have condemned some countries to remain indefinitely weak or failed.[29] Jeffrey Herbst takes this line of reasoning further, proposing that some deeply fragmented African states simply ought to be allowed to disintegrate so that more sustainable indigenous territorial units can take their place.[30]

Despite this ongoing debate in the literature, across the Muslim world we are currently witnessing the violent construction of unexpected new polities that challenge our preconceived notions about state formation. Out of the ashes of civil wars, Islamist proto-states have emerged across the Muslim world and bested their competitors. What explains these new polities? This book introduces two crucial intermediary economic processes to help explain the relationship between modern civil wars and Islamist political order.

In highlighting the oft-forgotten role of local economic elites, this book also speaks to some of the most recent and groundbreaking research on complex, multiactor civil wars. Although the traditional literature simplifies complex conflict environments into a tidy two-actor game,[31] recent scholarship has recognized that contemporary civil wars are multiplayer games,[32] with a range of complex and fragmented participants.[33] These players both cooperate and clash, engaging in messy, simultaneous interactions in a single-war theater.[34] This important new literature provides a much more realistic—albeit chaotic—portrayal of the modern civil war. Using a rationalist framework to explain the behavior of the local business class, an important and often-overlooked actor, adds to this vibrant ongoing scholarly discussion about multiple and diverse participants in civil wars.[35]

By bridging these disparate literatures, this book offers a new agency-based approach to the study of civil war economies that helps explain how Islamist political order can emerge out of anarchy. As the following chapters illustrate, the roots of Islamist power lay in the invisible hand of the civil war economy. The stories of the business elite in these war zones reveal a remarkably rational logic behind the rise of Islamist power. From Mogadishu to Peshawar, practical, everyday economic considerations compelled members of the business class to seek out creative ways to overcome the high costs of deep social fragmentation. At their core, these material interests were politically benign. But when these market forces colluded with jihadist passion, the explosive mix created a radically new proto-state polity that remade political order in an Islamist image.

2

Black Flags in the Bazaar

THE MAKING OF MODERN ISLAMIST PROTO-STATES

The Prophet (peace be upon him) said: "If you see the black flags coming from Khorasan, join that army, even if you have to climb over ice, for this is the army of the Caliph, the Mahdi, and no one can stop it until it reaches Jerusalem."

DAEEF HADITH, narrated by At-Tirmidhi and Ahmad

ACCORDING TO LEGEND, the rise of an army marching under black flags portends the start of the last great battle of the Islamic world at the very end of human civilization.[1] When al-Qaeda fighters first established bases in southern Afghanistan in the 1990s, they seemed to be dramatically enacting this ancient prophecy, raising their banners across what was once medieval Khorasan.[2] They then broadcast this emotionally charged symbol to aspiring jihadists around the world, inspiring an unparalleled modern global phenomenon.

Since the beginning of the twenty-first century, a wave of black standards has swept across the Muslim world, heralding a rising tide of militant Islamist power. From North Africa to the Middle East, these modern jihadists have not only been remarkably competitive on the battlefield but also demonstrated a surprising ability to reign over seemingly ungovernable spaces. They have captured territory across ethnic and tribal divisions, consolidated political power over their rivals, and brutally enforced their laws. From the mountains of Khorasan to the Maghrebi deserts, these black flags clearly signal the intent to rule.

From these jihadist conflicts, reactionary yet hypermodern Islamist proto-states have emerged both within and across existing borders. While these political entities are not fully formed states, they have appeared in parts of Iraq, Syria, Afghanistan, Pakistan, Somalia, Libya, Nigeria, and Mali. These polities construct legitimacy and authority from a divine mandate to return to a romanticized golden age that predates the miseries of the colonial era and draws on an imagined conception of an Islamic nation that transcends all other loyalties. The black banner represents a prophetic metanarrative that situates the proto-state at a critical juncture between an idealized mythical history and an inevitable apocalyptic future.[3]

Despite this homage to the past and reverence for prophecy, however, these jihadist-constructed polities resemble neither the old system of caliphates nor the futuristic warriors of the darkened end-time. Rather, the proto-state is an inherently modern political expression, born out of the abysmal performance of the postcolonial state. Across the Muslim world, the proto-state acts as a practical twenty-first-century political alternative to the contemporary failures of both nationalism and tribalism. This political entity is a fundamental rejection of the secular state construct that seeks to redraw the world map to reflect a new configuration of emergent Islamist polities.

The success of these jihadist-constructed polities has been striking. Across vastly different geographic, cultural, and linguistic spaces, these zealous jihadist groups have shown an unexpected flair for ruling over parts of the globe that are considered terribly difficult to govern. With an appetite for savage violence, they have bested other well-established factions on the frontlines and established control over highly divided societies. But why are some of these particular groups able to capture and consolidate their political power, while other highly competitive armed factions have failed? What explains the uncanny rise of these Islamist proto-states, especially in areas where chaos has reigned for years?

Unveiling the Proto-State

Much has been written about the surge in Islamist political power over the past decade. The conventional wisdom in the literature suggests that the success of Islamists must be due to either their religious convictions or their tribal networks.[4] First, given their obsession with apocalyptic prophecies, a lot of insightful work has been done on the extremist ideas and beliefs that inspire modern jihadist groups.[5] Ideology is certainly an important piece of the puzzle that helps to explain group motivations and actions, but alone it cannot explain the accumulation of power. Even within a single war zone, there are often many dedicated groups with similar philosophies and values, but not all of them create statelike political order. Ideology may help to explain insurgent motivations but not why proto-states have formed successfully in some cases and not others.

A second group of scholars argues that Islamist success is based on their successful co-option of local ethnic and tribal networks.[6] These scholars are surely correct that jihadists often build alliances with local tribal guerrillas to gain access to community resources.[7] This behavior, however, is not unique to Islamist groups; indeed, local factions constantly negotiate alliances in civil wars, and these collective efforts rarely lead to the consolidation of state power.[8] Furthermore, while it is fairly easy to uncover which communities supported particular jihadist groups after their victory, it is much more difficult to use tribal politics to predict the rise of Islamists before the fact. Even in deeply fragmented societies, there is no clear correlation, let alone causation, between tribalism and Islamism that explains variation in the emergence of these proto-state polities.

While ideology and identity are important factors in understanding jihadist behavior, these factors therefore cannot explain why certain Islamists succeed over other groups with similar religious and cultural endowments. Military victory and political power cannot be won on sentiment alone, and without material resources, even the most zealous believers will starve in the trenches. My analysis builds on the wealth of insights from this existing literature to provide a new economic framework for understanding how ideology and identity are practically operationalized in a conflict environment, revealing the agency of important and oft-overlooked local actors.

By focusing on the ground-level economics of Islamism, my economic argument also contributes to the research agenda on jihadist financing, the majority of which focuses on foreign sources of support from states or private actors.[9] External funding is certainly an important variable that affected outcomes in Afghanistan and Somalia; in war, access to foreign weapons, soldiers, and cash is essential for survival. In both cases, however, virtually every armed faction enjoyed substantial external backing from neighboring states, which was at times much greater than the amounts received by either the Taliban or the Islamic Courts Union. Yet none of these other foreign-supported armed groups achieved anything like decisive military victory, nor did they manage to re-create statelike power. Moreover, external funding for jihadist groups has grown increasingly uncertain due to successful international legal controls established over the past fifteen years.[10] While the foreign money supply has not completely dried up, it is not nearly as attractive as was historically the case. Foreign support alone cannot explain the emergence of these Islamist polities.[11]

What then is driving the creation of Islamist proto-states? Why have these new polities succeeded in so many divided and conflict-affected parts of the Muslim world? To answer these pressing questions, this book investigates the practical, financial sources of jihadist power at the domestic level, in order to provide a much-needed agent-based perspective to the ongoing scholarly debate. It finds that behind the shock factor and fanatical violence, the emergence of these new polities actually turns out to be a surprisingly rational—and predictable—enterprise. In fact, what we are witnessing in these troubled parts of the Muslim world is the messy business of creating political order.

Throughout history, building states has been a bloody, even gruesome ordeal. The earliest European states were first born as little more than monopolistic violence rackets, in which political entrepreneurs centralized their power by extorting taxes from citizens in exchange for protection from their own abuse.[12] As Charles Tilly argues, "If protection rackets represent organized crime at its smoothest, then war making and state making—quintessential protection rackets with the advantage of legitimacy—qualify as our largest examples of organized crime."[13]

These historical order-making processes provide important insight into what is happening in troubled parts of the Muslim world today. Behind the scenes of graphic violence, I propose that modern jihadist groups are establishing a similar type of extortion-protection agreement in civil wars. The difference today is that they are forging this security relationship with a particular class of powerful economic actors: the local business class.

Two processes explain this potent business-Islamist alliance. First of all, Islamic identity provides the business class with a valuable mechanism that works across ethnic and tribal lines. One of the biggest challenges that businesses face in civil war is the extraordinary hostility between rival groups, and emphasizing religion over other contentious identities can help overcome this trust deficit. In the Muslim world, Islamic identity acts as a potent social lubricant that can help build relationships with new partners across factional lines. Second, the business class chooses to support Islamist factions as a way to reduce its overall security costs. Because Islamists can sell security to a wider pool of consumers at a lower price, they can quickly outcompete their ethnic and clan rivals. By monopolizing the security market, the Islamists create a proto-state out of anarchy.

Together, these two ideal-type economic processes have played a critical role in the rise of the modern Islamist proto-state around the world. The need for trust drives the business class to embrace Islam, and its desire for lower costs thrusts it into the arms of Islamists. Out of this nexus of violence and opulence thus emerges the Islamist proto-state, which threatens the very nature of the international state system.

Trust and the Social Lubricant of Islam

Even for the power players, doing business in a civil war is an extraordinarily high-risk, high-reward game. There are countless variables that affect each gamble, and competition is fierce. Most rookies will barely scrape by, earning just enough to survive another day in the hustle. But the possibilities are intoxicating, and one big deal can suddenly catapult a lucky amateur into an elite class of high rollers. The windfall of new money feels exhilarating, and the thrill of winning can be addictive. Besides, once the connections are lined up, the next bet seems easier. In this casino-style capitalist marketplace, no one quits while they're ahead. The temptations of criminal business options also frequently prove irresistible.

The hawkers in the bazaar and the mob bosses in their estates are all playing a dangerous and unpredictable game. For the bold, untold riches lay ahead; but to err can be fatal. In their pursuit of fortune, the players must navigate a complex landscape of volatility and threat. Moving goods through rival warlord turfs requires creating a web of reciprocal deals with local partners, and even then an unexpected skirmish or a freelance checkpoint can thwart an entire operation. There is also always the lingering fear that even the most trusted associates might try to muscle out their own partners just to get a bigger share of the loot. Without a functioning government to guarantee transactions, there is no formal recourse against fraud or larceny. Too often, behind the lure of treasure is the deadly trap of betrayal.

The problem here is that all economic life relies on trust. As John Stuart Mill aptly states, "The most serious impediment to conducting business concerns on a large scale is the rarity of persons who are supposed fit to be trusted with the receipt and expenditure of large sums of money."[14] Whether trade occurs between large industrialized states or Somali merchants, business partners must be confident that agreements will be kept. Kenneth Arrow explains, "It can be plausibly argued that much of the economic backwardness in the world can be explained by the lack of mutual confidence."[15]

This crisis of trust is worsened in cases of conflict. In functioning states, corporations can rely on public institutions and the rule of law to back their contracts. But in the middle of a civil war, formal governing institutions are unable to enforce property rights and agreements, leaving the world of commerce in a state of anarchy.[16] Corruption and abuse by local militias further disrupts markets and undermines healthy competition.[17] This systemic lack of functioning institutions and regulations hikes up transaction costs and scares off prospective investors.[18]

Fear and xenophobia also stall the trade engine. This is especially true in cases where normal social relations are destroyed by ethnic or tribal violence. The development studies literature already shows that heterogeneity can undermine societal trust, leading to economic underperformance and low trade.[19] Economists have also discovered that people are more likely to enter into economic agreements with members of their own ethnic, racial, or tribal group than with outsiders.[20] Even under normal conditions, social diversity has been shown to increase civil discord and lower economic growth.[21] In war zones, these effects of distrust are dramatically amplified.

Given these factors, one might imagine vibrant trade to be virtually impossible in a civil war.[22] But this is not so. Businesspeople are not passive participants in this game; they actively work to change its rules to increase rewards and lower risks. In response to fragmentation, members of the business class must find new identities and institutions to override these problematic ethnic, racial, and tribal divisions.[23] They need to reconstruct categories of inclusion and exclusion so that they can better secure deals and gain access to new markets.[24] The challenge, however, is that existing cultural identities too often overlap with fault lines of intrastate violence. What the business class needs is a more versatile identity that can soothe tensions, facilitate intergroup cooperation, and evoke feelings of trust and confidence.[25]

For well over a millennium, Islam has played exactly this role in commercial life. As far back as the seventh century, the rapid expansion of Arab Islamic power increased economic interaction over a vast stretch of territory from Northwest Africa to Central Asia, connecting the Mediterranean Sea and Indian Ocean.[26] For traders seeking to profit from lucrative markets across the Muslim world, Islamic identity served as a useful form of social capital that could smooth business relations across a wide range of linguistic, ethnic, and cultural divides.[27] With Arab dominance over the ancient Silk Road, Islam became an important mediating force in easing economic interactions between distant communities. This winding 6,500-kilometer route connected agriculturalists, pastoralists, miners, and manufacturers to lucrative markets across numerous and varied dynastic empires, kingdoms, and princely states.[28] Long before the formation of the modern nation-state, Islam played an essential role in facilitating economic life across the diverse Muslim world.

More recently, this business-Islamist relationship has been documented in the literature on modern Iran.[29] During the shah's thirty-year authoritarian reign, the bazaar remained largely unregulated and off the books. Under these conditions, the Iranian traditional merchant class (*bazaari*) and the clergy (ulema) developed a reciprocal relationship to keep the informal economy alive.[30] The ulema provided the *bazaari* with reputational legitimacy and a moral "green light" to circumvent government regulations, making it easier to do business outside the purview of the state.[31] And in return, the bazaar privately financed the clerical class.[32] Over time, Islamic norms, laws, and institutions became the primary mechanisms for regulating business transactions in the bazaar, and the ulema cemented its financial and political independence from the state. After decades of mutually beneficial relations, this powerful *bazaari*-ulema alliance culminated in the dramatic 1979 Islamic Revolution.[33]

Although the Islamic Revolution in Iran occurred within a strong state, a similar and comparable type of business-Islamist relationship also emerges in cases where the modern state is weak or failed. In the absence of a normal, secure corporate environment, Islam offers businesspeople a versatile, practical set of solutions to the complex challenges of civil war. To start, it nurtures "feelings of loyalty and identity towards a large reference group that exceeds ethnic boundaries," thus creating a mechanism for businesses to work across factional lines.[34] It also provides a ready-made religious legal system, sharia, which can be used as an informal mechanism to govern and regulate social and economic life.[35] Islamic laws and institutions thus offer a set of religious rules and guidelines that can reduce uncertainty, facilitate contracts, and reduce transaction costs. Islam even offers reputational benefits and social capital to overcome a low-trust environment, making it easier to build new partnerships and expand enterprises.[36] Across diverse cultural and linguistic divides, Islamic identity provides a means of establishing relationships between prospective business partners. In a civil war, reviving and emphasizing this identity has tremendous practical and material value.

In fact, this social capital is so valuable that businesspeople operating in deeply fragmented societies often support Islamic foundations, schools, and institutions as a way to prove their religious credentials. While not a perfect guarantee of trustworthiness, such charitable demonstrations act as compelling information shortcuts that signal honesty and personal virtue. Having a reputation for religious piety and public charity makes the right impression in a violent, low-trust environment. A businessman who donates money to the local mosque, for example, seems unlikely to steal from his own business partners. He has not only confirmed that he is generous but also proven that his actions are governed by a higher power, even in the midst of a violent civil war. So while there may be no human laws that can punish him, his faith in God's judgment should prevent him from cheating. Demonstrating Islamic character proves trustworthiness, and trust makes business easier. In the absence of a functioning state, choosing a prayerful business partner seems like a safer bet.

Through this philanthropic investment in Islamic causes, the business class in a civil war therefore gains valuable social capital to overcome the trust deficit. This influx of charitable donations, however, also gives Islamic institutions more power over social and economic life. These Islamic institutions then act as a networking space that allows businesspeople to connect and further reinforces their reliance on Islam in commercial life. Over time, these religious institutions begin to fill many of the roles and responsibilities normally played by government.

As these interactions are repeated, the business community grows into its Islamic identity, and its outward religious symbolism gradually results in a social evolution within the elite class. Even though these religious identities, institutions, and symbols are adopted instrumentally, in time they nurture the formation of an Islamist culture within the business class operating in a civil war environment. Not unlike the union of the bazaar and ulema in Iran, this symbiotic relationship creates the conditions for a future surge of Islamist power.

Islam has always played a central role in the bazaar. But in the middle of an active fight, the need for social trust and institutional rules is particularly acute, and Islam provides a valuable set of tools for surviving and thriving. While the game remains unpredictable and dangerous, there are ways to improve the odds. To win in this venture, the players need to simultaneously signal that they are both good Muslims and tough gangsters—that they are to be trusted and feared at the same time. But as members of the business class turn to Islam to reduce their costs and create new opportunities, they also develop and cultivate these identities in a way that changes the political landscape. Once the spark of modern jihadism catches in these civil wars, this latent identity makes it possible for the business class to shift its financial support to Islamists, thus creating a new proto-state.

The Islamist Discount

Although the need for trust drives members of the business community to embrace Islamist identities, it is their desire for lower overhead costs that explains their support for Islamist groups. To understand why Islamist groups rise to power, we must first see how the business community operates in these theaters at a very practical level. At the heart of the matter is the fact that all businesses operating in civil wars must factor the cost of security into every single one of their transactions. In addition to paying for trucks, drivers, and fuel, businesspeople must also calculate the total price for security demanded from each warlord in each fiefdom that they cross, as well as the total price of extortion at militia checkpoints along major trading routes. These are the hard and measurable costs of moving from point A to point B across privately held warlord turfs. In the absence of a functioning government, these compound security prices are constitutive of the business community's overall tax burden. These costs are then added to the price of goods, dramatically affecting supply and demand in target markets.

Imagine, for example, that you live in Mogadishu but you want to sell floral cotton prints in Baidoa, a promising in-land market where there is a big demand among young women for summer fabrics. First, you call your local partner in Baidoa to check that no one else is already selling the prints and to investigate how much these women are willing to pay for them. Because there are no local manufacturers, you then contact your overseas suppliers in Pakistan, negotiate a low price for a container of fabric rolls from Karachi, and arrange to ship your goods to the Mogadishu port. The overseas shipping costs, port and loading fees, driving and truck rental, protection payments, percentages paid to local partners, and routine checkpoints along the major roadway from Mogadishu to Baidoa are all factored into the overhead cost of the operation. And because the shipment will be passing through multiple fiefdoms, you add an extra contingency to the budget, just in case a freelance checkpoint stops your truck.

All of these overhead costs are then added to the price of each roll of fabric in the container. The final price of your prints cannot exceed the maximum amount the women are willing to pay. Otherwise, you will have to offload the cotton rolls at a loss, or they will sit in a storage room and rot. You must buy low enough to be able to afford the security costs and sell high enough for the deal to have been profitable.

These compound security costs are obvious and easily calculable for the fabric trader, but they also matter to virtually every businessperson that relies on the movement of goods through rebel-held territory. A telecom giant that wants to expand wireless operations will need to move steel and copper to build new towers. A local pharmaceutical company needs to successfully bring ingredients from markets to their laboratories. Even a tea seller on the side of the road will notice fluctuations in the cost of the tea leaves if his supplier paid too much to militias. In a civil war, everyone is paying security prices.

But how do these cost calculations affect political order? Why should warlords care about fabric prices in Baidoa? Actually, these everyday cost calculations have a very real and dramatic effect on the security environment. Armed groups rely on the hard currency extracted from the business class to pay foot soldiers and purchase supplies to support the war effort. This supply of cash is more important to keeping a warlord in power than the possession of land or other capital. If, after evaluating these transaction costs, the businessperson decides not to buy the floral prints, then the warlord loses all of the potential revenue he could have gained from that deal. It is on this delicate equilibrium—between the businessperson and the warlord—that the civil war economy and formation of political order rest.

To illustrate this relationship, I develop a model of civil war as a competitive security market. Here Tilly's description of the state as a protection racket finds an apt parallel in the warlord fiefdom.[37] When a state descends into civil war, no party has a clear monopoly on force, and security must be purchased from competing warlord protection rackets.[38] Each of these rackets not only protects its clients but also threatens them and attacks other rackets. When there are multiple warlords engaged in active combat, protection is expensive and in demand.[39]

If these security costs are too high, however, businesses will lose their profit margin, the trade engine will break down, and the warlord will have bankrupted his own financial base.[40] The very survival of a warlord is contingent on his ability to continue to extract rents from his subjugated population. As Mancur Olson sharply states, "The stationary bandit [warlord] keeps on gaining from reducing his rate of tax theft down to the point where what he gains (from tax theft on larger output) is just offset by what he loses (from taking a smaller share of that output). He is left at the revenue-maximizing rate of tax theft."[41] By this logic, the successful warlord ought to rein in his extortion to meet market conditions; if his fees are too high, then his business community supporters lose their comparative advantage and cannot sell. It is in the best financial interest of all the parties involved that the women in Baidoa get their floral prints.

It is also because the warlords rely on this cash flow that the business community has an ability to negotiate the conditions of its own subjugation. While the business class is coerced into making these security payments, it also retains a unique type of political power: access to large sums of cash. In this free-market security environment, moneyed individuals can vote for a warlord protection racket with their dollars. In fact, overextraction can lead to collective revolt against the warlord, either by withholding support or by financing a political alternative.[42] As Robert Bates explains:

> Should the [violence] specialist opportunistically seize the wealth of a member of a group, his defection would trigger punishment by that citizen's confederates: They can withhold tax payments or mobilize fighting. If not sufficiently paid for the provision of security, the specialist in violence can pay himself: he can turn from guardian to warlord. And if preyed upon or left undefended, then the citizens can furnish their own protection; they can take up arms.[43]

The successful warlord protection racket must therefore retain its support base by offering competitive terms of subjugation vis-à-vis its political rivals. The rate of extortion should remain at the equilibrium point: high enough so that the warlord can remain in power, but low enough so that the business class does not engage in rebellion.[44] Both the warlord and the patron alike must at some level agree to the terms of subjugation.[45]

So far this model overlooks one key factor, however: modern civil wars are often shaped by identity politics. Accordingly, warlords are often limited to selling security to their own ethnic and tribal constituencies to protect against rival groups. When a warlord primarily relies on a narrower pool of buyers, he must therefore charge each head a higher rate for security provision. Under these conditions, the business elite's ability to change to a less expensive racket is also restricted, as identity politics often makes it impossible to switch sides in a civil war.[46] Obviously, businesses simply cannot buy into a rival kin group's protection racket in the middle of a genocide, no matter how much more competitive its security rates are. When kinship ties predetermine political affiliation, businesspeople are forced to accept suboptimal and coercive arrangements in which warlords extort them with greater impunity. And if they want access to new markets, they must also create local partnerships across each turf and then pay into multiple protection rackets for each kin group.[47]

Even though civil war creates new opportunities in smuggling and other criminal activities, the cost of this social fragmentation gets steep. Purchasing protection from multiple warlord protection rackets is an expensive risk management strategy. As an alternative, businesspeople can try to hire their own private security. For example, a trader could invest in setting up her own checkpoints along a key route, thus turning her insecurity into another source of profit. She could also consider hiring her own militias to protect her businesses in order to pay less at checkpoints than her competitors. The price of salaries, weapons, and ammunition needed to build and maintain an adequately sized private army can greatly exceed the rates charged by warlords for protection, however, making this an expensive proposition for the businesswoman. Security in a civil war always comes at a price. Under multiple and competing ethnic or tribal factions, the cost of doing business skyrockets.

When the business community is held hostage by expensive ethnic or tribal politics in this way, Islamist groups can appear to be a convenient and affordable exit option.[48] It is at this critical moment that the long-term relationship between the mosque and the market can have a powerful transformative effect on the civil war. The Islamists cash in on the years of trust between the business class and Islamic institutions, calling for a new Islamist solution to the high costs of civil war. The resulting business-Islamist alliance catalyzes a rapid chain reaction that brings the conflict to a head.

The business community triggers these processes by investing in a new group of Islamist security providers, not only to demonstrate their religious credentials but also to hedge against ethnic and tribal protection rackets. Because the Islamists are able to sell security widely across ethnic and tribal divisions, however, they are able to offer more competitive prices than groups that primarily sell protection to a narrower pool of buyers. By charging lower margins across the board, Islamist groups are able to capture a larger share of the security market than ethnic or tribal factions. As their market share increases, they can further lower their rates to price out their rivals. The ethnic warlord reacts to this surge in Islamist revenue by desperately extorting more money from his base, which only expedites his loss of support.

In the short term, the Islamists appear to be offering the business elites much better value for their money. The Islamist not only provides businesses with the option to exit coercive relationships with ethnic or tribal protection rackets but also offers discount security prices to do so. And the lower the overhead costs, the greater the net revenue for businesses. As the price of financing the Islamists drops below the cost of maintaining the warlords, the business community is incentivized to collectively shift its support, thus bankrupting the old protection rackets. Once they have dominated the security market, the Islamists then have the ability to do what other armed groups cannot: win the civil war and capture the state.[49]

From Theory to Practice

The connection between the fabric merchant and the Islamist group is not an obvious one. Selling floral prints has no passionate ideology or identity

behind it. But the practical challenges of making these simple business transactions work lead to an unexpected union between the mosque and the market. Without kinship ties in Baidoa, choosing a religiously pious business
partner makes it easier to trust that you will receive a fair cut from the fabric
sales. In the long term, the bazaar adopts an Islamic identity and funds Islamic
institutions as a way to develop social trust across problematic local divisions.

Furthermore, paying off multiple warlords to move the fabric to Baidoa
also cuts into net revenues; paying Islamists to lower overhead costs means
higher profits per roll. In the short run, the business class dumps ethnic and
tribal warlords and collectively shifts support to Islamists. Many of the stories
of the business class recounted in this book mirror this example of the fabric
merchant, but with even greater unpredictability and complications. Their
experiences reveal an important connection between business and Islamism
that helps explain conflict dynamics in the contemporary Muslim world.

In order to truly understand this intersection between jihadist politics
and bazaar economics, however, we need to enter this volatile business world
at the ground level and meet the people behind the processes. Their stories
involve hustling multimillion-dollar shipments to illegal ports, negotiating
with drugged-up militiamen at checkpoints, and pushing products in gun-
infested street markets.

Afghanistan and Somalia provide a rare opportunity to explore this phenomenon. Both the Taliban and Islamic Courts Union dramatically broke
an enduring stalemate and established a surprising degree of statelike control over their populations, a feat that repeated international peace processes
failed to accomplish. They consolidated their military and political power,
routed their competitors on the battlefield, and enforced their rule of law.
From anarchy, they created a surprisingly stable form of political governance,
which was neither a traditional tribal system of order nor a conventional
authoritarian regime.

Turning to empirics, the stories of these business elites in the next four
chapters reveal their origins, interests, and evolving identities in their respective civil war economies. Profit-motivated business elites and ideologically
dedicated Islamists make for strange bedfellows; yet, as we discover on this
journey, it was through their unexpected marriage of convenience that the
modern Islamist proto-state was born.

3

Mafia and Mujahideen

TRAFFICKING AND TRUST BUILDING
UNDER SOVIET OCCUPATION

Whether you buy or sell, all is sorrow;
There is nothing else in the bazaar of this world.
They are all cheats and swindlers;
Those who sell and buy in this world.
They will never love the world;
If they sense its malignancy.
Those who have their eye on their religion and faith;
Won't look to this world.
Both the young and old are deceitful;
How can you trust the cunning of this world?
The friends of the world are all enemies;
There is no friend in this wide world.
"THE WAY OF THE WORLD," poem by Rahman Baba

THE SECRET GUN workshops of Darra Adam Khel are a dusty half-hour's drive away from the bustling smugglers' bazaars in Peshawar.[1] Nestled in the rugged Pakistani tribal belt, the sole industry in this remote town is weapons production. Inside the rows of dilapidated mud brick factories are skilled craftsmen building impressive replicas, their weathered brows muddied with sweat and soot. The storefronts of these makeshift smithies are artfully decorated with streamers of bullet belts and display large collections of newly manufactured AK-47s and antitank weapons. Day and night, droves of customers haggle over prices and test merchandise by firing into the thick air, heavily laden with the smell of molten metal, grease, and smoke. In these rough stone hills, war generates business.

During the Soviet-Afghan War of the 1980s, my siblings and I used to wander freely through these lively streets. "They're *Haji Sahib*'s grandchildren. No problem." As youngsters, we would stroll past the heavy guns while local merchants greeted us with a gentle pat on the head. These trust-based relationships were the foundation of the war economy, providing insiders with safe passage through the deadly terrain. Only known truckers, traders, and commanders were admitted into these underground markets. An outsider may not have survived the trip.

Even regulars in the arms market, however, took no chances. Given insecurity along the Pakistan-Afghanistan border during the war against the Soviets, every trader, trucker, and craftsman carried a weapon to protect his property. But force alone did not lead to profit; social trust was necessary for doing business in these war-torn bazaars. To keep the wheels of industry turning, the traders and traffickers therefore fashioned their own unwritten rules of the game, aimed at lowering their costs and increasing their opportunities. To create order amid the anarchy, they turned to Islam.

Though it seems ironic that such rough folk would place importance on religious piety, Islam actually provided this local business class with a practical set of tools for mitigating social chaos and facilitating economic life. As the stories in this chapter reveal, Islamic identities and institutions provided a valuable mechanism for increasing trust and cooperation amid unpredictability, violence, and insecurity. In time, these pragmatic considerations fostered a militant Islamist culture within the business elite, forged in the fires of war and industry.

It was not always like this. A generous and hospitable people, the tribal communities in the border region once earned their living through agriculture, pastoralism, barter, and trade. Elders will still reminisce about a time when the rich almonds and sweet pomegranates and raisins of Kandahar were so coveted that colorful camel caravans would trek these delicacies over dry mountain passes to markets throughout the subcontinent. Intricately handwoven Afghan carpets seduced wealthy buyers from around the world, while delicate Chinese porcelains and fragrant Indian teas were imported back to Afghanistan in exchange. For centuries, the tribal peoples used their common faith in Islam to build peaceful trade relations across their harsh and arid terrain.

The decade-long Soviet-Afghan War shattered this welcoming society and mutated the historic relationship between business and Islam in the border region. Moscow had been secretly planning an invasion for years, looking to expand its empire deeper into Asia. Then suddenly, between 1978 and 1979, the Kremlin staged a series of destabilizing coups d'état in Kabul, first ousting and assassinating the then president, Daoud Khan, and then rapidly switching sides between rival Khalq and Parcham communist factions of the Soviet-funded People's Democratic Party of Afghanistan (PDPA).[2] Once Moscow had installed its proxies in office, on December 29, 1979, tens of thousands of heavily armed Soviet troops marched into Afghanistan in defense of their new regime. Two days later, Soviet commandos assassinated President Hafizullah Amin of the PDPA-Khalq faction and then inaugurated their preferred man, Babrak Karmal from PDPA-Parcham, as a puppet head of state.[3] The result was catastrophic.

For ten years Afghanistan bled and starved under the hammer and sickle. The Soviet invasion resulted in an estimated one million deaths, six million refugees, and the complete destruction of the traditional Afghan economy.[4] Brutal aerial assaults demolished vital irrigation systems, and scorched earth campaigns napalmed the lush grape vineyards and pomegranate groves to ash.[5] Soviet helicopters airdropped millions of antipersonnel landmines onto fertile pastures; these mines were painted with bright colors to attract unsuspecting children playing in the fields. The farmlands became perilous and unusable. Ill-conceived communist land reforms also devastated poor sharecroppers when their landowning patrons lost their deeds.[6] With nearly 80 percent of Afghans dependent on traditional agriculture, these targeted attacks meant penury and death. There were no more almonds and raisins from Kandahar in the Peshawar markets.

After establishing control over the cities, the Soviets then began systematically assimilating the rural areas. The traditional authority of the khan was dismantled, and government operatives assumed control over villages.[7] Tribal communities across the country resisted, but they could not match the juggernaut of Soviet military power. "At first we managed to keep them out of our village, but when they started to shoot at us from tanks we were forced to retreat," reported one field commander. "When we ran out of ammunition, we were forced to escape and hide wherever we could. By then the defense of our village had already cost many deaths. Many people were unarmed and were killed in the field where they were working when the first attack came."[8] Most of these early fighters, called the *mujahideen*, were severely underresourced. They fought back against Soviet tanks, often with nothing more than a few rusty British Enfield rifles, and sometimes even with knives, swords, and farming tools. The mujahideen showed heart, but their tenacity was not enough to fight off the Soviet Bear.

Without sufficient arms and ammunition, the resistance was getting slaughtered. The burnt countryside became a cemetery, each grave marked

only by a humble pile of rocks. To honor each of the fallen, the survivors
added a special tribute to these nameless tombs of the mujahideen: they tied
a small green cloth to a dry branch and erected it atop the stones. As the
casualties mounted, these haunting graveyards extended for miles. The lush
orchards were replaced with a desolate landscape of thousands of parched
gray branches and tattered green flags: a forest of death. Parents comforted
their children with promises that all those who fell in the jihad would mag-
ically transform into green birds and fly to heaven. Six million refugees fled
to Pakistan and Iran.[9] By the early 1980s, hundreds of thousands of Afghans
crowded into the sprawling Jalozai refugee camp in the suburbs of Peshawar.[10]

The mujahideen who stayed behind to fight knew that they desperately
needed better supplies, and they took extraordinary risks to advance their
cause. A common desperation tactic at the time was for a small group to enlist
in the Kremlin-funded Afghan army, complete basic training, and receive an
AK-47. The moment they received their weapons, however, they would then
stage an assault from inside the base against their commanding officers. They
were usually killed on the spot for trying, but sometimes these firebrands
could escape with a truck full of the latest-model assault rifles. In the early
stages, almost all of the new guns in the hands of the rebellion had been stolen
directly from the Soviets.

The arms bazaars in Pakistan's Federally Administered Tribal Areas (FATA)
thus responded to an urgent need to survive. A rebel who managed to kill a
Soviet could take the gun off his dead body, bring it across the border to Darra
Adam Khel, ask the blacksmiths to replicate ten more Kalashnikovs just like
it, and then head back into the fight. The arms manufacturers in these back-
alley workshops and bazaars were the first real lifelines for the mujahideen,
giving them a fool's hope on the battlefield. These gritty handcrafted assault
rifles proved to be surprisingly effective, especially since the local manufacturing industry was underresourced. Once the rebels had these new weapons in
hand, however, they began to defy the odds and inflict pain on the Soviets.

As the Americans witnessed the determination of the mujahideen, it
became clear that Afghanistan was not yet a lost cause. Representatives from
the Pentagon soon met with Pakistani Inter-Services Intelligence (ISI) in
Islamabad. The Central Intelligence Agency (CIA) needed to halt the Red
Army's advance into Asia, and the ISI wanted to prevent the PDPA in Kabul
from allying with Soviet-friendly India to flank its western border.[11] Together,
they devised a covert plan. The CIA agreed to secretly channel arms to the
anti-Soviet rebels through the ISI, via the rugged Pakistani mountain passes
in tribal areas.

This American strategy rested on Pakistan's ability to arm rebels in Afghanistan. Indeed, Islamabad had already been supplying jihadists in the tribal belt since the early 1970s, as part of its long-standing tit-for-tat border conflict against the Afghan state. The ISI had established deep links with the powerful Haqqani family network in North Waziristan, which had declared a jihad against Afghanistan's then president Daoud Khan as early as 1973.[12] By the time the Soviets invaded, the stage had already been set for a new jihadist rebellion, and Islamabad was perfectly positioned to take the lead in channeling arms to the mujahideen on behalf of the Americans. "The purpose of coordinating with the Pakistanis will be to make the Soviets bleed," explained US national security adviser Zbigniew Brzezinski, "for as much and as long as is possible."[13] These Cold War calculations set Afghanistan ablaze.

As the Americans and Pakistanis began to covertly traffic new weapons across the border region, local traders quickly became a lifeline to the Afghan mujahideen, providing crucial supplies to fighters on the ground. The economy of the entire border region adapted to the war. With every battlefield success, the Americans gradually increased their contributions.[14] Emboldened by this support, multiple mujahideen groups emerged, each representing an ethnic or tribal community but all committed to the common anti-Soviet cause.[15] Rebel commanders flocked to Peshawar to receive support from the ISI, even from distant communities in the far northern and western provinces of Afghanistan. Pakistani intelligence agents used their refugee camps as a cover for fighters to move back and forth across the border, from battlefields to arms bazaars.[16] Under the guise of seeking asylum, the mujahideen would cross into Pakistan and then be welcomed by ISI field operatives who had new weapons and ammunition waiting. These supplies were also trafficked directly to ISI bases established within the Pakistani tribal areas, which acted as safe havens for mujahideen commanders crossing the border back into Pakistan.

The situation escalated to critical levels, however, when the PDPA discovered that the Americans and Pakistanis had teamed up to supply the mujahideen resistance. "The Soviet high command was acutely sensitive to the activities of the Mujahideen in the eastern border provinces of Kunar, Nangarhar and Paktia," explained ISI Brigadier General Mohammad Yousaf. "Just across the frontier in Pakistan were the Mujahideen's forward supply bases, training facilities, and scores of refugee camps. From this area the great bulk of arms and ammunition poured into Afghanistan in an endless stream of caravans, or pack trains of animals, moving along the tracks and trails through the mountains."[17] Indeed, these forward operating bases were critical to the war effort. The ISI and CIA even established and defended a base at Zhawara, located five kilometers inside Afghan territory, which was controlled by their partners in the Haqqani network.[18]

Realizing these mountains were the key supply route, the communists immediately started hunting down the mujahideen and the smugglers who were supporting them. The Soviets created a KGB-styled secret police force, the KHAD, and appointed Muhammad Najibullah as its head of operations. Under Najibullah's iron fist, the KHAD infiltrated, spied on, and terrorized any communities that were sympathetic to the rebels.[19] Tens of thousands of civilians were captured. Men, women, and children were dragged out of their homes and disappeared forever. The notorious Pul-i-Charkhi penitentiary quickly gained infamy for being a death camp, full of horror stories of rape, torture, and summary executions.

"The biggest execution operation was the one carried out on 23 December 1983, when from 350 to 400 inmates were picked up for execution from half past five in the evening until one o'clock the next morning, mainly from cell-block number 1, where I had been held," shared Mohammad Hassan Kakar, a prominent Afghan historian and former inmate. "In a little over four years (until May 1984), between 16,500 and 17,000 inmates were taken out for execution to places in Dasht-e-Chamtala beyond Khair Khana to the north of the city."[20] The gray stone fortress reeked of human filth and decay. Whispers told of how inside its thick walls, the KHAD used electrodes and boiling oil on screaming prisoners to extract information.[21] Others would sexually brutalize a suspect's daughter in front of her father to break his will. As droves of newly arrested victims were marched through the front doors of the prison, thousands of disfigured corpses were dumped into mass graves out the back.

At the height of the war, there were a hundred thousand informants on the PDPA payroll. The KHAD had eyes inside every single mujahideen faction in Afghanistan, and its agents followed the rebels back through the mountains and into the Peshawar bazaars. Soviet infiltration and espionage had put everyone on edge. Entire communities fell into terrified silence, not knowing who among them was a spy. If the trade trucks didn't move, however, then the war would have been over in a month. The jihadists pushed back hard.

Leading the operation on the ground was the ISI special operative Sultan Amir Tarar, aka Colonel Imam, who specialized in irregular guerrilla warfare and was the chief agent responsible for coordinating ISI operations and developing close relationships with Afghan commanders. To balance against the KHAD, the Pakistani ISI tracked down the communist moles and worked to secure safe passage for supplies through the off-road smuggling routes in the mountains. "My job was training and operations. There [were] over two hundred officers and junior commissioned officers on my teams," explained Imam. "We had ten to twelve teams [and] a number of secret camps. All of my officers were majors and colonels, experts in their field, and I being the senior most, was the coordinator. I was in charge [of them all]. I used to make the selection of [which commanders and officers could] come [to the camps] and who not, and then I would monitor whether the training was being imparted correctly or not."[22]

Through Imam's selection process, the ISI developed a special relationship with the most powerful mujahideen parties in the fight, known as the Peshawar Seven: Jamiat-i-Islami (Islamic Society of Afghanistan); Hizb-i-Islami-Gulbuddin (HIG, Islamic Party–Gulbuddin); Hizb-i-Islami-Khalis (HIK, Islamic Party–Khalis); Harakat-i-Inqilab-i-Islami (Islamic Revolutionary Party); Ittehad al-Islami (Islamic Union); Mahaz-i-Milli-i-Islami-i-Afghanistan (National Islamic Front of Afghanistan); and Jebhe-i-Nejat-i-Milli (National Liberation Front). Of the seven, the two largest groups that received the most support were the Jamiat-i-Islami Party, headed by Tajik leader Burhanuddin Rabbani, and the Hizb-i-Islami (HIG) faction, led by Pashtun commander Gulbuddin Hekmatyar.[23]

"We were not only supporting Gulbuddin Hekmatyar. We were supporting seven parties," explained former ISI Director-General Hamid Gul, who was the highest-ranking general in the agency from 1987 to 1989 and directly responsible for Pakistani covert assistance to the mujahideen. "But of course, Rabbani and Hekmatyar were the leading parties. And these two parties received the maximum share because they had the ability. So they received an almost equal share."[24] It was more than just talent, however, that put these two commanders at the forefront of Pakistani generosity. Indeed, both Rabbani and Hekmatyar had already earned the favor of the ISI, having previously protested against the Afghan government and fled to Pakistan in the mid-1970s. These old relationships gave them a keen advantage during the anti-Soviet campaign.

Supporting so many diverse groups, however, was a massive covert operation that required tremendous logistical coordination. "I used to make the distribution to the parties," explained Colonel Imam. "[But even more] important was logistics . . . getting hundreds of thousands of tonnes of explosives, weapons, and ammunition from various countries by ship coming to Karachi, then from Karachi putting them onto trains and secretly bringing [them] to various places near to the border, then putting them into the trucks, [and] then distributing to the parties. I was in the field collecting people in Peshawar and Quetta, carrying out selections [of mujahideen commanders],

IMAGE 3.1 Interview with Pakistani ISI officer Colonel Sultan Amir Tarar, aka Colonel Imam, at his office on base in Rawalpindi, Pakistan.

getting the weapons from the logistics [team], and giving them [to the mujahideen]."[25] Within this covert operation, the existing trade and smuggling infrastructure became an essential conduit for moving goods across the border.

The entire economy of the border region was transformed by this secret operation. In lieu of household goods, the truck caravans started carrying weapons, ammunition, and medical supplies. Traders unloaded these goods on the Pakistani side of the tribal belt, then onto donkeys and camels that could traverse the back-road passes and cavernous tunnels through the rough mountains to rebel bases. And back in Afghanistan, amid the burnt orchards, farmers that dared to stay behind started growing opium-producing poppies in their poisoned and damaged fields.[26] Heroin factories sprang up in the mountains, processing the harvests into pure white powder for the global black market. Guns flowed into the country, and drugs moved out. By the mid-1980s, business in the border region had become militarized, criminalized, and dangerous.

To ensure that the operation ran smoothly, Colonel Imam sent in highly skilled field operatives to probe every insurgent commander and cross-border trader in the region, building powerful trust-based relationships to keep the KHAD at bay. These agents also provided training to the Peshawar Seven. "There were over twelve subjects [that ISI operatives taught to the mujahideen]: Stingers, antitank training, antiaircraft training, automatic weapons training, sabotage," explained Imam. "There were people in psychological operations, there were intelligence operations people, and there were protocol people."[27]

The rebels learned quickly, inflicting damage on their powerful opponents. Ambushes, raids, and subterfuge all helped the beleaguered underdogs take out Soviet tanks and convoys.[28] These guerrilla tactics created a frustrating military quagmire for Moscow inside Afghanistan. The mujahideen also made a bloody example of their Soviet captives, striking fear into the heart of the Kremlin. They mutilated, castrated, and skinned them alive as vengeance for their innocent daughters and sons, lost to the black abyss of Pul-i-Charkhi.

Despite their grit, however, the haggard mujahideen factions continued to be outgunned by superior Soviet military technology. As soon as the Soviets called in aerial reinforcements, even the most well-planned guerrilla attack could be crushed. Then finally, in 1986, the Americans dropped their thin pretense of noninvolvement and decided to back the insurgency with their own military hardware. After much pressure from Islamabad, the CIA agreed to deliver its newest state-of-the-art, portable, infrared surface-to-air missiles directly to the mujahideen. The ISI field agents then taught the Peshawar Seven commanders how to use these American Stingers against enemy aircraft, integrating the technological innovation into their flexible guerrilla style of warfare. Colonel Imam not only personally delivered the assets but also arranged for practical training for each of the top commanders, affectionately calling them his "best students." Under Colonel Imam's guidance, the mujahideen learned to balance the missile launchers on their shoulders and to fire accurately against moving targets while working cooperatively with a team of guerrillas.[29]

The Stinger missile program was a game-changer. With the new weapons and personalized training, the mujahideen took to the offensive. All of a sudden, the beleaguered Afghan rebels were downing Soviet helicopters with remarkable ease, neutralizing their air advantage. Colonel Imam praised his favorite students for their prowess and boasted of their success. As the tide of battle turned, the nightly news began to broadcast Cinderella stories of mujahideen victories while the Soviets watched their latest warbirds fall from the skies and burn in the fields.

When the Kremlin uncovered the details of the American Stinger missile initiative, the Soviets added new fire to their Cold War in Afghanistan. The

Soviets deposed Karmal and installed the former KHAD chief Najibullah as the new Afghan president.[30] Najibullah knew the traders were the critical link between the Americans and the mujahideen, and he redoubled his efforts in the border region. The KHAD set up military bases along the unmarked border to try to block the flow coming through Pakistan and also sent agents more aggressively into the mountains. The "Soviet border strategy was based on maintaining a multitude of posts, large and small, close to Pakistan. They were intended to seal the border and interdict our supply routes," explained Brigadier Yousaf, who personally supervised the arms convoys. "It was rather like a person trying to shut off a large tap by putting his hand over it."[31]

While the Soviets were unable to seal off the border region, however, they did radically destabilize its trust environment. To stay ahead of the double agents and keep arms safely moving under the many eyes of the KHAD, the cross-border traders had to build deep personal relationships with both the Afghan commanders and the Pakistani intelligence agents. In this hostile trust environment, Islam became a powerful shortcut for identifying "godless communists" and their supporters.

To forge the critical trust-based relationships needed to sustain the jihad, Pakistani agents, Afghan commanders, and cross-border traders therefore all rallied behind their common Islamic identity to weed out potential traitors. The fact that Pakistan, which held the purse strings of CIA money, had a staunchly Islamist political identity set the tone of these interactions.[32] The traders took bold actions to demonstrate their religious credentials, and all of the Peshawar Seven openly adopted an Islamist political platform to signal their commitment and smooth relations with Pakistani intelligence officers. The ISI patiently and consistently worked to train the Afghan commanders, and the traders kept the arms flowing through the mountainous caves and off-road smuggling routes. Together, these unlikely friends combined their unique abilities to stop the advance of the Soviets and bring down the empire once and for all.

In the process, the business class made a fortune. The trading tycoons that already dominated business in the border region became even more empowered by the infusion of new weapons. As they became critical players in the anti-Soviet campaign, the traders quickly learned how to leverage their financial influence. Far from being pawns in the political game, these business elites became an important linchpin between powerful spy agencies and battle-weathered guerrillas. They gave the Americans and Pakistanis instrumental use of their mountain passes, while using the influx of new resources and business opportunities to amass private power and build personal ties to the leading Afghan commanders.

The mafias that dominated the trade routes were already the toughest gangsters on the subcontinent, with a reputation for rough justice against their enemies. At the street level, they took hostages, issued death threats, and staged gun battles to settle any outstanding debts owed to them. For each illegal shipment, they forged papers, greased palms, and negotiated passage through unmapped back roads. To get rich in this business required political clout, business savvy, and private muscle. Tribes needed to be appeased, governments intimidated, rivals forced out, and alliances formed.

These power players all had friends in high places to avoid legal repercussions, and they had built their empires in plain sight of the Pakistani security forces. "It's not *exactly* legal," joked a prominent Peshawar-based smuggler, who regularly lunched with the former police chief.[33] Because the jihad depended so heavily on these business elites to keep the arms supply moving, however, the Pakistani government necessarily turned a blind eye to all of the traders' other illicit activities. As a result, smuggling surged throughout the 1980s and steadily grew into the most lucrative industry in the region, with annual revenues estimated at USD$5 billion.[34]

The Soviet invasion undoubtedly militarized and criminalized business life in the border region. But the truth is, long before the first Kalashnikov rifle arrived in Kabul, these trading titans were already positioned as dominant actors in the tribal areas, with tremendous sway over politics in their turfs. They had established their power over a hundred years by hedging against the government and perpetuating state weakness on both sides of the border. After securing a considerable degree of autonomy from both Afghanistan and Pakistan, they then developed a lucrative underground economy that had profited heavily from the circumvention of taxes and regulations. Starting in the 1950s, these original transit traders established a sophisticated and modern smuggling network that redefined economic life in the entire region. By the time the first Soviet soldiers entered Afghanistan, their well-oiled illicit trafficking system was perfectly in place to come to the aid of the mujahideen. Covert gunrunning was an easy transition for the business elite who knew all the secret ways and hidden passages through the mountains.

But how did these smugglers become such indispensable allies in the Soviet-Afghan War? What caused the uncanny alliance between the mafia and the mujahideen? To answer these critical questions, it is necessary to enter this treacherous business world at the ground level, from the surreptitious deals at seaports to the secret cave passages through rough mountains. The rest of this chapter illustrates how the need for trust drove the business class in the border region to embrace its Islamic identity and invest in Islamic institutions. The story begins in the shadow of a century of imperialist violence, and it takes off in the aftermath of state independence. With weak governments on both sides of the mountains, the old tribal traders transformed into new international smugglers, and they created the most powerful and dangerous illicit industry in the region. Unpacking the unscrupulous origins and evolution of their clandestine business—from camel caravans to tax evasion to gunrunning—reveals the symbiotic relationship between Islam, states, and smugglers that defined the volatile border region and changed the course of Afghanistan's future forever.

States and Smugglers: The Origins and Evolution of Industry in the Border Region

Traders in the border region are adamant: "Our camels and our families have crossed these mountains for generations," they swear. "No one can say this border is true." Indeed, caravans have been passing through their tribal communities for over a millennium, well before the modern state was even born.[35] Talk of smuggling is absurd to people who do not recognize borders and cannot even see where these boundaries have been drawn. To them, the unmarked Durand Line that separates modern-day Afghanistan and Pakistan is a baseless nineteenth-century British invention, an alien and invisible construct that arbitrarily divided close-knit families and tribes.[36] From the moment the Durand agreement was signed, the Pashtun traders ignored this imaginary line and continued to trek over the rugged mountain passes unimpeded.

There was no pushback from the state. The Afghan government had always given the tribes a wide berth, allowing them to continue their commercial interactions without undue imposition.[37] Even the first Afghan kings of the eighteenth century knew not to interfere with the livelihoods of their tribal peoples, granting them a remarkable degree of autonomy.[38] After several disastrous attempts, they also learned not to tax the tribes, lest they accidentally provoke a rebellion.[39] Instead, fatefully, the old kings turned to foreigners to help fill state coffers.

The British and Russians seized on this opportunity, eyeing the rugged mountains as a strategic buffer zone between their empires. At first, their foreign aid bought the Afghan state leeway with its unruly rural communities.[40] But from the late nineteenth to early twentieth centuries, the British and Russians used their economic influence to try to violently dominate Afghanistan in their so-called Great Game.[41] The tribes raised local militias to fight back against the repeated invasions, and the Afghan government tried to wrest itself from foreign rule. Without a domestic tax base, however, for almost a hundred years the Afghan state was being force-fed by the same hands that were strangling it.[42]

Ironically, it was as a result of this aid dependency and state weakness that the Afghan government was forced to accept the Durand Line in 1893, although Afghans have consistently and fiercely disputed their consent to the agreement. For over fifty years, this problematic border festered in the background, and the traders carried on their normal economic activities. But when Pakistan finally acquired its sovereign independence from British rule in 1947, through violent partition with India, it provoked another serious international crisis.[43] Afghanistan immediately refused to recognize the validity of the Durand Line and declared an irredentist claim over all of the Pashtun areas of Pakistan, a demand it has pursued to this day.[44] To rebuff this irredentist challenge from Kabul, the Pakistani government granted the Pashtun tribes in its western frontier a promise of considerable political and economic autonomy.[45] In return, the tribes tacitly accepted the new Pakistani government—and also largely ignored it.[46]

To defend against the territorial challenges from both Afghanistan and India, however, the Pakistani state badly needed cash. The government had received little foreign aid in the early years after independence,[47] and it was hesitant to directly tax restive ethnic and tribal communities, especially in contentious border regions.[48] To compensate, Pakistan decided to impose heavy customs duties on all imports arriving at its main Karachi Port in the southernmost point in the country. Because these indirect taxes would be less noticeable than household or property taxes, the government hoped to increase its revenues without provoking uprisings against the new state.[49]

To implement these new tax codes in accordance with international laws and norms, in 1950 Pakistan and Afghanistan signed the Afghanistan Transit Trade Agreement (ATTA), which allowed goods entering landlocked Afghanistan to bypass the Pakistani customs duties while still allowing traders to use the Pakistani seaport at Karachi.[50] Because Afghanistan is not connected to the sea, and yet relied on Karachi Port for imports, this agreement was necessary to avoid double-taxing imports heading for Afghan markets. Under the ATTA, goods earmarked for consumption in Pakistan would therefore be subject to the Pakistani government tax at the point of entry in Karachi, whereas those destined for Afghanistan could bypass the duties.

The entire smuggling industry was created in reaction to this legal instrument. Although the customs duties seemed innocuous in Islamabad, the Pashtun tribes in the border region regularly imported goods through the

Karachi Port and controlled the movement of goods across their mountainous trade routes. The state was weak and the informal economy was strong. As soon as Pakistan's new tax law came into effect, the traders quickly devised a system to exploit the ATTA by falsely earmarking goods they intended to sell in Pakistan as if they were destined for Afghanistan, thus allowing them to evade the higher Pakistani customs duties and sell their goods at duty-free prices on the black market.

The tax code created an irresistible opportunity for the prospective smugglers. According to the law, to import goods directly into Afghanistan via Pakistan, a transit trader needed to acquire paperwork through the Ministry of Trade and Commerce in Kabul, paying a bank guarantee of 1.5 percent of the total value of the trade shipment. With this permit, he could then ship the goods in a sealed container to the port at Karachi, where the transit trader's consignment would be verified by Pakistani customs agents and approved to bypass the Pakistani customs duty. The container would then travel to the Peshawar Dry Port, where traders would present an official document called *ilm-o-khabar*, the formal import license issued by the Afghan trade commissioner in Peshawar.[51] The Pakistani customs officers at the Peshawar Dry Port would then cross-check the packing list with the *ilm-o-khabar* to make sure that the goods in the container matched the license. Once verified, the customs officer would stamp his approval for continued transit onward to Afghanistan. The Peshawar-to-Jalalabad trucks could then bring the goods across the border to Torkham in Afghanistan, where the transit trader would then pay the much lower Afghan customs fee at the border crossing.

Realizing that the new Pakistani customs duties were going to dramatically undercut their profits, the traders developed a scheme to circumvent the system. Under the ATTA, all that was needed to avoid the hefty Pakistani duties was a letter of credit acquired in Kabul to ship goods directly from the Karachi seaport to Afghanistan. The traders therefore arranged to import a surplus of goods beyond the demands of the Afghan market, and then they secretly brought the excess back through the porous border.[52] To succeed, the traders built networks from Karachi to Kabul. The population of Afghanistan was just over eight million at that time, whereas Pakistanis were nearly five times that number. The math was simple, the markets were enticing, and the loophole in the agreement was big enough to gross billions of dollars in duty-free sales.

To capitalize on this opportunity, the traders devised a series of steps to get from the port to the smugglers' market. Imagine, for example, that a businessman wanted to sell a popular style of Chinese-made winter blankets, on which the Pakistani government had placed a fairly heavy tax. He estimated the demand in Afghanistan to be twenty containers worth of blankets, and in Pakistan one hundred containers. The first step was to contact his partner in Kabul to secure a letter of credit to import 120 containers into Afghanistan, thus bypassing the heavy Pakistani customs duty for the entire shipment. He would then set up his base of operations in Peshawar and arrange for the blankets to be shipped wholesale from China to the Karachi Port. His partner in Karachi would then pay clearing charges, inspection fees, demurrage payments, and an extra sweetener to expedite the process.

Next, the goods would move on to the Peshawar Dry Port via train and would then be reloaded into trucks heading for Afghanistan under the inspection of the Peshawar customs officers. Here the trader would pay standard baseline bribes per truck. The heaviest graft, however, happened at the Afghan Trade Commission in Peshawar, which would approve the original permit from Kabul, double-check the *ilm-o-khabar*, and confirm that the blankets were indeed destined for Afghanistan. The trader needed a friendly relationship with the Afghan trade commissioner to avoid getting fleeced. (Notably, if the contents of the shipment did not match that of the original permit, then additional payoffs might be required at this stage.)

With a green light from the trade office, the blankets could then move on to the border post at Torkham.[53] There, the customs clearing agent would charge a nominal inspection charge and allow the trucks to cross. Once these palms were greased, the trader's local Afghan partner could receive the trucks at the Jalalabad-Gomrak trading post inside Afghanistan. At this point, the partner would ship twenty containers' worth of the blankets onward to Kabul and then smuggle one hundred of them back to Pakistan through the back roads in the tribal areas, paying a modest transit fee to the local communities. The trader could then sell his blankets to the larger Pakistani market in local smugglers' bazaars, courting buyers with discounted duty-free prices.

In time, the wealthiest business elites simplified and expedited this process. The biggest bosses paid a larger bribe at the outset, falsified all of their paperwork, and unloaded their blankets directly in Pakistani territory, while hosting the police chief for lunch.

Afghans and Pakistanis from all walks of life took advantage of this new opportunity. Afghan traders serviced their interior, and they also set up shops in Peshawar's lucrative smuggling bazaars to sell to the larger Pakistani market. The tribal communities living in the border region also did well. They charged the trade community for *rahdari*, or "safe passage," and earned money doing

IMAGE 3.2 A truck passing through the Torkham border crossing at the Pakistani-Afghan border en route to Peshawar via the Khyber Pass.

the labor of moving the goods through their rugged territory. Because there was already a traditional exchange of goods coming across the border, smuggled goods were seamlessly integrated into the existing flow of trade. As profits surged, the downtown bazaars bustled with commercial activity, and the rising titans of the smuggling industry moved into newly constructed manors in the posh suburbs of Peshawar.

The ATTA loophole created a windfall for the entire cross-border trade community, but it came at the direct expense of the Pakistani state. Faced with multiple ethnic uprisings, however, the government was disinclined to target the informal economy. Because the Pakistani government had already granted the tribal belt autonomy, forcibly undercutting the traders risked disrupting delicate political relations in the restive border region. Pakistan did have the capacity to close its borders, but rather than upset its own population, the government used its power to punish Afghanistan for its irredentist claim. When Afghan forces made incursions into Bajawar in the summer of 1960, for example, Pakistan severed its diplomatic relations for nearly two years and closed its main road to Afghan goods moving into and through Pakistan, including the critical sale of pomegranates and grapes.[54] The closure of the formal roads sent a clear message to Kabul.

When it came to cracking down on smuggling activities in its own backyard, however, the Pakistani government took a hands-off approach. In fact, some officials actually saw this boon in the informal economy as a way to buy the loyalty of the Pashtun tribes and prevent rebellion. They even sponsored the construction of new smugglers' markets in Landi Kotal in Khyber Agency and Angor Adda in South Waziristan Agency, which created jobs and money-making opportunities for the more marginalized tribes.[55]

Accordingly, those participating in customs duty evasion were resolute that the business was not truly illegal, even though they admitted that it violated Pakistan's tax code. Most viewed their business as a natural extension of the historic trade between Afghanistan and Pakistan that had occurred for many centuries. The transit traders were also quick to point to the apparent acquiescence and even support of the Pakistani government in this tax evasion. The biggest players often rubbed shoulders with police chiefs and state officials, lunching together at their lavish estates. For the most part such relationships were based on mutual private gains. But turning a blind eye to these transactions also bought the Pakistani state political points with communities in the unruly border region. By allowing the industry to continue, Pakistan could drown out Afghanistan's irredentist claims in a sea of smuggled goods.

In this permissive environment, the volume of smuggled goods gradually increased over the years as the players got better at the game. The states on both sides of the border remained weak, but the underground economy grew stronger. The traders established better contacts in each city, and customs officials set more standardized bribes. As the participants grew more practiced, it became easier to predict and calculate the costs and benefits of each shipment. By the time that the first Russian tank rolled into Afghanistan, the ATTA had already transformed traditional trade into a powerful, multibillion-dollar illicit smuggling industry, with tremendous influence over the mountain passes.[56]

The Mafia and the Mujahideen: Arms Trafficking and the Anticommunist Jihad

When the Soviets launched their assault on Afghanistan in 1979, they used the northern roads carved into the towering Hindu Kush Mountains. Their first move was to establish control over the strategic Salang Pass, which connected their bases in Soviet-controlled Central Asia to their newly installed PDPA government in Kabul. The pass cut through snowy peaks over three thousand meters high, a winding corridor of rough tracks and dark tunnels bored through frozen rock. In neat procession, Russian tanks and convoys steadily moved along the treacherously narrow path, supplying their puppet regime in Kabul with the instruments of war. The Soviets seized the state apparatus and oil fields, giving the PDPA a clear economic advantage.[57] With their puppet regime wholly dependent on Soviet aid and loans, the Kremlin held Kabul firmly.[58]

Because Moscow controlled the major roads connecting the north and west of Afghanistan, the mujahideen needed to launch their operations from the south and east. To do so, the mujahideen set up headquarters in neighboring Pakistan while preparing their guerrilla war against the communist regime back in Afghanistan. The well-established smuggling networks in the border region were perfectly placed to facilitate these operations. The transit traders had already built a highly effective smuggling infrastructure through the rugged mountains, and their back roads and caves also provided an accessible route for Pakistani intelligence agents to reach the mujahideen. Members of the trade community who had intimate knowledge of the terrain became key points of contact for the commanders who had been using the tribal belt as a base. The smugglers also assumed responsibility for moving resources on behalf of the mujahideen.

At the start, the Americans wanted to maintain plausible deniability of their involvement in Afghanistan, so the Pakistanis established a covert system to co-opt the transit trade routes. Because the verification of Afghan permits and bank guarantees occurred in Karachi, the ISI was easily able to forge this paperwork. Pakistani forces set up parallel operations alongside import-exporters at the Karachi Port and directly managed the covert shipment of weapons via train to an arms storage facility in Rawalpindi; they then had them trucked to the markets in Peshawar.[59] Once in Peshawar, the ISI then used the traders as an effective cover to move arms into Afghanistan through the off-road routes.[60] Moving the goods through the secret mountain passes to the mujahideen base camps was a critical step that the traders were positioned to execute. The traders took the supplies from Peshawar along the main road in the Khyber Pass, and then they offloaded the goods near Landi Kotal in the Pakistani tribal areas, just a few kilometers from the Afghan border.[61] They then smuggled them over the Afghan border on donkeys and camels through the circuitous off-road routes and secret cave networks, thus dodging the KHAD at the Torkham border post.

Peshawar was the primary conduit that funded all mujahideen groups, but the CIA and ISI also created a secondary channel from the Karachi Port to the Pakistani city of Quetta via train. Local traders in Quetta would receive

MAP 3.1 Soviet and Mujahideen Supply Routes

CIA and ISI supply route from Karachi to mujahideen forces in Afghanistan, via Quetta and Peshawar

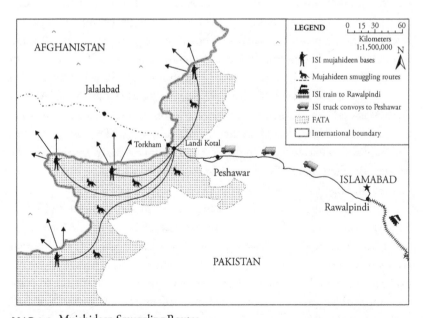

MAP 3.2 Mujahideen Smuggling Routes

ISI supply routes to secret mujahideen bases, via Peshawar and FATA backroads

the weapons via train, truck them to the Chaman border post, and then smuggle them across the border on pack animals along the southern hills and deserts, thereby also eluding the KHAD-controlled Spin Boldak border post on the Afghan side of the border. The Quetta route became the critical supply line supporting mujahideen factions in Kandahar and Helmand provinces in the desert region of Afghanistan.

On the ground, Colonel Imam was personally responsible for coordinating Pakistan's material support to the mujahideen factions, and he worked closely on these relationships. "The good mujahideen used to get maximum aid; [first] the best mujahideen, then good, then lesser good, then average, then low average, and then the worst," he explained. "Even the worst we used to give them; even Esmatullah Muslim from Chaman—who was against jihad—he was a chronic communist. He was a [PDPA] pilot, he deserted, he joined the jihad, he fought, and then he again joined the communists. Still I used to send to his wives living in Quetta a ration now and then, just to maintain [Pakistan's] relations with him."[62] Colonel Imam was a primary contact between the ISI generals in Rawalpindi and the commanders of the leading rebel factions, ensuring that Pakistani intelligence had eyes inside all of these groups.

The majority of the support went to Rabbani and Hekmatyar. In the northern regions, Rabbani's predominantly Tajik Jamiat-i-Islami Party was strategically positioned to target Soviet supply routes through the mountain passes. Rabbani's group proved its talents by bottlenecking Soviet convoys coming through the treacherous Hindu Kush Mountains and Salang Pass, blowing up tanks and trucks with brazen ambushes and cunning sabotage.[63] Rabbani also built an important relationship with popular Tajik Field Commander Ahmad Shah Massoud, who earned the nickname "Lion of the Panjsher Valley" for his prowess on the battlefield. In the Pashtun southern and eastern provinces, Gulbuddin Hekmatyar built the largest and strongest party. Inspired by the Muslim Brotherhood in Egypt, his Hizb-i-Islami-Gulbuddin (HIG) faction secured the largest share of ISI support as well as funding from Arab sponsors.

There were several other significant parties in the Pashtun regions of Afghanistan, however. In the eastern province of Nangarhar, Mohammad Yunus Khalis created a breakaway group, Hizb-i-Islami-Khalis (HIK), which espoused a more indigenous Deobandi Islamist approach that is widely practiced in the subcontinent. In the southern provinces, Mohammad Nabi Mohammadi led the Harakat-i-Inqilab movement, also from the Deobandi tradition. In the center-south, Abdul Rasool Sayyaf's Ittehad faction adopted a radical Salafi doctrine of Arab origins, which was foreign to Afghanistan but won him private funding from Gulf and Saudi sponsors.[64] Mahaz-i-Milli, and Jebhe-i-Nejat-i-Milli both followed a traditional Sufi philosophy, and they were the weakest Pashtun parties. Even these smaller parties, however, received significant external backing through the secret Pakistani mountain routes to support the fight against the Soviets.

Back at ISI headquarters in Rawalpindi, the directorate tried to control the flow of weapons to ensure that the resources had a maximum effect inside Afghanistan. "You see, we had a job. We had a task to defeat the Russians out of Afghanistan. And that was a professional requirement," explained ISI Director-General Gul.

> And in that professional requirement, we had professional criteria [for determining who would receive Pakistani support]. [First], that the party should be large enough and it should have representation in the whole of Afghanistan so that it can assimilate the materials that we give them. Second was the performance: how well they are performing on the battlefield. Were they really attacking the Russians and gaining some ground? And third was discipline, that they would not sell the weapons on the open market, whatever we gave them.[65]

Despite this concerted effort, however, after the ISI handed weapons over to Afghan commanders in Peshawar and Quetta, all of these mujahideen factions still needed the traders to assist with the final leg of delivery of their goods across the border. Rabbani, Hekmatyar, Khalis, Sayyaf, and the others each built personal relationships with the smuggling community to secure the transport of critically needed supplies, which could only be acquired through Pakistan. To get the materials that they needed, they often had no choice but to sell a percentage of their weapons in the smugglers' markets to help pay for shipping and other critically needed goods.[66] At one point, there were so many arms in the theater that it was actually easier to barter with guns. Commanders even drove captured Russian tanks across the border to exchange with the smugglers. "There is probably no commander in Afghanistan who has not, at some point, sold or bartered weapons [to pay transit and other costs]," explained Brigadier Yousaf.[67] With the influx of weapons from the mujahideen, the smuggling community grew increasingly militarized, and every leading business tycoon in Peshawar amassed a private stockpile of arms to secure his growing business interests.

In addition to their ongoing daily business of smuggling food, clothes, and household items, the traders thus took a lead role in this new war economy.

IMAGE 3.3 Assault rifles from the Soviet-Afghan era, held in shipping containers at a weapons facility in Kabul, Afghanistan.

The rebels armed the smugglers through their bartering of weapons, and the factions also gave them a tremendous amount of new business. In addition to weapons, the mujahideen needed everything from antibiotics to blankets, and they needed these supplies delivered covertly. Because the transit trade relied on the acquisition of permits from Kabul, the rebels were unable to directly import emergency supplies for the jihad without inadvertently drawing the attention of the Soviets' watchful eye. For example, as the war continued to take its toll, medical supplies for the mujahideen were in high demand. The PDPA, however, knew which shipments of medical supplies were being imported for its own troops and government-run medical facilities; a large unauthorized shipment of sutures or bandages to an unknown recipient would surely tip off the Soviets. The supplies might be confiscated, or even worse, the strategic locations of mujahideen bases could be discovered. The formal transit trade was much too dangerous for the mujahideen.

Because they were unable to import these goods directly, the rebels therefore asked the smugglers to acquire and move materials needed for the jihad to Peshawar, and then traffic them to the mujahideen through clandestine routes in the tribal areas. The price of these goods was sometimes higher because either the Pakistani customs duty had to be paid or the goods were locally manufactured, but the smuggling channels provided a safer option for commanders. Transit traders experienced in using the off-road passes for smuggling purposes were well positioned to provide this service to the mujahideen.

The burgeoning heroin trade was also a new windfall for the smugglers, who served as middlemen between Afghan commanders and international drug dealers. The mujahideen collected opium harvests from poppy farmers within their local ethnic and tribal communities and then brought the dry resins across the Pakistani border for processing. Heroin labs cropped up in the tribal areas so that local producers could sell a more value-added product on the global black market. As the supply surged, the smugglers developed new relationships with global criminal networks, which secured the export of white powder out of the Karachi Port and into lucrative western markets. As the traders established ties with these clandestine international buyers, opium provided the Afghan mujahideen with a valuable product to barter for other desperately needed supplies.

As they systematically built their wealth and influence, the smugglers found new political allies in Pakistan. Not only could established traders ensure that drugs, guns, and other contraband evaded scrutiny by the authorities, but they could also acquire police assistance to guarantee safe delivery through Pakistani territory. The very same police officers that were responsible for investigating the contents of trucks were also on the payroll of the largest transit traders. Clients could request that they not be bothered about a particular container.[68] The trader could then call their police contact, request that they look the other way for that specific consignment, and ensure that no one else inspected its contents. Other special requests were also accommodated, such as expedited shipment and security guarantees for more complex deliveries. These business elites enjoyed legal impunity and political perks from the Pakistani government in exchange for their cooperation with the war effort.

Drugs and guns were obvious moneymakers in the new war economy; however, the conflict also increased opportunities in the trade of everyday goods like food, clothing, and construction materials. In practical terms, the covert arms smuggling operation increased the number of trucks on the roads approaching the border with Afghanistan. These trucks were loaded with weapons heading toward Torkham and Chaman, but they were empty coming back. Traders took advantage of the surplus transportation capacity and began filling the returning trucks with both licit and illicit goods destined for Peshawar's bazaars. Instead of relying on the back roads through the tribal belt, they made use of the extra trucks in the Khyber Pass to facilitate their deliveries. Business life in the border region thus turned into a sophisticated illicit enterprise, composed of arms smugglers, human traffickers, and drug dealers. While traditional trade continued, most traders became increasingly involved in a blend of legal and illegal activities.

The formal transit trade lulled under the Soviets, but the smugglers benefited from the boon in clandestine business opportunities. They covertly supplied arms to the rebels and then transported opiates and people back across the border. The war had not only been good for business but also granted the traders a remarkable degree of influence. Afghan commanders became loyal customers of the wealthy Peshawar-based traders, and the mujahideen found a second home along the Pakistani border. The arms bazaars were well supplied with a wide selection of foreign-manufactured small arms, light weapons, and ammunition, which provided the rebels with a safe space to regroup and resupply.[69] The ISI even set up offices for the leaders of the disparate mujahideen groups in Peshawar in an effort to coordinate their military and political activities.[70] By the later stages of the war, each of the major rebel factions had a suburban base on the outskirts of Peshawar, a short drive from the business elite's stately mansions.

The traditional trading community thus transformed into a powerful illicit enterprise that both served the purpose of war and profited from its destruction. The covert arms channels militarized the smuggling industry, and the surge in narcotics trafficking further criminalized it. On the one hand, the invasion generated a powerful Islamist narrative that socially constructed the jihad around the highest religious ideals. On the other, the mujahideen heavily relied on revenues from narcotics trafficking, which is considered fundamentally un-Islamic. The cross-border trading community found itself caught at the nexus of these two contradictory forces. In response, as the business class became more involved in illicit activities, they simultaneously increased their outwardly religious commitments and efforts. By the time the last Soviet left Afghanistan, the smuggling industry had evolved into a militarized criminal network with a decidedly Islamist political character.

Heroes and Heroin: Islam and Drug Smuggling in the Soviet Era

The Red Army invasion of Afghanistan made it easy for the rebels to frame their struggle as a moral battle for the very soul of the Muslim world. The atheistic nature of the communist system and the aggressive social reforms imposed by the PDPA justified the rebels' resistance on religious grounds, as communist policies were widely seen as an assault on traditional life and the sanctity of Islam.[71] Stories surfaced about Afghan girls being forced at gunpoint to attend Soviet schools dressed in uniforms with short skirts, which was a violation of traditional customs of dress. The stories of rape and torture from Pul-i-Charkhi also made their way into the narrative. The violent excesses of the KHAD, the indiscriminate Soviet air raids, and the notorious colorfully painted landmines all added to popular disgust toward the regime. In mosques around the world, sermons expressed outrage over Soviet depravity and concluded with prayers of support for the mujahideen. After the services, collections were taken in support of the cause, and excited young men gossiped about how they too might join the rebels. Across the Muslim world, the Afghan jihad was framed as a battle between pious believers and godless communists.

A multitude of popular myths emerged that told of miracles and divine interventions on the battlefield. In the Khyber Mountains, it was common to hear tales of angels wearing bright green turbans arriving suddenly in the middle of a gun battle. These spirits would come to the defense of besieged and outmatched rebels, saving the day with critical military reinforcements. Answering the prayers of the true believers, these heavenly agents would blow up Russian tanks and aircraft and then disappear into thin air. As the stories were retold, these virtuous angels were said to be no less than seven feet tall, with perfectly unblemished white robes and shining black beards. Every community had its legend. Villagers from Khanabad swear that, from inside the shrine of a fallen mujahideen leader, a great fireball flew from the ground to down a Russian helicopter. Countless stories of spiritual magic and bold heroism surrounded mujahideen, each of which signified divine support for their cause.

Islam thus became the rallying point for the anti-Soviet cause, building a common language to define the political struggle. On the international stage, the mujahideen inspired thousands of fervent believers from around the world to join their fight, including those who would later form the original al-Qaeda network. These motivated foreign fighters pledged their fealty to the jihad and their willingness to make the ultimate sacrifice. They traveled to Pakistan and then crossed the mountains to stand shoulder to shoulder with the mujahideen on the front lines.

Members of the business community in the border region chimed in on the emotional narrative, declaring their own devotion and commitment to the Afghan cause. The traders signaled their loyalty by outwardly adopting a strict and devout ethos and by making donations to Islamic charities. Their religious credentials also helped the Pashtun traders to solidify their relationships with mujahideen from diverse ethnic and tribal backgrounds, including those from remote parts of Afghanistan who spoke in foreign languages and dialects and with whom they had little else in common. Islamic identity became an essential way for businesspeople to display their moral solidarity with the mujahideen across these other lines. Most of all, demonstrating solid Islamist values was necessary to secure the lucrative arms contracts with the ISI, which had a staunchly Islamist political identity. Although originally from Punjab, Colonel Imam grew a flowing beard and wore a traditional Afghan *patkay* (turban), commonly worn by Pashtun men. Even his nickname translated to "the one who leads the prayer," which signaled his personal piety to the mujahideen commanders. To fill the trust deficit created by the Soviets, the smugglers, intelligence agents, and rebels all leaned more heavily on religion to build trust.

Religion played a particularly important role in creating a sense of safety among these parties, especially as a way to buffer against infiltration by the KHAD. While not a flawless strategy, religion did provide some strategic value to all participants in the jihad. To start, Islam gave rebels from different geographic and linguistic backgrounds a point of connection, which built a sense of camaraderie and unity against the Soviets in what was otherwise a highly fragmented operation. Furthermore, emphasizing religiosity created a way to screen for suspected unbelievers. Islam is a demanding religion that requires frequent action from its adherents. Indeed, a Soviet mole might have a hard time playing the role of a true devotee who consistently prayed five times a day, fasted under difficult conditions, memorized passages of the Holy Quran, and gave regular alms to the mosques.

The mujahideen woke an hour before the crack of dawn to make the first of their five daily prayers (*fajr*), and it became common for the rebels and their supporters to mock the communists for being too weak and lazy to rise so early. In fact, in mujahideen-controlled territory, first graders were explicitly taught that "[PDPA] Khalqis and Parchamis wake up late and do not pray."[72] Religious observance therefore distinguished the mujahideen from their opponents, and it also put a premium on espionage. In this cloak-and-dagger world, these arduous baseline metrics of religious piety made it labor-intensive for a nonbeliever to convincingly fake camaraderie with the mujahideen. In the battle against godless communism, Islam became a critical shortcut for establishing trust.

This reliance on Islamic identity to build trust was not new, especially for the business class.[73] For over a thousand years, caravan traders have relied on their common religious identity to move goods across the mountains, connecting distant and diverse communities.[74] Sharia law worked alongside other local cultural institutions, such as the consensus-based *jirga* system, to smooth economic and social relations and settle disputes between tribes.[75] The business class in particular had always used Islamic laws, norms, and institutions to facilitate commercial life and build trust-based partnerships. Because of the high premium placed on economic integrity in Islam, religious adherence was already widely used by the traders as a way to evaluate the reliability of a prospective partner. Outward displays of piety were a social necessity.

For example, almost all businessmen in the region conformed to a traditional comportment, which includes wearing a traditional head covering and growing a beard.[76] Many businessmen also carry prayer beads into their business meetings, signaling that throughout their worldly endeavors they are also engaged in a constant reflection on the divine.[77] All prominent traders also carry the title of haji, meaning "one who has performed the pilgrimage," and are addressed by this honorific in their professional affairs.[78] So important is this distinction that a businessman who has not performed the hajj by middle age would be met with scorn.[79]

Successful traders were also expected to donate money for the upkeep of mosques and madrasas, sometimes even establishing a charitable trust (waqf).[80] If a businessman failed to make these contributions, he would not only be showing his lack of regard for widely held Islamic rules and norms but also his greed and stinginess. Indeed, a trader who was willing to cut corners with God might also be seen as more likely to rip off his own associates. Support for local Islamic institutions and charities was a must to be included in elite business circles.

The business class did not just invest in these institutions, however; it also actively participated in their social activities at the community level. For example, traders often attended events sponsored by the apolitical missionary group Tablighi-Jamaat, which preaches spiritual purification within the popular Deobandi revivalist tradition of Islam.[81] Every Thursday, Tablighi-Jamaat held an overnight gathering for men, called *Shabi Jummah*, at their main center in Peshawar, the *Markaz*.[82] The traders would pack into the Peshawar Markaz on these nights, using the venue to network and meet. Many traders spent several nights of dedicated prayers in the Markaz as a way to indicate even greater spiritual commitment and build more trust-based relationships. Tablighi-Jamaat's annual three-day-long gathering at Raiwand was also a key event for the traders, and attendance on the final day was considered a social necessity for the elite.

Islam had long been a social lubricant for the business class. During the Soviet-Afghan War, however, the traders built on these long-standing relationships with Islamic charities and organizations to further demonstrate their solidarity with the mujahideen, investing heavily in initiatives that supported the cause. Because traders dominated the markets, they played an important middleman role in linking aid donations to both the humanitarian effort and the jihad. Given their strong relations with both Islamic charities and the Afghan commanders, cross-border traders could also transform cash donations from around the world into the material supplies required by mujahideen in the field as well as for humanitarian causes in the refugee camps. "Buying arms for fighters was not done very secretly," explained a prominent Peshawar-based trader. "Actually, donation of arms was considered legitimate."[83] Donations were also used to pay for medicine, food, equipment, and transportation costs, all in support of the anti-Soviet campaign.

In addition to their direct support for the jihad, some traders also engaged in their own humanitarian activities in the camps, providing food, shelter, and other emergency supplies to the poor. Much of this aid effort was channeled through the mosque and madrasa system, which the business elite already had a long history of supporting. Local imams would announce a general collection at the conclusion of Friday prayers, and the traders assumed a lead role in responding to these calls. Tradition dictated that the business class take greater responsibility for charity in their communities, and a trader's reputation depended on his generosity and piety in such matters. Islamic charities and organizations also directly approached members of the business community, going door-to-door to solicit donations from well-known shops and offices.[84] Islamic charities also held fundraising events in support of the Afghan cause, which were attended by rich patrons from the business community who wanted to see and be seen.

Over the course of the war, however, the business class in the border region also became increasingly involved in violent and illicit business, some of which quite obviously contradicted Islamic law. Its members would trade in clothes and fruit on one day and then participate in gun and drug trafficking on another. The traders could find moral arguments to justify gunrunning and smuggling, which were supporting the jihad, but in Islamic law both the production and the consumption of intoxicants are explicitly forbidden. Narcotraffickers had a difficult time explaining themselves. "But these are natural botanical products," one midsize drug dealer tried to argue. "They are plants, which are created by God."[85] When challenged on this claim, he muttered that he could not be held accountable for the end-user drug addicts and that these consumers were non-Muslims and thus not his moral responsibility. Others tried to hide their involvement in the drug trade behind their devotions. In one case, two Peshawar-based traders undertook a forty-night commitment to prayer, called a *Chilla*, in which they remained in the Markaz throughout their pledge. Despite this outward display of piety, however, these businessmen were actually waiting on a large consignment of heroin that was to be delivered by the end of their forty days.[86]

The surging heroin industry created an awkward conflict with the traditional religious culture of the smuggling community. To resolve this moral dilemma, some traders sought special Islamic rulings (fatwas) justifying their activities. Many rightly argued that the drug trade was created by the brutal Soviet air raids and that without poppy crops poor Afghan farmers could not survive. This humanitarian excuse allowed the drug trade to take off at first, but it quickly became clear that the lion's share of the profits went to the traffickers, not the farmers. Participation in the heroin industry was hardly a charitable endeavor, and it was clearly a violation of Islamic law. Businessmen who wanted to profit from the narcotics industry therefore needed a way to restore their reputations.

To counter criticism and protect their interests, the smugglers who transitioned into the drug trafficking industry therefore made particularly generous charitable contributions to Islamic and humanitarian causes. One clear example is the case of a pioneer drug dealer in the tribal region who made his fortune in the heroin trade by developing one of the first networks that connected opium farmers in Afghanistan to heroin labs in Pakistan and then to clandestine international buyers around the world. This drug lord built a powerful empire in the tribal areas, which he ran from his heavily guarded estate.

Notably, not only did this businessman hold the title of haji, but he was also a well-known philanthropist in the tribal belt. In fact, he regularly approached the local hospital in his district and paid the medical expenses of every single patient in need, often for several months at a time. He insisted to the hospital administrator that if any patients were refused care, he would stop this financial arrangement. He was also widely known to give generously to the neediest families in his community.[87] These high-impact donations won him the favor of his local constituency and improved his reputation within the wider business community.[88]

The drug lord also refrained from vain displays and simply and quietly stated that he was doing this "for the sake of God alone." The powerful gossip networks then spread the news of his piety and generosity. His seeming humility won him praise. In fact, in a closed-door meeting of the most powerful businessmen in the region, the dealer's colleagues fiercely defended his professional and personal reputation. One of the most prominent traders in the region (who did not trade in drugs himself) outlined his extensive charitable activities, thus rebutting any allegations that the dealer was a *badmash*, or gangster.[89] The drug lord's philanthropy had successfully cleansed his professional reputation and bought him friends in high places.

Many other drug lords engaged in similar activities, building schools, funding hospitals, and providing emergency relief for the refugees of the Soviet-Afghan War. "Once you get a reputation for doing powder, you have to counteract it," quipped one trader who opposed drugs on religious grounds.[90] In the conservative tribal region, maintaining an honest religious reputation was a necessity to building trust-based partnerships. As the smuggling industry became increasingly militarized and criminalized over the course of the war, Islamic charity actually became a perverse antidote to the reputational costs of engaging in un-Islamic business.

This toxic cocktail of insurgency, criminality, and religiosity consumed the border region throughout the ruinous decade-long war. The impoverished mujahideen turned to their faith to steel themselves against the onslaught of Russian tanks and helicopters. The ISI used religion to screen for potential moles in their spy wars against the KHAD. The traders who dominated the arms trafficking industry relied on Islam to build trust with ISI field operatives and establish partnerships with the mujahideen. Islamic charities rallied around the cause of the jihad, declaring the mujahideen the heroes of the Muslim world. And the heroin dealers invested in Islamic charities and institutions to wash their illicit business dealings. For ten years, everyone had rallied around religion in this fight.

When the Red Army finally withdrew from Afghanistan in defeat, believers around the world praised it as a victory for God over the unbelievers. In reality, there were no such happy endings, no great triumphs of good over evil. In the aftermath of God's great victory over the Soviets, the devil of civil war was unleashed on Afghanistan.

The Coming Anarchy

In February 1989, the last Soviet troops withdrew from Afghanistan. Their defeat was followed by the dramatic dissolution of the Soviet Union in 1991 and an end to the Cold War. For a brief moment, there was elation. An impoverished yet pious people had routed a superpower from its homeland

and then broken its back on the world stage. To the supporters of the muja-hideen, it was a feat that testified to the tenacity, resilience, and faith of the Afghans. To the ISI and the CIA, it was a well-executed collaboration, and their victory was toasted in the halls of power.

The Soviet retreat was celebrated in Islamabad and Washington, but there was also so much to mourn on the ground. One million people had died, and most families had been separated, traumatized, and displaced. Millions more were maimed and disabled by the fighting, decimating the working popula-tion. The intelligentsia had been killed and technocrats had fled. Fields and villages were ravaged and turned to graveyards. The traditional agricultural economy was destroyed and replaced with the booming narcotics traffick-ing business. Smuggling was the only multibillion-dollar industry left in the country.

Najibullah tried to remain in power after the Soviet retreat. Despite a last-minute flood of Soviet economic aid to his regime between 1989 and 1991, the communist government in Kabul was so dependent on the Kremlin that the withdrawal had a catastrophic effect on its power. As the Soviet Union collapsed in 1991, the new Russian regime no longer saw its interests reflected in the PDPA government. Once the Cold War was over, the CIA also immediately lost interest in Afghanistan and terminated material support for the mujahideen. America dropped its anticommunist heroes overnight. Hekmatyar, Rabbani, and the rest of the Peshawar Seven quickly found them-selves scrambling for supplies. The Pakistani ISI stayed in the game, but now with a fraction of the resources. Islamabad kept pumping money and weapons to multiple factions inside Afghanistan, hoping that one of their many prox-ies would win out. But the situation was spiraling out of control.

"The Afghans were greedy for weapons . . . they always wanted more," complained former Director-General Asad Durrani, who led the ISI from 1990 to 1992. "Whenever they fired ten rounds, they would say they fired one hundred to get more. They wanted more weapons for illicit trade."[91] The Afghan militias had come to rely on weapons and ammunition from the Pakistani smuggling routes; with the Americans out of the picture, they now found themselves in competition over an ever-shrinking supply of foreign resources.

Without Soviet support, the PDPA government also found itself insol-vent. The regime went bankrupt. Najibullah's lack of funds and his inabil-ity to either reconcile or repress the Peshawar Seven led to his resignation in 1992. As the last remnants of communist rule crumbled, the mujahideen fac-tions seized control of the capital city of Kabul. In the vacuum of Najibullah's ouster, they quickly declared Hazrat Sibghatullah Mojaddedi of the relatively weak Jebhe-i-Nejat-i-Milli faction the new interim president of Afghanistan. While Mojaddedi was a respected Islamic scholar and the symbolic head of state, the real power lay with Rabbani, Massoud, Hekmatyar, Sayyaf, and a slew of other ethnic commanders. Members of the former PDPA Khalqi and Parcham factions knew their days were numbered. They fled, switched sides, or were killed. Even staunchly procommunist Uzbek commander General Rashid Dostum rebranded his ethnonationalist Junbesh-i-Milli Party as Junbesh-i-Milli-Islami, feigning an Islamic identity to remain relevant in the new era of mujahideen rule.

Although the mujahideen were skilled guerrillas, it quickly became clear that they had no idea how to govern, especially in a cosmopolitan and modern city like Kabul. In one jarring example, the rebels dismantled the Soviet elementary school system and replaced it with a new, jihad-friendly education program. As seen in Figure 3.1, by the early 1990s, the mujahideen had designed new textbooks for schoolchildren that featured weapons and ammunition. "For subtraction and addition they would use death and bullets," explained a Kabul-based schoolteacher who witnessed the transformation. "A question would ask: 'One bullet plus one bullet equals?' with an illustration. Or, 'A Mujahid encounters a group of five Russians. He kills three of them and captures the rest. How many Russians has he captured?'"[92]

The mujahideen also changed the elementary schools' reading textbooks to reflect the values of their jihad, added the schoolteacher: "The word for letter A [alef] was previously pomegranate [annar], but it was Allah in the new textbooks. For letter T [tae] they replaced mulberry [toot] with gun [tofang]. For J [jeam] it was corn [jawar] but they changed it to jihad. Z [Zae] was carrot [zardak] and now it was alms [Zakat]."[93] After ten years on the battlefield, the mujahideen brought their harrowing experiences of guerrilla war into their new state institutions, from their economic policies to their education platform. It was a disaster.

In addition to being hypermilitarized, the new mujahideen-run government was also deeply divided along ethnic lines. Within two months, Rabbani formally replaced Mojaddedi as the president, and the political competition with his rivals began to spiral. The mujahideen had always been a loosely organized guerrilla alliance that relied heavily on tribal networks for recruitment and leadership. To keep the rebels safe from the KHAD, there had never been a central command structure that governed all of these disparate factions. This strategy made sense for fighting an effective guerrilla war against the Soviets. Once Najibullah fell, however, this loose coalition

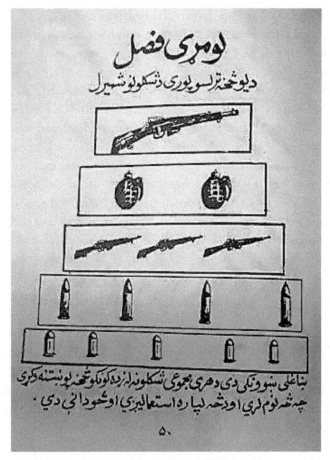

FIGURE 3.1 Page from mujahideen-era math schoolbook

between the powerful commanders fell apart and the rivalries between the groups grew violent. These ethnically divided militias quickly turned from allies to opponents. The former mujahideen commanders turned away from their Islamic jihad and began a campaign of ethnic hatred; they transformed into ethnic warlords.

Some of the older mujahideen went home after the Soviet withdrawal, unwilling to participate in this violent bid for power. The younger fighters, however, had grown up on the battlefield and knew nothing other than war. Many of them had lost their families and friends as children, and then joined the jihad as soon as they were able to carry a gun. Accustomed to scavenging for scraps, the militias cut power lines across the capital city so that they could sell the copper and aluminum quickly. Entire neighborhoods went dark

without electricity. The foot soldiers also raided former Soviet schools, burn-
ing high-quality furniture and desks from the classrooms as firewood rather
than repurposing them. Uncertain of how to live in a city, they then began
looting residences and occupying the homes of families who had fled.

For the young men who grew up fighting the Soviets, war had become a way
of life. They had no families and they had never known peace. After ten years
in the trenches, the adrenaline of battle was in their blood, and the only skills
they had developed were in violence and murder. Traumatized and broken,
the mujahideen factions turned against each other, warring over key positions
of power in an imagined future government. They raided the heavily stocked
Soviet weapons depots, and with this upgraded military hardware they turned
Kabul into a veritable gang war fought with mortar rounds and tanks.

As Rabbani's Jamiat-i-Islami Party failed to consolidate power, political
competition between the factions escalated. Hekmatyar demanded greater
concessions and began aimlessly shelling Kabul from the outskirts of the city,
killing thousands of civilians. Dostum's Uzbek faction from the north staked
out control over a strategically positioned neighborhood in Kabul, just opposite to the Jamiat-i-Islami stronghold.[94] His militias not only bombarded residential neighborhoods under Rabbani's control but also positioned snipers
to kill Pashtun and Tajik children playing across the river.

Sayyaf's ultraextremist Ittehad faction established a base in Paghman, to
the west of Kabul, and his Pashtun militias began systematically raping and
pillaging civilians from the minority Shiite-Hazara communities. To protect
the Hazara population from these brutal ethnic cleansing campaigns, Abdul
Ali Mazari led the Hizb-i-Wahdat Party, which built a fiefdom in western
Kabul. These Shiite-Hazara militias then began systematically killing Pashtun
and Tajik minorities in their turfs.[95] Militias loyal to Rabbani, Massoud,
Hekmatyar, and Dostum all retaliated against both the Hazaras and each
other. In the aftermath of the Soviet war, these latent ethnic and tribal divisions became the fault lines of a new ethnogenocidal civil war. The mujahideen commanders who had so gloriously defeated the Soviets had now turned
into rapacious ethnic warlords who brutalized and robbed their own people.

As the security environment deteriorated, life in the bazaar was also
deeply affected. Security costs for the traders skyrocketed, and the honey-
moon between the smuggling community and the Afghan commanders
began to sour. While the Soviet war may have been a boon for business, the
civil war in Afghanistan was something else altogether. The American supply
lines had dried up, and the wheat fields were awash with opium-producing
poppies for the heroin industry. Poor families starved. As the cash-strapped

mujahideen turned against each other in a bitter ethnic contest, they became more desperate to refill their war chests. There was nowhere else to turn but the business class. The relationship between the commanders and the smugglers thus shifted from being reciprocal to predatory. As the ethnic warlords carved bloody fiefdoms into the Afghan countryside, the traders desperately needed a way out.

Out of this anarchy, a new band of Islamists gave them one.

4

Traders and Taliban

BUSINESS INTERESTS AND ISLAMIST POWER IN AFGHANISTAN

Do not be concerned for worldly gain;
Look to your religion and faith. Don't lose your religion.
O unfortunate one! Every problem has a solution;
Do not lose hope in God, or frown in despair.
It's a great shame that the well-fed snatch food from others;
While you have food and water, don't steal from others. . . .
If they don't have piety and honesty,
Then don't sit with such companions.

"YOUR RELIGION," poem by Rahman Baba

BY THE TIME the Soviets left Afghanistan in 1989, the smugglers had built an extensive empire on both sides of the border.[1] The leading magnates had done especially well. The president of a leading business association, the Pak-Afghan Transit Trade Association (PATTA), the veritable godfather of the smugglers' bazaars, had built himself a heavily gated courtyard mansion in the posh suburbs, directly across the road from the main army base in Peshawar. His lavish manor featured towering white marble columns, four separate family wings, a forty-square-foot handwoven Persian carpet, and a golden chandelier hanging from the center of the intricately decorated domed ceiling in the main hall. From the balcony of his plush estate, the trade president could watch Pakistani soldiers patrolling the army compound just across the road. In the main hall, he frequently served chai and lunch to Rabbani's, Mojaddedi's, and Hekmatyar's top deputies, each looking to negotiate deals that would supply their militias.

Even for the heavyweights, however, the cost of doing business in the early 1990s was getting steep. With the end of the Cold War, foreign money disappeared and profit margins narrowed.[2] Pakistan was still pumping in supplies, but the superpowers had gone home. As the mujahideen clawed at each other for resources, the business community also began to feel the pinch. Local ethnic militias extorted money from trucks along every major road across Afghanistan, cutting off the Peshawar business elite from traditionally valuable inland markets. The tycoons were well off enough to have a buffer against these rising costs on the roads, but the smaller players were priced right out of the game. As the stories in this chapter reveal, as the civil war raged and the costs of business increased, the traders grew increasingly frustrated with the high costs of militia checkpoints and warlord extortion. Even the godfather, in his opulent suburban manor, was starting to get annoyed with the mujahideen commanders.

Meanwhile, the situation inside Afghanistan deteriorated into horrifying anarchy. The countryside had been carved into an array of ethnic fiefdoms, each under the command of a local warlord.[3] The strongest factions made a bid for Kabul, rolling tanks through residential streets and turning apartment buildings into military bases. The commanders divided the city into warring turfs, each of them declaring their right to rule the central government. At the neighborhood level, the militias began specifically targeting civilians from rival ethnic groups, setting up checkpoints in each of their territories to screen for minorities. They stopped civilians on the roads and asked them to pronounce different words to determine their ethnic backgrounds, murdering anyone who responded with the wrong inflection. Tajik and Hazara militias executed those who responded with a Pashtun accent, and vice versa.[4]

The ethnic fragmentation of the old mujahideen may have worked well against the Soviets, but in the aftermath it fueled a wave of genocidal violence. As these factions took control of the streets, Kabul's cosmopolitan residents suddenly found themselves in the middle of a rival warlord's turf. Families fled for their lives. Hundreds of civilians packed into decrepit vans and buses, desperately seeking transport to any destination that took them out of the capital. Those who stayed behind risked everything. "If you were wise, you ran," shared one family member who escaped the fighting.[5]

Women were especially vulnerable. Roving militias dragged screaming girls off the streets into their jeeps, to be brutally assaulted for days. Some chose death over rape. One Kabul resident recounted:

There was a girl next door named Nahid. She went outside either to fetch water or distribute *Halawa* [a sweet dish] for *khairat* [charity] when the gunmen saw her. They stalked her and found out which apartment she was in. They came during the night to break into their house to kidnap her, but she jumped off the fifth floor balcony to escape rape and save her family's honor. Her father and neighbors put her dead body on a stretcher and started marching toward the presidential palace, but the demonstrators were soon dispersed when a mujahideen check post started firing live ammunition at them.[6]

The civil war violence spread from Kabul to every remote village across the desolate countryside, as the former mujahideen turned into ethnic warlords and rapacious gangs. In the north and west of Afghanistan, Hazara, Tajik, and Uzbek commanders competed for control over key cities and mining resources. "Hazaras raped Tajiks; Tajiks raped Uzbeks," said the head of a women's civil society organization in Mazar-e-Sharif. "We had a lot of ethnic problems. At that time, [there were many] militia commanders."[7] In the south and east, rival Pashtun factions competed for power, fighting along tribal lines. "No one was safe," explained a medical doctor from Kandahar. "You could not walk the streets or carry money. Girls and boys would just disappear off the streets."[8]

As the ethnic violence spiraled out of control, the militias that once defended Afghanistan had now become its predators. "They would come inside the purdah and tie up the men by gunpoint," said a humanitarian worker from rural Kandahar province. "They would take the women and rape them in front of their fathers, husbands, and brothers. After they finished, they would leave them alive [as a mark of dishonor on the family]."[9] Driven by the need to retaliate, the militias grew ever more sadistic. "One of my neighbors was an older lady," said a man who was a resident of Kabul during the civil war. "Her family had fled, but she was too weak and frail to travel, so she stayed behind. When the militia came for her, they beat her so badly her skin was inflated [with blood]. They were joking that she didn't look so wrinkled when red and swollen. Once they had beaten her raw, they gang-raped her many times and left her for dead."[10]

The gangs also gained a reputation for capturing and sodomizing young boys, then selling them in the infamous and archaic pederastic rape practice known as *bacha bazi*, or "dancing boys." Militias not only brutalized these young boys themselves but also trafficked them into prostitution to wealthy buyers who purchased the kidnapped children as sexual slaves. This monstrous depravity of the civil war was a sharp contrast to the lofty and self-righteous religious proclamations of the mujahideen during the anti-Soviet campaign.

After the Soviet withdrawal, these ethnic militias dropped the pious performance and unleashed a torrent of sadism and sin.

It was from this moral abyss that the Islamists took their stand. The Taliban movement emerged as a fierce, puritanical reaction to these atrocities. The movement was born in a remote village called Sangesar, in rural Kandahar province, in the spring of 1994.[11] According to the oft-repeated legend, a notorious local commander named Saleh had kidnapped two girls at one of his checkpoints at Pashmool. After seizing the girls, he shaved their heads, assaulted them, and then handed them to his entire militia to be repeatedly gang-raped inside his base.[12] Horrified by these atrocities, the relatives and villagers from the community approached their local cleric, a religious schoolteacher named Mullah Muhammad Omar, and asked him to save the girls. Mullah Omar had a reputation for piety and courage during the anti-Soviet campaign, and the villagers beseeched him to take action against the malevolent warlord.

In response, Mullah Omar rallied two dozen of his religious students, or Taliban, and held an emergency meeting. "A group of Taliban gathered and chose the late Mullah Sahib [Omar], May God forgive him, as the leader and pledged allegiance to him," explained Mullah Abdul Salam Zaeef, a former senior-level Taliban member who helped found the early movement. "These were not tribal or ethnic elders. They were Mujahideen, former Taliban Mujahideen who pledged allegiance. These were around thirty to forty Taliban who came to the White Mosque [in Kandahar] and the movement rose from here. This is where the campaign started. People were interested because the situation in Afghanistan was intolerable. They wanted somebody to stop these [militias] and when Taliban announced their existence, the people knew that the Taliban could save Afghanistan."[13]

Indeed, rescuing the girls from the warlord's clutches became a rallying point for the Taliban. According to the story, Mullah Omar and his supporters had only sixteen rifles between them and no heavy weapons. But armed with their convictions, this small band of firebrands attacked the heavily guarded base to rescue the distressed daughters against extraordinary odds.[14] According to the fable as told in villages and towns across Afghanistan, the Taliban then freed the kidnapped girls, killed the evil commander Saleh, and hung his dead body from the barrel of a captured tank. Mullah Omar then triumphantly drove the tank through the village, parading the warlord's dangling body before the cheering villagers as a warning to anyone who dared molest the girls of his village.

IMAGE 4.1 Tanks compounded from the Afghan civil war era, stockpiled at a Heavy Weapons Cantonment facility on the outskirts of Kabul, Afghanistan.

Of course, this never actually happened. "Saleh had kept [the girls] with himself at the checkpoint and after doing whatever he did with them, he had them killed and left their bodies on a desert," explained Mullah Zaeef. "I had witnessed this with my own eyes. I was there when we found the abandoned bodies. Then we found [their families] to hand over [the deceased] to the Herati people. Their bodies had decomposed."[15] Another former Taliban official confirmed the heavy truth about the notorious commander: "The Taliban killed some of Saleh's men but Saleh himself fled the scene unharmed. The reality was a bit mundane and depressing. Saleh was killed a few months later in another encounter in [the] Del Aram district of Nimroz province and the kidnapped girls were never really found. The Taliban only found the remains of two dead bodies in a nearby trench that were hardly recognizable."[16] There had been no heroic rescue or cheering villagers; like so many others, the story of the girls had ended with a small pile of stones in Afghanistan's endless graveyard.

The Afghan population, however, had already had enough of these tragic tales of woe. In war, people need heroes and miracles. And so, with all of its embellishments and inventions, the legend of Mullah Omar continued to spread. As excited villagers and refugees retold the fanciful tale of the Taliban saving the two girls, popular enthusiasm for the movement grew. Under the banner of a new Islamic revolution, the Taliban also refused to give up and continued to charge forth against the heavily entrenched warlords. "At the time many even among the Taliban thought it was a suicidal folly," mused the former Taliban official. "The prospects of a ragtag Taliban group defeating a well-armed militia commander were apparently slim. But Mullah Omar believed that 'trust in God has no failure.'"[17] In time, their tenacity and commitment paid off and they gradually got better at staging rescue missions. Despite their failure to save the two young girls in the fable, "in subsequent operations the Taliban did free large numbers of teenage sex-slaves from their warlord captors."[18]

As these legends of valor and gallantry spread far and wide, the Taliban attracted supporters and recruits from across the southern and eastern provinces, as well as thousands of disaffected young men who were living in Pakistani refugee camps.[19] "We need[ed] enough men to stand up to other groups of bandits and robbers," explained Mullah Zaeef, "a group that cannot just defend itself, but also other people's rights."[20] By late autumn 1994, between forty and fifty commanders pledged their allegiance to Mullah Omar and declared their dedication to sharia as the guiding source of law and order.[21]

Despite these lofty ideals, however, the early Taliban were deeply pragmatic in their objectives. "Mullah Omar wasn't a man of big talk. His plans were modest in the beginning of the movement," explained another former Taliban official.[22] "After consulting his friends among the former Mujahideen members in Zangawat village of Panjwai district, Mullah Omar's initial intention was to remove the system of checkpoints installed by various warlords on the main highways in Kandahar."[23] Their success in clearing these predatory checkpoints added to their legitimacy and further boosted their recruitment. By the end of that year, approximately twelve thousand Afghan and Pakistani madrasa students had arrived in Kandahar to support the movement.[24]

With support swelling for his movement, Mullah Omar announced the Taliban's mandate to purge the rapacious ethnic and tribal factions terrorizing Afghan civilians and to rebuild order and stability by returning to Islamic law. From the outset, the Taliban movement built its political platform on a Sunni religious identity, rooted in a conservative Deobandi approach, rather than exclusive ethnic or tribal criteria. This religious identification allowed foot soldiers from rival factions to defect to the Islamists. The first to switch sides were Pashtun foot soldiers from the Hizb-i-Islami-Khalis (HIK) and Harakat-i-Inqilab factions, who were easily absorbed into the new movement;

both groups espoused a Deobandi religious identity and refused to fight their own brethren. When the Taliban rolled into Kandahar, they made the southern city their new de facto capital and the home of their burgeoning Islamist movement.

Gulbuddin Hekmatyar, however, pushed back hard against the new Islamists that were challenging his turf. Since the anti-Soviet campaign, Hizb-i-Islami-Gulbuddin (HIG) had been the leading Pashtun Islamist faction in Afghanistan. Hekmatyar had also adopted an Ikhwani ideology that was closer to Egypt's Muslim Brotherhood than it was to South Asia's Deobandi Islamism, which further separated him from HIK, Harakat, and the Taliban. To rebuff the rising Islamists from Kandahar, Hekmatyar reasserted himself as the rightful leader in the south and the east.

At the beginning, Rabbani's Jamiat-i-Islami Party assumed that the Taliban could provide them with a strategic advantage against Hekmatyar by splitting the Pashtun base, and they even unwisely offered support to Mullah Omar's group. As the Taliban gained momentum, however, the ethnic warlords in Kabul realized that the Taliban represented an existential threat to all of their fiefdoms, regardless of ethnic identity. Several commanders tried to build alliances with the Taliban to avoid the confrontation, but Mullah Omar refused to compromise with any groups that had a history of atrocities. His spiritually motivated warriors pushed further north toward Kabul and declared all the ethnic warlords, including other Pashtun factions that resisted them, to be the enemies of Islam and Afghanistan.

After consolidating Pashtun support across tribal divisions in the south and east, Mullah Omar's government then courted Islamist sympathizers from Tajik and Uzbek communities in the center, west, and north. With every battlefield success, the Taliban assimilated Sunni militiamen across ethnic and tribal divisions into their fold and brutally enforced discipline within their new ranks to ensure that their foot soldiers were compliant with sharia. Against this rising tide of Islamist power, the ethnic warlords frantically banded together, forming a loose network called the Northern Alliance. But these measures came too little and too late. The Taliban's rise to power could no longer be stopped, and the Islamist government in Kandahar had set its sights on Kabul.

Within less than two years, the Taliban movement systematically crushed Hekmatyar, Rabbani, Dostum, and Sayyaf on the battlefield. The Northern Alliance was forced to retreat to a small strip in the northernmost part of Afghanistan, where it was politically marginalized. Only Tajik commander Ahmad Shah Massoud from the Jamiat-i-Islami network maintained his base in the Panjsher Valley, but even his influence was limited.[25] By 1996, Mullah Omar's group held the entire southern and eastern regions, had successfully captured Kabul, controlled well over two-thirds of the Afghan countryside, and established itself as a primitive but powerful Islamist proto-state.

Having expelled their enemies, these Islamist newcomers built a powerfully centralized government based in Kandahar and began to impose radical social and economic policies across the countryside. The Taliban banned flying kites and playing music. They enforced severe punishments (*hadd*) for violations of Islamic law, such as stoning, flogging, and amputations for offenses ranging from adultery to theft.

After the brutal rape campaigns, the Taliban also declared that all women must remain inside their homes, unless accompanied by a male relative (*mahram*) for their protection. Women were prohibited from working, going to school, and participating in public life. In urban centers like Kabul, Mazar-e-Sharif, and Kandahar, these edicts had a devastating effect on women's livelihoods and security, especially for the large number of widows and other women who did not have male relatives to support them. Steeped in a deeply fundamentalist Deobandi religious tradition, the Taliban also brutally laid siege on the minority Shiite-Hazara people in the center and west. Although the Taliban had rejected ethnic divisions, they had just as much fierce sectarian prejudice against Shiite Muslims as many of the warlords they had deposed.

The Taliban's repressive capabilities also allowed them to extract revenues directly from their subjugated population. Most strikingly, after consolidating their power the Islamists fully implemented a countrywide taxation system for the annual collection of *zakat*, a 2.5 percent tax on accumulated assets after subsistence, and *'ushr*, a 10 percent tax on agricultural produce from solvent farmers that was collected at the local level. The fact that the Taliban were able to subjugate the countryside to abide by their writ, especially in the collection of taxes, is indicative of their remarkable degree of centralized political power. After fourteen years of continuous war, the Taliban seized control over the majority of the countryside and rebuilt a dominant, new Islamist political order out of anarchy.

Given Afghanistan's long history of extreme decentralization and weak governance, the Taliban's relative consolidation of power is remarkable. Why was the Taliban movement able to centralize political authority, especially at a time of such deep social fragmentation? The existing literature points to three main causes of the Taliban's success: Pashtun ethnic politics,[26] Islamist ideology,[27] and material support from neighboring states.[28] While these explanations provide important insights on the Taliban's rise to power, they cannot explain why the Taliban were able to achieve victory when other comparable groups failed. During the civil war, there were several Pashtun factions that espoused an Islamist political platform and received significant external support.[29] Pakistan had remained involved in Afghanistan and continued to finance the leading armed Afghan factions, the Peshawar Seven, throughout this period. Officials in Islamabad were still primarily concerned with making sure that a friendly regime took power in Kabul, and they had chosen Hekmatyar's faction, which was both Pashtun and Islamist, as a political favorite in the competition.[30] The HIG faction was the largest and most powerful Pashtun political party in the competition, and it had a long-standing relationship with Pakistan. Hoping to use these ethnic and religious ties to extend its reach across the Durand Line, the Pakistani Inter-Services Intelligence (ISI) had invested hundreds of millions of dollars in Hekmatyar's faction, more than it gave to any other Afghan group at any point in history.[31] Even after the Soviet withdrawal, Pakistan gave HIG greater financial and military support than any other group. Yet none of these Pashtun, Islamist,

Table 4.1 Mujahideen Groups Active in Afghanistan in 1994

Faction	Ethnicity	Ideology	Foreign Support	Local Business Support
Taliban	Pashtun-dominated	Deobandi - Sunni	Pakistan	High
Hizb-i-Islami (G)	Pashtun	Ikhwani - Sunni	Pakistan	Low
Hizb-i-Islami (K)	Pashtun	Deobandi - Sunni	Pakistan	Low
Ittehad al-Islami	Pashtun	Salafi - Sunni	Saudi Arabia; Gulf States	Low
Jamiat-i-Islami	Tajik-dominated	Nationalist - Sunni	Pakistan, United States, India, Central Asia	Low
Harakat-i-Inqilab	Pashtun	Deobandi - Sunni	Pakistan	Low
Hizb-i-Wahdat	Hazara	Shiite	Iran	Low
Junbesh-i-Milli	Uzbek	Ethnonationalist	Uzbekistan	Low
Mahaz-i-Milli	Pashtun	Sufi - Sunni	Pakistan	Low
Jebhe-Nejat-i-Milli	Pashtun	Sufi - Sunni; Nationalist	Pakistan	Low

and foreign-funded factions, including HIG, were able to achieve a similar level of success as the Taliban movement.

Why then were the Taliban able to create statelike control by 1996 while many other comparable factions failed to gain and consolidate power throughout the civil war? If all that mattered was Pashtun ethnicity, Islamist ideology, and Pakistani support, then Hekmatyar should have won the civil war outright instead of faltering and failing. To understand the Taliban's success, we need to return to the bazaars that funded and armed the mujahideen factions during the Soviet era between 1979 and 1989 as well as to the wealthy estates of the smuggling tycoons. By looking behind the fervent ideological rhetoric, we discover that these trading titans played a critical role in the early formation of the Taliban movement in 1994.[32]

Using detailed evidence from the field, this chapter illustrates how the high costs of doing business during the Afghan civil war era precipitated the rise of the Taliban. As the ethnic fragmentation worsened, the traders found themselves paying heavy security prices along the main roads. As the overhead of doing business in the civil war skyrocketed, the traders began to seek out an alternative. At a critical moment in the conflict, the business class made the collective decision to fund the Islamist newcomers as a cost-effective alternative to the ethnic warlords, which catalyzed a dramatic shift on the battlefield.[33] It was this influence of the traders that tipped the scales in favor of the Taliban, setting in motion an unstoppable Islamist juggernaut.

Transit Trade in the Civil War Era

By 1992, the Afghan civil war was in full swing and the Peshawar business elites were becoming increasingly agitated. Insecurity was rampant, costs had skyrocketed, and even the leading tycoons were struggling to stay afloat. Inside his stately domed manor, the president of the Pak-Afghan Transit Trade Association (PATTA) was irate. One of his sons had gotten caught up in the drug trade and lost a ton of money, creating much domestic discord in the mansion. As a traditional smuggler and a respected haji, the president of the trade association was infuriated that his son's illicit activities might affect his professional and personal reputation. It was one thing to do business with mujahideen commanders but entirely another to work in the heroin trade. Debts were settled, blood feuds fought, and relatives disowned. In addition to this domestic strife, the conflict in Afghanistan was also eating into his profit margins. The anti-Soviet jihad had been a tremendous boon for this trading titan throughout the 1980s, but the new ethnic civil war raging across Afghanistan was creating dramatically different opportunities and challenges for his business.

On the plus side, the ouster of the Afghan government opened up business opportunities for the tycoon. Once the paranoid Soviet-backed government was expelled, it became much easier for the trade association's president
to acquire transit trade permits to import all sorts of previously blacklisted
materials directly through the Karachi Port. With the Peshawar Seven commanders now holding power in Kabul, the president's personal relationships
with these powerful elites played in his favor. It also became easier to acquire
falsified documentation to dodge Pakistani customs duties at the Karachi Port
and thus increase sales in the Peshawar markets. Afghan militiamen continued to barter weapons in Pakistani bazaars, and Darra Adam Khel was busy
with customers looking to purchase locally manufactured ammunition and
ordnance. As foreign supplies waned, the ethnic factions relied more heavily on the domestic producers, creating new opportunities in the Pakistani
border towns.

On the other hand, infighting between the commanders also made it
tremendously difficult for the godfather to trade commodities inside of
Afghanistan. Kabul had become a key battleground between the factions.
Rabbani's Jamiat-i-Islami Party fought fierce battles against Dostum's ethnonationalist Uzbek faction in the city center, while Mazari's Shiite-Hazara
militias and Sayyaf's Sunni extremist faction clashed in the west of the capital.
Even more irritating was the fact that both Rabbani and Dostum had issued
their own currencies, the Daulati and Junbishi, making business transactions
in each of their turfs confusing and laborious.[34] To make matters worse,
Hekmatyar had laid siege to the city from the eastern hills, hoping to starve
his rivals into submission. The HIG militias blockaded the roads connecting
Jalalabad to Kabul so that Hekmatyar could both extort and manipulate trade
along this strategic route. Traders looking to move goods across the Khyber
Pass could hustle past Jalalabad, but they often found themselves obstructed
before they reached Kabul. The president's rogue son used his personal relationship with Hekmatyar to secure passage, but in the early stages of the civil
war, both the embargo and the violence had a significant impact on the Kabul
market.

The political conflict in Afghanistan directly impacted the traders in
Pakistan. As the fighting escalated and resources grew thin, higher-level
Afghan commanders began to compete over government posts, including
jobs that profited from the lucrative transit-trade business.[35] One of the
most lucrative posts was that of Afghan trade commissioner, the Peshawar-
based position that was responsible for licensing traders to import duty-free
goods from Pakistan onward to Afghanistan. The commissioner personally

sanctioned each shipment arriving in Peshawar headed for Afghanistan, and he could revoke a trader's license or veto any shipment simply by denying his stamp of approval. With this immense discretionary power, the commissioner could demand that traders pay a percentage on every single shipment crossing the border; these bribes were euphemized as *kharcha*, expenses for getting something done, or *shirini*, a "sweet" for doing special favors. This Kabul-appointed position was necessary to approve the movement of goods, which was essential for both transit traders looking to sell inside Afghanistan and smugglers who wanted to use the Afghanistan Transit Trade Agreement (ATTA) loophole to bring goods to the Afghan border and then back into Pakistani black markets.

In 1992, the position of Afghan trade commissioner was awarded to Commander Haji Masto Khan, who was directly appointed by Harakat-i-Inqilab leader Mohammadi. So valuable was this position that Masto Khan quickly became an important player in the social and business life in Peshawar, profiting from the traders who relied on his office. In December 1994, however, Mohammadi tried to recall Masto Khan and appoint as commissioner another Harakat-i-Inqilab commander, Haji Ahmed Khan Ahmedzai. Unwilling to resign from his plush position, Masto Khan mobilized his personal militia from Paktia province to ward off any attempt by Ahmedzai to occupy the Trade Commission office in Peshawar.[36]

Masto Khan then drove his militias to the suburbs to meet with the president of the trade association at his manor, hoping to secure his loyalty in the dispute. "I am being hung by my feet, and you have to help me to send this usurper back," demanded Masto Khan of the smuggling tycoon, who tried not to take sides.[37] The dispute grew so fierce that Pakistani security agencies stepped in to prevent a full-scale war between Afghan commanders in Peshawar. After withdrawing his troops from the disputed office, Masto Khan personally visited Mohammadi in Kabul and pressured him to extend his tenure as commissioner before letting his successor Ahmedzai assume the post. So profitable were the payoffs that an extension of his tenure was well worth the mobilization of Masto Khan's entire ground force.

As Harakat-i-Inqilab waned in political and military power in Afghanistan, however, Ahmedzai was also eventually pushed out of this plush position in Peshawar. In February 1996, the Jamiat-i-Islami president, Rabbani, appointed Aman Khan of the Mahaz-i-Milli faction as the new trade commissioner. Aman was the brother of the powerful Nangarhar commander Haji Zaman, whom Rabbani had needed as an ally in his fight against Gulbuddin Hekmatyar.[38] In this way, the factions used the Trade Commission office as an exploitable resource to finance the war effort and buy allies. Although the trade office bought the armed groups political leverage, the economic impact of these deals was profound. The bribes demanded by the commissioner came directly out of the profits of the traders themselves.

The corruption was not limited to these official channels, however. Along the main roads connecting the big cities, competing militias set up checkpoints to tax truckers, traders, and civilian passengers. Rather than paying militia salaries, lazy commanders provided their soldiers with positions along potentially lucrative trade routes, thus outsourcing the costs of maintaining their own forces. Militiamen publicly held territory for their respective factions while earning their commissions through extortion activities.[39] This strategy took the pressure off of the commanders' pocketbooks, but it also made their foot soldiers less dedicated to their factions. Their checkpoints were a paycheck, not a calling. Under minimal supervision, these militias used increasingly thuggish tactics to extort the business class.

For the beleaguered Afghan traders, this meant that they "now had to pay duty to regional authorities in Herat and [Kandahar] as well as booties to these checkpoints."[40] Anarchy had bred a new rapacity across the countryside. "The government was nonexistent and regional commanders or thieves had taken control of the area," explained Mullah Zaeef. "When a person was traveling from Kandahar to Kabul, there were about a hundred checkpoints where they would take money [from the traveler], calling it 'commission.' Similarly, if one were coming from Herat to Kandahar, money would be taken from them. Even on byway roads there were chains and checkpoints where money would be taken in the name of commission."[41]

This proliferation of militia checkpoints along key transit routes had a dramatic effect on business life in the early 1990s. Although smugglers retained the ability to sell goods on the Pakistani black market, the checkpoints dramatically increased prices in Afghan markets and made in-land markets inaccessible. Truck drivers not only added checkpoint taxes to their delivery estimates but also increased their fees in response to the risk premium. The additional costs of the checkpoints and shipping were therefore added to the price of the goods at the point of sale.

The farther into Afghanistan a good was to be sold, the more checkpoints it had to clear and the higher its price would be. Remote interior markets became completely unprofitable because the cost of transportation increased prices to the point that they collapsed demand for the goods. Drivers fretted that if they didn't pay up, their goods would be held up and looted or they could be killed. Traders complained that truckers were using insecurity on the

IMAGE 4.2 A street merchant sells fresh oranges at his stall in Old Kabul. The heavy shelling during the civil war era ravaged these neighborhoods and crushed small businesses.

roads as an excuse to overcharge for their delivery services.[42] The civil war kept these costs unstable and unpredictable.

A well-known trader from Jalalabad, frustrated with the difficulty of moving his imports from Peshawar to Kabul, described the scene in his colorful Kuchi dialect:

> Who could have told me that the road to Kabul will be ablaze like this? Wandering like a bewildered head I could not find a single driver willing to move my goods across Torkham no matter how many *kaldars* [rupees] I put in front of them. Those *topaki* [armed] thieves are popping up everywhere, becoming greedier all the time. At least I have bought a machine [a light or medium machine gun], which I am going to mount in my village for these descendants of donkeys. They should not come closer.[43]

An electronics importer further explained the impact of the checkpoints on his business in the early 1990s: "I was told that new checkpoints were emerging on the transit route in an unpredictable way. They said that a gunman with few accomplices may appear at a point—sometimes a new point—saying 'bring out the tax.' When I asked how much a truck was supposed to pay, they said one or two hundred rupees [USD$3–6 per checkpoint] are invariably demanded."[44] While these rates may have been manageable for larger businesses, with increasingly rapacious checkpoints stationed at every rock and turn, many small-scale traders were unable to compete.

Those traders who could navigate the security environment without being overextorted, however, were able to sell at a hefty profit margin. In fact, in exceptional cases, a special relationship with an elite commander could assure safe passage along key transit routes, allowing a trader to circumvent the checkpoints. Street militias were often unruly when left to their own devices, but when their bosses sent down distinct orders, the foot soldiers complied with their directives. Having preferential status with a top commander could therefore give a trader a rare economic advantage over his competition.

At the height of the civil war, for example, Gulbuddin Hekmatyar's HIG forces were in need of intravenous (IV) drips to treat wounded fighters. At that time, many of the IV supplies in Peshawar markets were either counterfeit or contaminated with a bacterial infection that would cause fatal toxic shocks to patients. The impact of these contaminated IVs on wounded HIG troops was significant. To resolve the problem, Hekmatyar made a deal with a wealthy businessman with whom he had many prior dealings: the rogue son of the president of the PATTA trade association. This chosen smuggler became the sole supplier of IV supplies to all HIG militias during the civil war period. Hekmatyar issued the smuggler a letter of authorization indicating this special relationship, allowing his trucks to bypass all HIG checkpoints along the Peshawar-Jalalabad road. The rogue son not only saved on checkpoint prices but also dominated the local market and guaranteed sales.[45]

In an attempt to capitalize on this opportunity, some businessmen also tried to create trade cartels within Afghanistan. Smuggling cartels brought together powerful traders with links to the local commanders from each turf along the trade route. Members of the cartel could collectively negotiate safe passage for their goods all the way from Peshawar to Kabul, thus creating a near monopoly in the Kabul markets. The goal of these cartels was to distribute risk across the entire transit corridor and maximize profits for shareholders. These efforts to capture key markets were not only costly but also met with violent resistance from both political opponents and business rivals, especially when their deals appeared to be favoring one ethnic warlord over another.

In 1995, for example, a team of three wealthy smuggling families—the president's rogue son and two families from the tribal areas—developed a cartel to distribute medicine in Kabul's markets.[46] They each leveraged their elite contacts so that they could successfully negotiate passage through the Peshawar-Kabul corridor without being frustrated by the multiple warlord rackets along the road. Once they had successfully bypassed the heavy fees, they opened a new office in Kabul to begin distribution of their merchandise. Before they could capitalize on the advantage of their much lower prices, however, the cartel office in Kabul was attacked by gunmen sent by a rival wholesaler, destroying the infrastructure. While their cartel had the ability to hit back against their rival, the cost of the fighting made the entire initiative much less financially attractive. Given the added security costs of continuing the medicine cartel, the businessmen decided that it was an unprofitable undertaking. The PATTA president's son and his colleagues decided to invest in other more lucrative options instead. They were, to say the least, quite vexed.

Most lower-level traders, however, had no opportunity to even dare to try such bold endeavors. For the average businessperson, trade into Afghan markets had to become a game of chance. In each gamble, the smugglers struggled to calculate the prospective costs and benefits of moving goods along the same two routes that the ISI had once used to supply the mujahideen factions. Along the northern mountain pass, the Peshawar-based transit traders brought imported goods into Afghanistan through the Khyber Pass and Peshawar-Jalalabad road, and unloaded them at the Jalalabad-Gomrak customs post at the Afghan border. The bigger traders centralized their efforts in Peshawar, which was the larger market. To access the smaller but important southern markets, however, Quetta-based traders would drive through the desert road past the Pakistani border post at Chaman, and then unload their goods in the Afghan border town of Spin Boldak. Once at these border points, the traders in both Gomrak and Spin Boldak would then have to decide whether to smuggle goods back to Pakistan for a lower but more predictable profit or take the risk to bring those goods further into Afghanistan and hope to sell at a much higher margin.

The potential gains in the Afghan markets were attractive, but the risk of losing the entire shipment was too high for many traders. Some bet that they could clear the militia checkpoints, and won big; others went bankrupt playing the odds or were killed when they couldn't pay up. Faced with the tremendous uncertainty and volatility of the Afghan markets, the transit traders increasingly rerouted their goods back into the safer Pakistani markets, using back-road smuggling channels. This resulted in a massive spike in customs duty evasion during the Afghan civil war period: "[Pakistan's] Central Board of Revenue estimated that Pakistan lost $US87.5 million in customs revenue in the financial year 1992–93, $275 million during 1993–94, and $500 million during 1994–95—a staggering increase."[47] These lost customs revenues signaled an exponential growth in the smuggling of licit goods back into Pakistan, like tea and clothing, during the Afghan civil war. The volume of both licit and illicit business, however, was even greater; Rashid argues that smuggling and narcotics trafficking together were likely valued at over USD$1 billion per annum.[48] Indeed, by 1994, the Pakistani markets were awash with weapons, drugs, contraband, and other smuggled goods. The relative safety of the Pakistani markets clearly appealed to the majority of the merchant classes in the border region, who wanted a guaranteed return on their investments.

Dumping goods in Pakistani smugglers' bazaars, however, also meant forgoing the lucrative Afghan market and its connecting routes through Central Asia. As transit traders opted to smuggle their goods back to Pakistan, the supply shortage kept prices high in Afghanistan, whereas the flood of smuggled goods to the Pakistani markets reduced the prices of goods. These market fluctuations were flamboyantly described by a trader in Peshawar, whose quick fortune from smuggling *sopari* (betel nut, which carried a high excise duty in Pakistan) for *paan* (a popular chewable spice medley) prompted his fellow traders to jump on the bandwagon: "I spotted a severe shortage of sopari in Karachi and decided to bring five containers full of sopari from Singapore and sold it quickly for almost a 300 percent profit in the Bara market [main smugglers' bazaar in Peshawar]. We Afridis are a greedy lot, so my envious colleagues rushed to get [sopari] and lost a lot of money. The market got flooded, [and so there were] no buyers [of sopari] to be found for a long time. Most of the demand for sopari comes from Karachi, and no one else in Pakistan or Afghanistan wants it."[49]

While Pakistani markets were flooded with surplus smuggled goods, in Afghan markets demand far outweighed supply. The result was a dramatic shortage of badly needed resources in Afghanistan, which caused tremendous suffering in the interior. This also created an opportunity, however. If a trader could dodge or navigate checkpoints from the Pakistani border posts right up to Mazar-e-Sharif or Herat, he could potentially sell the same goods in Afghanistan for a much higher margin. The roads north and west also led to lucrative Central Asian markets that traditionally relied on the Afghan trade route for imported goods. Central Asia was also an important channel for the booming narcotics trade. In order to navigate these roads, however, the

Afghan trader would have to forge multiple agreements with each faction that held the territory through which the goods were traveling. Even well-established businesspeople gambled with hefty unforeseen losses.

The hard fact was that the ethnic fragmentation and violence had made it very expensive to do business across factional lines in Afghanistan. As a result, more often than not, Afghan traders would simply operate inside their local tribal region, bidding on goods arriving at the Jalalabad-Gomrak and Spin Boldak customs posts at the Pakistan-Afghanistan border. Rather than try to move the goods to faraway markets, the traders would transport them shorter distances and then sell them to traders in the adjacent regions. That way the traders only had to pay for security from within their own ethnic and tribal community rather than trying to work across these lines.

Working within these divisions, however, dramatically affected prices. Every time the goods exchanged hands, the buyers needed to add another premium to the price, both for their own profit and also to pay for the next round of checkpoints or protection racket charges. By the time the goods reached more remote markets, the prices would therefore skyrocket and the demand would consequently plummet. This led the entire supply chain to stall all the way back to Karachi.

As the ethnic conflict between the factions intensified, businesses struggled to protect themselves from the blatant extortion. Convoys were looted and shipments were held up until obscenely high bribes were paid. Along the major trading routes, there were militia checkpoints every few kilometers. In a classic security dilemma, the more one faction taxed its base, the more another needed to squeeze its population to stay competitive. Social fragmentation in Afghanistan had proven enormously costly to the most lucrative industries in the region and had created ire among traders who could no longer profit under warlord rule. The smugglers needed a way out. When the Taliban movement emerged in Kandahar, it gave the business class exactly the sort of alternative it was looking for.

Transit Trade and Taliban

The Taliban's legendary appearance in the spring of 1994 caught the attention not only of besieged rural communities but also of the frustrated business class working on both sides of the border. Indeed, as soon as the Taliban established their control in Sangesar, the business class began to provide charitable donations to Mullah Omar's burgeoning group. "Businessmen were very eager and willing to aid the Taliban because prior to the Taliban it was a state of anarchy," explained Mullah Zaeef. "When the Taliban started organizing and campaigning and took weapons away from them [the commanders and thieves], the businessmen wanted peace and security of their lives and their goods. It was a national awakening. The nation, including the traders, took part. Traders supported a lot because they not only had the wealth, but also were facing problems daily."[50] By clearing the checkpoints and disarming the militias, the Islamists quickly won the favor of the trading community.

As members of the early Taliban movement explained, the reason that they were able to compete against rival commanders without setting up checkpoints of their own was because they relied on donations rather than extortion to fund their operations. According to one senior official, every Taliban fighter received "free food, clothes, shoes, transport costs (to their villages and back to their duty station), and some irregular pocket money, the amount of which depended on the amount of funds and charities available at a given time and place to a group leader. In fact the Taliban abhorred the idea of regular salaries because then it would seem like they were mercenaries. Even senior commanders who spent most of their time in war fronts did not ask for regular salaries; however, their families were supplied with rations and irregular cash from time to time. Those who came from land-owning families did not accept the rations either."[51] These Taliban officials insisted that their financial reliance on voluntary donations, rather than extortion, helped them to cultivate better and more disciplined fighters than their rivals. "The Taliban's costs were not that much either because their government was not like the other governments, as 99 percent of the Taliban were volunteers," added Mullah Zaeef. "Only one percent relied on salaries, which they could easily support with their income. This was one of the reasons behind the Taliban's success, that their costs were lower and their work was voluntary and with honesty."[52]

The Taliban indeed cultivated their reputation for economic honesty. One popular anecdote told of how several Taliban foot soldiers were desperately in need of food, so they broke into a store to eat some melons. But when the shopkeeper looked under the scraps, he found that the fighters had not only paid him for the food but also left him a surplus of cash. Countless stories of this variety, whether real or fanciful, emerged through the powerful gossip networks, broadcast via audiocassettes and videos and embellished further in gatherings at mosques, madrasas, *hujrahs* (common sitting rooms in villages), and *chai khanas* (tea houses). Compared to the rapacious ethnic militias, the new Taliban movement seemed to be providing desperately needed relief to terrorized civilians and frustrated business elites alike. "From the beginning, when the Taliban started, people were very much supportive," explained Mullah Zaeef. "Not only the businessmen and traders, but also the common people. I even remember that when Taliban had not yet reached Kandahar city, some sisters from Kandahar city were giving away their gold jewelry, which is very valuable to women, to support the Taliban. I had never seen such emotions of people as I saw the support back then."[53]

The Taliban's zero tolerance policy on extortion and corruption was, however, of particular interest to traders operating along the heavily obstructed Quetta-Chaman-Kandahar route. The transit traders noted that the territories under Taliban control were free of checkpoints and provided a degree of order and predictability. Frustrated with debilitating checkpoint prices, many local traders turned to the Taliban as a possible political alternative. The business class was therefore both motivated and well positioned to take the lead in supporting the new Islamist movement.

Over the course of the anti-Soviet campaign, members of the business class had developed close relationships with Pakistan-based Islamic charities and causes, which they sponsored as a way to establish their religious credentials. Support for the Taliban during the early stage of the movement was thus channeled through these types of donations via the mosque and madrasa system. Providing food and shelter to poor madrasa students had long been considered a conventional and apolitical charitable activity. In the early stages of the movement, supporting the Taliban, many of whom were indeed madrasa students from Afghanistan and Pakistan, therefore appeared to be a seemingly routine and inconspicuous form of philanthropy. Accordingly, while the ethnic militias were aggressively extorting people at checkpoints, the Taliban benefited from these voluntary charitable donations, which thus made it easier for them to win public favor.

Shortly after the Sangesar incident in May 1994, the religious holiday of Eid-ul-Adha provided the Taliban with an additional opportunity to appeal for charitable donations to help feed and support their students-turned-soldiers.[54] In response to this call for aid, Pakistani mosques and madrasas not only provided food and cash donations but also collected cow and lamb hides left over from the Eid feasts and donated them to the Taliban. "On Eid-ul-Adha we advertised the number of our mujahideen and asked for money and meat donations. Most of the Pakistani masjids and madrasas donated to us," explained another member of the early Taliban movement who was directly responsible for fundraising. "This was a major source of income for us. The Taliban were pious people and the leadership was pious. So these donations we collected were from individual philanthropy. The donations from the business community were completely voluntary. This was *sadaqa* [charity]."[55]

The Eid donations provided food for the Taliban, and the hides were sold to tanneries to manufacture high-quality leather for local and international markets, which served as another important source of revenue for the movement during its early stages.

These nonmonetary donations were an important source of material support during the early stages of the Taliban movement. "These aids were not merely monetary," Mullah Zaeef elaborated. "It was four or five [different] types of aid. Some people brought food, sheeps and cows to slaughter and provide [food] for the people [Taliban], and some people brought clothing and other aid. Some were monetary aid. And some were campaigning and preaching for them. And some, the Mujahideen, the good Mujahideen who had weaponry and ammunition, provided the Taliban with that."[56]

Cash donations, however, were channeled to the Taliban using covert money transfer agencies in Pakistan. "We used the *hundi* [hawala] system to receive money from our donors,"[57] explained the former Taliban fundraiser. "Rahim Afridi was the biggest money transfer person and he would transfer money from Pakistani donors to the Taliban. He had a currency exchange office in Peshawar, but it was an undercover money transfer system."[58] During the early summer of 1994, the Taliban movement developed its capabilities through these types of philanthropic donations from businesses and individuals.

The business community framed this early support as charitable donations while continuing to conduct business as usual. Because it did not stop paying other militia checkpoints, the business community's support for the Taliban was far less risky than if it had presented an outright challenge to powerful commanders. This clandestine charitable approach kept the business community safe while covertly developing the Taliban's material capabilities. The danger to the traders in this arrangement was relatively low: if the Taliban failed to rout the militias, there would be no immediate backlash against the business community because the traders did not take any obvious actions against the commanders. If the Taliban succeeded, the traders would be free of costly checkpoints and could benefit from a more direct economic relationship with the Taliban leadership. These charitable endeavors provided the business class with an avenue to quietly influence the balance of power on the battlefield.

These valuable offerings of food, cash, and in-kind donations from the business community also provided the Taliban movement with the ability to support its foot soldiers directly. While Taliban leaders financed their foot soldiers through the voluntary contributions of the business community, other commanders—who had tightened their belts after the Soviet withdrawal—fed their militias by telling them to directly tax the traders along the road. Even Hekmatyar's well-supported HIG faction had grown accustomed to the easy money of extortion. As a result, while the ethnic militias robbed the business class to pay themselves, the Taliban were free to provide security along the roads because they could pay their forces using donations from their business sponsors.

As the movement gained traction, more powerful members of the business class began to directly finance the Taliban with food and cash donations in addition to more covert charitable activity. The Quetta-based traders in particular began to work collectively to provide direct financial support to the Taliban movement. "Many businessmen and traders began to donate money to support the movement," explained Mullah Zaeef. "One man came to the checkpoint lugging a sack of money behind him. I remember when we counted the notes that the total came to over ninety million Afghanis.[59] This was an unimaginable sum of money at the time; I had never even dreamed of an amount that large. We were stunned by the man's generosity and told him that we would give him a receipt that recognized his donation and charity, but he said, 'I have donated this money for the sake of God alone. I don't need anyone to know about it. There is no need for a receipt or for my name to be known.' Many others came to donate whatever they could afford."[60] It was not only the wealthiest businesspeople who offered charitable donations to the Taliban. In fact, smaller businesses were even more desperate to have these roads cleared, as the checkpoints had completely stifled opportunities for players that could not afford the high risk of extortion.

The business community made these extraordinary financial donations because the Islamists not only removed rival checkpoints but also did not set up checkpoints of their own. The Taliban defined itself as a religiously inspired anticorruption movement, forged in opposition to the abuses and extortion of the ethnic warlords. Given the extortionist tendencies of other factions, members of the transit trade community were delighted with the seeming material asceticism of the Taliban movement. "The Taliban didn't go after our money or materials," explained one trader.[61] Rather, these spiritually motivated Islamists requested modest amounts of voluntary material support, often only their most basic subsistence, which further distinguished them from their rapacious rivals.

When the new Taliban movement therefore offered to remove checkpoints from rival commanders, without installing any new taxes of its own beyond the modest import duty paid at the Afghan border, the traders began to finance their new Islamist allies against the old tribal protection rackets. Because small and midsize traders were losing so much opportunity to do business, they were actually willing to pay higher start-up costs to finance the Taliban to remove the checkpoints. "With the removal of checkpoints the transportation expenses are lower," the traders explained.[62] The more successful the Taliban were at driving out local commanders and clearing the roads, the more resources they received from the transit trade.

In time, the Taliban's revenue generation became more formal and efficient. "When the Taliban reached Kandahar and took over the city, they created an organizational system which reactivated the customs, the taxes," explained Mullah Zaeef. "Therefore, people were supporting the Taliban legally now, and the Taliban could reach their income needs through the taxes and customs. There was no need for people's aid now. And, in [the] meantime, they created the 'ushr and zakat system through the Afghanistan Bank and the Pashtanay Tejarati Bank. Therefore, in about six months, Taliban were stable and independent to stand on their own."[63]

Even more striking was the fact that the Taliban were able to recruit this support from the business class across factional lines. Because the Taliban adopted an Islamist identity over any particular ethnic or tribal group, it was possible for traders from a wide range of communities to support the movement, thus widening the pool from which resources could be drawn. Because the Taliban espoused a fundamentally Islamist identity, they presented themselves as a viable political alternative for ethnic and tribal minorities. By courting support from the business class across local divisions, the Taliban generated enough start-up capital to launch an effective military campaign against the warlords, which in turn generated even broader support, creating a cascade effect on the battlefield.

With this support, by the midsummer of 1994, the Taliban shura (leadership council) had both the material and confidence to challenge Hekmatyar's HIG commanders and other local militias that were dominant in the southern region. Armed with the resources of the business community, the Taliban built their forces and gradually expanded their area of influence within Kandahar province. Pakistan had remained involved in Afghanistan throughout this period, but the Taliban had yet to prove themselves as a viable contender in the competition. Rather, at this time, Pakistani interior minister Naseerullah Babar was engaged in direct negotiations with local commanders in Kandahar and Herat to secure the coveted transit route to Central Asia, which could open up the area for the lucrative UNOCAL-Delta oil pipeline and connect Central Asia to international markets through Pakistan.[64] The Taliban were not even considered players in these high-level negotiations. In the summer of 1994, Hekmatyar was still considered the political favorite of the ISI, even though the Pakistanis were growing frustrated with his poor performance in winning the war.

The Taliban, however, had yet to prove their mettle to those controlling the purse strings in Islamabad, and the Islamic movement therefore relied only on the voluntary donations of local communities and business patrons that had grown frustrated by the political status quo. "In the beginning it was the traders of Afghanistan who wanted the trade routes to Central Asia to be open," argued Director-General Hamid Gul. "Before Taliban appeared on the scene, by the fall of 1994, the warlords had set up no less than 72 posts between Chaman [at the Pakistan border] and Torghundi [at the Turkmenistan border]. And at each post these traders had to pay the price, and sometimes with their life. So really, people were fed up and they started funding Taliban when they appeared."[65] With this support of the business class, the Taliban built their momentum and siphoned support away from other Afghan factions, soon attracting the attention of these key figures within the ISI.

At this time, Colonel Imam was the Pakistani consul general to Herat, and he was one of the first persons from the Pakistani establishment to connect with the new Islamist movement. He described these Taliban commanders as his old leftover mujahideen fighters from the Soviet era, whom he remembered training on the front lines. He claimed to have met with them just days before their first offensive against Hekmatyar: "I went to Mazar-e-Jami— they [the Taliban commanders] also came because many people go—I saw them. I was surprised. My favorite students are here, very good Stinger firers. Abdurrazak was there. There were about six of them, all very senior people."[66] Colonel Imam's patronizing attitude, however, irked some of the original Taliban leadership. "The truth is that behind every successful person you see, even in a university when a student graduates and becomes known, all the teachers argue that this was my student," quipped Mullah Zaeef in retort.[67]

Despite their pride, however, the Taliban did indeed seek Pakistani support to continue their campaign and soon went to Herat to connect with the ISI. "They said, 'We are coming to you,'" recounted Colonel Imam. "I said, 'I have nothing [no financial support] to give you. I am now a [civil] servant.' They said, 'we are not going to demand [money from] you, but we are going to tell you what is our plan.' They came at night. They said, 'We are going to Kabul. We didn't have resources. We came to Ismail Khan [the ethnic commander who controlled Herat province] and he said he is giving us an aircraft.

We are going to Kabul, tell Rabbani we are going to get on to his road and finish all of these checkpoints.'"[68]

Colonel Imam was impressed with their gall and saw that the Taliban were leveraging the ethnic conflict to their advantage. As the warlords balanced against each other, their opposition to Hekmatyar earned the Taliban special support from both Ismail Khan in Herat and Rabbani in Kabul.[69] In fact, Rabbani regarded the Taliban as a local movement that would split the Pashtun population, and thus undermine his rival Hekmatyar by flanking HIG forces in the east. "Rabbani was very happy. He told his commanders to help the Taliban," explained Imam. "He gave him 3 lakhs [300,000 rupees] and a lot of ammunition.[70] Only Hekmatyar decided to fight with them. Rabbani thought, 'Good enough, let them fight among each other. My job will be facilitated.' Taliban came back [to me] and said we have told Rabbani and he agreed. I said, 'OK I can only pray for you.' I thought, 'Look, these guys, they are suicidal. They are going to fight. And they'll be killed. Good luck.'"[71]

In the early stages of the fight, these Islamist firebrands were still newcomers and underdogs, not yet considered a real contender for the Pakistanis. All this would change, however, when the Taliban captured the strategic border town of Spin Boldak, which had been under the control of Hekmatyar's forces. In early October, the Taliban conducted their first serious military operation against HIG commanders in the Afghan border town along the Quetta-Chaman road. Spin Boldak was an incredibly important trading hub, which served as one of the key transit points for Pakistani traders to offload goods headed to Afghanistan or to be smuggled back to Pakistan. Hekmatyar's control over this border point had resulted in heavy delays and debilitating extortion. Trucks could be held until the traders agreed to pay whatever fee the local HIG gunmen demanded. As militia roamed freely through the unruly border town, traders also feared being looted or abducted. The transit traders were desperate to release Hekmatyar's bottleneck at Spin Boldak. In the summer months of 1994, traders in Quetta "had already donated several hundred thousand Pakistani rupees to Mullah Omar and promised a monthly stipend to the Taliban, if they would clear the roads of chain and bandits and guarantee the security for truck traffic" through this vital trading hub.[72] With these start-up funds, the Taliban mobilized a dedicated group of fighters to capture the border post and subsequently earn the attention and support of Islamabad.

With support from the business class, the Taliban strategically targeted Spin Boldak as a direct move against Hekmatyar. The shura's decision was based on three factors. First, HIG and other Pashtun militias were the main cause of resentment for the transit trade community on the Chaman-Kandahar route. Capturing Spin Boldak would earn the Taliban even more support from their business backers, who had specifically asked for the corridor to be cleared of checkpoints. Second, Spin Boldak was home to a major arms and ammunition depot, which could provide the desperately underequipped Taliban forces with necessary supplies. And third, capturing Spin Boldak could help develop relations with Pakistan, which had until that point largely ignored the Taliban and had continued to favor Hekmatyar.

On October 7, 1994, Mullah Omar sent notice to Hekmatyar's forces to hand over Spin Boldak.[73] Colonel Imam explained that Mullah Omar sent two separate warnings to HIG forces to leave Spin Boldak in the early part of October: "He told [Hekmatyar's commanders], 'I will give you seven days to vacate. Talk to your party leaders and vacate.' After seven days, they were still there. The Taliban asked, 'Why?' [The commander said], 'Our party leader [Hekmatyar] says we do not vacate.' The Taliban said, 'I will give you another five days. I don't want to fight.' After five days again he went back and they were still there."[74]

Hekmatyar refused, arguing that he was legitimately manning a transnational port under international law. Making good on his threat, Mullah Omar mobilized his ground forces against the HIG militia at the border post. Financed primarily by the Quetta-Chaman transit traders, the Taliban rallied two hundred fighters to attack Hekmatyar's forces at Spin Boldak.[75] After a brief firefight that left seven HIG fighters and one Taliban fighter dead, Hekmatyar's militia fled. For these soldiers of fortune, the base was worth killing for, but not dying for.

As Hekmatyar withdrew, the Taliban claimed the border town. The capture of Spin Boldak also provided the Taliban with a massive supply of weapons from their defeated rivals that were stockpiled in a nearby arms depot; the supply was estimated at seven thousand tons, enough to equip tens of thousands of soldiers.[76] The battle of Spin Boldak thus gave the Taliban the material resources to successfully secure the most lucrative and strategic transport routes in the southern belt.

They then proceeded to eliminate all checkpoints along the transit route, much to the satisfaction of the business class. "The businesspeople were grateful to have the checkpoints removed," explained the former Taliban fundraiser. "The Taliban did not ask for any taxes whatsoever. They only collected *zakat* and *'ushr*."[77] Colonel Imam described the aftermath of the battle for Spin Boldak: "No check post anywhere! The area was clear. The transport mafia—the transporters of goods—the businessmen, they were very jubilant! They used to be paying a lot of money on the check post to everybody. Then they [the business community] gave a big package to Mullah Omar, thank you very much."[78] With the help of the business class, the Taliban proved capable of challenging well-entrenched commanders.

The Taliban's capture of Spin Boldak caught the attention of key decision-makers in Islamabad who had been watching their standoff with HIG. Pakistan remained keenly interested and involved in its "backyard" and had ambitions to develop a modern transit corridor through Afghanistan to Central Asia, which had been obstructed by insecurity on the roads. Prime Minister Benazir Bhutto had been actively seeking to negotiate safe passage of goods from Quetta through southern Afghanistan and to Central Asian markets since 1993, hoping to increase Pakistan's dominance in regional trade.[79] Hekmatyar's commanders, however, saw the possibility of expanded trade as a potential boon for their faction and had thus increased their extortionist activities. Frustrated with their inability to access lucrative Central Asian markets, the Pakistani intelligence community began to explore the possibility of allying with the Taliban. In spite of its decade of support for Hekmatyar's group, by late 1994 the ISI was impressed with the Taliban's dramatic rising power in the south and began backing both sides. Although support for Hekmatyar continued well into 1995, it now overlapped with aid to the Taliban.[80] The Pakistanis then sat back and watched the fight play out. When the Taliban won, Islamabad took note.

After being ousted from the border post, Hekmatyar complained that the Taliban had Pakistani support at Spin Boldak, although evidence of involvement is disputed.[81] A 1995 declassified cable from the American embassy in Islamabad "denied the report that the Taliban were supported in seizing the armory [at Spin Boldak] by Pakistani Interior Minister's Babar's Frontier Corps."[82] The declassified cable also made reference to the support of the business community, stating that the initial financial support for the Taliban came from "family resources and local business and political connections (including the bazaaris and Jamiat commander Naqibullah), [which] raised 8 million Pakistan rupees (USD$250,000) for the cause and contributed six trucks.[83] Arms and ammunition came initially from stocks left over from the jehad."[84]

Regardless of how much interest the ISI had in the Taliban before they captured the strategic border town, however, the Islamists certainly received Pakistan's full attention shortly thereafter. On October 29, 1994, the Pakistani government had sent a military convoy through Quetta to Herat on a mission to explore development of a trade corridor to Central Asia. According to the declassified cable, the Pakistani authorities "had not even consulted with the fledging Taliban movement when planning the GOP [Government of Pakistan] Central Asian convoy, preferring to deal with more established Kandahari commanders."[85] Along the road, however, the convoy ran into trouble. Three local commanders—Amir Lalai, Mansur Achakzai, and Ustad Halim—held up the Pakistanis for ransom.[86] "And incidentally, I was there," added Colonel Imam with a wink. "I was taking that transport convoy."[87]

Colonel Imam attempted to use his elite position to negotiate the release of the convoy, but the commanders were aggressive. According to Rashid's interview with an unnamed Pakistani official, when the commanders proved uncooperative, Pakistan requested the Taliban's aid: "So we considered all the military options to rescue the convoy such as a raid by the Special Services Group (Pakistan army commandos) or a parachute drop. These options were considered too dangerous so we asked the Taliban to free the convoy."[88]

In response to this call, the Taliban engaged in a brazen military offensive against Lalai, Achakzai, and Halim's forces. "Pakistan sent a group from Quetta," explained Mullah Zaeef. "[Pakistan then] officially asked the Taliban to help find the looted cars and drivers, which the Taliban found for them. At that time, the Taliban desired to have good ties with the neighboring countries, especially with Pakistan, so the Taliban handed over whatever was under their control. This is when the relationship with Pakistan started."[89]

Indeed, their efforts were rewarded. The Taliban released the convoy, freed Colonel Imam and his associates, and killed the field commander who had detained the Pakistanis. Buoyed by their battlefield success, that very evening Taliban forces rallied their eager troops and proceeded to capture Kandahar city. Realizing that they were outmatched, the warlords of Kandahar abandoned their forces and withdrew. Riding the wave of their victory, the Taliban claimed the city with minimal resistance, forcing the surrender of the lower-level commanders and collecting their heavy weapons, aircraft, and military supplies.[90]

The Taliban's release of the convoy and their successful offensives in Spin Boldak and Kandahar city earned them a reputation for being a serious contender in the battle for Afghanistan and won the favor of major players in the Pakistani ISI, including Colonel Imam. Their decisive capture of Kandahar city caught the attention of key decision-makers in Islamabad, who began to discuss dropping their old favorite Hekmatyar in support of this promising new Islamist movement. "The Taliban appeared to be more popular and winning," shrugged General Ali Jan Aurakzai, who was the Core Commander in Peshawar. "Hekmatyar was not winning, so why bet on a losing horse?"[91]

Some Hekmatyar loyalists in the Pakistani establishment begrudged the change, and they managed to secure continued support for HIG until mid-1995. But the smugglers and traders had found their new champion. "Under the Taliban, checkpoints are not seen," was their mantra.[92] Backed by the business class and now by Pakistan, the Taliban quickly became the frontrunner in the competition. They consolidated their material and military resources and began a countrywide campaign against Afghanistan's most heavily entrenched warlords. By 1996, they held the majority of the countryside and successfully constructed the most invasive and domineering government in the history of Afghanistan. The timely donations of the smugglers proved to be a pivotal factor in transforming the nascent Taliban movement into a force that would shape the history of Afghanistan for decades to come.

Afghanistan's Islamist Leviathan

Out of civil war anarchy, the Taliban movement created a groundswell of Islamist power across the southern provinces. Public rage and frustration against the ethnic warlords fueled their momentum and drew support from disaffected communities. After integrating HIK and Harakat militias into their ranks and pushing HIG out of its strongholds, the Taliban began to extend their influence into adjacent fiefdoms. As regional commanders in the southern and eastern provinces surrendered or fell back, the Islamists absorbed their weapons depots and assimilated defecting militias. Coupled with the influx of madrasa students from the Afghan refugee camps across the Pakistani border region, this increase in manpower transformed the Taliban into a serious political contender in the fight.

As the Taliban movement expanded, it set its sights on Kabul. By 1996, the Taliban had established their control over the majority of the Afghan countryside and captured the capital city from the Northern Alliance. As Rabbani, Hekmatyar, Sayyaf, and Dostum all fled, the Taliban removed all of their militia checkpoints and opened up the trade routes. The business community had succeeded in creating its Islamist alternative.

The Taliban government was not all that the transit traders had hoped for, however. Despite their elimination of militia checkpoints, the newly entrenched Taliban government began to affect trade in a way that the business community had not at first predicted. Most significantly, once checkpoints were cleared, the Taliban turned their anticorruption agenda toward the business community itself. Bribery and other forms of corruption that had long served as a social lubricant for facilitating transactions in the transit trade community were now deemed un-Islamic. After the capture of Kabul in 1996, the Taliban sent a new trade commissioner to Peshawar named Haji Mohamad Sadiq Amir Mohammad (aka Maulvi Amir Mohammad). The new commissioner took immediate action against corruption within the trading community. He personally visited the president of PATTA at his domed estate and said, "If I find out that any money was paid to the staff in the Trade Commission, I will cancel that trader's license completely." Such a strong action by the commissioner could have eliminated the offending trader from participating in Afghan markets entirely. The smuggling tycoon was incensed. "With these Taliban, I can't even give 100 rupees!" he griped. "They are making a nuisance for me."[93]

This staunch attitude drew immediate ire from transit traders, whose institutionalized system of corruption was an intrinsic component of their regular business interactions. Without bribe payments, truck deliveries passing through Pakistan would be stalled or held up, potentially jeopardizing the delivery of time-sensitive goods into lucrative markets. This policy shift inadvertently jammed the trade right back to Karachi. But by this point, the traders were powerless to do anything to circumvent the new Taliban laws.

Furthermore, though fierce on the battlefield, the Taliban proved utterly ineffectual when it came to modern economic governance. They were thoroughly ignorant about monetary and fiscal policy, and they forwent the development of industry and enterprise in their relentless pursuit of social and cultural domination. As inflation skyrocketed, the Afghani became worthless, and it became easier for traders to deal in Pakistani rupees on both sides of the border. The exclusion of educated and qualified women from the workforce further depressed the talent-drained economy in the cities. In rural areas, the narcotics trade provided farmers with just enough to survive until the Taliban abruptly banned opium production in 2000 and sent poor farmers into destitution. Economic interests may have helped the Taliban rise to power, but once Mullah Omar had control, ideology ruled in the marketplace.

The Taliban's radical and violent enforcement of sharia law was also a serious deterrent to international investors. Over time, the Taliban's alarming domestic policies and ties to transnational extremists also attracted strong condemnation by the international community. On October 15, 1999, United Nations Security Council Resolution 1267 authorized a sanctions regime against the Taliban and al-Qaeda in Afghanistan. Economic sanctions further depressed the already weak Afghan national economy, which had failed to improve under the Taliban's inept management.

Despite their frustrations, however, the smugglers had sealed their own fate. By ousting their political rivals, the Taliban movement had established itself as the only game in town. By sidelining Rabbani, Hekmatyar, and others, the business community had eliminated the Taliban's political competition, thus giving them a free hand to rule as they saw fit. As Pakistan solidified its relationship with Mullah Omar's shura, the Taliban government dug in its heels. The business elites no longer exercised power over the movement.

Instead, they had created an Islamist leviathan.

5

Beards for Business

THE ORIGINS AND EVOLUTION OF
THE MOGADISHU MAFIA

One day Prophet Muhammad (peace be upon him) noticed a Bedouin
  leaving his camel without tying it and he asked the Bedouin, "Why
  don't you tie down your camel?"
The Bedouin answered: "I put my trust in Allah."
The Prophet then said: "Tie your camel first, then put your trust in Allah."
HASAN HADITH, narrated by At-Tirmidhi

THE LEGENDARY BAKARA market in downtown Mogadishu was a central hub of smuggling activities in East Africa, infamously known for weapons
trafficking through war-torn Somalia into neighboring states. The arms district showcased a diverse collection of assault rifles, machine guns, and rocket-
propelled grenade launchers. Some were stolen from government depots, and
others were smuggled into the country by international dealers in violation
of the United Nations (UN) embargo. Throughout the civil war, roving clan
militias roamed through this volatile bazaar in search of new supplies, testing
their merchandise by firing raucously into the air. Bullet holes pockmarked all
of the derelict shops.

Suuq Bakara featured much more than the instruments of death, however; customers could find everything from narcotics to sweet candies to cell
phones in these crowded streets. The unruly bazaar was a winding maze of
thousands of makeshift fruit stands, clothing stores, pharmacies, and electronics outlets. Vendors of every sort hustled their wares in this cosmopolitan open-air fair. Established merchants had well-protected storefronts, while
smaller players tried their luck selling goods from hand-pulled wagons that
served as rudimentary stalls.

With no police or legal protections, however, working in these markets during the civil war was risky business. Con artists, fraudsters, and criminals crept on every corner, looking for the next sucker to bamboozle. The great fear of every business executive was that these unsavory characters might infiltrate their operations and run off with the company loot. Finding trustworthy business partners was difficult, and fear makes entrepreneurs and investors cautious and conservative. In the absence of a functioning government, foreign investment and access to international markets were also limited. Lawlessness and social fragmentation made Somalia a high-risk, low-trust business environment.

Yet out of this anarchy emerged an elite class of wealthy Somali entrepreneurs who built vast personal fortunes out of the war. To deal with the insecurity and unpredictability, these business tycoons turned to Islam to build trust, lower costs, and increase access to markets. As the civil war dragged on, all of the power players in the Bakara market eventually adopted a new Islamist identity and business culture to mitigate the frustrating social fragmentation. As their stories in this chapter show, Islam helped the elite to create multimillion-dollar empires and connect to markets in nearby Gulf States. Over time, these Islamist businesspeople grew rich and powerful, while millions of ordinary civilians suffered the hopeless penury and misery of war.

Somalia was not always so broken. With its classical architecture and stunning beaches, the ancient city of Mogadishu was once hailed as the jewel of East Africa. Situated along its sandy three-thousand-kilometer coastline, Mogadishu's pristine seaport was a key point of entry for traders looking to sell in markets throughout the region. Overlooking sparkling turquoise waters, the welcoming city served as an important trading post that bridged the Middle East, the Indian subcontinent, and the Greater Horn of Africa. For many centuries, it linked the historic Indian Ocean shipping routes with markets along the Silk Road and connected the Somali coast to profitable markets across the Muslim world, using Islam as a common language to build networks across vast distances. In time, Mogadishu grew into a wealthy and multicultural entrepôt that attracted Persian, Indian, Arab, and Berber merchants to its plush bazaars, renowned for selling everything from fine Egyptian cottons to prized white she-camels.

After decades of external interference, however, this sparkling gem of East Africa descended into an abyss of political chaos and fragmentation. In 1969, a military coup installed leftist dictator Major General Mohammed Siyyad Barre of the Darod-Marehan clan as the head of state. For twenty-two years, his regime was propped up by Soviet support, and then later by American aid, allowing Barre to rule with an iron fist. Then suddenly, in 1991, the Cold War ended and this proxy war in the Horn of Africa was abandoned. After years of reckless economic mismanagement and political divisiveness, Barre's authoritarian government went bankrupt and collapsed. In the ensuing political vacuum, a brutal civil war broke out along tribal lines.[1] As society collapsed, violent lawlessness defined the new war economy and warped the historic relationship between Islam and business.

The magnitude of the violence was extraordinary. Mogadishu became the key battleground between two factions from the powerful Hawiye clan: the United Somali Congress (USC) party, led by interim President Ali Mahdi of the Abgal subclan; and the breakaway Somali National Alliance (SNA), headed by General Mohamed Farah Aideed of the Habr-Gidir tribe. The Hawiye factions immediately targeted Barre's Darod-Marehan brethren, who had benefited from the regime. After seizing control of the city, however, these Hawiye subclans then turned against each other in violent internecine conflict. Mogadishu became the frontline of a genocidal civil war.

At the street level, heavily armed gangs marauded through residential neighborhoods, gunning down rival militias and civilians alike. Drugged-up on a local narcotic called khat, these roving gangs of young men hunted for their clan rivals, especially those they believed had benefited under the former government. As the hostilities intensified, these militias began looting houses and stores, trafficking weapons and drugs, and violently extorting civilians to fund their fight.

Hundreds of thousands of people fled the capital to save their lives. "I hid in the back of a donkey cart for three days with no food or water," recalled a Mogadishu resident from the Darod-Marehan clan who survived the fighting by fleeing to the southern Gedo region.[2] "I still remember the horrific violence on the street," shared another survivor, "people being chased and killed."[3] Even those who escaped the violence of the cities were not safe; many found themselves lost in the middle of the barren desert, without food, water, and protection from predators, both man and beast.

Adding to the misery, the crushing 1991–1993 drought catalyzed an environmental and humanitarian crisis of biblical proportions. In the absence of functioning government institutions, the drought resulted in one of the most devastating famines in modern history, claiming 300,000 lives in less than two years. As scenes of violence, hunger, and despair hit the airwaves, public outcry called for an international solution to the crisis. In response, on April 24, 1992, the UN Security Council resolved to deploy a peacekeeping force to protect the delivery of humanitarian aid to the victims of the famine. The UN

Operation in Somalia (UNOSOM) was charged with providing emergency humanitarian assistance to famine victims and monitoring a weak ceasefire agreement between Mahdi and Aideed.[4]

As the UN peacekeepers tried to deliver food aid, however, the clan militias systematically targeted their convoys and raided their supplies. Mahdi and Aideed also ignored the blue helmets and continued to fight each other in the streets. The humanitarian intervention quickly became a new source of revenue for these armed groups, inadvertently financing their civil war.[5] While thousands of civilians died of starvation in the interior, Mogadishu's markets were flooded with pillaged food aid stolen from the intervention and used as a currency for exchange in the bazaars.

The international community realized that the mission was failing to resolve the crisis and thus expanded the scope of its operations to include a series of broad peacebuilding and state-building objectives. By 1993, the Americans ratcheted up their presence in Somalia, siding with Mahdi's Abgal faction over Aideed's Habr-Gidir group. But as the UN intervention became embroiled in the clan conflict, the peacekeepers became implicated in brutal human rights violations against Somali civilians.[6] In retaliation, Aideed's SNA militias targeted peacekeepers, culminating in the infamous Black Hawk Down incident in which eighteen American soldiers were killed, their burnt and mutilated bodies dragged through the streets by angry mobs.[7]

With no conceivable resolution in sight, the last of the blue helmets withdrew from Somalia in 1995, leaving the countryside to the mercy of the clan factions.[8] For the next decade, Somalia remained in a state of enduring anarchy. The children of the war grew up knowing nothing other than fighting, some joining their clan militias as soon as they were old enough to carry a gun. With no central government, a plethora of new warlords seized control over the countryside, carving it into an array of privately held clan fiefdoms. A perverse political equilibrium was created in which warlords balanced against each other to prevent any single faction from establishing control over the state, resulting in a perpetual state of political anarchy.[9] Fourteen internationally sponsored peace processes aimed at creating a coalition government were hosted in neighboring Kenya, Ethiopia, and Djibouti, to no avail.

While countless efforts at finding a political solution failed, Somalia's clan warlords remained deeply entrenched in their turfs. The situation inside the country was so unstable that it was impossible to gather reliable data on even the most basic human development indicators. Life expectancy was generously estimated at fifty years, one of the lowest scores in the world, and local communities suffered shockingly high rates of maternal death, infant mortality, and child malnourishment. The displacement also devastated traditional agriculture, including nomadic pastoralism. The country had grown so dependent on food aid donations that the farming industry had gone bankrupt, and most croplands were left untilled.

Out of this poverty and devastation, however, a powerful and wealthy new business class emerged in the Somali marketplace. Surprisingly, trade not only continued but also expanded. The bazaars that once sold cotton and camels became the largest trafficking operations in the Horn of Africa. The absence of government created a slew of new opportunities in tax- and regulation-free trade. The arms dealers fared especially well in this civil war economy. "When there is fighting, the demand is higher and this is good for our business," explained a smiling arms trader from Bula Hawa, with a twinkle in his eye.[10] The traders also learned to smuggle drugs and stolen food aid, as well as normal goods, such as fabrics, sugar, tea, and electronics.

Over time, these hustlers evolved into a more sophisticated entrepreneurial class. They created countrywide industries that provided a wide array of goods and services across clan divisions. While political change remained elusive, Somalia's economic transformation was profound. In the absence of government, the market took on an increasingly important role in social life. Amid the rubble and ruin, Somali entrepreneurs built private companies to meet public demands, which grew into multimillion-dollar enterprises. While the state was failing, the market was thriving.

The clan conflict, however, continued to obstruct access to profitable inland markets and undermine business expansion. Due to the violence, social trust had understandably plummeted among the Somali clans, thereby dramatically increasing the costs of doing business across tribal lines. To compensate for this trust deficit, the Somali business community leaned more heavily on Islamic identity and institutions to facilitate economic activities between groups. Without a state to guarantee their transactions, Islam provided a critical source of social capital that allowed the traders to reduce uncertainty, develop business partnerships across local divisions, and gain access to profitable markets in Gulf States. Religious piety proved to be an effective way to profit within the political anarchy.

How did the business class manage to leverage religious identities and institutions to their material advantage? Why did the bazaar turn to Islam in the midst of the civil war? To answer this question, it is necessary to understand how business in Somalia worked, from the rowdy shipping seaports to the volatile back roads in the hinterland. This business world started centuries ago with ancient shipping routes that connected Somalia to the Arab and

Persian sultanates; but as the state failed and the old system collapsed, the traders transformed into a powerful and secretive transnational criminal network, spread across the Horn of Africa.

By entering these war-torn markets and talking to the merchant class, the accounts in this chapter uncover the critical relationship between Islam and business that formed in Somalia and how it evolved under the extreme pressures of the civil war. The stories reveal that terrible fragmentation drove the Somali business community to turn to Islamic identities and institutions to increase trust, reduce their transaction costs, and increase their access to markets, thus changing the course of Somali history.

Camels and Coastlines: The Origins of Islam and Industry in Somalia

"The herd of a man who knows only one place [pasture] does not grow," goes the old Somali proverb. For thousands of years, Somalis were masters in the art of nomadic pastoralism, moving vast distances across their land to optimally produce goat, cattle, and camel products for both consumption and trade. The astonishing nine-thousand-year-old cave paintings in Laas Geyl, found in northern Somaliland, are some of the world's earliest representations of pastoral life, preserved almost in entirety because of the arid climate. These early Neolithic remnants depict the development of a nascent agricultural production economy that set the foundation for a vibrant trading community.

Somalia's largely nomadic pastoralist population, however, made it difficult for early city-states and sultanates to tax and control this transient and mobile people.[11] Instead, urban and rural communities in the Horn of Africa developed their social links through mutually beneficial trade.[12] The merchant class worked cooperatively with nomadic pastoralists to connect the hinterland to the coastal cities and consequently to overseas markets. Long before the existence of the state, the Somali people had established a lively informal economy based on sophisticated commercial linkages between disparate communities.

The introduction of Islam in the early eighth century facilitated the trade between Somalia's ancient coastal kingdoms and the Arab and Persian sultanates across the Gulf. The sea trade also served as a medium for the spread of Islam in Africa, as increased interaction with the Arab world led to the complete religious conversion of the Somali population.[13] "Islam was the faith of urban, mercantile, literate South-West Asia and its adoption brought East Africa into a huge common market," explains Graham Connah. "In particular it ensured commercial and cultural intercourse with the Arab lands to the north."[14] Increased economic interaction between Arab and African traders also helped to develop vibrant cities along the Somali coastline, such as Berbera, Merka, and Baraawe. Like Mogadishu, these coastal cities became key emporia linking East African traders to wealthy Arab and Persian markets.

Islam also provided an important social lubricant to facilitate social and economic interactions within Somalia. Although the Somali people are religiously, linguistically, and ethnically homogeneous, their society is divided between five major clan families: Darod, Hawiye, Isaaq, Dir, and Rahanweyn (also often called Digil-Mirifle). Within each of these families, there are many subclans and sub-subclans that order social and political life. As Islam spread through the Horn of Africa, sharia law melded with existing cultural institutions, including the Somali customary legal code known as *xeer*.[15] Together, sharia and *xeer* served as robust mechanisms for resolving local disputes and enforcing economic agreements between different clans. These informal religious and cultural institutions provided a common legal framework for organizing social and economic life.

The colonial era radically transformed these traditional social, economic, and political systems.[16] By the nineteenth century, Ethiopian and European imperialists had violently carved the ethnically and linguistically homogenous Somali population into five territorial zones: Italian Somaliland (on the eastern coast), British Somaliland (on the northern coast), French Somaliland (present-day Djibouti), Ethiopian Somaliland (the Ogaden region), and the Northern Frontier District of British Kenya (in northern Kenya). These foreign powers then immediately began a series of large-scale development projects aimed at extracting the most profit from their newly conquered colonies.[17] These incursions provoked a fierce domestic resistance against the Ethiopians and Europeans, led by religious leader and anticolonial fighter Sayyid Muhammad Abdullah Hassan during the period 1900–1920.[18] But the rebellion failed, and for another four decades Somalia was subjugated by British, Italian, and Ethiopian colonizers.

This prolonged era of foreign subjugation had a long-term impact on Somalia's economic, political, and social development. To start, the Europeans implemented a system of indirect taxation, such as customs duties, to quickly profit from their Somali colonies without building robust state institutions. "In the case of the Italian colony indirect taxes constituted about 73 percent of the state's locally generated revenues between 1950 and 1958," explains Abdi Ismail Samatar. "In the British Protectorate indirect taxes, mainly in the form of customs duties, accounted for more than 80 percent of the local revenues from 1955 to 1959."[19] Imposing these indirect taxes gave the imperial powers an easy way to extract revenue from the import-export business. The impact of this policy, however, was that the Somali state never bothered to develop a normal protection-taxation relationship with its citizens. In the long run, this tax policy actually undermined the state's capacity, distorted market prices by adding taxes to imports and exports, and undermined trade.

These legacies of colonial subjugation endured long after Somalia won its independence in 1960. The governing institutions inherited from the colonial era perpetuated the system of indirect taxation, keeping the state weak and separated from its citizenry. Imperialist borders became the sovereign boundaries of newly independent African states, thus dividing the Somali people between Kenya, Ethiopia, Djibouti, and Somalia. As a rejection of these colonial borders, the new Somali national flag showcased a white five-pointed star—each point representing one of the five colonies—a defiant symbol of Mogadishu's irredentist claim over its lost ethnic territories.

From Cold War to Collapse: Foreign Interference and Market Shocks

The legacy of these colonial borders created regional tensions, but the Cold War inflamed them. Shortly after gaining independence, Somalia became embroiled in an extended American and Soviet proxy war in the Horn of Africa. From the early 1970s, Barre's socialist regime received significant funding from the Soviet Union, as part of the Kremlin's Cold War strategy of balancing against the pro-American regime in Ethiopia. Barre was heavily dependent on support from Moscow, and he worked desperately to secure aid money to prop up his regime. To appease his Soviet sponsors, Barre adopted a countrywide policy of "scientific socialism," signaling his loyalty to the communist agenda. Soviet aid allowed Barre to amass his personal power, but these radical socialist reforms also led to an underutilization of the manufacturing sector and drastic inefficiencies in the market.[20]

Foreign support also allowed Barre to establish powerful networks of patronage and corruption, which further undermined private-sector growth. Import-export permits were consistently only issued to a handful of elites within Barre's inner circle.[21] Faced with exclusion from the licit economy and a worsening economic crisis, Somalis survived by participating in informal trade. The government attempted to control the expanding black market by introducing the *franco valuta* system in 1977, which was designed to create incentives for participation in licit trade.[22] Yet Barre also manipulated this system to his advantage in order to maintain control over import permit licensing to benefit his personal networks.[23]

Although Barre's policies were flawed from the outset, the political situation worsened dramatically when, in 1974, a Marxist rebellion called "the Derg" overthrew US-backed emperor Haile Selassie of Ethiopia. At first, Barre saw the turmoil in Addis Ababa as an opportunity to reclaim the Somali territories in Ethiopia's Ogaden region, and he launched an attack in 1977. Much to his surprise, however, the Kremlin switched its support to the new Marxist regime in Ethiopia, leaving Somalia without a sponsor. As Barre found himself abandoned and betrayed by his Soviet allies, he promptly expelled all Soviet advisers from Somalia and began pursuing an alliance with the United States instead. The Soviets and Americans essentially swapped positions in their chess match in the Horn of Africa.

To ingratiate himself with his new American patrons, by 1980 Barre had abandoned the socialist economic model and adopted dramatic liberal economic reforms and structural adjustment programs. According to Jamil Mubarak, his economic policies were "erratic, inconsistent, and often moved from one set of objectives to another, thereby confusing the domestic market."[24] To compensate for these shocks, the regime then printed money, causing a sharp increase in inflation rates in the 1980s. "Between 1983 and 1990, average annual depreciation of the Somali shilling against the US$ was over 100 percent," argued Peter Leeson.[25] These rapid and radical changes in economic policy proved disastrous.[26]

Barre not only mismanaged the national economy, but his regime provoked such serious clan conflict that by the late 1980s there was a nationwide rebellion against the state.[27] Systematic assaults by Barre's forces on the Isaaq, Majerteen, Ogaden, and Hawiye clans led to the formation of multiple armed political opposition groups, each representing a particular clan community. The state attempted to quell the uprising with brute force and collective punishment against civilians from rebellious clans, which further galvanized the resistance and increased the pressure on Barre to step down. By the late 1980s, pressure was mounting on the fledgling US-backed government.

When the Cold War ended abruptly in 1991, the jig was up. As American dollars and weapons dried up, the aid-dependent Somali government found itself without a foreign patron. The regime went bankrupt and dissolved, and Barre resigned and fled. As the state collapsed, rebel factions rolled into the capital city and raided government depots stocked with American- and Soviet-grade weapons. As authority disintegrated, scores of warring groups took control of the countryside, targeting members of rival clans in systematic cleansing campaigns.

The clan rivalries that were inflamed during Barre's last years in power spread like a wildfire that engulfed the capital city. The genocidal campaigns not only purged members of Barre's Darod-Marehan clan but also quickly spiraled into retaliatory attacks among all clan communities. The famine exacerbated the humanitarian crisis, killing hundreds of thousands and displacing millions more. Shocked by the magnitude of the suffering, international peacekeepers and aid agencies landed on Somali shores to respond to the disaster. Little did they know that their presence would inadvertently create a new civil war economy that would endure for decades to come.

Anarchy and Industry: Getting Rich off of the Poor

The collapse of the state was a game changer for the traders. On the one hand, many businesspeople, particularly those from Barre's Darod-Marehan clan, lost everything. In fact, all those who had done well under the Barre government were specifically targeted by newcomers to the business world. As one Mogadishu-based businessman explained, "I was in business [for] around 40 years, from when I was 16 years old. After the fall of the Siyyad Barre regime, a new phase of business started, which was very dangerous. All rules governing business were destroyed. All illegal business was possible [and], with no taxation, people got rich."[28] Several other Mogadishu businesspeople who lost out after the government fell argued that these new businessmen allied with local warlords to push out the old guard. A prominent Mogadishu-based warlord from the early civil war period gave a frank assessment: "After the civil war, all the businesspeople were thrown out. Property was looted and stolen. The old business community left the country with whatever they had. The new businessmen supported and gave money to the warlords so that they could secure their transactions."[29]

On the other hand, for these newcomers, the end of Barre's corrupt government put an end to nepotism, taxation, industry regulations, and crippling bureaucratic red tape. This opened the door to new traders that wished to capitalize on tax- and regulation-free opportunities in both licit and illicit goods. Rampant looting and criminality generated the start-up capital for business development.[30] Many new Somali businesspeople got their start by pillaging the wealth of rival clans.

State collapse also meant that criminal elements could operate without the rule of law. The removal of all industry regulation and taxation provided lucrative new opportunities in the trade and transport business for smugglers, arms dealers, drug lords, and racketeers. The absence of Somali customs duties and taxes meant that local traders could sell smuggled goods at a discounted rate in the Kenyan and Ethiopian interior, thereby monopolizing regional markets. These new business entrepreneurs also established relationships with local warlords to shield themselves from their economic and political rivals. For these newcomers, civil war proved to be a boon.

Indeed, during the early stages of the war, the UN intervention provided extraordinary sources of revenue for this new business class. The intervention had imported large amounts of emergency food and medical aid to the Mogadishu port through various intergovernmental and nongovernmental organizations, which needed to be distributed across the country.[31] Opportunistic businesspeople won multimillion-dollar contracts for transportation and handling of donated food aid, much of which was illicitly siphoned off and sold on the black market.[32] Because the countryside was so dangerous, aid organizations had to rely on these businesspeople for transportation of their goods.[33] A prominent trader from the Yaqshiid district Suuq Ba'ad market in Mogadishu explained: "UNOSOM brought heavy investment and money. After 1990, the greatest opportunity was UNOSOM. Many businesspeople got contracts. There were contractors for everything. Without UNOSOM, the business community couldn't make any money. Small businesspeople became millionaires. Aid helped the humanitarian and the business side too."[34]

The most lucrative international contracts were in food aid delivery, worth hundreds of millions of dollars. During the famine and civil war, demand for relief was extremely high, which made food aid a type of liquid asset. Food became an informal currency in Somalia. "Food aid is the only source of revenue for the majority of society," explained humanitarian medical doctor Deqo Mohamed from Afgooye. "In the whole country, there is no income except food distribution. Everyone is trying to make money on this food distribution. If you are living in the bush and you want sugar or cloths, you have to sell half your sack so you can buy something else. Where are you going to get money to buy the gun? There is no bank to steal. There is only WFP [the World Food Programme]."[35]

Those businesses that had the strongest ties to warlords were best positioned to loot the international aid agencies. Because warlords controlled security on the roads, contractors that had relationships with warlords were able to demonstrate that they could get aid into the otherwise inaccessible countryside for a price. A Mogadishu-based businessman who worked in

IMAGE 5.1   Food aid delivery at a camp for internally displaced persons during the 2012 famine crisis, near the northern Somali border with Somaliland.

water distribution described how this aid distribution worked: "Say they want aid delivered from point A to point B. The contractor tells them that it is too dangerous on the road, so he says that he is forced to take a much longer off-road path to get to point B." As the businessman drew a map of this long and unnecessary side-trip, he clarified, "Because the aid agencies can't independently verify the security on the road, they must pay this extra transportation expense."[36]

These aid contractors were not necessarily inhibited on the roads, nor did they actually take the longer side routes. What these businesspeople did, however, was forge agreements with local strongmen to ensure delivery, either into the countryside or simply to an adjacent market, paying off the local strongmen. They would then fake their transportation records and charge the aid agencies an exorbitant rate for transiting the supplies, plus an added security cost. "We were one of the three major World Food Programme contractors," boasted the executive of a large firm. "WFP operations are everywhere and in contact with everyone. We could work anywhere and with everyone unimpeded."[37] The business elites got rich off the aid contracts and gave the warlords the resources to create and maintain their private power.

As the humanitarian mission faltered, the UN stepped up its operations and began delivering aid directly to distribution hubs in the Somali interior. When UN peacekeepers cleared the roads of checkpoints to facilitate the delivery of humanitarian aid, they prompted General Aideed to find a new source of income. In response, the SNA and its business associates colluded to create fake nongovernmental organizations (NGOs) to acquire cash and food resources from the international community. They initiated a trend that quickly became popular among Somali factions of all stripes: the "suitcase NGO."[38]

"There were three angles [to the suitcase NGO business]: connection to warlords because they needed to access the roads; connection to business people because they had to sell to them; and connection to heads of international organizations in Somalia, so that they could continue to get the aid," explained Dr. Hawa Abdi Dibwaale, who was actively engaged with the aid community throughout the war period.[39] To make this scam work, the warlord entered into an agreement with a member of the business community with whom he had established a relationship. With the help of a skilled professional, they then drafted a proposal requesting support for an imaginary camp of internally displaced people somewhere in the interior, preferably in a location that could not easily be verified.

The businessman then sent one of his employees to pose as a local NGO representative and present the proposal to the Somali official within the international aid organization. The Somali official approved the bogus request in exchange for either a percentage of the aid profits or a flat-rate fee. Once approved, the businessman collected the aid resources, paid his warlord security-provider the agreed-on percentage, and then transported the remaining supplies to the market for sale. "They used to write a good proposal saying they are running a camp, school, everything," said Dr. Hawa. "Then they take the money. Some of them disappear and never come back. They call it, 'Hit one time and run.' "[40] This fake NGO industry provided a highly lucrative cash-grab opportunity for both businessmen and warlords, which further solidified their elite-level partnership.

This windfall was short-lived, however. As the last UN peacekeepers withdrew from Somalia in 1995, the foreign resources that the warlords had grown accustomed to stealing suddenly disappeared. The lucrative aid contracts that had been the backbone of the new Mogadishu business elite were also drastically reduced. As these foreign resources dwindled, the number of armed subclan groups in Somalia proliferated. The warlords were the first to feel the pinch, and they sought out new sources of revenue. Some cut down trees to export charcoal, causing mass desertification. Others allegedly allowed European companies to dump toxic waste inside their turfs, in exchange for cash and weapons, poisoning Somalia's fields and waters in perpetuity.[41]

They also turned to their partners in the business world, demanding fees for protection.

With dwindling access to foreign resources, members of the business class watched their profits shrink and became increasingly aware of their losses. The internecine conflict had also made it difficult, if not impossible, for members of different clans to maintain normal economic relations with each other. Clan violence eroded social trust between rival groups to the point where normal business activities and partnerships were no longer viable. As such, most Somali business owners predominantly operated within their own clans. It was simply easier and safer for them to build partnerships within their own communities than work with out-group members.

If an employee from a businesswoman's own clan were to steal from her business, for example, the businesswoman could therefore work within the existing clan social structure to hold the rogue employee responsible. But if the businesswoman had hired from outside her clan, pursuing the rogue employee could provoke violent reprisals and instigate clan conflict. Given these constraints, most Somali businesses hired their staff from within their own communities, and as a result, each private-sector company was colored with a clan affiliation. Conducting business within the boundaries of clan and subclan groups therefore exacerbated social fragmentation and undermined prospects for expanding business into new markets.

Being a fellow clan member didn't make an employee honest, however, and business owners often found that navigating clan hierarchies was inefficient and ineffective. Personal familial relations between rogue employees and clan leaders complicated human resource management. Firing a lazy or corrupt employee might upset fellow clan members who had personal ties to the dismissed worker. Also, by selecting only within their own clan, businesspeople found that they were limiting their talent pool and selecting candidates that were not ideally suited for the job.

Tribalism therefore may have been the most prevalent social institution in civil war Somalia, but it was certainly not the most profitable. Faced with these high costs, businesspeople who had established their fortunes through clan conflict now sought out a way to overcome the crippling social fragmentation that they had helped perpetuate. In the political vacuum, religious identity and institutions quickly became a valuable mechanism for the Somali business community to reduce uncertainty, build trust, develop business partnerships across tribal divisions, and gain access to lucrative markets in Gulf States. With no government and no security, the business class turned to the only available source of social capital that had sway across clan lines: Islam.

Beards for Business: Islam as an Industry Solution

Beginning in the mid- to late 1990s, the business community began to realize the potential of Islamic identity as a mechanism to expand business opportunities into markets outside their clans. Aspiring and established business-people alike attempted to bolster their Islamic identities over their clan identities. Much like the traders working in the Pakistan-Afghanistan border region, adopting an Islamic identity was a way of building trust across these lines and providing reassurances against risk. Outward indications of religiosity were displayed as symbols of trustworthiness; growing a beard and dressing in Islamic clothing, for example, were ways of telling a member of another clan that you were an honest and morally upright business partner. This information shortcut held depth and weight, as the majority of Somali Muslims believed that strong religious practice meant that a person was likely to be truthful, spiritual, and not materialistic.[42] Through Islamic symbols, businesspeople could therefore utilize these widely held perceptions to reduce uncertainty across clan divisions.

As a result, almost comically, even criminal bosses grew long beards and began wearing traditional clothing. They carried religious paraphernalia, such as prayer beads, and took on the label of "Sheikh" (Islamic scholar) despite having no religious training to warrant the title. The head of a leading Mogadishu business school explained, "Since there is no regulatory or law enforcement agency and everything is based on trust, this is where Islamists come in. Most companies are led by people who look like sheikhs."[43] By the mid-1990s, Mogadishu experienced an overnight boom in its "sheikh" population, as the business community sought to gain from the social capital afforded by Islamic identity and association. While clan divisions didn't at all disappear, Islamic identity became an increasingly important reputational tool and mechanism for navigating clan divisions at home and securing international contracts abroad.

Islamic identity provided Somali businesspeople with a reputational edge, even for those that had questionable or outright criminal pasts. "With no government, Islamic adherence was a way to get the trust of the people," explained a prominent Somali lawyer who supported the early Islamist movement. "If you take the title of sheikh and grow a beard, then you will be more trustworthy than a person smoking a cigarette, with no beard."[44] A Mogadishu-based economist added, "[Imagine] if you have two stores: one is run by someone who is smoking cigarettes and chewing khat and the other owner is dressed nicely and looks like a practicing Muslim; then the people will buy from the person that is dressed like a good Muslim. They will believe that he is less likely to cheat them."[45]

Notably, many members of the Mogadishu business elite who had acquired their fortunes through dubious methods were now concerned with the social and reputational consequences of their criminal actions. A history of looting, corruption, and theft would undoubtedly act as a serious deterrent to building new trust-based business partnerships. Adopting outwardly visible symbols of Islam was thus a mechanism used by such businesspeople to disguise their criminal pasts and improve their public images.

For the most part, this approach worked. While there were a handful of cases where a purported Islamist businessperson would shave his beard and abscond with company money, Islamic trust was largely an effective way to navigate interclan dynamics. The results from my survey of over a thousand members of the business community suggest that these sentiments were widespread. As seen in Figure 5.1, 80 percent of the business community strongly agreed that Islam is a good way to assess trustworthiness in business, whereas only 17 percent felt strongly that clan identity was a good measure of trust. Also, 88 percent of respondents reported that Islamic identity was more important than clan identity in business affairs.

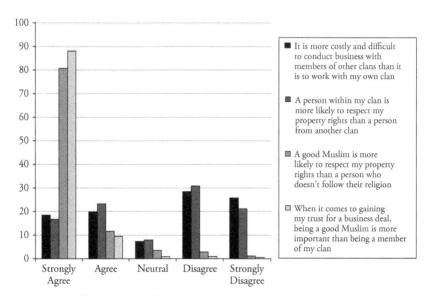

FIGURE 5.1 Clan Trust and Islamic Trust

Survey of Somali business owners operating in Mogadishu from 2004 to 2006. N = 1,003.

Most businesspeople whom I interviewed, however, considered reliance on Islam to be a temporary or second-best substitute for formal governing institutions. It was state failure that caused the business community to turn to Islam. As the head of a large business association in Mogadishu explained, "With the rule of law, this reliance on Islamic merit and trustworthiness would be greatly reduced."[46] Nonetheless, in the absence of a functioning state, Islam provided a valuable utility to members of the business class, which allowed them to expand their reach into the countryside.

Over time, these businesspeople created large, multiclan nationwide corporations with partners from different parts of the country using Islam as a social glue between the clans. The largest nationwide businesses in Somalia are hawalas (money transfer agencies) and telecommunication firms, which provide cell phone and Internet services.[47] Hawalas take the place of the formal banking system and operate entirely on the basis of personal trust; customers send and receive money through the hawala company on the promise that it will deliver the funds to the intended recipient. A successful hawala cannot have errors or corruption, nor can insecurity be an excuse for failure of delivery; one story of a lost or stolen transaction could bankrupt the company. Trustworthiness is essential for success in the money transfer industry.

The telecom industry was born out of the success of hawala companies. In many cases a hawala and a telecom are part of one larger parent enterprise, with the same owners and shareholders.[48] Both hawalas and telecom companies are countrywide and have a pan-clan shareholder structure representing all regions where business is active. During their initial formation, these companies strategically expanded into new regional markets by procuring local partners and agents from the dominant clan group in each region and by developing multiclan shareholder structures and business models. By 2000, all major telecommunication and money transfer companies in Somalia had adopted an Islamic framework for managing business relations, using religious identity as a mechanism for working across clan divisions and attracting shareholders from diverse clan backgrounds.

These companies even began utilizing Islamic trust as a platform for hiring staff. One of the largest Somali telecom companies, for example, posted an open job search in a local Mogadishu newspaper. The company announced that it was hiring for ten new positions that required specialized technical expertise. In response to the posting, the company received around a hundred applications and shortlisted thirty candidates. The shortlisted candidates were then asked to sit for an exam to determine who would be hired. Among the shortlisted was the top student at one of Mogadishu's best private business education institutions. Surprisingly, the star student failed to get a position while other, less technically proficient, candidates were hired.

What went wrong? The dean of the university approached his best student to ask why he had been unsuccessful. "At least 50 percent of the exam was *Amana* [Islamic trustworthiness and integrity]," the star student explained. "I am not very good at *Islamiyyat* [religious studies]." The dean was struck by this response and approached the owner of the large telecom about this policy. He asked the telecom owner why the company would allot half of its exam on technical expertise and the other half on religious knowledge. The owner responded: "Because we can train in the specialization that he has learned in the past two years, but we cannot teach a 22-year-old boy 20 years of Islamic education. We cannot control thousands of staff, so we want someone who controls himself."[49]

For companies like this telecom, Islam was a form of risk management. These businesses determined that it was more cost effective to hire a trustworthy person who needed some additional technical training than someone who might put the company at risk. In this Islamic meritocracy, merit equals skill plus trustworthiness, and trust is measured by religious adherence. As Figure 5.2 shows, a striking 75 percent of respondents preferred to work with someone who has a reputation as a good Muslim, whereas only 20 percent said they would prefer someone who was a successful businessperson. Though still imperfect, Islamic trust allowed the business community to more confidently recruit from a wider pool of applicants than those provided by clan-based networks while still controlling for potential corruption.

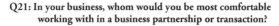

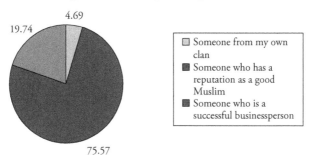

Q21: In your business, whom would you be most comfortable working with in a business partnership or transaction?

4.69
19.74
75.57

☐ Someone from my own clan
■ Someone who has a reputation as a good Muslim
■ Someone who is a successful businessperson

FIGURE 5.2 Identity and Trust in Business Partnerships
Survey of Somali business owners operating in Mogadishu from 2004 to 2006. N = 1,003.

Islamic identity also had great utility in establishing trust-based business partnerships in the Gulf States, where demonstrating high Islamic credentials allowed some Somali businessmen to secure lucrative loans and contracts from their Arab partners with nothing more than a handshake. In much the same way that Islam provided Somali merchants with better access to Arab and Persian markets in the thirteenth century, the external adoption of Islamic symbols, norms, and rhetoric also helped Somali traders to gain better access to markets in the Gulf States after the collapse of the modern state.

Indeed, because of its geographic location, Somalia had a long history of trade with the Arab world. When the state collapsed, however, there was no guarantee that agreements would be honored, and Gulf businesses shied away from prospective Somali partners. The risk of betrayal was exorbitantly high. If a Somali partner were to run away with the company loot, the Gulf business would have absolutely no legal or practical recourse for their lost revenues. Despite this risk, however, Somali ports were highly attractive and lucrative entry points into East African markets. The primary obstacle to initiating business partnerships was the lack of trust.

Adopting an Islamic (and in particular a Salafi or Wahhabi) identity provided Somali businesspeople with the opportunity to build trust-based relations with prospective business partners outside Somalia, especially in Saudi Arabia and the wealthy Gulf States.[50] Establishing these relations between Gulf and Somali partners was a long-term process, involving repeated interactions over time. One could not gain access to the elite Salafi business club simply by outwardly displaying Islamic symbols, although such symbols were necessary prerequisites. Rather, Somali businesspeople developed personal networks of trust with Gulf colleagues by using their common Salafi identity as an initial basis for interaction and then gradually proving their personal credibility.

Several members of the Mogadishu business community explained that, in the mid-1990s, their contracts with Gulf partners were smaller, reflecting the level of trust between the parties. A Somali businessman might have an agreement worth no more than a few thousand dollars. Because there was no government to enforce these deals there were no written contracts, and parties relied entirely on verbal agreement. These early investments allowed Somali businesspeople to demonstrate their trustworthiness, with less dollar-value risk to their Arab partners. Anyone who defected with the loot was out of the club for life, whereas those that demonstrated that they could be trusted gained incrementally larger contracts.

Eventually, trust-based relationships translated into multimillion-dollar loans from Gulf partners, with no enforcement mechanisms for repayment. The largest and most well-connected Somali businesspeople adopted a Salafi approach to Islam and developed strong ties to the Gulf business network. Resources from wealthy Gulf business partners allowed these businesses to outcompete their non-Salafi rivals, thus resulting in a domination of Salafi elites in the Somali marketplace. Through these interactions, Gulf businesses helped to select the winners and losers in the Somali business community.

The Somali business class therefore took on a Salafi identity, and those elites who demonstrated the greatest Islamic credentials became the most wealthy and powerful. The most prominent countrywide industries in Somalia adopted Salafi business culture, which they reinforced through their hiring practices. Whether a particular businessperson was sincere in his or her increased religiosity, or whether religiosity was used for purely strategic objectives, is impossible to ascertain. When asked if these businesspeople were truly Salafi (or Wahhabi, the Saudi version of Salafism), however, the chief legal counsel for the Islamic Courts Union held up his right hand, bent his index finger, and said, "If I tie a string around this finger and leave it like this for 10 years, when I untie it, my finger will stay like this. The business community is the same. After years of pretending to be a Wahhabi, you become a Wahhabi."[51] Thus, while the adoption of Salafi identity within the business community may have been driven by rational self-interest, in the long run, it also had a transformative effect on the identity of the business community as a whole.

Given these advantages, how then could a businessperson effectively demonstrate that his or her religious commitment was sincere and not just a superficial adoption of outward symbols? An important aspect of building solid Islamic credentials was the financing and sponsorship of local Islamic charities and institutions. There were plenty of opportunities for these activities, as the collapse of the state had created a humanitarian catastrophe and an enormous need for public services. With millions of Somalis internally displaced by the war, the magnitude of the crisis was profound. The incidences of infant mortality, maternal death, malnutrition, and disease in Somalia were among the highest in the world. Most significantly, after the withdrawal of the failed UN mission, international aid organizations cited inaccessibility and insecurity as reasons to not engage the failed state. Without the state to provide services or the ability for international nongovernmental organizations to operate in-country, the Somali population was largely displaced, disrupted, and underserviced. Islamic institutions played a significant role in responding to this dire humanitarian situation.

With no government to provide healthcare, education, and water, for example, public goods provision in Somalia was left to either the private sector or charitable organizations. Somali businesses were keen to provide services, such as drinking water supply and power generation, for a profit.[52] Those services that were less easily profitable, however, such as education, orphanages, and emergency healthcare, were often left to local Islamic charities to provide.[53] A large businessperson could therefore improve his or her standing in the community by financing a hospital or school. Saudi Arabia and the Gulf States also supported these charitable endeavors, adding to the religious character of humanitarian aid in Somalia.[54] Backed by these powerful financiers, Islamic charitable enterprises proved competent in public goods provision, thus legitimating and propagating the concept of Islamic governance as a solution to state failure.

Among the most important of these public services was the provision of pockets of law and order, which were provided by local clan-based Islamic courts. Because Somali communities had relied on sharia and *xeer* for nearly a millennium, these institutions were considered traditionally legitimate sources of law and order. Following the collapse of the government, these local clan-based Islamic courts took on more central roles in administering juridical decisions. Over time, these courts provided pockets of governance and rule of law for local communities and gained popularity for their demonstrations of effective arbitration of both family and corporate matters. The business community, which needed these informal governing institutions to reduce its transaction costs, already had a material interest in sponsoring the courts. The Islamic courts could facilitate their economic transactions and resolve disputes between business partners, making it easier for them to work across local divisions.

Islamic identities and institutions thus provided the business community with a valuable mechanism for mitigating the lack of trust between the clans, making business easier and more profitable. Insecurity, however, continued to disrupt economic life. The warlords demanded their protection payments, and the militias kept up their extortion along the roads. No matter how much trust and order the business class created for itself, Somalia remained anarchic, unpredictable, and expensive. Turning to Islam did not solve these problems. After a decade of war, however, a new band of political Islamists promised to do so.

The Islamist Exit Strategy

The rise of Islamism in Somalia emerged as a direct response to violent clan fragmentation in the civil war. Leading the Islamist initiative were members of the "Salafi club," the group of business elites who had grown frustrated with the high costs of social fragmentation that were undermining economic growth and thus adopted a new Salafi Islamist identity to overcome these problems. Frustrated with the political stalemate, starting in 2000 the business elite began to play a more active role in the political process, investing in the Somali peace talks held in Arta, Djibouti. With the material support of the business community and the leadership of Somali religious and civil society actors, the Arta process created the Transitional National Government (TNG), the first attempt at a new government since the collapse of the Barre regime. The TNG was constructed on what is known as the 4.5 system, which divided power equally among the four dominant Somali clans and offered a one-half share to all other minority clans. It was designed to balance power between Somali clans, and it included strong representation from both Islamic civil society organizations and business lobbies.[55]

The prospect of a new Somali government increased consumer confidence and attracted investment and development aid.[56] However, while the TNG was supported by a range of traditional elders, Islamic organizations, and elites from the business class, it excluded Somalia's strongmen. As a result, the new TNG was vehemently opposed by clan warlords who felt excluded from the new political system and were unwilling to relinquish their economic and military control. These warlords formed a joint military alliance called the Somalia Reconstruction and Restoration Council (SRRC), which effectively challenged the legitimacy and undermined the practical abilities of the TNG throughout its reign.[57] As the TNG failed, businesspeople found themselves supporting a powerless paper government while continuing to pay protection fees to the warlords.

On the ground, the political situation in Somalia therefore remained stagnant. After four years of stalemate and under pressure from the international community, in 2004 the TNG and the SRRC initiated a new peace process hosted in Mbagathi, Kenya. Through the 2004 peace process, the SRRC formally reconciled with the TNG on the promise that the clan warlords would be included in the formal political process and would be given power in the next government. The Mbagathi process thus created the new Transitional Federal Government (TFG), led by a warlord named Abdullahi Yusuf from the Darod-Majerteen clan, whose faction had built friendly ties to neighboring Ethiopia.

Yusuf's presidential inauguration was held at a stadium in Nairobi, Kenya, where members of the new TFG were being hosted. The inauguration was attended by power holders from across the Horn of Africa, and clan warlords found themselves awkwardly placed next to civil society actors and foreign dignitaries. Somali musicians and poets performed cheerfully as the VIPs were seated, while audience members across the stadium whispered and pointed around the crowd, gossiping about which commander had received what post and whether those excluded from the process would act as spoilers.

Once everyone was seated, to start the ceremony, officials made impassioned remarks about Somalia's bright future. Uganda's authoritarian president Yoweri Museveni offered a long-winded and ironic rant about his dedication to democracy, before handing the stage over to Yusuf. The new warlord-turned-president then gave a highly rhetorical speech about his commitment to peace in Somalia. Across the stadium, eyes rolled and heads shook.[58]

Despite the enormous skepticism, however, the initial hope had been that including the warlords in the political process would have pacified them on the battlefield. To do so, the TFG gave parliamentary positions to nearly every clan-based strongman with spoiler capability and offered the warlords accommodations and stipends for participating in the government. The result was a bloated government held in exile in Nairobi, run by warlord-parliamentarians. Most warlords took up residence in posh downtown Kenyan hotels to hustle donor funds and secure official titles in the TFG. As they grew used to these perks, many of these warlords could be found lounging poolside, casually sending battle orders to deputy field commanders on their mobile phones. The TFG proved to be wholly ineffective, and disagreements between the warlord-parliamentarians prompted new skirmishes between their respective militias.

Back in Somalia, the traders were still getting fleeced by local militias. With the warlords frequently out of the country, busy enjoying the comforts of Nairobi's five-star air-conditioned hotels, security within their fiefdoms deteriorated. Freelance gangs became more aggressive, setting up their own checkpoints inside the warlords' turfs. Conflicts between the warlord-parliamentarians in Nairobi also prompted them to increase their extortion of the business class. The warlords threatened the traders with targeted violence if they refused to pay up, but they did nothing to provide the business class with greater security within their own turfs. Businesspeople were therefore paying heavy protection moneys to the warlords, while also getting extorted by a slew of militia checkpoints on the road. Exasperated by these high levels of extortion, Somalia's merchant titans actively sought a political alternative to warlord rule.

At this pivotal moment, the Islamic Courts Union offered the business elites exactly what they were looking for.

6

The Price of Protection

THE RISE OF THE ISLAMIC COURTS UNION

Haste can give birth to a bit of money, patience to a bag of it.

The world is like a shadow: in the morning it is turned towards one direction, in the evening towards the opposite one.

SOMALI PROVERBS

BY THE TIME the last United Nations (UN) troops left Somalia, the bazaars of Mogadishu had been completely transformed by the war. A new class of business heavyweights had displaced the old elite and now controlled the local economy. After making a fortune during the UN era, the powerful Adani family of the Hawiye-Abgal clan decided to expand its operations and established the El Ma'an Port Authority at a natural seaport located fifteen kilometers north of war-torn Mogadishu. "When the UN pulled out of Somalia, Mogadishu Seaport was closed," explained the chief executive of El Ma'an at a posh air-conditioned hotel in Dubai. "The warlords closed the seaport. . . . So [we] opened El Ma'an in 1995. We purchased barges and invested in port development."[1] This new port connected Somalia to international markets, and El Ma'an quickly became the only channel to import and export goods from Mogadishu and the Middle Shabelle region. By charging import taxes and handling fees to every trader using its new port, the Adani family quickly amassed a vast private fortune.

Even the wealthiest business elites, however, were growing increasingly frustrated by the high costs of the Somali civil war. Following the UN withdrawal, plush aid contracts had shrunk and foreign resources dwindled. As the clan warlords felt the pinch, they began increasing their extortion of the business class to keep afloat and maintain a balance against their rivals. Local militias responded to the economic downturn by setting up checkpoints along major roads, demanding payment from traders and truckers as they moved goods through the privately held turfs. Even the Adani family felt bullied: "They [the warlords] were the ones who shut down every single attempt at Somali government," explained the executive. "Every warlord wanted to take over and charge taxes that we couldn't afford."[2] The stories of this chapter reveal that as members of the business community grew increasingly frustrated with these skyrocketing costs, they began to invest in an Islamist alternative to the costly warlords in the hopes that this would increase their profit margins. Through their pursuit of greater wealth and security, these Somali business elites inadvertently transformed the trajectory of the Somali civil war forever.

For the impoverished and disempowered masses across Somalia, however, the civil war had meant nothing but penury and death. Unlike the wealthy elite, most civilians had no such power to change their circumstances. Millions were languishing in improvised and underserviced camps for internally displaced persons (IDPs) scattered throughout the interior, unsure of when the next ration would arrive. They were easy prey for drugged-up militiamen who robbed and raped with impunity.

To try to protect their families from the predation, individuals paid off their local strongmen, hoping to defend against attacks from neighboring clan factions. These protection payments, however, did not shield them from abuses at the hands of their own clan militias, which grew increasingly violent and exploitative as the war dragged on. These unruly gangs often engaged in murder, extortion, and rape against their own communities. Militias set up hundreds of checkpoints along every major road in the country, terrorizing travelers who dared to move through their turfs. Most Somalis lived in a state of constant fear and stress.

Doped up on khat, these militiamen spent their afternoons sitting under trees at makeshift checkpoints: "I have years of experience in establishing checkpoints in this area," boasted one gunman, casually waving his AK-47 as he spoke.

"Watch it man, that gun is loaded!" interrupted his comrade, his mouth full of narcotics. He pointed an AK-47 back at his boastful friend, roughly gesturing at him to back down. "You have no manners!"

"Don't worry, it's facing up," the cocky gunman replied nonchalantly, carrying on with his story. "As I was saying, I have more experience than you in capturing and robbing people. We have to kill everyone we rob so there will be no witnesses."[3]

On the receiving end of the assaults were the civilians. Families were separated, and fathers bid tearful farewells to their wives and children, who had better chances of getting refugee status alone. Many never saw each other again. The luckier ones made it out of the country, seeking sanctuary in crowded Kenyan and Ethiopian refugee camps along the Somali border. The Dadaab camp was the largest, set up by the United Nations High Commissioner for Refugees (UNHCR) in the middle of a parched red desert at the Kenyan border. It was originally designed to accommodate ninety thousand refugees, but as the crisis escalated, their numbers swelled to nearly half a million. The camp grew into a sprawling landscape of densely packed makeshift huts, built out of nothing more than dry branches and plastic UN tarps, spread across a fifty-square-kilometer zone.

Aid workers scrambled to get emergency resources to the refugees, mostly women and children, but could not protect them from the militias that were hunting them down across the unmarked and unregulated border. "Women are afraid to go out into the bush [to collect firewood]," explained one woman in the Dadaab camp. "We are chased by men with guns." Another refugee added: "If they catch us, they will rape us." The same tribal militias that had been terrorizing them in Somalia had followed the women into the camps. "We went into the bush to fetch wood, and that's where the gang caught us and raped us," shared an elderly woman who was assaulted by two armed men. "On that day, the militia were everywhere in the bush. Since that day, I have been very sick, very upset, and very sad."[4]

The gangsters in their turfs were remorseless. "Everyone has their own gun. Some got it through conflict, others in secret trade," slurred a stoned militiaman from Bula Hawa, Somalia, which is near to both the Kenyan and Ethiopian borders. "There's no economy in this town, so we use our guns to rob people to feed our families," added his friend. "We won't put these guns down. We protect our lives and our property with them."

A third gunman interrupted, shouting: "We steal things and rape women with it!" The entire militia laughed, egging him on. "Man, we [rape] women with it!" he declared, lifting his AK-47 in a lewd gesture. His red-eyed comrades howled in approval. "Do you understand now?" the first asked again, once the laughter subsided. "It's clan warfare."[5]

The Islamic Courts Union (ICU) movement in Somalia first emerged as a grassroots response to the predatory behavior of these local militias. According to the story, in 2003 a cleric named Sheikh Ahmed Sheikh Sharif was working as a schoolteacher at Jubba Secondary School in the crime-ridden Siisii neighborhood of northern Mogadishu. During the school year, a group of local gangsters kidnapped one of Sheikh Sharif's young students, a twelve-year-old boy named Abdulkadir. The thugs demanded a huge ransom from his family for his safe return.[6] Hearing the news, Sheikh Sharif mobilized a grassroots community movement to create a new Islamic court in the Siisii district. He then rallied the community's power through the newly established court and successfully pressured the kidnappers to release Abdulkadir and return him safely to his parents.

The triumph of the new Siisii court in northern Mogadishu inspired a new wave of optimism for the Islamic courts as a model of effective governance. Sheikh Sharif's heroic rescue increased popular support for the courts, which offered better security provision and public service than the warlords. Buoyed by this success, Sheikh Sharif was appointed chairman of a group of Mogadishu courts and began work on organizing the courts into a coherent group. Although still loyal to their respective subclan groups, these disparate Islamic courts began to recruit and train young men from their communities into the courts' militias. They affectionately named the courts' militias *al-Shabaab*, or "the youth."

Over the next year, the Islamists coordinated their efforts. Sheikh Sharif joined forces with militant Salafi Islamist leader Sheikh Hassan Dahir Aweys on a mission to transform the clan courts in Mogadishu into one overarching political entity. Notably, since the mid-1990s, Aweys had been involved with the powerful Ifka Halane court that represented his dominant Hawiye-Habr-Gidir-Ayr subclan; he therefore saw an alliance with Sharif's Siisii court as an effective way to advance his Islamist cause.[7] The resources and power of the Ifka Halane court also helped to boost the influence and muscle of the Islamists based at the Siisii court. Together, they gave birth to a new Islamist force that had influence in the Somali civil war. With this foundation, starting in 2004, Sharif and Aweys began to systematically work to create an Islamist movement that brought more local clan-based courts into their system.

At first, these Islamic courts maintained cooperative and respectful relationships with Mogadishu-based warlords, coordinating their efforts only to improve community policing. Keeping their distance from the warlords' private militias, al-Shabaab focused their efforts on removing freelance criminals and unaffiliated gangs from their own neighborhoods. These freelancers were a drain on the business community, but they were of no consequence to the warlords.

In early 2006, however, Sharif and Aweys announced the formal unification of the courts into a single group, the Islamic Courts Union.[8] The ICU brought together the leaders of all the Mogadishu-based courts into a Supreme Council and merged their clan militias into one military force. This official unification created a dramatic change in the political environment.

The amalgamation of al-Shabaab fighters into one military force transformed the courts' small clan contingents into a sizable Islamist army. The ICU emerged as a powerful political and military contender, with enough muscle to effectively challenge the heavily entrenched warlords.

This shift in the balance of power had a dramatic effect on the political landscape. The ICU declared clan politics to be the scourge of Somalia and challenged the warlords for their excesses against civilians. Under the banner of Islam, the ICU set forth a mandate to reconstruct the Somali state and establish order over the unruly countryside. By July 2006, the ICU had expelled all of the most heavily entrenched warlords in Mogadishu and opened its seaports and airports for the first time in a decade. The checkpoints were cleared, and the ICU established a rudimentary legal system, based on Islamic law, and a new taxation system. Six months later, the ICU had captured 90 percent of southern Somalia, bringing the majority of the country under a single government. For the first time in fifteen years of an uninterrupted civil war stalemate, the ICU and al-Shabaab had established centralized political and military control across clan and subclan divisions.[9]

Given the magnitude and durability of state failure in Somalia, the success of the ICU is highly significant for two reasons. First, the ICU effectively utilized Islamic identity to create a central government that commanded the support of multiple clans. Although the core Mogadishu courts drew from the Ayr subclan of the Hawiye-Habr-Gidir, there was significant support for the movement from many other clan factions, including the rival Abgal. The ICU's Supreme Council also made concrete efforts to include meaningful representation from other clan backgrounds and acquired supporters across clan divisions.

Second, the ICU demonstrated a striking ability to establish centralized control over the countryside and impose its will on society. One of the most significant indications of the ICU's capabilities was its ability to implement unpopular laws without incurring insurrection. For example, after assuming control of Mogadishu, the Supreme Council imposed a number of new regulations that caused immediate ire within the business community. The Islamists banned the widely consumed narcotic khat and cigarettes and prohibited watching soccer matches and participating in other popular social activities.[10] Although these new rules were incredibly unpopular among Somalis, the ICU remained resolute. The ICU also implemented a tax system and quality control regulations, the absence of which had been an advantage for the business community in the past. The new quality control regulations on imports eliminated the highly profitable business of selling expired food and medicine. Despite opposition to these edicts, however, the Islamists were able to effectively impose their writ across multiple clan communities.

How was the ICU able to centralize political power in the midst of such intense fragmentation? And why was the ICU able to achieve this striking political victory over other heavily armed warlord groups? Given the enduring legacy of identity politics in Somalia, most existing scholarship understandably points to the role of clan identity,[11] or Islamic ideology,[12] to explain the rise of the ICU. Some scholars show that eleven out of twelve of the Islamic courts in the original movement were from the Hawiye clan, and that the majority of the ICU leadership drew from the powerful Hawiye-Habr-Gidir-Ayr subclan, whereas members of the Hawiye-Abgal and other clans were underrepresented.[13] This explanation, however, overlooks the role of key Abgal and non-Hawiye supporters, without whom the collective action would not have been possible. "The ICU was not about clan," claimed a high-ranking Darod member of the original ICU movement. "It was an Islamic government that included all the clans."[14] While there was staunch resistance to the ICU from then–Transitional Federal Government (TFG) president Abdullahi Yusuf's Darod-Majerteen clan in the north, the ICU successfully incorporated Isaaq, Hawiye-Abgal, Darod-Marehan, Darod-Ogaden, and Rahanweyn members into its umbrella organization.

In fact, as the ICU advanced into the Middle Shabelle and then the Bay and Bakool regions in the summer of 2006, fighters from the Rahanweyn Resistance Army (RRA) and other factions surrendered to the ICU.[15] In a clear demonstration of its Islamist political identity, military leader Sheikh Mukhtar Robow (aka Abu Mansour) declared that the ICU was willing to accept any soldiers defecting from the government, regardless of their clan affiliation.[16] Most significantly, by opening up membership to different clan backgrounds, the ICU was able to construct a pan-clan Islamist identity that allowed it to extend its influence across the country. Much like the Taliban in Afghanistan, this emphasis on Islamist identity over clan fragmentation gave the ICU the ability to draw support from multiple clan groups, thus tipping the balance of power in its favor.

Other researchers have looked to the role of religious ideology to explain the rise of the Islamic courts.[17] Political Islam has a very long history in Somalia, however, and there were many predecessor Islamist movements over the course of the civil war, such as al-Ittihaad al-Islamiyya, al-Islah, and Ahle Sunna Waljama'. In fact, many former al-Ittihaad and al-Islah members became supporters of the ICU movement, but none of these predecessor Islamic groups generated a comparable level of political success in their own right.

The Islamic courts themselves had been in existence for quite some time but did not gain any significant ground until the mid-2000s. The religious argument alone fails to explain why the ICU gained political ground when and how it did.

Why then was the ICU able to establish political control out of chaos? To understand this rise in Islamist power, it is essential to look at the interests and choices of the Somali business class at the moment of ascent.[18] This chapter uncovers the costs of doing business during the Somali civil war and how these costs directly contributed to the success of the Islamists over rival clan warlords. Using both interview and survey data, the stories in this chapter show that at a critical juncture the business community collectively abandoned its long-standing alliances with warlords and switched sides to support the Islamic Courts Union movement.

Indeed, by 2006, 70 to 75 percent of the Mogadishu business community had voluntarily contributed resources to the ICU.[19] They also systematically withheld support from clan-based warlords at the exact same moment. As the business community withdrew its funds from the clan fiefdoms, the warlords were unable to pay their foot soldiers, and the ICU absorbed their defecting militias into the swelling ranks of al-Shabaab. The logic behind this collective action was simple: the ICU lowered security prices for the business community across clan lines. Taxation, far more than ideology, helped propel the Islamists to power.

Trade and Tax in the Somali Civil War

For members of the Somali business class, calculating their expenses and profits was terribly frustrating. To start with, all businesspeople had to budget for two different types of security payments just to stay alive. The first were the protection moneys paid directly to local strongmen. Small businesses were extorted at their storefronts by local henchmen as the price of doing business within a warlord's turf. For large businesses, however, these payments were extorted directly by the warlord himself, who would simply call the business owner on the phone and demand a certain amount of money. For the shopkeeper and the tycoon alike, however, denial of payment would result in physical reprisals. "The warlords were demanding much from the business community," explained a top executive from one of the largest companies in Somalia. "They sent freelancers to scare the business community into paying up. The warlords just demanded money and threatened violence. A businessperson would have to calculate what you have, what you would lose, and then pay up."[20] Members of the business community were forced to make these protection racket payments not only to warlords within their own clan's turf but also to every subsequent warlord who held territory through which they wanted to move their goods. These compound protection prices were getting very steep.

The second type of "taxation" that the business community faced was extortion by militias along major trade routes. As the armed groups fragmented into a plethora of smaller subclan factions, the number of checkpoints that a businessperson would have to cross to secure passage along a trade route also skyrocketed. "After UNOSOM left, the two main factions broke down into many groups based on clan," explained one of the biggest business owners in Mogadishu. "As the number of factions increased, the number of checkpoints increased. Therefore, the business community all needed their own private security. This was like taxation. Everywhere you paid more at each checkpoint. For example, at one checkpoint you used to pay 1,000 [Somali] Shillings and two years later you would have to pay 100,000 Shillings. This was because of both inflation and greediness."[21]

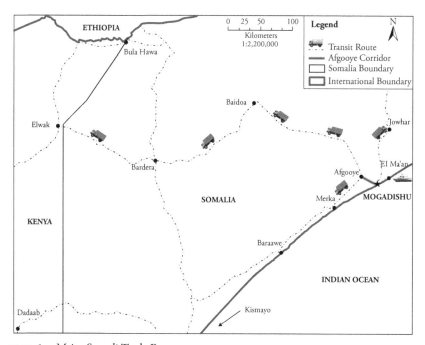

MAP 6.1 Major Somali Trade Routes

Key transit routes from El Ma'an and Mogadishu to Jowhar, Afgooye, Baidoa, and Baraawe.

The business community therefore found itself engaged in complex, multi-actor negotiations in order to move goods from one region into another. Important trade routes were now divided among multiple groups, each of which held a portion of territory along the road. As traders passed through different clan turfs, they required multiple clearances to ensure safe passage for their goods. As a result, Somali businesspeople and clan powerbrokers created a noisy system of reciprocal agreements to help move goods across territory. Even after securing permissions and paying fees, however, businesspeople regularly complained that they could still be held up on the roads by freelance gangs or unruly militia and lose everything.[22]

One trader who moved goods from Bardera, Somalia, to Elwak, Kenya, told how his colleague was held up by a gang of thugs 110 kilometers outside of Mogadishu in the town of Lego: "The checkpoint asked for 60 percent [of the entire product]. The leader of the militia arrived and [my colleague] tried to negotiate, but the leader refused. At last, the leader said, 'Go ask the man who was sleeping there [in a nearby shelter] and whatever he asks, I will accept.' My colleague went inside and saw that it was a dead man. He agreed to their amount."[23] In essence, the business community was being fleeced twice: first by the warlord protection payments, and second by gunmen on the roads. "The warlords were taking money for 'security,' but the insecurity was still there," explained the Bardera-to-Elwak trader. "A certain amount would be agreed with a warlord, but another militia would then come and ask for money."[24]

One of the most important transit routes in Somalia is the strategically significant Afgooye corridor, a 250-kilometer east–west road that connects Mogadishu to the important inland city of Baidoa. The head of the Suuq Ba'ad market, the second-largest market in Mogadishu, explained how the extraordinary number of checkpoints in Afgooye produced a dramatic shift in prices for goods in Baidoa. "During [the reign of] warlords, there was an increase in the number of checkpoints, so we added this to the price of the commodity before sale," he said. "The difference between a sack of sugar in Mogadishu and Baidoa was approximately USD$2 more, including the cost of the car rental, fuel, and checkpoints."[25]

The Bardera-to-Elwak businessman complained bitterly about the impact of this extortion on his ability to compete on the market. "The price of sugar per sack went up USD$4 to $5 because of checkpoints on the Afgooye corridor," he explained. "I practiced. I took [sugar] from Mogadishu to Baidoa. The lowest price difference was USD$3.50. Lower than this was impossible due to insecurity."[26] For this businessman, plowing through the checkpoints increased the price of his goods at sale, subsequently reducing his overall competitiveness.

Other inland markets were similarly affected. The town of Jowhar, located ninety kilometers north of Mogadishu, is an important economic center in the Middle Shabelle region and a key trade conduit from Mogadishu to other domestic markets. The cost of warlord taxes, however, was so debilitating to trade in Jowhar that it completely frustrated business development. As the head of a prominent Mogadishu business school explained, "Jowhar was under warlord Mohamed Dheere's control and he imposed very high taxes on incoming goods that really affected the economy. A sack of sugar was USD$3 to $5 more expensive in Jowhar than in Mogadishu. The price of goods in Jowhar was so high that people from Middle Shabelle started going directly to Mogadishu instead of buying in Jowhar. It became less expensive to go to Mogadishu than to buy goods in Jowhar."[27]

Not all businesses suffered equally under the system of warlord rule, however. Businesspeople that had ties to the security establishment could negotiate better protection payments than those who lacked such connections. For example, one savvy and well-connected businesswoman from Mogadishu bested her beleaguered competitors by negotiating an agreement that allowed her to bypass the checkpoints. "I could buy sugar through El Ma'an port for USD$12.00/sack, plus a USD$1.80/sack charge for transport to Mogadishu," she explained. "It arrived in Mogadishu markets for USD$13.80, but I sold for USD$15.00 in Mogadishu markets with a USD$1.20 profit margin. I sent to Baidoa paying USD$1.00/sack transportation costs, so it was USD$16.00 to get to Baidoa, with a USD$0.50 profit. To send to Jowhar it was approximately USD$0.70 to USD$0.80/sack, with a USD$0.50 profit. In Jowhar I could sell for USD$16.20."[28]

This businesswoman, known for her powerful kinship connections, easily outclassed her competitors by paying a lower rate on the roads. While other businesspeople had to pay an additional premium to move their goods from Mogadishu to Baidoa, her ties to the security establishment allowed her to negotiate a USD$1 per sack transportation cost. Notably, according to the head of the business school, the price of transportation from Mogadishu to Baidoa for fuel and trucking fees was USD$1 per sack, which suggests that the well-connected businesswoman had managed to negotiate her trucks through the Afgooye corridor without paying any checkpoints at all.[29] The businesswoman herself suggested as much, saying, "In most cases, it is better for our business when there is no government, as we make more profit."[30]

For the overwhelming majority of the business community, however, this was simply not the case. "Under the warlords, the price of goods was high and the demand was low," griped a frustrated trader. "It took two days to get the goods from the port to the market."[31] Extortion by warlords and militia had limited the business community's ability to service potentially profitable inland markets. For most traders, political fragmentation proved to be incredibly costly to business.

By the mid-2000s, the number of freelance militia targeting the business community on the streets of Mogadishu also dramatically increased. These freelancers lacked any particular factional affiliation or leadership, and they operated primarily as armed criminal gangs.[32] "A new face of kidnappers and bandits emerged, a new wave of second-level independent warlords, with no politics and no clan," explained the prominent Mogadishu import-exporter. "They were just opportunists. They were the cruelest of all."[33] The unpredictability of this extortion created the most aggravation. "You could not plan," explained the trader who worked from Bardera to Elwak. "You plan to waste a certain amount of money [on checkpoints], and then someone would increase it on you."[34]

Even the largest and most well-connected businesspeople were affected by this increase. For example, Mogadishu has a functioning Coca-Cola manufacturing plant with the production capacity to supply the countryside; however, the company remained underproductive because of the checkpoints on the roads. "In the time of warlords, I couldn't sell Coke outside of Mogadishu," explained the head of the Coca-Cola Company at his posh office in Dubai. "My average production was 500 cases/day and 15,000 cases/month. But my actual production capacity was 285,000 produced per month, but I couldn't sell this because of the insecurity on the roads." Because the militia at checkpoints perceived soft drinks as a luxury item, they were keen to tax trucks carrying Coke bottles. However, because Coke is a nonessential good, it could not sell when the price was inflated. As a result, production and sales were both under capacity. "With the checkpoints, we lost both time and money," he added. "Delays on the road also reduce profits because you make only one trip when you could have made two or three trips back and forth with the same truck."[35]

Extortion of the business community therefore created two sources of ire. First, the business community was forced to pay protection rents to local warlords, despite the unwillingness or inability of those warlords to furnish an adequate degree of protection. And second, the business community was directly extorted on the roads by militia and freelance criminals, who made it impossible to predict the cost of transportation to inland markets. "The risk reduced growth by 40 percent," explained the beleaguered small businessman. "Because of the inability to access the countryside, people reduced their business, froze it in the markets, and decided not to take risks."[36] Even the wealthy and well-connected businesswoman agreed that the increase in unpredictable freelance criminals reduced her opportunities: "Because of the checkpoints, I calculate that I am losing 50 percent of business profits overall. I cannot import what I want. I don't have the freedom to do what I want."[37]

Indeed, even Adani's powerful El Ma'an Port Authority was frustrated by the high cost. Unlike most businesses, the Adani family was so wealthy that it could afford to hire its own private security forces to secure passage between its port and the markets in downtown Mogadishu. "By 2005 we controlled the road from El Ma'an to Mogadishu," explained one of Adani's associate executives. "The businessman who brings a ship to El Ma'an pays USD$2,000–USD$3,000 just to bring the ship to dock. The full amount [for safe passage] was then paid in advance at the port in one lump sum for transit all the way to Mogadishu. If you received any problems on the way to Bakara or Suuq Ba'ad markets, the Benadir Company [one of the subsidiaries of the Port Authority] will help to resolve any problems of freelancer thieves."[38]

The El Ma'an Port Authority therefore not only was able to bypass checkpoints but also charged its own security fees to all other traders that wanted to use their port and roads. The Adani family profited, but also paid hefty overhead costs. As his chief executive explained, the price of maintaining his private security force along the roads was astronomical: "Just to provide security we needed one thousand soldiers and one hundred technicals [light improvised military vehicles]," he grumbled, furrowing his brow as he calculated these expenses. "Eighty percent of our revenues were spent on security. We never saved anything from El Ma'an."[39]

Large and small businesspeople alike grew increasingly frustrated with the high costs of doing business under the warlords. The business community desperately tried to mitigate these costs, becoming increasingly involved in the political process, to no avail. As the warlords and their militias continued to extort the business class, however, members of the business class began to seek out an alternative to the clan fragmentation. One of the most promising avenues for catalyzing this change, they found, was through their local Islamic courts.

The Business Class and the Islamic Courts

Islamic courts have a long history of providing law and order at the community level in Somalia. Since the collapse of the state, however, these courts have taken on a much larger role in local governance. From the early 1990s, Somalis invested in local sharia courts to help create pockets of law and order in the midst of the civil war. Given the fragmentation, these courts were only able to exercise jurisdiction over their own specific subclan groups and did not exercise legal power over members of other clans.[40]

As early as 1994, businesspeople from Mogadishu's dominant Hawiye clan began to invest in their courts as a practical means of reducing transaction costs and resolving disputes with associates. Although each court exercised authority only over its own subclan constituency, these informal legal institutions provided businesses with a mechanism to mitigate uncertainty and facilitate contracts. Business owners continued to pay for security from warlord protection rackets but increasingly relied on these clan-based courts to provide the rule of law. Buoyed by investment from the business community, the courts were able to create a small degree of order in the otherwise lawless capital.

"At first, every clan worked in their own areas," explained the import-exporter, who is a longtime financier of the courts. "The first assignment was that every clan was to reduce insecurity and bandits in their own areas. This was led by local leaders. Every clan was willing to fight against freelancing bandits. At this stage, the courts could only fight low-level bandits, not against warlords who had heavy weapons. There was even a relationship between the warlords and the original clan-based courts. The elders balanced the security situation to coexist with the warlords."[41]

Over time, the success of the courts at the local level increased their material capabilities and political aspirations. By the late 1990s, these disparate, clan-based Islamic courts were collectively becoming an emerging political contender in their own right. Pleased with the courts' demonstrated ability to provide effective adjudication over disputes, members of the business community invested in the maintenance and expansion of their respective clan courts, including the hiring of religiously trained clan militias to safeguard the court's neighborhood. Through this support, the courts gradually became powerful enough to oppose warlord power. In this way, the courts provided the business community with a mechanism through which it could exercise its political voice. In fact, Kenneth Menkhaus describes the business community's 1999 boost in support for local Islamic courts as a "coup" against warlord protection rackets:

> Frustrated with having to pay tribute to militias that provided no security in return (and that were usually the source of insecurity and banditry), leading businesspeople in Mogadishu refused to pay taxes to the warlords associated with their clans. Instead, they bought out

the militiamen from beneath the warlords and assigned the gunmen to the command of local sharia courts. The sharia militias promptly became an impressive source of law and order, at the expense of the much-weakened warlords.[42]

The 1999 enthusiasm for the courts generated momentum for a joint Islamic courts project, which could unify the courts in southern Mogadishu and adjacent neighborhoods.[43] The courts had a history of providing order for local communities, which positioned the Islamists to present themselves as a credible alternative to the unruly militias. By the late 1990s, businesspeople had already started funding the Islamic courts to mitigate the violent fragmentation that was cutting into their profit margins. "With every small court, there was a necessity for coordination," explained a longtime financier of the courts. "It was necessary to unite because thieves run from one district to another."[44]

This support was short-lived, however. By 2000, the business community opted for a more formal solution and thus shifted its support to the new TNG.[45] The general enthusiasm for the prospect of a new Somali government increased consumer confidence and investment, creating a short-term economic boom. The TNG also attracted development assistance dollars and refrained from imposing any new taxes, which brought business supporters on board for the initiative.

The excitement for the TNG was, however, overblown. The business community quickly realized that the TNG was nothing more than a paper government, so ineffectual that it posed no real challenge to the warlords who continued to run the country in private fiefdoms. "Both the business community and the civil society backed the TNG," explained a prominent businessman in the import-export business. "But it excluded warlords, so it was ineffective. That government never succeeded in removing even one checkpoint."[46] The business community thus found itself footing the bill for the TNG, while also paying the exact same amount of protection fees to the warlords. These double charges were tremendously irksome.

As these political processes floundered, the Mogadishu business community further subcontracted practical aspects of providing security to its local Islamic courts. By the time the warlord-dominated TFG took power in 2004, the Islamic courts had already developed a working relationship with their local communities. At first, the courts did not appear to be a threat. The business class continued paying protection fees to warlords and seemed to be funding the courts as a philanthropic side project. The courts had only hired young boys with religious backgrounds to police their neighborhoods for freelance criminals but had taken no aggressive action against the warlords themselves. Preoccupied with their power struggles over high offices, the warlords allowed the courts to arrest unaffiliated bandits and gangs so long as they posed no challenge to their official clan militias.

Business support for the Islamic courts gradually increased between 2004 and 2006, primarily channeled through this voluntary sponsorship of local clan-based courts.[47] The goal of this support was to clear the roads of the unpredictable and debilitating freelance checkpoints but not those of the warlords' militias. The prominent Mogadishu trader who was a leader in financing the courts for many years described how the business community systematically worked together during this critical period:

> There was a regular budget paid by the business community and the clans to the ICU. At first, it was only to your own area, your own clan. Every clan took money to his own court only. Then upon centralization, taxes and fees were given at the district level. These were not taxes, but voluntary contributions. There [was] a committee of 65 elders who collected for them. In the beginning of 2004, [the business community] allocated USD$1,000 per month, per district. By the end of 2004 until mid-2005, we gave USD$3,000 per month, per district. From mid-2005 to 2006, we gave USD$10,000 per month, per district. In Yaqshiid district, near Suuq Ba'ad market, the amount of our contributions increased over time, as [the courts'] activities increased. In 2006, [the ICU] took the whole city, so there was no more need for voluntary contributions. We went from voluntary contributions to taxation, paid by all people for the security of their own houses.[48]

The biggest businesspeople played a lead role in the collective initiative. "To start, there were two key individuals financing the ICU: Ahmed Nur Jim'ale and Omar Adani," explained the head of the Mogadishu Coca-Cola Company. "During the initial stages, Jim'ale and Adani were supporting 50–60 percent of the ICU [to remove freelancers]. Everyone else jumped on board after seeing some success."[49] Adani took a lead role in the early Islamic courts movement, hoping to reduce the high costs he was paying for security. The other leading financier was the primary shareholder in the powerful Hormud telecommunications firm (and former owner of the Barakat hawala company), Ahmed Nur Jim'ale. Adani and Jim'ale were two of the biggest businessmen in Somalia. Together, they laid the financial foundations for the rise of the ICU.

The underlying relationship between these business elites and the burgeoning Islamist movement soon came to a head. According to the chief
executive of the El Ma'an Port Authority, in January 2006 Adani came into
confrontation with one of Mogadishu's most established warlords, Bashir
Rage. The Adani family had an interest in a strip of land in Galgalato, located
in the northeast outskirts of Mogadishu along the coast, which was inside
the territory held by Rage. "We bought land in the Galgalato area," explained
the chief executive. "We bought this land, but Bashir felt threatened. Bashir
said, 'You can't buy here, it's my territory.' We used to ally with Bashir against
warlord Muse Sudi.[50] Rage is from the same clan as us."[51] Financial interests,
however, trumped this clan connection; the Adanis dug in their heels against
Rage and turned to the Islamic courts for backup.

The Adani-Rage battle became a watershed moment for the nascent
Islamic courts movement. Having invested so heavily in the courts, Adani
called in a favor from the ICU leadership. "We fought against Rage with the
moral and material support of the ICU," explained the chief executive. "After
twenty years, people were fed up with fighting. It was four months of continuous fighting, from February/March to June 2006."[52] At the same time, Rage
rallied members of the business community from his own turf to financially
support him in this battle against Adani. These businesspeople were now
faced with a choice between supporting their warlord protection racket and
backing the Islamic courts movement. They chose the ICU. In a seismic shift
in the balance of power, 70 percent of the business community suddenly and
collectively shifted its support to the new Islamist movement.[53]

Alarmed by the ICU's display of power, other warlords mobilized to
defend their turfs. To balance against the surging Islamists, a group of TFG
warlords had formed the Alliance for the Restoration of Peace and Counter-
Terrorism (ARPCT) in order to gain access to covert financial support from
the Pentagon. By early 2006, "CIA operatives based in Nairobi funneled
$100,000 to $150,000 (£80,000) a month to their proxies," hoping to prevent
an Islamist takeover.[54] But it was too late.

The fact that the Islamic Courts Union drew its support from multiple clan backgrounds gave it a comparative advantage over the warlords.
Tribalism had prevented the warlords from expanding their base, but the
ICU was able to acquire support across clan lines. By widening the pool from
which they could draw support, the courts were able to amass a powerful military force. As the ICU pushed into the countryside, al-Shabaab absorbed the
foot soldiers of clan-based factions across southern Somalia. Unlike encroach-
ments by other armed groups in Somalia, the ICU provided clan militias with

the option of defection. Because al-Shabaab had a fundamentally pan-clan, Islamist political identity, rival militiamen could join the Islamists without fear of extermination. The Islamists then systematically indoctrinated and assimilated the clans' foot soldiers into their ranks, giving the ICU a substantial army that could compete against even the largest clan militias.

The Islamists also outmatched their rivals in revenue generation. Because the warlords relied on funding from their clans, they had a narrower base of support and subsequently had to charge higher margins for protection. In contrast, because the courts drew support across clan divisions, the Islamists were able to charge lower margins for security, giving the ICU a competitive edge over its rivals. The price differential made the Islamists an attractive political option for the business community.

How substantial was the discount? The chairman of one of the most lucrative markets in Mogadishu aptly stated: "For every USD$100 we were forced to pay to the warlords, we would give USD$35 to the Islamic Courts" to remove them.[55]

The Islamists won the support of the business class with these bargain security prices. "The reasons that the business community supported the ICU was because of the illegal taxes," said a prominent Mogadishu-based economics professor and businessman. "The ICU didn't say they wanted taxes. They only asked for *khidmat* [service charges] or *zakat*. People felt they were better off."[56] While the warlords prayed to the almighty dollar, the Islamists were fighting *Fi sabililah*, "for the cause of God."

The businessman who had been extorted along the Afgooye corridor was delighted with the reduction in checkpoints: "Overall, business increased by 10–15 percent under the ICU due to reduced prices and increased demand, not only in Jowhar and Baidoa but everywhere. We never saw this [the ICU contributions] as a cost. It was holy money to pay."[57] Even the shrewd businesswoman who could avoid the checkpoints was pleased: "[The ICU] was 'pay what you can.' They opened Mogadishu port, so I saved from what I used to pay for El Ma'an. There was increase in demand and the volume of goods. If the ICU stayed, we would have had expansion in business."[58] With this firm backing of the business elite, the Islamic Courts Union bested the warlord on the battlefield and consolidated its power over the Somali countryside.

Surveying Somali Businesses

Business support thus played a critical role in the rise of the ICU in Somalia. To understand why the business community engaged in this collective action, I examined the survey results against my interview data, using a multivariate

regression of the business community's interests, identities, and political preferences.[59] My survey asked Somali business owners about their experience of
the following four political systems: (1) the 2000–2004 Transitional National
Government; (2) the 2004–2006 Transitional Federal Government; (3) the
2006 Islamic Courts Union; and (4) no government at all. According to
the results, 54 percent of all respondents felt they did best under the TNG;
9.5 percent felt they fared better under the TFG; 20 percent preferred the
ICU; and 16.5 percent felt they do best with no government at all.

The survey also asked respondents two questions about their protection
payments: first, to estimate their total security costs under the reign of warlords from 2004 to 2006; and second, to estimate their costs under the ICU
in 2006. Both of the security costs questions were measured on the same
ascending five-point ordinal scale, ranging from none to very high. I also
asked several questions about clan identities, Islam, and trust. Looking at the
responses to all of these questions, I then examined what factors explained the
business community's support for the ICU over other options.

My analysis of these results indicated that how much a businessperson
remembered paying for security had a profound impact on his or her political
preferences.[60] As seen in Table 6.1 and Figure 6.1, higher warlord costs were
negatively correlated with preference for the TFG and positively correlated
with preference for the ICU.[61] Other things equal, a one-level increase on the
scale of warlord security prices made an individual 43 percent less likely to
prefer the TFG and 33 percent more likely to favor the ICU. Similarly, a one-
level increase in the level of recollected ICU security costs made 51 percent
less likely to prefer the ICU and 24 percent more likely to support the TFG.
A one-level increase in perceived ICU costs also made the odds 72 percent
higher that a businessperson would prefer having no government at all.[62]

These results reflect the reality of business life in Somalia. The fact was
that every businessperson had to calculate whether it was more cost effective to buy protection from their clan's warlord fiefdom, support the ICU,
or shoulder the costs of security alone by hiring their own militias. As the
results show, higher warlord security prices resulted in increased support for
the ICU, whereas high ICU costs led businesspeople to feel that they were
better off alone. There was no correlation between gender and political preference in any of these results; Somali businesswomen responded similarly to
their male counterparts, both for and against the ICU.

My interviews with the largest business owners signaled that the wealthiest businesspeople paid the highest rates of extortion to the warlords and
were also the front runners in funding the early ICU period.[63] The statistical

Table 6.1 Political Preference: Multinomial Logit Analysis

Independent Variables	Dependent Variable		
	Risk Ratio		
	Multinomial Logit Coefficient (Standard Error)		
	TFG	ICU	Prefer No Gov't
General Social Indicators			
Male	1.060	.899	1.311
	.059(.258)	−.106(.194)	.270(.210)
Size of Business	1.181	1.370**	.773*
	.166(.167)	.315(.131)	−.257(.135)
High School	.410***	.600*	.475***
	−.889(.332)	−.509(.308)	−.743(.269)
University	.799	2.006*	.677
	−.224(.537)	.696(.405)	−.388(.457)
Religious	.574*	1.099	.548**
Education	−.554(.312)	.095(.280)	−.601(.252)
Identity and Ideology			
Clan Trust	.679	.808	.673*
	−.386(.261)	−.212(.210)	−.395(.206)
Islam Trust	.840	.509***	1.571
	−.174(.326)	−.674(.222)	.451(.305)
Like Islamic Law	.640*	.846	.676**
	−.445(.241)	−.167(.191)	−.391(.193)
Taxes			
ICU Taxes	1.243*	.493****	1.716****
	.218(.122)	−.706(.109)	.540(.111)
Warlord Taxes	.570****	1.326***	1.039
	−.561(.116)	.282(.101)	.039(.106)
Constant	.410(.757)	.346(.628)	−2.582(.774)****

Note: Cells contain risk ratios with standard error indicated in parentheses. Number of observations= 1,003. *$p<.10$, ** $p<.05$, *** $p<.01$, **** $p<.001$. TNG as residual category.

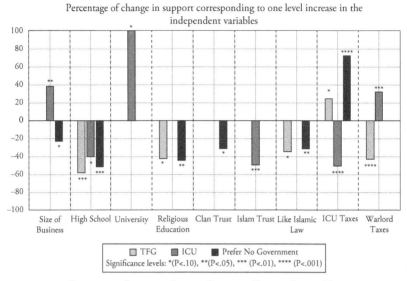

Percentage of change in support corresponding to one level increase in the independent variables

FIGURE 6.1 Illustration of statistically significant coefficients from table 6.1

results corroborated this interview data: a one-level increase in the size of a business made a businessperson 37 percent more likely to prefer the ICU and 23 percent less likely to want no government at all. Bigger businesses took the lead in rallying behind the ICU.

While these security costs had a significant effect on political preferences, the identity variables showed little explanatory power. Three other variables were included in the estimation to test the effects of clan and Islamic trust.[64] Surprisingly, the clan trust variables had no effect on preference for either the TFG or the ICU, and clan favoritism was negatively correlated with a preference for political anarchy. Clan sentiments did not provide an explanation of why the business community supported the ICU. In fact, only the residual category, the clan-based TNG, attracted the support of those who felt most positively about clan. Overall, respondents had a diverse but largely negative reaction toward clan-based trust. Two female business partners who operate a large khat-trading operation explained the waning centrality of clan politics: "We are both from different clans, but that doesn't matter. Clan is irrelevant in business. We are concerned with profit."[65] When asked about their preferences for selecting a business partnership, as seen in Table 6.2, only 5 percent of survey respondents opted to work with a member of their own clans. In contrast, over 80 percent of respondents thought that having solid Islamic credentials is a good way to determine trustworthiness.

Neither "Islamic trust" nor "support for Islamic law," however, had any clear statistical effect on preference for the ICU. In fact, those who felt most strongly

Table 6.2 Frequency Distributions for Identity and Trust Variables

SURVEY QUESTION:	Q8: It is more costly and difficult to conduct business with members of other clans than it is to work with my own clan	Q9: A person within my clan is more likely to respect my property rights than a person from another clan	Q10: A good Muslim is more likely to respect my property rights than a person who doesn't follow their religion
1. Strongly Agree	18.44%	16.65%	80.66%
2. Agree	19.84	23.33	11.67
3. Neutral	7.38	7.98	3.59
4. Disagree	28.51	30.91	2.89
5. Strongly Disagree	25.82	21.14	1.20

that Islamic identity is a good measure of trustworthiness were negatively correlated with preference for the ICU. Indeed, as seen in Figure 6.1 and Table 6.1, businesspeople who felt most strongly about Islamic trust were actually 49 percent less likely to favor the ICU. Furthermore, there was no statistically significant correlation between support for Islamic law and preference for the ICU. Respondents who strongly favored Islamic law as a way to regulate transactions among businesses were 36 percent less likely to support the TFG and 32 percent less likely to prefer no government at all. Strong feelings about Islamic law, however, did not correspond with increased support for the ICU.

Moreover, Islamic education had no obvious impact on support for the ICU. Religious education did make a respondent 43 percent less likely to support the TFG and 45 percent less likely to prefer no government at all compared to the TNG. There is no indication from the survey results, however, that religious training or strong religious sentiment explain why members of the business community might prefer the ICU. On the contrary, the data show that respondents who had a university-level education were twice as likely to feel positively about the ICU.[66]

Neither religious nor tribal sentiments provide a clear explanation for why the business community decided to support the ICU. Drawing from both the interviews and the survey data, however, the evidence suggests that security costs played a crucial role in shaping the political preferences of the business class at a critical juncture. As the Islamists lowered their overhead costs, the business community collectively shifted its support to back the ICU against the warlords, catalyzing a dramatic transformation in the balance of power in the Somali civil war.

Somalia's Islamist Juggernaut

The resounding success of the Islamic Courts Union came as a surprise not only to the warlords but also to the business elites who sponsored it. "We and Jim'ale had no political agenda," insisted the Adani executive. "We did not even expect to defeat the warlords. We were just acting out of our own interests."[67] Once the courts unified, however, the biggest ICU sponsors were rewarded with positions of political power in the new government. Because Adani and his family had contributed so much to the courts, they expected a return on that investment. "When the ICU took over in June 2006, [we] wanted to quit," explained his executive. "We had spent a lot of money and we wanted to be refunded for these costs."[68] Instead of quitting, however, Sheikh Sharif made an agreement with the Adani family, making Omar Adani's son Abdulkadir the secretary of finance in the ICU. Ahmed Nur Jim'ale was also rewarded for his contribution to the ICU, with his brother assuming the role of vice secretary of finance for the Islamic Courts.

Through his official position, Abdulkadir Adani reopened the Mogadishu port for the first time in a decade and began to charge baseline taxes on importers. These taxes helped to finance the ICU, but they also allowed the Adani family to extract a percentage in order to recollect on their investment. "We only charged fixed taxes from the seaport and the airport," explained the Adani executive. "Everyone paid the same."[69] However, this "fixed tax" proved to be deeply frustrating to some traders, who claimed that the ICU system was poorly conceived and unfairly applied. One beleaguered business-man exclaimed, "They charged you for the size of your crate, not the value of the product inside it!"[70] Another businessman, who was among the minority of traders who didn't support the ICU, argued that the taxes were even more debilitating than under the reign of warlords: "If you cannot pay to the war-lord, you can go to the clan elders or to another warlord to have the amount reduced. But for the ICU, there were two types of businesspeople: (1) those who gave a lot to the ICU voluntarily, and (2) those who benefited from secu-rity but were not with the ICU. For the latter, they had to pay 'forced volun-tary' taxes. You could not refuse these and there was no recourse."[71]

Even the supporters of the ICU, however, quickly realized that once the clan-based warlords had been expelled from Mogadishu, the business class no longer had any political options. The Islamists had seized power, which could now be used to control the business class. "The ICU came up with regulatory practices, such as stopping the khat trade and cigarettes, that were not attractive at the time," explained one of the most powerful businessmen in Somalia.[72] This businessman had taken a lead role in financing the ICU from 2004 to 2006, but ironically he was also the owner of a multimillion-dollar cigarette business. Once the ICU took power, he found he could no longer control its political decisions, even when the Islamists caused immense harm to his company through the cigarette ban. "If the business community had influence over the ICU, there would have been no mistakes," he said. "[But] we could not stop supporting them because they were a power to reckon with."[73] The business elites that had collectively mobilized their support for the ICU found that they could no longer control it.

They had created an Islamist juggernaut.

7

The Blowback Effect

INTERNATIONAL INTERVENTION AND
THE COLLAPSE OF THE PROTO-STATE

A scorpion and a frog met on the bank of a river. The scorpion asked the
  frog to carry him across the water on its back.
The frog asked, "How do I know you won't sting me?" The scorpion replied,
  "Because if I do, I will die too."
The frog accepted this logic and set out to cross the river with the scorpion.
  Then suddenly, midstream, the scorpion stung him. The frog grew
  numb and started to sink, knowing they would both drown.
The frog gasped, "Why?"
The scorpion replied, "It is my nature."

AFRICAN FABLE

THE ISLAMIST PROTO-STATE emerged out of despair. In the years leading up to the rise of the Taliban and Islamic Courts Union (ICU) movements, both Afghanistan and Somalia were quintessential failed states, ruled
by predatory ethnic and tribal warlords and bereft of hope. Entire generations
had been raised in refugee and internally displaced person (IDP) camps, ignorant of their own history, politics, and religion. In the enduring anarchy, traditional values were replaced with radicalism and gun culture. Most Afghans
and Somalis lived in desperate poverty, never having experienced peace. Yet
out of the ashes of these civil wars, a new business class arose, amassing tremendous private wealth and influence. In pursuit of greater fortunes, these
economic elites used their financial leverage to fund the creation of a new
Islamist political order.

Backed by the local business class, the Taliban and the ICU recruited
fighters across factional lines; routed the heavily entrenched warlords; and
established centralized control over their divided societies, bringing these
fragmented countries under a single authority for the first time in many years.

They cleared predatory checkpoints and expelled rapacious militias from their turfs, which brought desperately needed relief to their besieged populations. From ruin, they built a surprising degree of statelike power. Establishing firm control over their divided populations, the Islamists promised a new dawn after the dark era of brutal civil war.

This promise of a bright future, however, was soon overshadowed by extremism, dashing hopes of an end to the fighting. The Taliban and ICU not only failed to lift their societies out of political and economic misery but also, through unsuccessful international relations, propelled these societies into ever-greater suffering. The jihadist uprisings that the business elites had first believed to be their saving grace turned out to be a poisonous venom that would engulf both Afghanistan and Somalia in a new wave of violence.

Although the goal of this book is to uncover the domestic financial origins of the modern Islamist proto-state during its initial rise to power, the eventual failure and demise of these polities is an important final episode in this account. At first the Islamists appeared to be a new hope for these war-torn countries; but once in power, their story took a dark turn. After the business community sponsored the Islamists' initial formation of the proto-state, their mutual relationship quickly shifted to one of domination. In this chapter, the evidence shows that, as the Islamists continued down their ideological path, they not only alienated the local business class but also attracted the hostility of the international community. Faced with an impending global confrontation, the local business class found itself paralyzed, unable to rein in the Islamists to avoid the clash. Although the proto-state was born of endogenous processes, its death was the result of these powerful external forces.

In Afghanistan, the cross-border traders felt their influence drop very suddenly. After their victory at Spin Boldak, the Taliban found a new source of funding from neighboring Pakistan and were no longer beholden to their early business backers. "The Taliban were our baby," explained General Aurakzai. "It was an indigenous movement because of the internecine warfare going on in Afghanistan, [where] there were various groups fighting for supremacy. [The Taliban] emerged as a very potent force, and since we were always placing our stakes with the Pashtun community, who have also been the ruling elite in Afghanistan ... it was quite natural for the ISI to side with the Taliban, [and] give them a bit of [financial support] so that they succeed."[1] By 1996, these Pakistani assets gave Mullah Omar the freedom to rule and made the Taliban increasingly independent from the traders who first financed their rise to power in 1994.

As the Taliban's financial dependency shifted to Pakistan, their love affair with the business class therefore grew cold. Mullah Omar's council introduced new regulations that dramatically affected business in the border area. While the Taliban successfully purged the checkpoints, they also imposed harsh laws against bribery, which stalled trade from Peshawar back to Karachi. The smugglers had built their networks on the basis of an elaborate system of graft, which was suddenly under Taliban scrutiny. Business empires began to crumble, and even the trade association president was eventually forced to give up his stately domed manor.[2]

The Taliban also banned female employment, putting thousands of qualified women out of the workforce. "There was no more rape. The Taliban were good people in that regard," explained a village woman from Balkh province. "But we couldn't move. We couldn't go outside."[3] Female-headed families fell into crushing poverty, and many fled the country. Removing women from the already stressed workforce was economically disastrous, especially in the cities. International sanctions against the regime further hurt the already impoverished civilian population.

The heroin dealers would also soon get their comeuppance. In 2000, the Taliban imposed a countrywide ban on poppy cultivation, breaking the backbone of the drug trade.[4] They declared production of narcotics to be a violation of sharia and enforced strict punishments against any farmers caught contravening the law.[5] Within one year the opium harvest in Afghanistan dropped by a staggering 90 percent, creating a ripple effect on prices in the global market.[6] For the poor farmers who had grown dependent on opium smuggling networks, the injunction was devastating. The wealthy drug lords did not go hungry, but they too felt the hit. By this point, however, the smugglers in the border region had lost all control over the Taliban government. They had mortgaged their long-term economic interests for the short-term promise of security. They were trapped.

The Islamists in Somalia also turned on the business class. Although the Islamic Courts Union was only in power for a short time, as soon as the movement consolidated its power, its relationship with the traders soured. In a surprise move, the ICU forbade chewing khat, smoking cigarettes, watching movies, and listening to music. Drug addicts were irate, as the ban forced them into chemical withdrawal. But even the general population found the prohibitions on cinema and music to be extreme and inconsistent with their traditional understanding of Islam. The traders who dealt in these newly banned commodities were stunned. Having sponsored the Islamic Courts

Union, members of the business class thought that they would have influence over the new government. They quickly realized they had no such power.

Concerned that the ICU was taking Somalia down a dangerous path, the business community also grew anxious at the global hostility brewing against the Islamists. "The number one mistake the ICU made was having a bad relationship with the international community," argued a prominent cigarette trader. "If the business community had [retained] influence over the ICU, there would have been no mistakes."[7] As international pressures mounted against the ICU government, Somalia's business elites grew fearful that their association with the Islamists might result in legal charges against them or result in their assets being frozen on accusations of sponsoring terrorism. Fearing these reprisals, even the head of the El Ma'an Port Authority tried to distance the Adani family from the ICU. "We are just businesspeople," the chief executive desperately pleaded. "I swear, we only supported the ICU to create stability."[8] Their words now had little impact, however. These elites no longer had the ability to rein in the Islamists, who were primed for a head-on collision with the international community.

From Proto-State to Jihadist Insurgency: Islamist Power after the Taliban and ICU

Despite having their roots in local politics, both the Taliban and the ICU inevitably found themselves embroiled in international conflicts and intrigues beyond their original mandates, ultimately leading to their downfall on the world stage. Behind this global confrontation was the fear of transnational terrorism. Underfunded and diplomatically alienated from the international community, these two fragile Islamist regimes were easy targets for infiltration and manipulation by powerful terrorist networks that actively sought to exploit the local Islamists.[9]

In Afghanistan, al-Qaeda operatives first built ties with the Taliban leadership and then used the war-torn country as a secret base to coordinate their devastating September 11 attacks. In Somalia, al-Qaeda had limited contact with the Islamic Courts Union, but even this perceived link was enough to provoke a preemptive US-backed Ethiopian invasion in 2007, sparking a dramatic rise in extremist violence.

In both of these cases, al-Qaeda eventually successfully co-opted these domestic Islamist movements, provoking two large-scale international military interventions that radicalized the domestic Islamists. In response to these interventions, Islamist insurgencies in both Afghanistan and Somalia adopted a more transnational and networked jihadist identity and mandate.[10] The international interventions thus created an unintended and uncontrollable blowback effect: as these Islamist proto-states collapsed, they inspired a new era of globalized jihadist violence that swept across Afghanistan, Somalia, and beyond.

Afghanistan: From the Taliban to Transnational Terrorism

The early Taliban movement did not start out seeking a global confrontation.[11] After sixteen years of uninterrupted war, Afghans were tired of the violence. In fact, the Taliban were at first enthusiastic about establishing ties with the United States, which had supported the Islamic resistance against the Soviet invasion. Hoping to rekindle this relationship, in 1995 a Taliban official reached out to the US embassy in Pakistan, calling the Americans "an important and unbiased friend."[12] Mullah Omar also sent twenty-four-year-old Sayed Rahmatullah Hashemi, one of the few Taliban fighters with a command of the English language, to the United States as his international envoy. Young and inexperienced, Hashemi's diplomatic efforts in America failed to build confidence, despite his apparent desire to build bridges. Indeed, in 1996 the Taliban even invited the Americans to set up a consulate in Kandahar to establish direct relations with the regime, an invitation that was refused outright.[13]

Despite these awkward but well-meaning overtures, however, the Taliban government lacked both technocrats and diplomats, and its treatment of women and minorities isolated the regime on the world stage. Pakistan and Saudi Arabia were the only two countries that officially recognized the Taliban government, but neither was willing or able to assist with Afghanistan's political development. They simply propped up the regime financially and defended its more radical policies from international criticism. On the ground, the Taliban remained isolated, with limited skills, resources, and experience in governance.

The early al-Qaeda network was well positioned to take advantage of this miserable situation. Osama bin Laden had invested many years in Afghanistan in support of the anti-Soviet mujahideen, and his Arab comrades had built a relationship between Gulf financiers and various Afghan commanders, including Sayyaf's radical Ittehad faction.[14] Once the Soviets withdrew, however, bin Laden personally left Afghanistan, returning to Saudi Arabia in 1989 to pursue various other jihadist adventures around the world.[15] After failing to get Saudi support for a jihad in Kuwait, he was exiled for his extremist actions and then moved to Sudan.[16] Turning his attention to Africa, bin Laden and his supporters began to foment extremist violence in Egypt, Somalia, and Kenya.[17] His extremism soon caused him to wear out his welcome with the government in Khartoum, and he was again expelled in 1996.[18] Unable to return to either Saudi Arabia or Sudan, bin Laden then made his way back to Afghanistan, where state failure and civil war could allow him to operate freely. Upon arrival, he at once made contact with one of Sayyaf's commanders, using his ties from the Soviet era to find sanctuary in the Jalalabad area.[19]

As the tide of battle turned in the Taliban's favor, bin Laden also reached out to Mullah Omar. He ingratiated himself by offering the Taliban his support and playing up his contributions to the anti-Soviet jihad.[20] The deeply held Pashtun tradition of offering hospitality to foreign guests served bin Laden well, and he took advantage of the generosity offered by the Taliban leadership council. In time, bin Laden's menacing ways and bombastic media presence soon prompted many Taliban to call for his expulsion; this time, however, he could not be removed.[21] Not only were the Taliban too weak to curtail his activities, but he had also manipulated Mullah Omar and his inner circle to secure his safe haven. Over time, bin Laden used this sanctuary to establish a powerful base of operations inside Afghanistan.

Bin Laden's toxic presence in Afghanistan made it impossible for the Taliban to establish normal diplomatic relations with the United States, thus rendering young Hashemi's efforts futile. In thirty direct communications between the US government and the Taliban leadership between 1996 and 2001, the Americans informed the Taliban of bin Laden's involvement in international terrorism and demanded his extradition. The Americans presented a clear warning to the Taliban: "Because bin Laden has been in Afghanistan for so long and has committed so many terrorist acts, the US will hold the Taliban accountable if he commits any further acts."[22] Although Taliban leaders repeatedly tried to distance themselves from bin Laden's terrorist activities and extremist rhetoric, they refused to surrender him to the Americans.[23]

By 1998, the Taliban's refusal to extradite bin Laden had limited discourse between Washington and Kandahar. "I held four meetings with the US ambassador over the issue of Osama bin Laden, each without result," explained former senior Taliban official Mullah Zaeef. "Even though we had both tried to improve the relationship between our countries, and had a good personal rapport, nothing came of these encounters as neither of us had the power to take decisions. Other people were responsible for authorizing all of our meetings as well as our decisions and answers, all of which were negative."[24]

According to diplomatic cables, the Taliban's foreign minister to Pakistan, Mullah Wakil Ahmed Mutawakkil, insinuated that an internal political issue was preventing the Taliban from cooperating on the extradition. In a private conversation with the deputy chief of mission to the US embassy in Pakistan, Alan W. Eastham Jr., "Wakil then asked rhetorically [why] the Taliban still did not expel bin Laden. He said it should be obvious that there was an internal obstacle to doing so, since the easiest way to proceed would be to respect international laws and norms."[25]

The relationship between the Taliban and al-Qaeda grew increasingly tense, leading to a debate within the Taliban leadership council. Some senior Taliban officials felt that their Arab guests were taking advantage of their hospitality and co-opting their domestic politics. By 1998, the majority of the Taliban leadership council favored bin Laden's extradition. Taliban official Abdul Hakim Mujahid declared that "80 percent of Taliban officials oppose [bin Laden's presence]."[26] Yet the council ultimately decided to allow bin Laden to stay in Afghanistan, with "his political activities curtailed."[27] Despite evidence that bin Laden was "out of control," the Taliban leadership was either unable or unwilling to cooperate on the issue of extradition.[28] When pressed to explain, Mujahid was evasive and apologetic, saying, "The Taliban have 'shortcomings' and the world should not expect too much from them."[29] Behind the scenes, bin Laden's surreptitious activities escalated, but Mutawakkil insisted that he and his associates were not aware of the nefarious plot.[30] As a result, al-Qaeda not only succeeded in murdering nearly three thousand civilians on September 11, but less than one month later, the United States waged war on the Taliban and became embroiled in a multibillion-dollar military quagmire.

On October 7, 2001, the United States and its allies launched Operation Enduring Freedom, aimed at overthrowing the Taliban and creating a new interim government in Afghanistan. The ensuing international intervention not only destroyed the Taliban proto-state but also reinstalled the old ethnic warlords and sparked a new jihadist insurgency. Rather than staging a large ground invasion, the Americans decided to outsource the initial ground war to the former ethnic warlords of the Northern Alliance, including Dostum, Rabbani, Khan, and Sayyaf.[31] Armed with new military hardware, the old warlords quickly mobilized their troops against key Taliban strongholds, calling in American air reinforcements to crush the Islamists on the battlefield.

The committed jihadists stayed faithful to Mullah Omar, but many others jumped ship, shaving their beards and changing out of their uniforms before they were slaughtered. Knowing they could not defend against the aerial bombardment, the Taliban loyalists withdrew from the front lines and prepared for a long, drawn-out guerrilla war, using a similar strategy that they employed against the Soviets. Mullah Omar remained the symbolic leader of the jihad, but at ground level the Islamists adopted a more decentralized approach to their insurgent operations.

With their backs against the wall, the Taliban leadership also dropped its pious pretense when it came to the drug trade, using heroin revenues to stay afloat. Realizing the movement would need fast money to sustain its fight, Mullah Omar rescinded his ban on opium production, and the Taliban began to tax and profit from narcotics trafficking. Over time, the Islamists increased this involvement. "While the Taliban have long profited from the taxation and protection of the drug trade in Afghanistan," explains Azam Ahmed, "insurgents are taking more direct roles and claiming spots higher up in the opium chain, according to interviews with dozens of Afghan and Western officials, as well as smugglers and members of the communities where they reside."[32] Becoming narco-gangsters in their own right, the Taliban established a solid economic foundation to fund their insurgency.

As the Islamists pulled back and focused on their guerrilla war, the old ethnic warlords reestablished their private fiefdoms. Ismail Khan reclaimed control over his native province of Herat, located to the west of the country. Rabbani's faction established its control over the Tajik communities in the northeast. Dostum's Uzbek militias captured the northern Balkh, Jowzjan, Faryab, and Sar-i-Pol provinces. As their ethnic commanders seized control of the countryside, they not only brutalized the Taliban and their supporters but also once again turned on each other in a violent bid for power.

Dostum's men were savage, rounding up women from their households and brutalizing them. The US-backed warlord was unabashed about his violence. "If you upset me . . . God may protect you, but down here, if I don't look after you, no one will," Dostum warned a room full of terrified village elders, who visibly shook before the towering warlord. "You will lose your honor and dignity. You will be killed. You will be robbed. Even your [women's] honor will be trampled under [men's] feet."[33] But the Uzbeks were not the only group guilty of the renewed ethnic violence. Reports of targeted violence and systematic sexual assault of women and children erupted across the country immediately after the fall of the Taliban.[34]

These grisly human rights violations, however, had no effect on the international community's support for the warlords; rather, the ethnic warlords
and their deputy commanders assumed positions of power in the new US-
backed Afghan government under newly appointed president Hamid Karzai.
Former Jamiat-i-Islami Field Commander Mohammad Qasim Fahim, who
had fought with Ahmed Shah Massoud faction until his 2001 assassination,
became the defense minister in 2002 and then served as vice president starting in 2009. Ismail Khan was given governorship of Herat until 2005 and was
then appointed the minister of water and energy for the next ten years. After
securing his base in the north, Dostum was appointed the deputy defense
minister and then took over the vice presidency in 2014. Sayyaf became an
influential parliamentarian in the new government, alongside his deputies.

The result was a new internationally sponsored, warlord-run Afghan government rife with corruption and abuse. Between parliamentary sessions,
Sayyaf's men took turns taunting the female parliamentarians in the new government. "*Fahesha! Fahesha!* [Prostitute! Prostitute!] Take her and rape her!"
they jeered at the few women who dared speak out against the resurgence of
violence.[35] The newly minted warlord-government also wasted no time in
seizing control of Afghanistan's poppy fields, emerald mines, and trafficking
networks, accruing enormous private wealth. So extensive was this corruption
that Ahmed Wali Karzai, the late brother of the then president, ran Kandahar
province as his private warlord fiefdom. The shadowy brother of Hamid Karzai
used aid monies and projects to establish his dominance over Kandahar province, building himself into one of the biggest drug lords in the country.

The Americans knew about this corruption, but they did little to stop it.
"Much of the real business of running Kandahar takes place out of public
sight, where [Ahmed Wali Karzai] operates, parallel to formal government
structures, through a network of political clans that use state institutions to
protect and enable licit and illicit enterprises," diplomatic cables reveal. "In
Kandahar's political realm, he is an unrivaled strongman. For example, the
Kandahar Provincial Council, which is made up largely of individuals who
are personally beholden to him, wields serious influence, despite its lack of
statutory powers."[36] Yet because the Karzai family was the domestic political
face of the intervention, the Americans kept quiet.

These staggering levels of corruption, however, shattered public confidence in the intervention. Countrywide surveys found that government
corruption presented the single greatest challenge to the legitimacy of the
state-building project in Afghanistan: "For an overwhelming 59 percent of
the population the daily experience of public dishonesty is a bigger concern

than insecurity (54 percent) and unemployment (52 percent)."[37] Making these warlord-run bureaucracies transparent and scrupulous, however, was an impossible task for the international community. "There is virtually no chance that the Afghan government will tackle corruption—and everyone knows it," quipped Roland Paris, an expert on peacebuilding, after the 2012 aid donors' conference in Tokyo.[38]

Government corruption not only undermined confidence in the international community, however, but also gave credence to the Taliban's call for jihad. To start, local Taliban commanders established shadow governments in every province across the country, running parallel to the new Afghan government institutions. These Taliban offices then worked hard to eliminate corruption in their ranks, especially in fence-sitting and bellwether districts. The Islamist leadership even publicly sacked several of its own shadow governors and political officials to prove itself more accountable than the Afghan government.[39]

The strategy worked. Countrywide survey data revealed that "50 percent of the respondents consider that [government] corruption fosters expansion of the Taliban [and] one third of respondents said they had heard the Taliban were mobilizing against the government on the basis of corruption allegations."[40] In the same spirit that Mullah Omar's movement differentiated itself from the rapacious militias during the civil war era, the Taliban's crackdown enhanced their popularity over the warlord-parliamentarians in the new government. In the competition for political legitimacy, anticorruption gave the Taliban an important advantage.

On the battlefield, however, they remained outmatched. Knowing that they were in for a protracted fight, the Taliban urged patience: "If you take your revenge in one hundred years, you've acted in haste," goes the old Pashto proverb.[41] The Taliban embraced the long game, and Mullah Omar was popularly quoted as saying, "The Americans have all the watches, but we have all the time." The Taliban therefore worked to maintain their economic and military power, while frustrating the foreign forces with a sustained campaign of guerrilla and terrorist tactics. They planned to wait for the foreign occupation to withdraw, and then fully mobilize to take down the warlord-dominated Afghan government and reestablish their sharia-based rule of law. Their patience paid off. Despite facing tremendous international pressure for over ten years, the Taliban insurgency defied the odds and maintained its influence across the Afghan countryside.

As time passed, however, the insurgency also underwent an ideological evolution. The original Taliban movement had been born out of a conservative Deobandi tradition, which is not wholly incompatible with peace or even democratization. Because the international community treated the Taliban as if they were synonymous with al-Qaeda, however, the conflict actually increased bin Laden's influence over the Islamists. Over the course of the lengthy war, many fighters shifted to a fringe version of militant Salafi extremism popular among jihadist groups in the Arab world.[42] With every passing year, the Taliban insurgency grew more extreme and less reconcilable.

Meanwhile, Pakistan played both sides of the conflict. On the one hand, the Pakistani government appeased its American allies by facilitating NATO supply lines through Karachi and launching large-scale counterterrorism operations in the border region. The Inter-Services Intelligence (ISI) also arrested leading Taliban commanders and secretly allowed the Americans to send unmanned military drones into Pakistani territory to kill terrorist suspects, especially those that were attacking Pakistani targets. On the other hand, the government was accused of keeping the top-level Taliban leadership hidden inside Pakistan as a tool of leverage over what it perceived to be a more pro-India government inside Kabul. When the Americans finally found and killed Osama bin Laden in his heavily guarded estate in Abbottabad, a short drive from Islamabad, the fact that the infamous terrorist leader had been living less than a mile away from the Pakistani Military Academy for years proved to many observers that the ISI has been involved in a double game.[43]

Despite this seeming duplicity, the future of the fledging government in Kabul rests on the prospects of peace negotiations with the Taliban leadership, a process that Islamabad has worked tirelessly to control. Yet since the Taliban's public acknowledgment of the death of Mullah Omar in 2015, serious internal divisions within the ranks have also emerged. With a proliferating number of factions splintering from the original Taliban movement, initiating effective talks between the warring parties in the region has become a bewildering business, one that even Pakistan does not appear able to contain. After decades of war, a meaningful political resolution to the conflict remains elusive.

Somalia: From Islamic Courts to Al-Qaeda Franchise

After fifteen years of uninterrupted clan conflict, the ICU finally put an end to the scourge of clan warfare in Somalia. The Islamists' success at home, however, also provoked a new international crisis abroad. The Taliban experience weighed heavily on decision makers in Washington, who feared an extremist takeover in East Africa. "The first concern, of course, would be to make sure that Somalia does not become an al-Qaeda safe haven, [that] it doesn't become a place from which terrorists can plot and plan," said then-president George W. Bush on the rise of the ICU.[44] Sean McCormack, the US State Department spokesman, added, "We certainly want to work with people in Somalia who are interested in combating terrorism. The presence of foreign terrorists in Somalia is a destabilising fact."[45]

While these fears were intense, however, the fact is that they were largely unfounded. In 2006, the number of foreign extremists in Somalia was actually limited to a small handful with little political influence.[46] Although al-Qaeda had long sought to infiltrate Somali Islamist organizations, transnational terrorists consistently found local Islamists in the xenophobic country to be much less hospitable than the Afghan theater.[47] In the Somali case, American attitudes toward the ICU were based more on fear and misinformation than hard evidence of terrorist infiltration. After their disastrous relations with the Taliban, however, the Americans had little confidence that Somalia's new Islamist government would be moderate.

To assuage these fears and prevent a clash, the ICU tried to extend an olive branch. Sheikh Sharif penned an open letter to the United States, the United Nations, the African Union, the Arab League, and the Organization of Islamic Countries (*sic*), introducing the ICU to the world.[48] "We categorically deny and reject any accusation that we are harbouring any terrorists or supporters of terrorism in the areas where the courts operate," the letter stated. "We share no objectives, goals or methods with groups that sponsor or support terrorism."[49] The statement then specifically invited the international community to engage with the ICU on the issue of terrorism, saying:

> We invite the International Community to visit the area where the court operates and see for themselves if there are any terrorists elements being harbored or living in this area. We commit ourselves and our clan elders to this position: to be open and honest in order to spare the Somali people the violence and the suffering being perpetrated by the warlords. *We have nothing to hide from the international community and we strongly believe that, once they realize what we do and what we have achieved, they will support our initiative and efforts to bring peace and stability to Somalia.*[50]

Sharif then sent an invitation to the international media, saying, "It is my pleasure to invite you to come to Mogadishu and see it yourself what we have achieved."[51]

While Sharif presented the moderate, diplomatic face of the Islamic Courts Union, behind the scenes a number of less savory figures set off alarm bells about possible links to transnational terrorists. Most disconcerting was Sheikh Hassan Dahir Aweys, the former leader of the now-defunct al-Ittihaad al-Islamiyya (AIAI) movement that had links to the early al-Qaeda network in Africa, which was responsible for the 1998 embassy attacks in Kenya and Tanzania.[52] Aweys' participation in the ICU project thus raised suspicions that the new Islamists posed a threat to international peace and security.

The senior ranks of the ICU also showed signs that they espoused an illiberal Islamist ideology. Their imposition of harsh sentences, such as amputations and capital punishment, alarmed Somalis and international observers alike.[53] Their bans on soccer, cinema, and cigarettes seemed eerily reminiscent of the Taliban's authoritarian rule. A string of unexplained and shadowy assassination plots against foreign workers, journalists, and TFG officials fueled suspicions that the ICU's military wing, al-Shabaab, was dangerous and extremist.[54]

Amid this climate of fear, the clan warlords who had been expelled by the ICU mounted a campaign to recapture Somalia. They fed misinformation to security analysts and political officials in Nairobi in order to squeeze the international community for financial support. Based on this faulty data, the 2006 UN Monitoring Group team produced a report that erroneously claimed that the ICU was receiving funds from Iran and had sent over seven hundred Somali fighters to Lebanon to join Hezbollah in its fight against Israel.[55] These sensationalist allegations, which did not even distinguish between Shiite and Sunni Islamists, eventually proved baseless. Yet at the time, the tone of these faulty messages resonated deeply in Washington.[56]

The Ethiopians also had an interest in checking their regional Somali rivals and played into the conflict. Officials in Addis Ababa were irate that the ICU had ousted pro-Ethiopian TFG president Abdullahi Yusuf from office. In response, in secret diplomatic cables from the US embassy, Ethiopian prime minister Meles Zenawi reportedly "called the rise of extremism in Somalia the greatest long-term security threat facing the region" and said that Somalia's "ports were the focal point for organized crime and links with Al Qaeda."[57]

By December 2006, the Americans were sufficiently convinced that the ICU was a threat to their interests. Hoping that they could quickly expel the Islamists and return to the status quo, they supplied military and financial support for a large-scale Ethiopian ground invasion of Somalia aimed at overthrowing the ICU and reinstalling the warlords of the TFG in their fiefdoms.[58] The Americans were right that the Islamist government would crumble quickly, but they gravely miscalculated the effect of the intervention on local conflict dynamics. Rather than returning to the previous era of clan conflict, the Ethiopian presence gave birth to a fierce new Islamist insurgency that redefined the civil war.[59]

As Ethiopian tanks rolled into Somalia, the ICU dissolved and the Islamists went on the defensive. Sharif and Aweys both fled to Djibouti together, becoming the symbolic political leadership of the resistance. Back on the home front, anti-Ethiopian sentiment afforded the Islamists fairly broad popular support across multiple clan constituencies.[60] Appalled by the invasion, the Somali public galvanized its support behind al-Shabaab as the vanguard of Somali independence.[61]

Although only a small handful of foreigners was present in Somalia before the invasion, the Ethiopian presence attracted a new wave of foreign fighters, including experienced commanders from Yemen, Pakistan, and Afghanistan who assumed deputy leadership roles within al-Shabaab.[62] As more international fighters arrived in Somalia, they provided both guidance and technical expertise on how to attract and indoctrinate new recruits, produce propaganda materials, and stage effective insurgent attacks against a much larger conventional military opponent.

Child soldier recruitment and ideological indoctrination also increased under the tutelage of these foreign commanders, and the recruitment of young men from the Somali diaspora swelled the ranks of al-Shabaab and gave the insurgency an international character.[63] A new generation of fighters with stronger transnational ties emerged out of al-Shabaab's ranks, some even more extreme than Aweys and the old guard. Suicide bombings, which were previously unheard of in Somalia, became a common occurrence.[64] As the jihadists advanced, they tore down Somalia's national flag, which was pale blue with a white star, symbolizing an ethnic irredentist vision, and replaced it with the black standard of global jihad.

By August 2008, al-Shabaab and its Islamist allies held the majority of south and central Somalia, cornering the Ethiopian forces into just a few neighborhoods in Mogadishu. Their control over key trade routes in the Afgooye corridor of the Middle Shabelle region and the lucrative port city of Kismayo in southern Somalia provided the Islamist coalition with a steady income from domestic sources, worth tens of millions of dollars per year.[65] Al-Shabaab continued to tax its population, pay its foot soldiers, and function like a jihadist proto-state; as the intervention faltered, al-Shabaab's forces remained strong and committed.

Faced with the Islamists' surging economic and military power, the international community tried to initiate a reconciliation process between the ICU and TFG. By late January 2009, Ethiopian forces had withdrawn from the Somali theater, and the mission was handed over to the African Union Mission in Somalia (AMISOM). In an effort to unite the TFG and the Islamists and rein in the jihadist insurgency, in January 2009 former ICU leader Sheikh Sharif was sworn in as the new president of the Somali TFG.

The plan backfired. Although Sharif loyalists supported the new government, these more conciliatory Islamists failed to bring in the hard-line base that had been fighting the ground war in Somalia. Al-Shabaab's commanders denounced the reconciliation process and declared Sharif an apostate for joining the TFG. Aweys also rejected the deal and the new government and called for continued fighting. Without support from its core Islamist fighters, Sharif's new government quickly proved to be as impotent and ineffectual as the previous TFG administration had been.

Sharif's weakness was met by a surge in Islamist power.[66] Aweys became a symbolic spiritual leader of the insurgency, but the real military strength remained with al-Shabaab's younger, battle-hardened field commanders, particularly leader Ahmed Godane (aka Mukhtar Abu al-Zubayr). With a global Islamist vision, Godane courted the al-Qaeda network and declared his fealty to Osama bin Laden. Bin Laden signaled back to Somalia's surging jihadists: "Oh, how desire for wealth, eminence, and status has ruined our leaderships! These sorts of presidents are the surrogates of our enemies, and their authority is null and void in the first place," declared bin Laden in an al-Shabaab insurgent video message. "And as Sheikh Sharif is one of them, he must be dethroned and fought."[67] Taking advantage of the divisions among Somalia's Islamists, al-Qaeda spread its poison.

By February 2012, Godane declared a formal merger with al-Qaeda in the Horn of Africa, turning al-Shabaab into a formal regional al-Qaeda affiliate. On the day of the announcement, a group of al-Shabaab militiamen arrived at Dr. Hawa's doorstep in Lafoole, located in the strategically significant Afgooye corridor. The gunmen went directly into the elementary school adjacent to her hospital and forcibly loaded all the male schoolchildren onto four buses.[68] The medical staff and teachers were held up, while the boys were taken to the nearby city of Baidoa to participate in the al-Qaeda celebrations. Still in their school uniforms, these kidnapped schoolboys can be seen sitting despondently in a row at the 15:50-minute mark of al-Shabaab's official al-Qaeda merger film, titled *The Year of Unity 1433*.[69]

The move crossed the red line for the Americans, who backed a forceful AMISOM military offensive against al-Shabaab strongholds. The international community went in heavy. By October 2012, the Islamists had been routed from the strategically significant Afgooye corridor and had lost Kismayo Port, along with its extraordinary revenues. Although al-Shabaab shifted its focus to exporting illegal charcoal, this loss of territory in key trading areas weakened its financial base.[70] With fewer taxation revenues, al-Shabaab started behaving more like a terrorist group than a proto-state. As the Islamists fell back, the international community funded the warlords to reclaim their territories.

The warlord-parliamentarians used this opportunity to systematically fleece the donor community out of hundreds of millions of dollars. The UN Monitoring Group alleged that "the real scale of corruption is probably even higher, since millions of dollars of revenue go unrecorded. In other words, out of every US$10 received by the TFG in 2009–10, US$7 never made it into state coffers."[71] The intervention was a windfall for the clan warlords, who were well positioned to profit from foreign donations.

The system encouraged graft. In 2012, a new internationally sponsored Somali Federal Government (SFG) was inaugurated, which transitioned the old TFG into a permanent government system. The old power players used their newly funded official positions to climb the corruption ladder: "It's a good post, worth at least 50 percent [of government funding] off the top," whispered a senior SFG official to his junior colleague, lounging poolside at a posh hotel in Nairobi. The senior official was moving to a higher position and was hustling to fill his old position with a trusted subordinate. The junior colleague declined, and then quipped behind his back: "If he offered me 50 percent, then he's probably skimming 90 percent."[72]

For poorer businesspeople, however, the corruption and fragmentation in the new government created much ire. "All the drivers said they thought life was better under al-Shabab—less corrupt and more secure, so long as you stayed out of politics," said journalist Gabriel Gatehouse, who interviewed traders unloading their goods at the Mogadishu port. "In al-Shabab areas, we don't see guns everywhere," a local trader named Mahmood Abdullahi told Gatehouse. "If the government disarmed the militias and got rid of the checkpoints that steal money from us, then we would support the government."[73]

The wealthy business elites also returned to paying for protection from strongmen and checkpoints; however, those that sided with the intervention enjoyed the windfall of new foreign investment. With the international community reengaged in Somalia, these power players won lucrative new

IMAGE 7.1 Meeting with civilian Somali political leaders to discuss the challenges of state building amid insurgency and corruption. *From left to right*: Dr. Ibrahim Farah, Speaker of the Federal Parliament Mohamed Osman Jawari, Aisha Ahmad, and First Deputy Speaker of the Federal Parliament Jeylani Nur Ikar.

construction and development contracts from the donor community. Yet, when asked whether they would be willing to pay for their new government through formal taxes, rather than aid donations, members of Mogadishu's new Chamber of Commerce replied in unison, "It depends on how much it will cost us."[74]

As the SFG hustled the international donors, however, al-Shabaab continued to clash with the US-backed AMISOM forces across southern Somalia. Having lost its prime revenue streams in Afgooye and Kismayo, the new al-Qaeda affiliate in East Africa shifted to a cheaper version of insurgent violence, attacking schools, shopping centers, hotels, and other soft targets in Somalia and neighboring Kenya. The Americans responded to this surge in violence against civilians by increasing support to AMISOM and the SFG and amplifying their drone war campaign to target al-Shabaab's top-level leadership.

In September 2014, Godane was killed in a targeted air strike, leading to widespread speculation that al-Shabaab was destined to split apart.[75] Yet the Islamists would not break; shortly after the strike, al-Shabaab's media wing announced Ahmed Umar, also known as "Abu Ubaida," as its new leader. Abu Ubaida kept the jihadists cohesive and reaffirmed their affiliation with al-Qaeda. Despite countless predictions that the group would fragment or collapse, al-Shabaab remained surprisingly unified and resilient on the battlefield. After twenty-five years, the Somali civil war still had no end in sight.

International Interventions and the Rise of Global Jihadist Power

The Islamist proto-state was born of domestic economic forces, but its death was the result of its failed international relations. In both cases, Islamist proto-states provoked a violent clash with the international community, which culminated in the demise of these polities. Even these large-scale global confrontations, however, did not eradicate jihadist power in the war theaters; rather, these interventions fueled new Islamist insurgencies and worsened the prospects of peace in these volatile regions. The interventions in Afghanistan and Somalia successfully dismantled the proto-states, but they also simultaneously mobilized and empowered new insurgencies that are even more extreme than their predecessors. The jihadists that emerged out of the rubble of these failed proto-states evolved into a plethora of radical and irreconcilable militant factions. Counterinsurgency and counterterrorism strategies aimed at curtailing these groups also helped to popularize these groups and amplify the influence of al-Qaeda over local jihadists.[76] Ironically, these interventions inadvertently fostered the spread of the very same extremist ideologies that they originally intended to combat.[77]

These new jihadist groups fared well on the battlefield. Despite being outgunned by the international community, they adapted their military strategies, shifting their focus from governance to guerrilla tactics whenever necessary. They aimed to bleed and frustrate their opponents until they withdrew and then recapture their lost territories and govern once again. Fighting against this type of opponent proved frustrating and futile: even after investing hundreds of billions of dollars in elaborate peacebuilding and state-building operations, these large-scale international interventions empowered and granted legitimacy to predatory warlords who engaged in relentless corruption and infighting. While these foreign-backed warlord-run governments faltered, the international community also barely managed to prevent a jihadist takeover and proved unable to defeat the Islamists outright. The past fifteen years have made one fact tremendously clear: it is much easier to destroy states than to rebuild them.

Meanwhile, a new generation of jihadists emerged in response to these international interventions. Its members built networks, shared ideas, and signaled solidarity across vast geographic distances.[78] They learned to use film and social media to build a common narrative around their struggle while signaling support to other like-minded groups around the world. Afghan fighters lauded Palestinian rebels for defending Jerusalem, and Somali insurgents praised the "lions in Chechnya and the Caucasus." From Iraq to Pakistan to Yemen, local jihadists sent shout-outs to other Islamists in their messages. The Islamist proto-state became a global phenomenon. As these ideas spread, waves of radical new jihadist polities rose up across the Middle East, North and West Africa, and South Asia.[79]

Their black flags heralded a rising tide of Islamist power in the modern era.

8

The Proto-State Goes Global

BUSINESS-ISLAMIST ALLIANCES ACROSS
THE MUSLIM WORLD

Sharp like the sword, the wind, the billows in abundance.
Strong like the horse, the lion, the thunder, sparkling.
Bold, he seeks his upheaval and sees good tidings in death.

"SHARP LIKE THE SWORD," Jihadist nasheed

THE MODERN JIHADIST proto-state is a rapidly evolving global phenom-enon.[1] In the Middle East, a new band of ultra-extremists seized power and established a radical proto-state across Iraq and Syria. In the north and west of Africa, al-Qaeda in the Islamic Maghreb (AQIM) built a powerful regional operation across the border region of Mali and Algeria and into neighbor-ing Mauritania and Niger.[2] In the Pakistani tribal region, a multitude of new Taliban splinter groups declared war on both sides of the Afghan border. Across the Muslim world, these jihadists all claim to have the legitimate right to rule.

What explains this global phenomenon? The challenge of conducting rig-orous scholarly research on these trends is that most of these Islamist groups are involved in ongoing conflicts, building new alliances and then switch-ing sides to advance their causes. All the modern jihadist movements in the Middle East, North and West Africa, and South Asia are in a state of rapid flux. To investigate this puzzle, this book has examined two modern histor-ical cases of Islamist proto-state formation: Afghanistan and Somalia. The evidence from the field showed a strong causal link between business and Islamist interests in these violent places.

Looking beyond these two classic cases, in this chapter I extend my anal-ysis to three other cases in the modern Muslim world: Iraq and Syria, Mali, and Pakistan. I examine the financial origins of the leading jihadist groups in these three regions in order to identify their relationships with business networks during their early formation. My preliminary evidence from these three cases reveals that local business-Islamist alliances helped fuel the rise of jihadist power.

Because these are ongoing conflicts, I focus specifically on business-Islamist relations during the early stages of these jihadist movements rather than their rapidly evolving organizational structures, alliance patterns, or political mandates. I examine the financial foundations of the leading jihadist polities in each region, drawing on both original fieldwork and existing scholarly sources to gain insight into these hidden processes. My meetings with researchers and analysts in Lebanon, and trips to the Syrian border region, helped me understand how regional trafficking networks have helped finance Daesh. I also traveled to Bamako to conduct in-depth interviews with Malian academics, journalists, and civil society actors working on the conflict in the northern region, in order to understand the relationships between al-Qaeda militants along the Algerian border and transnational narcotrafficking networks. My analysis of the Pakistani case is based on fieldwork conducted during the height of the new Pakistani Taliban insurgency between 2006 and 2009 and includes observational research from Peshawar and key informant interviews in Islamabad.

In each of these cases, I look at how the dynamics of these war economies contributed to the rise of jihadist groups. My preliminary evidence from the field indicates that a business-Islamist dynamic is at play in each one of these three civil war theaters. To understand how these war economies operate at the ground level, we need to return to the bazaar.

Iraq and Syria: Smuggling Networks and the Rise of Daesh

The smugglers' market on the outskirts of Beirut is a clamorous maze of clothing stalls, confectioneries, and cheap Chinese electronics. Underneath a heavily spray-painted concrete highway overpass, hundreds of vendors set up makeshift booths to sell housewares, tchotchkes, and trinkets at heavily discounted prices. Every week, thousands of shoppers weave through these crowded alleyways, haggling over merchandise to get the best deal. Among these sundry stalls is a collection of quaint souvenir shops, each showcasing replica antiques from the region. Clay pots claiming to be fashioned in a Roman era sell for USD$20 dollars. A golden-colored sword hangs

IMAGE 8.1 Antiquities shopping in a Lebanese bazaar. These are licit replica artifacts.

on the wall, with freshly added marks of distress to mimic relics from the crusader era. The real antiquities, however, lie farther into the market.

Since the outbreak of wars in Iraq and Syria, the illicit sale of antiquities has grown into a billion-dollar industry. As armed groups ransacked the museums and historical sites, they built an elaborate trafficking network to sell stolen artifacts to shady art dealers around the world, secretly moving them through the region. So profitable is this illegal business that some jihadists have even pretended to destroy these priceless antiquities, publicly declaring them un-Islamic, while secretly hoarding them for sale. By faking the widespread destruction of these artifacts, buyers were tricked into believing that the surviving relics were rare; the militants could then sell the stolen goods at inflated prices on the black market.

Some of these rare Byzantine artifacts found their way into the back alleys of Beirut, amid the many souvenir stalls in the smugglers' bazaar. Most of the colorful antiques in the storefronts were clearly cheap replicas meant for the casual tourist; proximity to the Syrian and Iraqi conflicts, however, also brought in the valuable stolen goods. Like all such markets, both licit and illicit merchandise can be found for a price.

"I have mostly Ottoman artifacts," said one shopkeeper. "For Byzantine, go further ahead and turn right. Ask for Abu Athar."[3] At first glance Abu Athar's shop looks exactly like the rest of the souvenir stalls, with piles of fake shiny swords, rusted lanterns, and terra-cotta clay pots out front in a motley display. A towering man with a heavy brow, Abu Athar has more than cheap trinkets in his collection, however. "These things are very expensive," he said quietly, standing behind the cash register. He kept his collection of smaller Byzantine artifacts in a large plastic box under the counter for safekeeping, but he was quick to show them off to potential customers. The tiny statues could fit in the palm of your hand, and they were priced at around USD$500 each. "The bigger pieces we keep off-site, depending on how much you're willing to spend," he said.[4] Indeed, the ancient cuneiform tablets Abu Athar was known to have in his possession were of the type last seen in the museums of Iraq.

From antiquities to oil smuggling, these types of illicit networks are the lifeblood of the war economy in the modern Middle East. "There has always been a relation between money, finance of war, and middlemen," explained Amine Lebbos of The Lebanese University, who has been tracking the war across the border in Syria. "It is normal that there is a relation between the jihadists and the business people; we find this relationship everywhere."[5] This business-Islamist alliance played a key role in the rise of jihadist power in Iraq and Syria. As these jihadists melded with regional criminal networks, they rapidly seized power and built a radical new form of order. Out of the rubble, they used this financial power to build an expansive and deadly jihadist proto-state.

Their story begins after the disastrous, decade-long 2003 US-led invasion and occupation of Iraq, a turning point in the region's history. The American invasion not only destabilized the regional neighborhood and gave birth to a new wave of extremism but also unleashed an unprecedented, toxic mix of sectarian, tribal, and political violence from which these militant Islamists emerged and mutated. Although a multitude of jihadist groups has arisen in Iraq and Syria since the invasion, dominating this battleground is the ultra-extremist militant group that haughtily calls itself the "Islamic State" but which most free people in the Arab world derisively refer to by the slur *Daesh*. The scornful moniker Daesh is an acronym of the group's Arabic name that sounds close to another word, *daes*, meaning "to crush or trample."

Daesh rose from the ashes of the now-defunct al-Qaeda in Iraq (AQI). Unlike predecessor groups, however, these new jihadists broke new ideological ground by claiming to have created a caliphate, a new polity that they believed replaced all other borders and authorities across the entire Muslim world.[6] In 2014, these ex-al-Qaeda militants announced their formation of a new caliphate, anointed former AQI leader Abu Bakr al-Baghdadi as their new caliph, and declared him to be the only legitimate commander of the global jihad.

In so doing, they garnered the support of groups that had been disenfranchised in post-Saddam Iraq, including former Baathist soldiers and commanders with valuable combat experience. Indeed, "as the Iraqi army was demobilized in 2003–05, a great part of these Baathists were transformed into jihadists," explained Lebbos. "[One jihadist leader] was the number three in the Baathist regime; [he] transformed from being a secularist Baathist into a jihadist. Religion is the best thing to fix people around a fight."[7]

By claiming to be a caliphate, however, Daesh also awarded itself the highest possible authority in the Muslim world, sparking controversy and conflict with other established jihadist movements.[8] As the original leaders of the global jihad, for example, top al-Qaeda commanders dismissed al-Baghdadi's supposed revival of the caliphate as bombastic, illegitimate, and in clear violation of the rules and regulations set by Islamic law. On the western Syrian battlefront, al-Qaeda's franchise, Jabhat al-Nusra, rejected the caliphate and reaffirmed its pledge of allegiance to global al-Qaeda leader Ayman al-Zawahiri.[9] Nonetheless, despite these vocal objections, al-Qaeda lost ground in the global jihad while Daesh surged in popularity, inspiring a number of radical factions in Libya, Egypt, Pakistan, and Nigeria to symbolically pledge their allegiances to the new caliph.[10]

On the home front, Daesh brazenly seized control of the north and west of Iraq and captured large swaths of territory in the north and east of Syria. Heralding its expansionist and totalitarian objectives, the caliphate announced, "The legality of all emirates, groups, states and organisations becomes null by the expansion of the caliphate's authority and arrival of its troops to their areas."[11] Its leaders also declared state boundaries void and tore down border crossings. "As you can see, this is the so-called border of Sykes-Picot," declared Abu Safiyya, a fighter and spokesperson for Daesh, standing at an overrun Iraqi-Syrian border post, referring to the infamous 1916 secret Sykes-Picot agreement that plotted to divide the Middle East between the British and French. "We don't recognize it and we will never recognize it. We will break all of the borders. We will break the barriers of Iraq, Jordan, Lebanon, all of the countries until we reach Quds [Jerusalem]."[12]

Daesh not only achieved tremendous battlefield success but also demonstrated an uncanny capacity to govern. In a few short months in 2014, the extremists seized control of major cities and towns across northern Iraq, including the majority of al-Anbar province. They also established a powerful presence in eastern Syria, expanding their influence as far as Raqqa and even Aleppo. Al-Baghdadi then focused on building his caliphate's political presence, issuing new laws and taxes over the populations that he now ruled under his iron fist.

Al-Baghdadi's proto-state enforced these laws with savage violence ranging from crucifixions to burnings. As Daesh expanded its reach into northern Iraq and eastern Syria, it both absorbed and repressed the many Sunni tribal communities that held power in these territories.[13] When local communities resisted, Daesh used collective punishment against them, such as the grisly murders of hundreds of civilians from the Shueitat tribe in Syria and from the Albu Nimr tribe in the Anbar province.[14] Dissenters were deemed apostates and summarily executed by public beheading. Religious minorities, such as the Shiite and Yazidi peoples, were specifically targeted. In a brutal campaign of genocidal violence against the Yazidi, Daesh slaughtered the men and sold the women as sex slaves in open-air markets.

Alongside this savage violence, however, was the construction of government bureaucracies and legal institutions. To bolster its claims of statehood, the militant leadership also invested heavily in creating and promoting its symbols and structures of governance. They created administrative offices and tax bureaus and dispensed official documents and receipts; they even announced—albeit somewhat fancifully—a new caliphate-issued currency welded out of gold, silver, and copper.[15] Daesh was not only a bloodthirsty insurgent group; it was also actively building a proto-state.

Why was Daesh able to consolidate its political power so rapidly? The evidence from the field shows that behind al-Baghdadi's success were the well-established criminal networks that extended across the Iraqi, Syrian, and Turkish borders. At its peak in 2014, Daesh was widely considered to be the wealthiest jihadist group in the world, with total assets estimated at an astonishing USD$2 billion.[16] Al-Baghdadi developed this massive fortune through a multitude of criminal activities across the region, including extortion, theft, kidnapping, bank robberies, slavery, human trafficking, and the smuggling of antiquities and oil.[17] With these tremendous revenues, more than any other jihadist group in modern history, Daesh then developed its statelike capabilities in both extraction and coercion.

Although the revenue sources behind the formation of Daesh were diverse, the evidence suggests that al-Baghdadi's largest source of revenue was drawn from the oil smuggling industry.[18] These well-established underground networks had long connected Iraqi smugglers to the global black market through northeastern Syria, southern Turkey, and Iran.[19] "It's important to keep in mind that oil smuggling in Iraq has been going on from the 1990s when there were sanctions on Saddam," explained Renad Mansour, a visiting scholar at Chatham House who works on the ground in Iraq and Syria along these major smuggling routes. "These networks were there. These guys, it was their trade. They knew how to smuggle oil. So [Daesh] basically co-opted the system. [For] the Sunni oil smugglers who had been very wealthy under the time of Saddam, who had lost a lot after 2003 once the [Shiite] and the Kurds emerged as the kingmakers of the new country, [Daesh] was an opportunity [for them] to revamp that system."[20]

The failure of the Iraqi government created a perfect breeding ground for this new business-Islamist alliance. Then Iraqi prime minister Nouri al-Maliki, a Shiite politician who actively excluded Sunni Arabs from political power, had fostered deep ethnic and sectarian resentment with both the Arab and Kurdish populations in the north and west of the country. His government was also accused of extraordinary levels of corruption and extortion, provoking ire within the smuggling class. "Maliki really started creating a difficult business space for them," explains Mansour. "He was preferring his own people. Even the Iraqi military under Maliki, his [army] people in these areas were taxing people, outside of the formal [system]. They were asking for bribes; they were *forcing* bribes."[21] This sectarian and economic resentment provided the jihadists with a perfect window of opportunity to court the support of the business community. "Since 2011, Daesh was cultivating these ties," continued Mansour. "They didn't just conquer. It wasn't that easy. These guys were creating networks for years, slowly, and trying to establish preferable business relations with major stakeholders and elites."[22]

Some of the most important economic ties were with the oil smuggling class. During its 2014 blitz campaign, Daesh seized control of six out of ten Syrian oilfields, as well as four small fields in Iraq. Once in control of the supply, Daesh was then able to increase smuggling up to an estimated eighty thousand barrels of oil per day across its borders.[23] Global oil prices were at a high, and so Daesh began to sell looted oil to the truckers and smugglers at heavily discounted prices, which Louise Shelley estimates at USD$25–30 per barrel; at that stage, she says, the "crude [then] gets to refiners [via the smugglers] at around $60 per barrel, which is still under market price."[24] According to George Masse, who tracks conflict dynamics in the region, "around 70 percent of Syrian oil [was] controlled by Daesh. The biggest part used to [be smuggled] to Turkey and from there, to other—often European—countries. These connections with smugglers helped Daesh at the beginning."[25]

To profit from these illicit channels, the smugglers acted as middlemen, trafficking the oil from the refineries to the well-established underground markets across the region.[26] "You always have intermediaries who are very eager to do the brokerage deal," explained Lebanese scholar Georges Labaki, whose research examines the intersection between religion and conflict. "[These are] brokers who can get through all different parties, to make money and to service both sides."[27] These intermediaries played a critical role in this war economy, both paying off the armed groups and selectively supporting the ones they believed would get them the best deal for security.

During their initial rise to power, Daesh was careful to ensure it was offering these brokers a better deal than its competition. "This was the difference between al-Qaeda in Iraq and [Daesh]," explained Mansour. "[Daesh] was very well aware that upsetting these business elites would mean that they are out the door in a few years again. So they had to accommodate. That's what helped them survive. Which meant that they gave [the business class] very favorable rates, but nonetheless taxed them."[28] These lower tax rates and oil prices under Daesh created a short-term boon in the oil smuggling business, which thus gave the jihadists a clear market advantage across the region.

During this formative period, the jihadists not only lowered taxes but also simplified the method of payment. With Daesh, "when you pay a tax, like a trade import tax or an income tax, to one local body or office, or border checkpoint, that was the end of it," explained Yezid Sayigh, a senior associate at the Carnegie Middle East Center, whose research networks extend across these jihadist-held areas. "You could travel throughout [Daesh] territory after that and never have to pay that tax again, unlike the system under Assad or under the Syrian opposition, where every time you come to a checkpoint you pay an informal protection tax."[29] According to Sayigh, the proliferation of checkpoints actually helped Daesh gain support from the grassroots. "There was a very strong feeling among Syrians of wanting to be finished with this constant rapacious system, and they found that the opposition militias and armed groups did more or less the same [in terms of extortion] . . . and that was a disappointment. So for farmers, traders, anyone who needed to move goods around, the relief of not having to pay a fee at every single road block was immense."[30]

Because Daesh held the oilfields, simplified its taxation system, and kept its rates low, it quickly won the favor of the smuggling class and solidified this business-jihadist relationship. Using the hawala money transfer system to move cash through this underground economy undetected, Daesh quickly dominated the black market for oil and other illicit goods. The smugglers and their business associates in the hawala industry grew rich. According to Margaret Coker, who investigated the hawala system under Daesh, "Money-exchange offices in the Iraqi cities of Mosul, Sulimaniyah, Erbil, and Hit charge as much as 10% to transfer cash in and out of militant territory—twice normal rates." The hawala owners flourished: "I don't ask questions," said Abu Omar, the money-changer who spoke to Coker. "Islamic State is good for business."[31] With these deep ties to the underground economy, plus the bonus moneys from looting and other criminal business, Daesh grew into the wealthiest and most powerful extremist group in the world.

As al-Baghdadi's forces expanded their control, Daesh also established a robust statelike apparatus that could directly tax its citizens at the household level.[32] The new proto-state taxed everything from the trade trucks to personal incomes.[33] Although violent purges reduced the number of non-Muslims living in their strongholds, any Christians or Jews that remained were also forced to pay the added *jizya* (unbelievers) tax.[34] Such an invasive taxation strategy necessarily required a high level of institutional control, a deep level of penetration into peripheral territories, and uncontested dominance over its people.

As part of this new taxation system, Daesh tapped into Islamic jurisprudence that demands that all Muslims pay *zakat,* or Islamic charity, which is a mandatory donation of 2.5 percent of each person's total wealth allocated toward helping the poor. Using this principle, Daesh institutionalized the *zakat* system by creating a medieval, caliphate-style collection system called *Bayt al-Mal*.[35] With millions of people under Daesh's control, this household taxation system created a massive source of revenue for the group.[36]

As the so-called caliphate grew increasingly powerful, however, al-Baghdadi's taxation system began taking much more than just the modest 2.5 percent. Daesh also taxed the cross-border traders, and rates were reported to be as high as USD$800 per truck.[37] This taxation of the traders and truckers was thinly veiled as charity for the poor, and indeed the evidence betrays these claims. According to Raheem Salman and Yara Bayoumy, "In the eastern Syrian city of Mayadin, an Islamic State supporter who goes by the name of Abu Hamza al-Masri, said the militants had set up checkpoints in the last few months demanding money from passing cars and trucks. The money purportedly goes into a 'zakat' or 'alms' fund, but Abu Hamza admitted some sums go to pay bonuses or salaries of fighters."[38] By this point, however, the traders who had profited from the initially low taxation rates and the boon in oil smuggling were no longer in any position to object to al-Baghdadi's blatant extortion. Daesh had complete control over its turf, and the smugglers were trapped.

What started as a symbiotic relationship between the smugglers and the jihadists thus quickly turned into a parasitic one. "I've talked to people from Mosul right now who say that taxes have gone to a crazy level," explained Mansour, describing the increased extortion under Daesh in 2016. "People are not happy with how the financial model is going. Increasingly the social contract is no longer 'we give you money and you give us protection'; it's more 'we fear you and you're taking money from us.' "[39] As the jihadists fell onto harder times, the corruption worsened and the religious justifications grew more unconvincing. For example, Daesh instituted a land tax called *khāraj*; however, "since the Koran contains no references to khāraj, which was a later innovation," argues Mara Revkin, "the taxation of land is one area of policymaking in which [Daesh] exercises considerable discretion."[40] Telecommunications, cash withdrawals from banks, and goods sold by vendors were also subject to added taxation.[41] The more the international community attacked the oilfields and other sources of Daesh revenue, the more the jihadists extorted their subjugated population. As a resident living under Daesh rule in the Syrian city of Raqqa aptly stated, "Only the air people breathe is not taxed."[42]

Indeed, although Daesh got its initial boost from a symbiotic relationship with the smuggling class, its centralized, hypercoercive taxation system helped the group grow into a more financially independent and stable polity. Describing the situation in early 2016, Revkin explains that "the organization is far more dependent on the cooperation of ordinary civilians than was previously believed," whereas oil revenues have "been dwarfed by taxation." She adds, "the ratio of money brought in from taxes to money from oil extraction now stands at an estimated 6:1."[43] With millions of people under its control, forcible taxation provided a massive and reliable source of revenue for the proto-state.[44]

It remains challenging to conduct intensive field research on the criminal and jihadist networks in this region, but early evidence on this case reveals that clandestine business interests were instrumental during the initial formation of the Daesh proto-state. The American-led invasion of Iraq created the conditions in which these connections could take deep root, but it was their relationship with the oil smuggling networks that gave the jihadists the resources they needed to consolidate their power. Although big oil companies and some Iraqi elites profited from the occupation, the invasion had overwhelmingly plunged Iraq into political and economic disarray. Existing criminal and smuggling networks in the region were thus primed to take advantage of the chaos, and the jihadists were well positioned to ally with them. The resulting business-Islamist alliance gave birth to a powerful and extreme jihadist proto-state, which at its peak in 2014 was equipped with a sizable tax base and the ability to spread its influence into South Asia, North Africa, and beyond.

Mali: Cigarette and Cocaine Trafficking in the Maghreb and Sahel

The Artisanal Bazaar is a historic commercial and cultural hub in the very heart of downtown Bamako. A crowded labyrinth of narrow lanes and densely packed storefront booths, this famous Malian market boasts a colorful display of homemade musical instruments, sacks of West African spices and seeds, and intricately crafted cultural trinkets with designs from Timbuktu. Once a bustling tourist destination, customers are now scarce. Since 2012, jihadist violence and political turmoil have destabilized Mali and thrust the troubled country into a crushing depression.

As the economic engine in Mali stalled, goods of all sorts piled up in the bazaar, with no demand from buyers to consume the surplus. Mountains of beautifully carved wooden masks, each representing hours of expert labor, collected dust on the back shelves. Instead of customers, the alleyways were flooded with hungry hawkers and peddlers, all desperate to find a buyer for any salable item that they could offload for a profit. As the hawkers roamed aimlessly, hundreds of impoverished Malian artisans continued to sit in their storefronts fashioning their next pieces, carving and hammering scraps of supplies into stunning art. Despite knowing that their handiwork would soon be added to their dusty heaps of unsold goods, these stoic artists have chosen to assert their dignity by focusing on their craft.

Above the noisy despair of the bazaar, the call to prayer echoes from the minaret. Next to the market is the mosque, a large white concrete building with green-painted trim, where thousands of men and women congregate for prayers. Once one steps through its arched gates, the clamor and hustle of the bazaar feel distant, masked by the gentle serenity of the spiritual oasis. For most Malians, religion helps soothe the sharp pain of poverty.

For the jihadists in the northern region, however, Islam provided a cunning disguise for a plethora of illicit business activities, allowing the militants to amass a great fortune. As in all war economies, this horrific poverty was juxtaposed with extraordinary riches. The opportunities for profit were abundant. Violent conflict, state weakness, and porous borders create a permissive space for smugglers to operate across the unruly region. "The North of Mali, the Sahel, is a very extensive zone of thousands and thousands of kilometers that is in fact controlled by no one," said a peace researcher in Bamako who works in the northern region. "Many have exploited this situation [of border porousness] . . . to seek different ends: . . . illegal smugglings of human beings, through immigrant networks, and the smuggling of cigarettes."[45]

At first, the Islamists of the Sahel and Maghreb regions started out building protection-taxation relationships with these wealthy smuggling networks, much like their counterparts in South Asia, East Africa, and the Middle East. As the jihadists got a taste of the profits, however, they increasingly began to take over these industries themselves. Unlike their militant brethren around the world, the jihadists of northern Mali soon developed a reputation for being more interested in wealth than in religion. Today, the interconnectedness between criminal and jihadist interests is arguably more powerful in North and West Africa than anywhere else the world.

Of course, most ordinary Malians have no power to profit from the chaos. "All are poor in the region," described a local analyst studying the northern border region. "The north is a desert; there is little water, [and] there is little space if one wants to practice agriculture or pastoralism. Young people must travel 10 kilometers [on donkeys] just to search for water."[46] This desperation in the northern region repeatedly sparked violent conflict against the government in the south, resulting in a vicious cycle. As this analyst aptly stated: "The poverty creates war, and the war exacerbates poverty."[47]

During the early stages of the conflict, this economic disparity helped foment rebellion by giving jihadists an opportunity to capitalize on grievances. "The original economic conditions are unequal," explained the peace researcher. "Some people are privileged and given preferential treatment to the detriment of others. Those who are disadvantaged develop feelings of frustration, and this creates conflict between different communities."[48] As jihadist groups honed in on these sentiments, they used their Islamist identity to legitimate their claims.

Much like the Afghan and Somali cases, Islam helped build bridges across ethnic and tribal lines in the fragmented northern region. "For one to proclaim himself Islamist was to be on the right side of the [identity] barrier," the peace researcher continued. "It breaks the [tribal] barriers that were previously established."[49] This crosscutting identity was also essential for the jihadists to recruit support from different communities. "This is why in these movements you have a representation of all ethnicities," the researcher added, "whereas if one was limited to the clan movements you would only have those people from your clan. The Islamic label transcends these barriers."[50]

These jihadists also used their Islamist identity to cement their relations with the local business class and mask their involvement in illicit activities. At the outset, this cooperation took the form of a protection-taxation relationship, similar to the patterns observed in Afghanistan, Somalia, and Iraq. As the jihadists established their presence in the lawless border region, they forged these security agreements with local smugglers to move their goods across unruly and fragmented territories from the west coast of Africa through the deserts of North Africa and then across the Mediterranean Sea. "The armed groups ensure the security of businessmen's smuggling of goods, and in exchange businessmen give them a part of what they earn from the smuggling," explained the peace researcher. "These are very formal networks, worth millions of dollars, and based on mutual interests."[51] As these illicit businesses took off, local militants gradually accrued millions of dollars in taxation revenue. From Mali to Libya, this business-Islamist relationship helped finance jihadist power.

The most powerful jihadist group operating in this complex war theater is al-Qaeda in the Islamic Maghreb (AQIM). This regional al-Qaeda affiliate originated in Algeria, but it found sanctuary in the lawless deserts of the Malian-Algerian border region during the mid-2000s.[52] By establishing deep roots in local tribal communities, AQIM steadily extended its reach across the Maghreb and Sahara desert regions and grew into one of the wealthiest and most influential jihadist groups in Africa.

Illicit business networks played a key role in the rise of AQIM. Led by blacklisted Algerian terrorist Mokhtar Belmokhtar, AQIM developed its base of operations in the rough deserts along the Algerian-Malian border.[53] After amassing tens of millions of dollars in revenue from a string of high-profile kidnappings, Belmokhtar used this start-up capital to finance his jihadist group and build his smuggling empire across North and West Africa.[54] "They are dependent on this sort of trafficking," explained the peace researcher. "Cigarette smuggling [is] the most [sustainable source of] revenue, while smuggling weapons and kidnapping was [more common] at the beginning."[55]

These trafficking routes had been operating for decades before the rise of AQIM and were relatively easy to co-opt. The governments in the Maghreb and Sahel had allowed these smuggling networks to develop unimpeded, hoping to appease their unruly tribes. Much like the Afghan and Pakistani governments had done in their border region, these weak states had mostly turned a blind eye to the smuggling networks along their borders.[56] By doing so, however, these illicit business networks expanded, using tribal and nomadic communities to move contraband through the unmarked borders between Algeria, Mali, Tunisia, and Libya.

Starting in the 1980s, the traders began using these contraband networks to smuggle cigarettes, aiming to circumvent customs duties and taxes imposed by governments across the region. This cigarette trafficking business quickly evolved into a billion-dollar industry, dominated by a handful of elites. Over time, the smugglers also built expansive drug and human trafficking rings that connected the Sahel and Maghreb to illicit European markets.[57] These, argue local experts, "are very formalized networks that existed well before the advent of current rebellions, and this is why we think that these networks feed the rebel movements. These networks are not based on tribal lines. It is as if they were [purely] based on economic interest."[58]

Knowing full well the wealth and influence of these smuggling networks, Belmokhtar's AQIM faction moved into the border region and established a special relationship with the barons of the cigarette smuggling industry. "There is a single common link [between traffickers and Islamists]: it is money," explained a member of a group of civil society activists from the conflict-ridden northern Kidal region, at a meeting in Bamako. "To have the hereafter, they must have means to fight."[59]

To secure these links, Belmokhtar not only recruited supporters from the ethnic Tuareg communities in the northern Azawad region of Mali but also married his daughters into powerful tribal families in the region.[60] These personal ties to the tribes made it easier to access these mafias and negotiate favorable protection-taxation rates with them. Highlighting the similarities with other criminalized economies around the world, a Malian scholar explained that "it's like the mafia: to have peace of mind, you pay up. They ratchet up taxes; it is like this everywhere, whether in Italy, Venezuela, Indonesia, or in Northern Mali."[61]

Over time, AQIM and its allies became key players in this massive illicit cigarette-trafficking industry in North Africa, with the support and cooperation of the Tuareg tribes across southern Algeria and northern Mali. These connections to the tribes allowed Belmokhtar's AQIM brigade to capitalize on criminal opportunities in the region,[62] in a way that Shelley argues epitomized "the intersection of crime, corruption, and terror in the vast territory from North Africa to the Sahel."[63] Given his deep involvement in these business networks, according to Morten Bøås, Belmokhtar became "known as one of the more pragmatic figures, more interested in filling his own pockets than fighting jihad."[64] Malian analysts explained the logic behind this jihadist-business connection on the ground. "Sometimes mafias transform into jihadists for protection," explained one of the civil society activists from the north, "not because of convictions but to reinforce themselves. It is a cooperation."[65]

To ensure positive relations with the tribes, the jihadists were also careful to keep their taxes on this industry low. "The state adds to the prices," explained a leading Malian legal scholar, referring to the duties, taxes, and tariffs that states normally impose on goods. In contrast, he added, AQIM "allowed people to have [smuggled goods] at a much lower price because there was no tax on them."[66] By keeping their cigarettes tax-free, the smugglers quickly dominated the market. By 2009, illegal "cigarettes smuggled along these routes accounted for around 60 percent of the Libyan tobacco market (or $240 million in proceeds at the retail level) and 18 percent of the Algerian market (or $228 million)."[67]

Having established a strong financial base in these smuggling networks, AQIM was then well positioned to take advantage of existing ethnic tensions and political turmoil in the region to expand its power. In 2012, an alliance of ethnic Tuareg rebels in the northern Azawad region launched a campaign to separate from Mali, seizing control over the restive north and staging a coup d'état in the capital city of Bamako.[68] The rebellion, however, was both mixed and fragmented, allowing the jihadists to co-opt the uprising. Leading the uprising were three key armed groups: first, the relatively secular Mouvement National de Libération de l'Azawad (MNLA, National Movement for the Liberation of Azawad); second, the militant Islamist group Ansar Dine that had ties to AQIM; and third, the AQIM-affiliated Movement for Unity and Jihad in West Africa (MUJWA). Ansar Dine and MUJWA not only sought ethnic independence but also declared their intentions to create a new Islamic state in northern Mali. While Ansar Dine tried to distance itself from AQIM, fearing reprisals, MUJWA openly vocalized its radical views and alliance with Belmokhtar's AQIM brigade.[69]

Despite the fragmentation, the rebellion emboldened AQIM and increased its influence over the local factions. Once the rebels established their hold over the south, they also created even more coercive protection-taxation relationships with the businesspeople in their turfs. "The armed groups work[ed] with local mafias composed of barons and businessmen," explained the legal scholar. Consider, for example, "the passage of transport trucks on the Bamako-Gao road, after Islamists occupied the North [in 2012]: the [businesspeople] were forced to pay passage fees to the armed groups so that they could go to Gao, and from Gao to Niamey. For some time, even the person in charge of this passageway was suspected of being in cahoots with the armed groups."[70] With this new tax system in place, the jihadists declared that they had created a new independent Islamist state.

Their victory was short-lived, however. The al-Qaeda connection provoked the 2013 French-led military intervention in Mali, which quickly overran the Tuareg rebels and reestablished the government in Bamako. In response to the French operation, Belmokhtar's faction cemented its relationship with MUJWA.[71] By August 2013, the two groups announced "their union and fusion in one movement called al-Murabitoun to unify the ranks of Muslims around the same goal, from the Nile to the Atlantic."[72] The merger allowed al-Murabitoun to progressively develop its capabilities in the Sahel region, and Belmokhtar's financial power gave the new jihadist group significant influence across the Algerian-Malian border region.

By 2013, the total value of the illicit tobacco trade in North Africa was estimated at over USD$1 billion and analysts argued that "cigarette smuggling has provided the bulk of financing for AQIM."[73] Al-Qaeda in the Islamic Maghreb benefited from the underground tobacco industry both by participating in the trafficking and also by taxing smugglers for safe passage and transport.[74] Belmokhtar's personal involvement in this illicit business activity was so extensive that he earned the nickname "Mr. Marlboro."[75]

Profits from the illicit cigarette trade also made it easier for AQIM to expand into other criminal businesses that use similar distribution networks, such as trafficking fuel, weapons, human beings, and drugs.[76] Al-Qaeda in the Islamic Maghreb built strong ties to Latin American cocaine cartels, and narcotics quickly dwarfed the cigarette business. "The most important traffic is drugs," explained one of the civil society activists. "It's like a mafia."[77] As they entered into these powerful transnational criminal networks, AQIM leaders established new drug-smuggling operations across West Africa that connected to well-established Latin American cartels.[78] Their goal was to bolster the profitable West African trafficking routes connecting Latin America to Europe. "AQIM and al-Murabitoun protect a line of trafficking that passes through [Mali], but that is not consumed locally," another one of the activists explained. "They assure the transport of their [cocaine] merchandise, and they earn a lot for that. One passes by [Mali] and goes to Mauritania . . . the other goes to Morocco and passes through Algeria, to Tunisia, to the Libyan coasts, and goes up [to Europe] by boats, or toward Israel."[79]

Al-Qaeda in the Islamic Maghreb both taxed and participated in these illicit activities. According to a report from the Economic Community of West African States (ECOWAS), the taxation of cigarettes, drugs, and fuel became "one of AQIM's most lucrative activities," and these charges took "the form of a right-of-way fee paid by smugglers passing through territory under the control of AQIM, with the old salt caravan routes used today by trucks carrying smuggled cigarettes, weapons, illegal immigrants, hashish or cocaine."[80] This alliance between drug trafficking and terrorism represented a new "hybrid" of organizations that, David Brown argues, "blurs the traditional distinction between organized crime and terrorism [as] both groups exploit the same state weaknesses and are increasingly overlapping in using the same 'shadow facilitators'" for these illicit activities.[81]

As time passed and the profit margins increased, AQIM and al-Murabitoun ramped up their trafficking activities, cutting out the middlemen to secure a larger return for themselves. "They were usually taxing, but since it was so juicy, they started doing it themselves," explained a Malian journalist who covers the conflict in the north. "So now they are doing both [taxing and trafficking]."[82] Territorial control made it possible for the jihadists to co-opt and control these commercial activities. Given their deep roots in these criminal industries, most Malians now see these jihadists as driven more by the desire for profits than paradise. "They have no religious conviction," the civil society activists insisted. "It's just a money conviction."[83]

Indeed, ties between jihadist groups and regional smuggling networks have given the jihadists a remarkable degree of financial and military independence. The International Crisis Group reported that "criminality and radical Islamism gradually are intermingling in the suburbs of major cities and in poor peripheral villages. Over time, the emergence of a so-called Islamo-gangsterism could contribute to the rise of groups blending jihadism and organised crime within contraband networks operating at the borders—or, worse, to active cooperation between cartels and jihadis."[84] These extensive, historic relationships between regional criminal networks and transnational jihadists have created a volatile mix of economic and ideological interests.

As these contraband markets continue to boom, so too does the jihadist influence over the Maghreb and Sahel regions. The North and West African theater clearly shows that the nexus of business and jihadist interests played a critical role in the rise of Islamist power in the region. Al-Qaeda in the Islamic Maghreb not only established ties with smugglers across the Tuareg tribal areas but also actively participated in and taxed this massive underground economy. After a decade of evolution, this business-Islamist alliance has become so interwoven that its players are now practically indistinguishable.

In this way, the Malian case is a bit unusual. Al-Murabitoun appears to have always been more centrally motivated by profit seeking than most other jihadist groups. Although the financial origin story of AQIM follows a similar pattern to the Afghan, Somali, and Iraqi cases, these Malian militants seem to have been more driven by the desire for wealth than their ideologically impassioned jihadist brethren in other parts of the world. This unique feature of the Malian case suggests that engaging the jihadist problem in this theater will require a very nuanced approach.

Further complicating this conflict landscape is the emergence of competing jihadist polities, including the spread of Daesh affiliate groups. In the case of Libya, Daesh took advantage of the chaos that occurred after the botched 2011 international intervention against then-leader Muammar Gaddafi, which sparked a brutal civil war. As violence surged between government and rebel factions, this new Daesh group established a provincial capital in the city of Sirte, calling itself the "Libyan province of the caliphate." In Nigeria, Daesh expansion was far more symbolic than it was substantive; the militant group Boko Haram declared its allegiance to al-Baghdadi but retained independent control over its operations and finances. As Daesh tries to extend its reach, a new global war front has emerged in the Sahel region. Indeed, whether AQIM will continue to dominate this complex conflict landscape, or if Daesh will instead rise to power across the region, will be determined in great measure by the ability of these competing jihadists to capitalize on the existing war economy.

Pakistan: Narcotrafficking and Neo-Taliban Factions

By 2009 the situation in Peshawar had wholly deteriorated. Suicide bombings, kidnappings, and assassinations rocked the city on a near-daily basis. Driving along the dusty streets in the smog-filled downtown core was dangerous and difficult; every government-run military checkpoint was a potential target for an explosion, with the surrounding bottlenecked traffic its collateral damage. As the violence, poverty, and desperation surged, ordinary working folks were kidnapped off the streets and held for ransom under threat of death. No longer just the staging ground for war across the border, the blowback effect of militarizing the tribal areas and arming Afghan insurgencies for decades had now come back to haunt the Pakistani city.

A multitude of new groups rose up out of the chaos. Some of these were motivated primarily by economic gains, loosely feigning some sort of ethnic, tribal, or religious identity to disguise what was otherwise pure gangsterism. "The robbers will come into your house and steal everything, and then on their way out say, 'You should be saying [the five daily] prayers,'" mocked one resident of Peshawar. "They claim to be jihadists just to scare people."[85] Across the city, these stories are told with a mixture of disgust and derision.

Other factions, however, were indeed inspired by both ideology and grievance. Unlike the jihad in Afghanistan, these neo-Taliban factions' primary target was the Pakistani government, and they accused Islamabad of perfidy and apostasy. This hostility stemmed from Pakistan's seemingly schizophrenic approach to the Taliban: behind the scenes, Inter-Services Intelligence (ISI) secretly supported the insurgency in Afghanistan, hoping to leverage the Islamists against the pro-India regime in Kabul. Publicly, however, Islamabad cooperated with the Americans and assisted with their counterterrorism and counterinsurgency operations against Taliban factions based in Pakistan, and even deployed troops in 2002 into the restive Tirah Valley.[86] By 2004, Pakistan had quietly allowed the Americans to begin launching drone strikes against insurgents based in the Federally Administered Tribal Areas (FATA).[87] This double-cross prompted accusations of Pakistani treason among Taliban supporters and sparked a violent reaction in the border region.[88]

In response to Islamabad's duplicity, in 2007 a group called Tehrik-i-Taliban Pakistan (TTP) emerged as an offshoot of the Afghan Taliban movement, symbolically pledging allegiance to Mullah Omar but otherwise operating independently in its own strongholds. Under the leadership of a tribal commander named Beitullah Mehsud, the TTP seized control over key districts in the FATA. Unlike Mullah Omar's group, however, which focused its efforts on fighting the United States and North Atlantic Treaty Organization (NATO) in Afghanistan, the TTP aimed its aggression at the Pakistani government. Incensed by Islamabad's policies, Mehsud and his supporters mobilized tribal communities from across the tribal belt and the northwest frontier, united by their common goal of attacking the Pakistani government.[89] Together, they consolidated control over their turfs and built an umbrella alliance of self-governing jihadist fiefdoms.

As the TTP coordinated a wave of deadly suicide attacks in Pakistani cities, the government in Islamabad found itself in the absurd position of supporting Afghan Taliban factions across the border while fighting neo-Taliban factions at home. Some members of the ISI leadership tried to explain this contradiction by calling the Afghan factions "good Taliban," while labeling the new Pakistani insurgents "bad Taliban" and "terrorists."[90] Outside of Pakistan, however, security analysts and policymakers alike called foul on Islamabad's obvious double-game.[91] Amid this controversy, this jihadist insurgency in the Pakistani border region grew increasingly radical and powerful.

Behind the mid-2000s rise of this new TTP movement were the criminal business networks operating in the tribal areas. During its early formation, Mehsud's insurgent network relied on a wide range of revenue-generating strategies, including kidnapping, narcotics trafficking, extortion, and smuggling.[92] Business and taxation revenues, however, were a significant source of income that allowed the TTP to act like a nascent proto-state. Although many analysts at first assumed that private foreign donations were behind its success, the TTP proved to be "largely self-financing through low level criminal activities ranging from smuggling and kidnapping to extorting protection payments from businesses."[93]

Of course, the TTP is part of a very long legacy of jihadist conflict in the border region, and these factions inherited many of their links to criminal networks from previous armed groups. Given the long-standing connections between tribal leaders and criminal networks in the FATA, the TTP was therefore able to extract security fees from local traders and businesses, including from the booming narcotics industry in Afghanistan. Mehsud, for example, controlled the back-road smuggling routes across South Waziristan, a strategically located region between the Peshawar and Quetta trade corridors. His territory was a key conduit connecting Afghan opium farmers in Kandahar and surrounding provinces to heroin factories in the FATA. Control over the roads afforded Mehsud's faction considerable financial independence through both taxation and participation in the lucrative drug trade.[94]

Other jihadist commanders within the network were also well positioned to profit from these smuggling and taxation revenues. The TTP leaders in Mohmand, Bajaur, and Khyber were a short drive from Peshawar and the gun-manufacturing town of Darra Adam Khel and were also connected to these profitable underground markets. With these ties across the mountains, the TTP network dominated the extortion market and the lucrative smuggling corridor. Buoyed by revenues from their illicit businesses, the TTP established a remarkable level of military control over the FATA.

In the North Waziristan district, another Taliban-allied commander named Jalaluddin Haqqani coordinated attacks inside Afghanistan against American, NATO, and Afghan government targets.[95] The Haqqani network built its own powerful Taliban proto-state in North Waziristan, funding its operations by taxing and extorting protection moneys from traders operating in their turfs on both the Pakistani and Afghan sides of the border.[96] Construction contractors provided Haqqani with significant taxation revenues: this is "the most important source of funding for the Haqqanis," explained Maulavi Sardar Zadran, a former Haqqani commander. "The

Haqqanis know that the contractors make thousands and millions of dollars, so these contractors are very good sources of income for them."[97] The Haqqani network also participated in and taxed the illegal smuggling of minerals through the Khost, Paktia, and Paktika provinces of eastern Afghanistan and into Pakistan.[98]

In addition to smuggling and taxation, the TTP also directly profited from the international intervention in Afghanistan, using a similar strategy to the one employed during the Soviet era. In this case, Pakistan had agreed to assist NATO by opening a supply shipping line from the Karachi Port to Peshawar and then onward into Afghanistan. To profit from these channels, the TTP began taxing the Pashtun truckers who were responsible for transporting these NATO supplies from the Karachi Port to destinations in Afghanistan.[99] The fact that NATO transport trucks were paying protection moneys to the Taliban was scandalous; however, moving supplies from Karachi to Kabul required safe passage through TTP territory, and control over these roads gave the jihadists a key advantage.[100]

The TTP thus profited from and participated in a wide range of smuggling and criminal activities that financed its rise to power. Competition for control over these business connections, however, also spurred conflict among the jihadists.[101] Because the insurgency was an umbrella organization for many different local groups, not all commanders enjoyed the same level of support from the business class. Although the TTP worked to coordinate its finances, the decentralized nature of the insurgency also created inequality within the movement. Uneven access to extortion revenues exacerbated tensions and put a heavy strain on the TTP leadership.[102] After the drone war campaign not only killed Beitullah Mehsud but also his successor Hakimullah, infighting within the TTP intensified.

By 2013, external pressures and internal conflicts had caused the TTP leadership to fragment into multiple factions. In the aftermath of these splits, each TTP subgroup turned to its business base to finance its bid for power. As a result, businesspeople in the border town of Dera Ismail Khan reported that whereas they used to only have to pay off one group, the infighting resulted in a massive hike in extortion rates: "So many different people are demanding money that I have to move my business, because if you pay one, tomorrow another one will call," bemoaned a businessman from the border region. "How can we run our business in such a situation?"[103] As the TTP fragmented into multiple, competing tribal factions, the traders found they were paying out of pocket more than ever before, and once again they needed an exit strategy.

As this fragmentation worsened in 2014, Daesh attempted to make inroads into both Afghanistan and Pakistan. With his caliphate's appeal growing globally, al-Baghdadi took advantage of the TTP splits to try to spread the influence of his group. In November 2014, a TTP faction called Jundallah declared its allegiance to al-Baghdadi, hoping to gain prestige and importance from the caliphate label. Shortly thereafter, in January 2015, another TTP splinter group led by the late Hafiz Saeed Khan announced its fealty and obedience to Daesh.[104] As these former TTP fighters rebranded themselves and their group as followers of al-Baghdadi's movement, they adopted a new name that held great symbolic value for the purported caliphate, based on the ominous prophecy about the rise of the black flags: the Province of Khorasan.[105]

In the aftermath of Mullah Omar's death, and the assassination of his successor Mullah Akhtar Mansour Daesh seized the opportunity to co-opt and recruit support from disaffected Taliban members. As the wealthiest extremist group in the world at the time, Daesh allegedly courted these fighters with offers of higher salaries, allegedly ten times the ordinary rate paid to local Taliban foot soldiers.[106] Once part of al-Baghdadi's family, these local affiliates then reportedly began building their own self-sustaining income sources, particularly through the ecologically destructive timber-smuggling industry, cutting down trees in Afghanistan and selling the lumber to Pakistani markets.[107]

This Daesh expansionism raised alarms in Islamabad, which lacked control over these developments. The Pakistanis admitted that Daesh presence in Pakistan was growing, and not only among the fragmented TTP factions; in fact, al-Baghdadi's influence had extended into the Punjab[108] and was affecting other jihadist groups, such as Lashkar-e-Jhangvi and Sipah-e-Sahaba.[109] This Daesh infiltration into South Asia not only threatened the Pakistani state but also worsened fragmentation within the TTP network and further inflamed the conflict in neighboring Afghanistan.[110]

The Pakistan-Afghanistan border region has been a hotbed of criminal activity and jihadist violence for decades; indeed, these links run so deep that they may now be unbreakable. Considering this historical context, the Pakistan case can be seen as a continuation of the Afghan Taliban story, which has mutated and evolved multiple times. What the TTP case reveals, however, is that these long-standing business ties were critical in financing this new wave of jihadist activities during the mid-2000s as the new insurgency took hold of the FATA. Although recent fragmentation complicates this story, Pakistan's jihadists continue to enjoy strong roots in these regional criminal networks, which give them staying power in this complex war theater.

The Failure of the Business-Islamist Alliance

The preliminary evidence from these three mini case studies reveals the important and often overlooked role that businesses play in the rise of jihadist proto-states across the modern Muslim world. Each of these cases follows a surprisingly similar pattern to the Afghan and Somali stories: a seemingly symbiotic relationship between jihadists and the business class finances the rise of jihadist power. From Syria to Mali to Pakistan, these jihadist groups actively built protection-taxation relationships with local business elites, particularly those operating within cross-border criminal networks. The revenues from these business-Islamist alliances then gave these jihadists the financial power needed to succeed on the battlefield.

These business-Islamist relationships appear at first to be mutually beneficial. The business class needs order to protect its assets, and the jihadists need money to finance their cause. Cooperation seems natural. At this stage, the Islamists also seem to be offering a better deal than rival groups. Instead of paying off a plethora of armed groups, the business class can choose to buy into one Islamist system that offers lower protection rates and better access to markets. Leveraging this competitive edge, the Islamists use this support from the business class to oust competing factions from power and establish a new Islamist order out of the chaos.

Once they have established their dominance in the conflict theater, however, these jihadists have consistently turned against their own supporters, increasing taxes and extorting their populations at will. The business community thus finds itself trapped: having financed these Islamist protection rackets, it inadvertently created an Islamist monopoly on violence. The result is the creation of a self-sustaining jihadist proto-state with the coercive capacity to continue to extract revenue from its tax base.

Meanwhile, the overwhelming majority of people in these troubled places continue to live in destitution. While business elites whine about higher taxes, it is the poor who bear the brunt of these political and economic shocks. For most civilians, these grand transformations on the battlefield are felt most acutely in the price of milk and bread. As the cost of living increases alongside the spike in taxation, those with little power must pay. Too often, they pay with their lives.

9

Rising from the Ashes

THE DILEMMA OF MODERN JIHADIST PROTO-STATE FORMATION

We have risen, as lightning and thunder.
We have come, as eagles and lions.
We have come, as streams of soldiers.
We have moved forward, as companies.

We have destroyed fortresses; we have smashed the borders.
We lead the steeds; we break the bonds.
We direct fate; we strike the gatherings.
We embark on the clash; the sword is dented.

We have cut the heads; we have sought to rise.
We sipped the chalices; we bared the wound.
We slaughtered the soldiers; we filled the plane.
We were the fuel; so be the spectators.

We have cut throats; we have broken sheaths.
We have healed chests, and made victory of good fortunes.

"WE HAVE RISEN," Daesh anthem

HIGH ATOP THE arid mountains, the lush green fields and quaint rustic shacks of the Beqaa Valley look remarkably idyllic. Famous for its wheat and wine, this fertile agricultural vale on the Syrian-Lebanese border has been a breadbasket in the Levant region since the Roman era. If one descends into the gorge, however, this picturesque view quickly turns to horror. Amid the rich orchards and sweet vineyards are nearly one million shell-shocked, hollow-eyed refugees huddled together in crowded and underserviced settlements.

A short drive over the mountains leads to neighboring Syria, where a raging civil war has claimed hundreds of thousands of lives and turned the once shining cities of the Middle East to rubble. The ensuing anarchy gave birth to a multitude of new jihadist groups, each more violent and virulent than the one before, and all claiming to be the true champions of Islam. As chaos swept across the region, Beqaa became a magnet for terrorized civilians fleeing violence, extremism, and persecution. Millions of Syrians fled for their lives, many risking the treacherous waters of the Mediterranean to reach Europe. Those unable to make the perilous journey by sea clambered over the mountains on foot to neighboring Lebanon.

Among them was a father of three, who had sent his two teenage sons across the waters to Germany and then smuggled his wife and daughter into Lebanon. His family had spent their last cent on securing safe passage via the risky human trafficking networks, daring to escape with only the clothes on their backs. The exhaustion and trauma of the war weighed heavily on the beleaguered father's slouched shoulders, his eyes reddened and darkened by loss. Terrorized and separated from his sons, the father and his wife and daughter had just barely managed to flee from Raqqa, the self-declared capital city of Daesh.

They had to run. Notorious for their savagery and sadism, Daesh militias were known to forcibly recruit and brainwash young children, taking them away from their parents and indoctrinating them with a violent ideology. "There was no other solution!" said the refugee father mournfully, his wife nodding in agreement. "Because if [our sons] had stayed, they would have been brainwashed. . . . [Daesh] offers games and toys to the kids so that they start appreciating them, and then they start giving them [extremist] classes." Despite their terrible fear of sending their children across the stormy seas, the parents dared not risk losing their teenaged boys to the psychotic tyranny of the extremists. With tears in his eyes, the father resolutely stated: "Death is better than Daesh."[1]

THE WAR-RAVAGED CITIES of Iraq and Syria signal a disquieting trend that has spread across the modern Muslim world. From the mountains of Khorasan to the Maghrebi desert, jihadist movements have risen from the ashes of civil war and constructed a new type of political order. Born from the rubble of disastrous foreign invasions and domestic failures, all of these jihadist polities promise both a divine hope and inevitable doom. Their fervent adherents are inspired by an apocalyptic metanarrative in which the emergence of a sharia-based government foreshadows the fulfillment of an elaborate end-of-days prophecy. Unyielding and irreconcilable, this next generation of jihadists has provoked a global conflict and spread its toxic ideology further than ever before.

IMAGE 9.1 Connecting with communities in the refugee settlements in Beqaa Valley, ten kilometers from the Syrian border. This is a different family than the one in the story. Over one million Syrian refugees now reside in Lebanon.

As jihadist proto-states take root in weak and war-torn countries across the Middle East, North Africa, and South Asia, scholars and policymakers alike have been desperate for insight into this phenomenon. Despite the obvious importance of ideology and identity to these movements, the question remains how such groups have seized political power in the first place. The fact that they have repeatedly succeeded in building relatively robust proto-states in parts of the world that are exceptionally difficult to govern is a disturbing pattern. Why have these Islamists been able to capture and create statelike power when so many other seemingly comparable groups have failed?

To understand this global phenomenon, much attention and energy has been devoted to researching the identities and ideologies of these militant groups. Some scholars have carefully mapped Pakistani tribal networks, Tuareg ethnic politics in Mali, and Sunni Arab tribes in Iraq.[2] Others have compared different jihadist belief systems and teased out the ongoing tensions among al-Qaeda, Daesh, and other Islamists.[3] These important studies have all provided crucial insights into the ideas and goals of modern jihadists; they do not, however, explain the practical sources of their power. Challenging the conventional wisdom, the stories in this book revealed that underneath the terrible violence, fervent ideologies, and complex identity politics is an elite class of business actors with a fiercely rational set of material interests. From the outside, these conflicts appear to be driven by ideas and identities; but inside these war zones, everyone is talking about money.[4]

Following the money showed that these thriving civil war economies are made up of a diverse assortment of characters, including smugglers, gunrunners, money transfer companies, tech start-ups, and entrepreneurs of all sorts. From street hustlers to trading tycoons, the business elites in these bazaars are driven by the pursuit of prosperity, not paradise. They are pragmatists, not ideologues. Time and again, however, these elites have found themselves in bed with jihadist groups at critical junctures; and every time, this uncanny business alliance helped to propel the Islamists to power.

To investigate this dynamic, I traced the domestic financial origins of two classic cases of the modern Islamist proto-state: the Taliban in Afghanistan and the Islamic Courts Union (ICU) in Somalia. In each case, I discovered that business-Islamist alliances helped to finance these jihadist groups during the early stages of their formation. Through fieldwork, I engaged with these local business elites and uncovered the pragmatic reasons behind their decision to sponsor the Islamists over other armed groups, thus changing the balance of power on the battlefields. Their stories revealed that behind the fervent religious rhetoric and extremist violence were the cold, hard cost calculations of the local business class. Ideological beliefs may have inspired the Islamists, but rational economic interests explain why and how they were able to create political order out of chaos.

Delving into the evidence from Afghanistan and Somalia, these paradigmatic cases introduced the reader to a world of violence and affluence. While most people living in these war zones were desperately poor, the disorder also created a plethora of lucrative new opportunities, both licit and illicit, for a select few. There was opulence amid the anarchy. From seaports to smuggling routes, the business class that was born out of these civil wars not only profited from the violence but also transformed the marketplace into a vibrant underground economy. From their gated and guarded estates, powerful tycoons forged empires and established nationwide firms worth tens of millions of dollars.

The stories of these elites explained why and how their economic interests aligned with those of Islamists at a critical juncture and thus transformed the political destinies of their troubled countries. To understand this phenomenon, I systematically examined the two key reasons why these business elites found themselves in bed with Islamists: the need for higher trust and the desire for lower costs.

First of all, my research discovered that Islamic identity gave the business communities operating in conflict zones practical ways to build trust across ethnic and clan lines over the long term. In these civil wars, violent social fragmentation was costly, and the lack of trust hampered business development. The case evidence showed that Islam provided businesspeople with a robust type of social capital which lowered costs and mitigated the extreme trust deficit. Although its members adopted this outward religious character for instrumental purposes, over time the business class was socialized with this strong Islamist identity and culture.

For example, during the 1979–1989 Soviet-Afghan War, the old smugglers in the border region realized that touting their Islamic identity was an advantage in securing lucrative business deals. As Pakistani and American intelligence agents colluded to channel a massive amount of weaponry and ammunition to mujahideen fighters via the Pakistani border, the smugglers found themselves in a new war economy where Islam was a valuable currency. In the fight against godless communism, the smugglers' religious credentials became a critical form of social capital to demonstrate trustworthiness. Over time, the smugglers and the jihadists working in the border region built their relationships using this Islamist identity as a bridge.

In a similar story, religion also served as an important social lubricant for the business class during the height of the Somali civil war. After the state collapsed in 1991, the countryside fell into chaos between warring clan factions, frustrating business development and expansion. Unable to trade across clan lines, members of the Somali business class began actively emphasizing their religious identity over their tribal ties. Islam became essential for building trust and expanding business ventures across these divisions as well as for securing lucrative deals with prospective partners in the Gulf. As these elites increasingly relied on Islamic identities and institutions to lower their transaction costs and increase their market access, they cultivated a powerful new Islamist business culture that helped to fill the political vacuum.

Secondly, my research also revealed that the business community supported the Islamists over other armed groups as a way to lower overall costs. Under the reign of ethnic or tribal warlords, traders and tech giants alike were forced to pay two types of security costs, which were akin to taxes: first, they paid to the competing warlords who ran their fiefdoms like protection rackets; second, they were extorted by thugs at roadside checkpoints. The business class thus found itself paying steep extortion moneys just to stave off violence. Hoping to reduce compound security fees and increase their profit margins, these elites sought out an alternative to this expensive arrangement. Compared to ethnic or tribal protection rackets, they found that Islamists offered better-quality security at a lower price. Supporting Islamists against ethnic and tribal warlords therefore looked like a sensible, cost-effective choice. With support from the business class across ethnic and tribal lines, the Islamists were then able to oust their rivals on the battlefield and establish a new order.

As seen in the Afghan case, this rational, strategic business calculation was instrumental in financing the rise of the Taliban in 1994. During the 1992–1996 Afghan civil war, the smugglers and traders working along the Pakistan-Afghanistan border had become terribly frustrated with the high taxes they were forced to pay to the many ethnic warlords and militias that were running the countryside. With the roads overrun and their profits sinking, the traders in the border region sought an alternative to this costly ethnic and tribal fragmentation. When the Taliban emerged in 1994 in rural Kandahar, they quickly courted the support of the business class by clearing key trade routes of checkpoints and accepting only voluntary donations for their services. Unlike the rapacious ethnic warlords, the Taliban appeared to be a low-cost solution to the high costs of civil war. Rallying behind the new Islamist movement with their voluntary donations, members of the business class helped turn the Taliban into a surprisingly powerful new contender, which quickly ousted the well-established ethnic warlords on the battlefield. Out of failure and fragmentation, the Taliban then centralized power and built a robust new Islamist government that enforced its writ from Kandahar to Mazar-e-Sharif.

The Islamic Courts Union movement was equally successful in courting this type of widespread business support in Somalia. After suffering from fifteen years of violent clan warfare, from 2004 to 2006 the Somali business class actively mobilized its resources to create a solution to the deep social fragmentation. By this point, the civil war had become incredibly costly; traders and entrepreneurs were paying extortion moneys to multiple clan warlords and militias that controlled the countryside in privately held turfs and provided little protection in return. As these security costs compounded, members of the business class began voluntarily investing in their local Islamic courts, which offered an alternative model of security provision. Once the ICU formed into one coherent movement in 2006, the business community then yanked its support from the clan warlords and threw its support behind the Islamists. This collective action created a dramatic shift in the Somali civil war. With the support of the business class, the ICU crushed its heavily entrenched rivals on the battlefield, captured 90 percent of the countryside, and created a new centralized Islamist government out of the anarchy.

Afghanistan and Somalia provided unique opportunities to explore this two-staged dynamic in great detail. Given that the Islamist proto-state is a contemporary phenomenon, these historical cases made it possible to systematically investigate the two processes in depth. The evidence revealed that the alliance between ideologically motivated Islamists and profit-driven business elites was instrumental in the early rise of both the Taliban and the ICU. In both of these failed states, the business-Islamist alliance broke an intractable political stalemate and created statelike control out of chaos. These cases are not outliers, however; this dynamic has also occurred in several other parts of the modern Muslim world. A preliminary investigation into the rise of jihadist power in the Middle East, South Asia, and North and West Africa revealed similar patterns to the Afghan and Somali cases. As the evidence in chapter 8 on Iraq and Syria, Mali, and Pakistan reveals, in each of these war theaters a business-Islamist alliance appears to be instrumental in financing jihadist power.

Looking to the Middle East, my research uncovered a clear relationship between business and Islamist interests in the Iraqi and Syrian war theaters. Declaring itself a new caliphate in 2014, with a mandate to govern the entire Muslim world, the militant group Daesh created a robust and institutionalized jihadist proto-state that smashed through the troubled border. As Daesh emerged as the dominant jihadist player in the theater, these militants pursued a range of aggressive revenue-generation strategies, from bank robberies to kidnapping for ransom. At its core, however, the group relied heavily on the long-standing oil smuggling and criminal networks in the region. Following the 2003 American invasion of Iraq that overthrew the Baathist government of Saddam Hussein, a new war economy was born that gave the jihadists a key advantage. According to experts in the region, after the Baathists went underground, the mafias and criminal organizations in the Sunni-dominated northwest of Iraq built deep ties to the jihadists. As the civil war dragged on, the traffickers grew frustrated with having to pay off a multitude of armed groups for protection. In contrast, Daesh worked to keep its taxes low during its early formation, courting the support of these wealthy elites. Having secured this business support, Daesh was then able to capture large swaths of territory and build a coercive new proto-state that could tax and extort its population at will.

Moving to Mali, my research uncovered even more powerful connections between criminal networks and militant jihadists along the unruly Algerian border. Over the past decade, al-Qaeda in the Islamic Maghreb (AQIM) established its control over this wild desert region, using it as a base to launch a series of violent kidnappings and deadly terrorist attacks from Tunisia to the Ivory Coast. During the group's early period of formation, AQIM leader Mokhtar Belmokhtar invested heavily in building ties to the tribes in the northern Kidal region that dominated the lucrative cigarette smuggling industry; Belmokhtar even married into these tribes to gain access to these criminal networks, especially in cigarettes, drugs, and human trafficking. During its initial period of formation, his group taxed these smugglers, being careful to keep their rates competitive, but as the revenues from the cigarette and narcotics trade skyrocketed, the jihadists began to cut out the middlemen and take a higher cut. Unlike the Afghan, Somali, and Iraqi cases, however, AQIM has historically been more uniquely motivated by its desire for wealth than its commitment to jihad. Most Malians actually believe that AQIM is more interested in profit than religion, and they have even nicknamed Belmokhtar "Mr. Marlboro." Indeed, looking at its financial activities today, the links between AQIM and these regional criminal networks now appear so enmeshed that they are difficult to distinguish.

Turning next to Pakistan, my research revealed a clear link between criminal business and jihadist power in South Asia that built on the long legacy of jihadist financing in Afghanistan. The contemporary crisis, however, erupted as Pakistan attempted to play both sides of the conflict in Afghanistan, supporting the Americans overtly and the Afghan Taliban covertly. This double-game triggered accusations of treason in the unruly tribal areas and sparked a violent reaction in the border region. In response to perceived Pakistani perfidy, a radical new group of Pakistani Taliban (TTP) factions declared war on Islamabad and launched a wave of deadly terrorist attacks across the countryside, claiming tens of thousands of lives. Behind this surge in jihadist power were the long-standing criminal business networks that had been established in the border region over the course of Afghanistan's lengthy wars. Building on these deep roots, these TTP factions built their power base along the key smuggling routes in North and South Waziristan that connected the Afghan war economy to the global underground, both taxing and participating in the industries operating in their turfs. From narcotrafficking to minerals smuggling, these illicit businesses paid into these jihadist protection rackets, thus giving these TTP groups the financial independence to cement their hold over the tribal areas and unleash a reign of terror on their Pakistani targets.

As scholars and analysts try to make sense of the modern jihadist proto-state, the insights drawn from these cases reveal an important new agenda for future research. This phenomenon is important for the study not only of civil war economies but also of the very nature of violence and contemporary state formation. Understood this way, the evidence in this book points to practical guidance for the policy community to better address these global security problems. I thus conclude the book with a discussion of how the world can respond to the emergence of Islamist power, in the hope that this leads to a higher profit margin and a lower body count for all parties involved.

The Dilemma of Order Making in the Modern World

The emergence of modern jihadist proto-states presents a troubling predicament. Indeed, their revisionist agendas and expansionist ideologies challenge the existing global order and threaten international peace and security, and their extremist violence has shocked moral sensibilities across the planet. It is no surprise that the entire international community has rallied against these radical new jihadist polities.

Yet the fact is that these jihadist proto-states represent a new form of order making that has emerged in some of the most volatile and anarchic parts of the Muslim world. This endogenous process of state formation, built on the uncanny alliance between jihadists and the business class, has occurred across vast cultural, linguistic, and geographic distances. From the Pakistani mountains to the Malian deserts, the emergence of these proto-states creates a difficult dilemma for both scholars and policymakers alike.

On the one hand, these jihadist polities typically espouse an extremist, intolerant, and revisionist interpretation of sharia that shocks our moral conscience, terrifies mainstream religious communities, and comes into stark conflict with international human rights laws and norms. For the overwhelming majority of the Muslim world, these modern jihadist proto-states are alien and abhorrent constructs. The political and military expansionism of these new jihadist polities also threatens state sovereignty across the Muslim world. Since the creation of the United Nations in 1945, the international system has been predicated on the fundamental principle of territorial integrity; indeed, despite much political upheaval and conflict over the past seventy years, the international community has been highly resistant to changing borders and recognizing new states. The jihadist proto-state is thus a most unwelcome new actor on the world stage.

On the other hand, however, it is the failure of the sovereign state system in these parts of the world that has contributed to this rise in jihadist power in the first place. For most of the Muslim world, contemporary state borders were inherited from a toxic legacy of European imperial subjugation, drawn haphazardly across what were once unified populations.[5] Jihadist groups across the Middle East, North and West Africa, and South Asia have thus associated these problematic borders with their Islamist struggle. In Pakistan and Afghanistan, the Taliban built their support base on both sides of the disputed Durand Line in denial of the nineteenth-century British-imposed border.[6] Al-Qaeda in the Islamic Maghreb has extended its influence across the unmarked borders dividing Mali, Algeria, Libya, and Mauritania, which were drawn by French and Italian colonists in the early twentieth century.[7] Daesh has framed its expansionist agenda as a political rejection of the 1916 Sykes-Picot agreement, which divided the Arab provinces of the Ottoman Empire between the British, French, and Russians and subsequently influenced the borders of the modern Middle East.[8] These jihadist groups are not only fighting for the creation of a new Islamic political order; they are also reacting to the failure of the modern sovereign state across the Muslim world and raging against borders they associate with a humiliating era of colonial subjugation.

Underneath the seething anger and apparent chaos, however, is a powerful and endogenous process of order making. In some ways, the seemingly futile conflict in these troubled parts of the Muslim world is actually part of a lengthy and messy pathway to political development. Youssef Cohen, B. R. Brown, and A. F. K. Organski have argued that violence is a "usual feature of the process of primitive accumulation of power," which eventually leads to the development of modern statehood.[9] Charles Tilly's famous quote, "War made the state and the state made war," is indeed a grim prophecy.[10] The history of human civilization has shown violence to be part of the ordinary process of state formation—but one that exists on a very long time horizon.[11] The emergence of the jihadist proto-state fits with this established, albeit gruesome, pattern of political order making.

Violence alone, however, does not explain the origins of the proto-state. Looking at the hidden financial foundations of Islamist power, this book showed how civil war economies play an essential role in this state formation process. Bridging these disparate literatures, I put forward a new dynamic that shows how the nexus of economic and political interests can actually produce a robust type of order formation out of chaos. The evidence shows that as the interests of the bazaar intersected with those of the jihadists, this business-Islamist alliance helped finance the formation of these proto-states. Just as medieval European states were first born as coercive protection rackets that taxed citizens in exchange for security, Islamist proto-states also forge this social contract with the moneyed elite in contemporary civil wars. Money, ideology, and violence create an unholy trinity, out of which modern political order is born.

The emergence of the jihadist proto-state thus presents a conundrum. On the one hand, jihadist expansionism presents a violent threat to the modern international order, which gives primacy to the protection of sovereign states. On the other hand, despite all their violence and horror, the jihadist polities that have emerged across the Muslim world may also be exemplary of an ordinary process of order making in which the violent consolidation of power produces a more stable polity in the long term. Just as Henry VIII, Louis XIV, and Ivan the Terrible helped to build England, France, and Russia into strong states, these nascent jihadist polities may indeed be an example of an early evolutionary stage in the creation of viable states.[12]

From this lens, the violence perpetrated by modern jihadists looks relatively mild compared to the witch hunts, religious wars, torture chambers, inquisitions, and ethnic purges of medieval and early modern Europe. Even contemporary European borders, forged in the aftermath of World War II, emerged out of the ashes of trench warfare, aerial bombardments, and gas chambers. Hundreds of millions of people died in the making of modern Britain, France, Russia, and Germany. Considering the utterly gruesome history of European state formation, these jihadists seem to have built their proto-states with a comparatively modest amount of blood and treasure.

Nonetheless, even if these proto-states do hold the promise of order and stability on the distant horizon, this pathway to political development is now permanently closed. The world can no longer stomach the bloody and horrifying process of medieval state building. Awakening from the nightmares of Normandy and Auschwitz, we have created a new international order that, despite all its faults and failings, has created a surprisingly peaceful world for over seventy years. In this new world, we declared the inalienable rights of every single person on the planet in the 1948 Universal Declaration of Human Rights. It then became possible for the world's poorest people to overthrow the shackles of imperialism with the 1960 United Nations Declaration on the Granting of Independence to Colonial Countries and Peoples. The arc of our moral universe has bent, however slowly and haltingly, toward justice. We are thus unwilling to allow insurgent groups to commit acts of genocide and terror to advance an apocalyptic or mystical agenda. It is over. We have had enough.

The Islamist proto-state therefore finds itself at a crossroads. Despite its success in consolidating power at home, its future on the international stage is destined for failure and enduring hardship. The world will simply not allow these groups to repeat the long and bloody history of state forma-tion that once defined Europe. Yet as these jihadist movements spring up in civil wars around the world, this phenomenon appears uncontainable. The international community has thus far failed to effectively eliminate or pacify these groups; rather, these movements have actually multiplied over the past decade, causing entire regions to become infected with the spread of extremist violence. The international community is thus faced with a problem that it cannot accept and cannot control. This impasse is unsustainable.

Rational Policies toward Jihadist Polities

Dealing with the dilemma of modern jihadist proto-states requires a new approach to international security. This book put forward a dynamic to help explain how and why business and Islamist interests converge in civil wars, thus leading to the rise of these new Islamist polities. Over the past decade, hundreds of billions of dollars have been spent to fight against jihadist groups, yet the result has been a dramatic proliferation of these insurgencies. The extremism and violence is arguably worse now than it was before these costly interventions.

Considering the poor results of the international community's military ventures into Afghanistan, Iraq, Syria, Somalia, and Libya, a new engagement strategy for conflict-affected parts of the Muslim world is clearly necessary. Although this book has largely focused on explaining the phenomenon of the jihadist proto-state, this study also points to some important counsel for members of the security policy community. There is no silver bullet that can solve these complex crises. Building on the evidence from the field, however, I offer this policy community three modest considerations for building a new approach to engaging this problem: incentivizing the business class, engag-ing with area experts, and exercising restraint in new interventions in the Muslim world.

First, policymakers would do well to invest in creating meaningful incentive structures to encourage local businesspeople to behave cooperatively. As the stories in this book revealed, the business community in a civil war has a unique ability to influence political outcomes, and it uses this financial leverage to change the balance of power on the battlefield. This elite class is not, however, passionately partisan in any direction. Even businesspeople that offer tremendous material support to Islamists are not true ideologues. They are primarily motivated by profit, and their interests and choices are highly responsive to material incentives. In a very literal sense, the preferences and allegiances of these powerful business elites are up for sale.

Carefully designed economic incentives can have a powerful effect on this class of actors. To start, strengthening legal instruments that crack down on illicit activities changes the cost calculations of these elites. The business communities in these conflict zones, including the criminal class, are sensitive to legal sanctions, and like any good investors, they have no desire to have their assets frozen. Of course, these measures should be designed to avoid undermining the normal commercial activities in an informal economy. Aggressive sanctions can actually hurt licit industries and force businesspeople into criminal activities. For example, early efforts to crack down on jihadist financing involved freezing the assets of entire hawala money transfer companies; however, these sanctions also robbed millions of civilians, businesspeople, and humanitarian organizations of their normal sources of income. War economies are complex organisms that emerge out of chaos and play an essential role in survival. When targeting the toxic elements of these markets, policymakers should be careful not to poison the lifeblood of these vulnerable societies.

Dealing with these illicit business networks thus requires sophisticated instruments. Given the nexus between global jihadists and transnational criminal networks, coordination between counterinsurgency and international policing efforts is necessary for success. Cooperation between international security and law enforcement agencies has already afforded policymakers better tools to disrupt known criminal networks, target smuggling networks, and impose sanctions on specific supporters of blacklisted groups, which have arguably been effective in countering violent extremism.[13] Building on this success, these coordinated efforts can help to narrow the space in which criminal and extremist groups are able to converge.

Of course, while these legal measures are important, they do not tackle the problem at its root. As long as criminality and extremism are financially more attractive than licit activities, there will always be entrepreneurs who seek to dodge the law rather than abide by it. Nonetheless, it is essential to remember that even the most hardened smugglers, gunrunners, and drug dealers that I spoke to in these conflict zones are not committed criminals; rather, many openly stated that if they had access to other safer and more lucrative business ventures, they would switch trades in a heartbeat. Gun dealers in Somalia and Afghanistan explicitly stated that they would be keen to enter a new profession if there were better opportunities available. Opium farmers in Afghanistan said the only reason that they grow poppies is because no one will buy their wheat at a competitive price. Most people in these unruly places are making perfectly rational economic decisions.

It is also important to consider that these entrepreneurs are not committed to any particular political or ideological movement, including the Islamists they supported against other ethnic and tribal factions. In fact, the only real partisan position the business class has consistently supported is its preference for lower taxes. These liberal economic values are quite reconcilable with those of the international community; if wielded effectively, these interests may actually provide a common ground on which creative new initiatives toward peace and prosperity can be developed.

Alongside the stick must therefore be a carrot. Given the general lack of normal economic opportunities in conflict zones, businesspeople in these conflict-affected areas are certain to be receptive to the prospect of profitable new ventures and partnerships. Investing in productive, licit industries is therefore not only sound security policy, but it can also help lift these societies out of poverty. The players in this game all understand how to work in a free trade environment, and they are ready to compete. Creating new financial incentives to prompt the business class to behave positively can affect both the economic and political environment.[14]

In practical terms, this means increasing regional economic cooperation to improve the local business environment. For example, the 2016 trilateral transit trade agreement between Afghanistan, India, and Iran opens a lucrative new regional trade corridor through the Chabahar Port, which promises to expand business opportunities for the truckers and traders in the region. Of course, this new deal has rattled the Pakistani defense establishment, which sees Chabahar as a challenge to its well-established Karachi-to-Kabul route; however, there is no reason that this new deal should limit the future participation of Pakistan and even China. It would be folly for any of these parties to view trade as a weapon between regional rivals; opening these routes is a win-win game, not a zero-sum calculation. Increasing regional economic cooperation and integration is a job best left to the diplomats, not the army generals.

Second, policymakers would be well advised to rely on highly detailed and nuanced analyses of different jihadist groups in each individual war theater well before making any decisions about specific engagement strategies. When it comes to decisions about intervention, the policy community should be especially wary of sensationalist arguments that seem politically salable but that lack detailed evidence from the field. For example, in 2006 the United Nations (UN) Monitoring Group released a report alleging that the Islamic Courts Union sent hundreds of Somali foot soldiers to fight alongside Hezbollah.[15] Area experts easily identified the flaws in this argument, pointing to the deep sectarian differences between Somali-Sunni and Lebanese-Shiite Islamists; careful observers even asked for photographic evidence of African fighters in Lebanon, which of course did not exist. Although these allegations eventually proved baseless, at the time they fed into popular political narratives and prompted a large-scale international military operation against the ICU.[16] This intervention inadvertently created a new wave of jihadist violence that threatened the entire East African regional neighborhood.

The policy community can learn from this painful and unnecessary mistake. Early conversation with scholars who have conducted fieldwork can help the policy community to tease out these necessary details and ensure that engagement strategies toward specific Islamist groups are based on solid evidence. There are a handful of guiding principles in making these determinations. Suffice to say, any counsel that fails to account for the differences between Shiites and Sunnis, or haphazardly groups them together, ought to be summarily dismissed. The policy community would likewise do well to carefully distinguish between different Sunni Islamist schools of thought, such as Deobandi, Salafist, Ikhwani, and Takfiri approaches, as these constitute major fault lines of contention.[17] Furthermore, too often scholars and analysts have dangerously mischaracterized all Wahhabis as violent extremists; erroneously conflating a minority Takfiri jihadist doctrine with the millions of quietist Wahhabis around the world alienates these peaceful communities and gives space to extremist elements.[18] Without this level of nuance in designing an engagement strategy, policymakers are at risk of creating the very problems they wish to solve.

The fact is that Islamists and jihadists are a diverse set, and understanding this variation is necessary for developing effective policy responses toward each of these groups. It is entirely possible for jihadists that are fundamentalist and undemocratic at home to genuinely seek peaceful relations with the wider world. There are also global Islamist movements that seek the creation of a new caliphate but that expressly denounce any calls for violence and jihad.[19] Apocalyptic Islamists are also varied; some act like militant death cults, while others are quietists who patiently wait for what they believe to be an inevitable future. Knowing the difference between these typologies, and their implications for group behavior and alliance formation, is necessary to ensure that engagement strategies do not inadvertently give more space to the most extreme elements within this set. For too long, policymakers have been content to use an ax; the contemporary landscape of Islamist politics, however, demands a scalpel.

Third, the policy community would be wise to adopt a strategy of restraint and humility in any future international interventions in the Muslim world. The lessons of Afghanistan, Somalia, Iraq, Libya, and Syria are compelling: the chaos created by these international military operations has been unstoppable and uncontrollable. This new era of political disorder began with the 2001 US operation in Afghanistan, during which then-president George W. Bush said to his National Security Council, "Look, our strategy is to create chaos, to create a vacuum, to get the bad guys moving."[20] This disorder spread with the 2003 American invasion of Iraq, which not only removed Saddam Hussein from power but also completely disbanded his Baathist security forces, thus leaving the country without a functioning security apparatus.[21] The consequences of these political vacuums have been enduring state failure and escalating jihadist insurgencies.

As the international community kept pushing, the chaos spread even further across the Muslim world. In 2011, the UN Security Council declared its responsibility to protect civilians under threat in Benghazi, and NATO launched a military offensive in Libya that toppled President Muammar Gaddafi.[22] Building on the Libyan mission, when the Syrian government allegedly used chemical weapons against its civilian population, the Americans began covertly supplying weapons to opposition rebels fighting against President Bashar al-Assad.[23] The principles motivating the Libyan and Syrian interventions were largely humanitarian, and proponents rightly pointed to the extreme abuses of the Gaddafi and Assad regimes as justification for international action under the Responsibility to Protect doctrine.[24] By the principles and norms enshrined in the doctrine, the international community was morally obligated to come to the defense of these besieged civilians. Yet despite these lofty humanitarian ideals, in both cases, these interventions still unintentionally plunged these countries into utterly devastating civil wars.

The reasons behind each of these international interventions— Afghanistan, Somalia, Iraq, Libya, and Syria—have differed; security or economic interests motivated some military operations, and human security principles were the impetus for others. Although the inspirations varied, the strategies and consequences of these cases are alarmingly similar. Both well-intentioned interventions and self-interested invasions have produced extreme levels of disorder. And out of the ensuing political abyss has emerged the latest generation of jihadists, even more radical and irreconcilable than its predecessors. Anarchy has proven to be the breeding ground of extremism.

In all of these cases, Pandora's box has already been opened. Once the chaos has been unleashed, there is no easy way to contain it. The international community thus has no choice but to deal with the fallout of the crises it helped to create. Unfortunately, at this late stage in the game, there are no magic silver bullets that can put a quick end to these conflicts. Rather, the evidence suggests that continued confrontation with these jihadist groups has only led to ever-greater militancy and extremism, putting these troubled countries on a longer and more precarious path to recovery. For Afghanistan, Somalia, Iraq, Syria, and Libya, the goal of a durable, self-sustaining peace will now take decades to attain. The deed is done.

What the policy community can do, however, is to learn the fundamental lesson from these failed engagements and stop repeating them. This is a painful lesson, as interventions are sometimes justified by reasonable, even noble objectives. The humbling fact, however, is that the practical tools for successfully executing such interventions are often sorely lacking. In these modern conflicts, the instruments of war—whether drone strikes or cruise missiles—do not resolve the humanitarian or political crises that justify their use. Urgent outcry that the international community must "do something" therefore lacks an essential element of humility. It is akin to feeling strongly that a patient ought be cured of cancer but having only a kitchen knife and a bandage to achieve this goal. Having an emotional need to "do something" does not make it acceptable to stab the patient. Knowledge without action might be injustice, but action without knowledge is criminal.

The gap between our ideals and our instruments is vast. From air bombing campaigns to democratization projects, the outdated tools in our belt are ineffective in resolving contemporary intrastate conflicts and can even inadvertently create crises. Under such conditions, toppling governments is dangerous, foolish, illegal, and immoral. When faced with a potential new confrontation in the Muslim world, the policy community would therefore be wise to hold back on creating another uncontrollable war front and instead seek out a less invasive political solution. This is a much humbler approach to international politics, but one that is acutely warranted. Given the human costs of these interventions, an ounce of preventive diplomacy may indeed be worth a thousand pounds of cure for state failure.

At first blush, humility seems antithetical to conventional approaches to international security. States and rebel groups alike are socialized to posture and push in their pursuit of power. War inspires bravado, machismo, and nationalism and scorns all else as weakness. Yet as Proverbs 11:2 teaches: "When pride comes, then comes disgrace; but with the humble is wisdom." The dire fact is that these particular types of violent confrontations have the potential to destabilize the entire international system. The insurgents cannot lose, the states cannot win, and these conflicts spread across borders. The time horizon for these wars is indefinite, and the costs in blood and treasure are astronomical. In our desperate search for peace in the Muslim world, all parties must come to terms with their own helplessness. Without this necessary drop of humility, the prospects of a future détente and peace are bleak; there will be no victors, only victims.

The Islamists must also be nudged in this direction, perhaps heeding the words of the Prophet Muhammad, narrated in *Sahih al-Bukhari*: "Shall I not tell you about the companions of Paradise? They are every humble person considered weak, but if they gave an oath by Allah it would be fulfilled. Shall I not tell you about the companions of Hellfire? They are every harsh, haughty, and arrogant person."

This hellfire is already here, from the ruins of Palmyra to the shelled hospitals of Kunduz, and from the Sinjar Mountains to Guantanamo Bay. Interests alone are not enough to escape this torment; the path to peace will necessarily require overwhelming moral courage in order to begin to deescalate these tensions. Islamists are often defensive when asked to step back, pointing to the many humiliations the Muslim world has suffered, from colonialism to the Cold War. Humility is not a position of weakness or dishonor, however; rather, it is one of prudence, equanimity, and genuine power. As the Koran states:

> The servants of the Most Merciful are those who walk upon the earth
> in humility, and when the ignorant address them [harshly], they say
> [words of] peace.[25]

Methodology and Field Research

This book is concerned with the emergence of modern jihadist polities out of civil wars in the Muslim world. While there is an urgent need for new scholarship on this phenomenon, conducting empirical research in these field environments is fraught with complications. Given these dangers, few academics choose to conduct research on these conflicts, and even experienced scholars face frustrating security conditions in the field. Research is often delayed by unpredictable eruptions of violence, and it can be difficult to gain direct access to key players in the middle of an active fight.

Foreign academics are also at risk of being suspected of espionage by governments, substate armed groups, and local communities alike. Given this mistrustful social environment, even the slightest error in judgment by the researcher may jeopardize the security of his or her entire network. Scholars conducting field research in these volatile conflict zones are faced with an array of logistical, security, and ethical challenges throughout their studies.

Conducting academic research on current events also presents serious methodological difficulties. Because most contemporary jihadist groups are rapidly and continuously evolving, investigating their internal development can be frustrating. If the group is in a state of flux, a researcher's findings may become outdated almost immediately after leaving the field, long before they ever reach academic publication. To compensate, as events change on the ground, researchers may find themselves unintentionally chasing explosive headlines instead of testing theories, wasting valuable resources for little scholarly benefit. The challenges of studying current events can prevent even the most capable academics from successfully completing their projects.

The Afghan and Somali cases provided me with a historical window into a decidedly contemporary security question. By tracking the emergence and evolution of two recent Islamist proto-states that have already experienced both their rise and their fall, I avoided the potential pitfalls of chasing an ongoing investigation. I also enjoyed robust personal and professional networks in these troubled regions, which helped greatly with the problem of access. This mitigated many, but not all, of the serious security considerations that normally accompany this type of research. These two classic cases of Islamist power make up the majority of the empirical work in the book.

The three additional mini case studies involved a different type of fieldwork. I chose to examine these cases for the purpose of establishing external validity of my hypothesis, and I thus approached my interviewees with specific questions about the relationship between jihadists and business networks. My interviews for these cases were primarily with scholars, peace practitioners, and other key informants who had extensive knowledge of the conflicts in their home regions. There was no ethnographic element to these meetings, and all of my respondents were accustomed to these types of interviews with foreign researchers. Nonetheless, I was fortunate to have excellent local research assistants who assisted me in navigating these theaters and acquiring this preliminary evidence. My meetings in Beirut and Bamako helped me to compare the evidence from the Afghan and Somali cases to processes that were taking place in Syria, Iraq, and Mali, using the insights of local scholars and analysts to vet my ideas and highlight where these patterns were similar and where they were different.

In this appendix, I provide a detailed account of my research methods and address the particular security, logistical, ethical, and personal challenges of conducting fieldwork in active civil wars in the Muslim world. Building on the existing conflict literature that provides guidelines on field research, I explain the security and ethical considerations that affected my research on modern jihadist polities. I share my experiences openly here in order to provide clarity on my process and to contribute to important, ongoing discipline-wide discussion on field research broadly and in these complex conflict environments specifically.[1]

Field Research Methods

Completing this study required extensive preparatory work in the field in advance of my formal research. The research on the two main cases in this book involved travel across Kenya, Somalia, Pakistan, Afghanistan, and the United Arab Emirates. My study began with initial feasibility assessments in the field, which informed my research design and ethics review process. In practical terms, this meant that I invested thousands of hours of research time learning about my host societies, receiving basic language training, and building local networks before embarking on other forms of data collection.[2]

Undertaking field research on these subjects was therefore a time-consuming and labor-intensive endeavor. After conducting the initial assessments, I decided on a mixed-methods approach that included interviews, survey questionnaires, and participant and nonparticipant observations. Although there were immersive elements to my research, the ethnographic and observational data were primarily used to build the narrative style of the book. In contrast, my interview material constitutes the core evidence used to evaluate my hypothesis in both cases. To establish validity of these interview data, I also conducted a quantitative study for the Somalia case.

Importantly, this empirical work took place in complex cultural contexts with high levels of social diversity, fragmentation, unspoken signals, and threats of violence. While my basic linguistic and cultural training helped me navigate these rowdy bazaars, it was not nearly enough to capture the nuances of communication and social interactions. In Afghanistan and Pakistan, not only are Pashto dialects famous for local variation but the language is also full of colorful proverbs and references that have deep meaning and connotation. Indeed, in response to a research question about business success, a respondent might say, "If you plan to keep elephants, you need a big door." Similarly in Somalia, people express themselves using countless idiomatic sayings, which cannot be understood without detailed cultural knowledge. A Somali interviewee may respond to a question about their finances by saying, "a blind man does not forget his walking stick."

Without support from my local contacts and research associates, this interview material would have been utterly incomprehensible. I thus relied on my research team for both translation and interpretation. Beyond simple translation assistance, my cultural interlocutors were essential supports for navigating the challenges of communication in the field, and they assisted in both collection and analysis of the data. They also provided insights at the research design stage and were instrumental in ensuring that the fieldwork was conducted safely and ethically.

Interview Data

Interview research constitutes the backbone of the four main empirical chapters on Afghanistan and Somalia. To complete this work, I met with a wide range of interview respondents, including business elites, Islamists, warlords, political and intelligence officials, civil society organizations, and local scholars and analysts. My interview data were vetted through several processes. First, I triangulated the data by asking different respondents about the same events, with special attention paid to both class dynamics and the ethnic and tribal identities of my interviewees. Second, before leaving the field, I arranged for expert review sessions with local colleagues, using focus group discussions, research workshops, and scholarly presentations of my research. And third, I used member checking, both before and during the writing stage, to ensure that the interview quotes reflected the tone and intention of the subjects.

For the Taliban case study, I conducted lengthy unstructured and semistructured interviews with scores of respondents. My conversations with members and supporters of the original Taliban movement, Afghan militiamen, transit traders, Pakistani academics and analysts, and former members and heads of the Pakistani Inter-Services Intelligence (ISI) took place in both Afghanistan and Pakistan, starting with feasibility assessments in 2005 and 2006, continuing with formal interviews through 2009, and then finishing with member checks and expert review between 2011 and 2016.

In Afghanistan, I spoke with former militiamen from a wide range of ethnic and tribal backgrounds in Jalalabad, Kandahar, Kabul, and Mazar-e-Sharif. I also interviewed powerful traders and smugglers that worked across the Pakistan-Afghanistan border and members and supporters of the original Afghan Taliban movement. In all of these meetings and interviews with insurgents, Islamists, and businesspeople in Afghanistan and Pakistan, I was accompanied by a male relative, or *mahram*, who had access to these circles. Indeed, as a female researcher, having a *mahram* accompany me during these meetings was not only a sociocultural requirement for interacting with these respondents but also provided me with valuable assistance with translation of local dialects, interpreting nonverbal cues, and navigating complex cultural mores in both immersive research and interview work.

My research also capitalized on years of unfettered access to and observations of the everyday business decisions of traders and smugglers in the Pakistan-Afghanistan border region, including their deals with different Afghan commanders. Because of my personal connections to this business community, I had firsthand information about several of the anecdotes relayed in the book. For my research, I interviewed members of the business class who were present on the scene at the time of these historical events. In the case that the individual was deceased, I spoke to immediate relatives or associates who were best positioned to give eyewitness accounts and then used triangulation and member checks to confirm that my portrayals of incidents were accurate. These respondents confirmed and clarified the particular details of behind-the-scenes business deals and confrontations. My conversations with these traders and smugglers provide a vivid and intimate lens into the hidden social forces at play in this volatile war economy.

I also conducted in-depth interviews with Pakistani officials who played leading roles in the Afghan conflict throughout the 1980s and 1990s. I was a visiting researcher at the Institute for Policy Studies in Islamabad, where I met with local scholars, analysts, and members of the Pakistani political and intelligence community. My interviews in Rawalpindi involved many hours of conversations with the highest-ranking decision makers in the Pakistani intelligence, specifically those who were directly responsible for sponsoring armed Afghan groups throughout the Soviet war, the Afghan civil war, and the Taliban era. These interviews are treated as anonymous, except when several elite-level Pakistani intelligence officers and field commanders waived anonymity and agreed to be quoted, including General Asad Durrani, General Aurakzai, the late Colonel Imam, and the late General Hamid Gul.

To establish the validity of the qualitative data, I triangulated sources and verified stories told by different interviewees. For example, in order to ensure that my narrative depiction of Pakistani strategy during the Soviet-Afghan War was accurate, I met with a diverse range of elite Pakistani intelligence officials; in these one-on-one meetings, these elites gave me an account of their responsibilities in and experiences of key events. These different perspectives allowed me to examine the internal consistency of the narrative within the Pakistani intelligence community. Both during these interview sessions and in follow-up conversations, I used member checks and read back key quotes to make sure that I had written them down properly.

Furthermore, before leaving the field, I held a series of workshops, focus groups, and public talks to establish the validity of the data, review preliminary results, and debrief from the research process. These academic interactions did not require a *mahram*; rather, my relationships with local academic and policy institutions made these sessions possible. I spent several months as a visiting scholar and guest lecturer at Peshawar University, which allowed me to build these important scholarly networks. At Peshawar University, I held a focus group discussion with local scholars, journalists, and military officials to help contextualize my results. These informal conversations with faculty and graduate students in Peshawar were also tremendously helpful in vetting the data. In Islamabad, I was fortunate to be hosted for several excellent review sessions, including a half-day, closed-door focus group workshop with several high-ranking political and intelligence elites. As a guest lecturer in both Peshawar and Islamabad, I also reviewed the preliminary results by giving public talks on my findings; these open academic sessions not only allowed me to receive broad feedback on the research but also served as an opportunity to contribute to academic and scholarly life in my host society.

The Somalia case required an equal amount of qualitative fieldwork in Kenya, Somalia, Somaliland, and the United Arab Emirates. My interview respondents included Somali business elites, leaders of the Islamic Courts Union movement, clan warlords in the transitional government, political officials, local scholars and analysts, and civil society actors. Although I started working and building networks in East Africa in 2004, feasibility assessments for this particular project began in 2007. After months of consultations and expert review of the research design with my Somali colleagues, the formal interview work for the Somalia case study took place between 2009 and 2013, with member checks and expert reviews occurring between 2009 and 2015. Many of these interactions were repeated over several years.

Although Somali women do enjoy more social freedoms than Pashtuns, a similar set of gender dynamics shaped my research in East Africa. Like in all Muslim societies, Somali women are often expected to be accompanied when interacting with unfamiliar men; those who do not abide by such mores are seen as either foreigners or disreputable. To address this social requirement, in all of my interviews with Islamists, business elites, and clan warlords, I was accompanied by a well-regarded and senior Somali scholar, who introduced me as his student. Although this did not formally meet the standard of a *mahram*, establishing this relationship between a teacher and student added social respectability to the interaction, which made it possible for me to engage with my more conservative interview subjects in a productive manner. Not only did this make it much easier to build trust-based relationships with these interviewees, but having a type of *mahram* accompany me during these meetings also provided essential assistance with trust building, translation, and interpreting cultural cues.

My interviews with Islamists, clan warlords, and members of civil society organizations were open-ended and aimed at building a narrative around the rise of the Islamic Courts Union. For months I lived in the Somali refugee neighborhood of Eastleigh, where I met with many political entrepreneurs who had backed the Islamic Courts

Union movement. Other powerful actors from Somalia could be found in the lounges or lobbies of posh Kenyan hotels. In Mogadishu, I met with former Islamists who had been involved in the Islamic Courts Union project as well as with the local civil society organizations that assisted them. My conversations with these political actors focused on their experiences of mobilization leading up to the rise of the Islamists in 2006. I specifically asked these respondents to comment on the roles of clan, Islam, and business in Somali politics.

I also conducted scores of in-depth interviews in Mogadishu, Hargeisa, Nairobi, and Dubai with the most powerful business owners in Somalia, from across clan and subclan divisions, on their interests, identities, political leanings, and business experiences. These interviews included the chief executives of leading money transfer corporations, telecommunications firms, and trading conglomerates. In Mogadishu, I held official meetings with members of the new Somali Chamber of Commerce, composed of the biggest business owners in the country.

My interviews with Somali business elites were semistructured and asked about clan networks in business, Islamic identity in business, the cost of security under different warlord protection rackets, the relationship between security costs and the price of goods in different inland markets, the accessibility of inland markets, and business investment in the Islamic courts. These data were then cross-checked against each interviewee's subclan identity to determine how clan networks may have affected responses. To triangulate these data, I interviewed businesspersons from those subclans that are broadly perceived as being pro-ICU, such as the Habr-Gidir-Ayr, as well as those who were from subclans that are perceived to have been less supportive of the ICU, such as the Abgal.[3] I also interviewed a number of powerful non-Hawiye CEOs and shareholders from large nationwide corporations.

To evaluate my qualitative data, I held post-research workshops, scholarly meetings with faculty at the University of Nairobi, and expert review sessions. After completing my study in 2009, I hosted a half-day workshop with a team of Somali academics and policy experts to invite feedback on my data and preliminary analysis. Some of the participants had been consulted on the initial research design process and others were new to the project, which provided a valuable range of perspectives.

I also benefited from a number of one-on-one conversations with my Somali colleagues, who offered to review the findings, including civil society experts and academics from universities in both Nairobi and Mogadishu. These meetings not only allowed me to evaluate and review my interview data but also helped me to debrief from the fieldwork.

Survey Data

My survey work in 2009 was intended to triangulate and verify the interview results on the Somali case. To evaluate my argument against competing explanations, I conducted an original survey of 1,003 members of the Somali business community to explore the effects of security costs, Islamic trust, and clan trust on political preferences.[4] Surveys in Somalia are, for obvious reasons, extremely difficult to perform.[5] This study took advantage of a unique opportunity presented by an exodus of business refugees from Somalia to the Eastleigh district of Nairobi. From 2007 to 2009, intense fighting between al-Shabaab militias and Ethiopian and African Union forces in Somalia resulted in massive displacement in the Middle Shabelle region of Somalia. Mogadishu became a ghost town, while the Afgooye corridor was flooded with hundreds of thousands of internally displaced persons.

At this time, tens of thousands of businesspeople from Mogadishu migrated to Nairobi and set up remote offices in the Somali neighborhood of Eastleigh. Members of all dominant clans in Mogadishu shifted their operations to Kenya on an interim basis to avoid the clashes. So concentrated was this migration that several brand-new shopping malls were built in the heart of Eastleigh, creating an overnight economic boom in the neighborhood. Back in Mogadishu, the markets remained empty. This exodus therefore provided a unique opportunity to survey a representative sample of the Mogadishu business community. Virtually all nationwide trading firms, telecommunications companies, money transfer agencies, and other large industries have corporate offices in Mogadishu, so this sample also includes businesses that operate across the country.

The survey data were collected in 2009 from new arrivals in Eastleigh who were members of the Mogadishu business community throughout the period under investigation. I determined that it was most appropriate to survey this particular business community precisely because the Islamic Courts Union movement originated in Mogadishu. The criterion for entry into the study was therefore that the respondent must have owned a business in Mogadishu between 2004 and 2006. Each respondent was asked this qualifying question before being admitted into the study. There were no other conditions (such as clan, size of business, type of business, age, gender, etc.) that limited entry into the study. All prospective respondents were assured of their personal anonymity in the process of acquiring their consent to participate in the study.

The survey was administered by a team of five Somali field researchers from a range of clan backgrounds. Before commencing the study, the field team attended a full-day training session on interview and survey techniques that I hosted alongside faculty from the University of Nairobi, which covered sampling, informed consent, anonymity, and other aspects of our data collection process. After the training session, the field team began the study by identifying key blocks and shopping malls in Eastleigh, which were used as the survey area.

Over the course of six weeks, each of the five trained interviewers, two women and three men, began by selecting a random starting point within the fixed survey area and then walking from that location, door to door, seeking to speak to the owners of the business, with an objective of completing up to seven questionnaires per day. Given the open culture of the Somali bazaar, both male and female interviewers were able to interview male and female respondents. It is worth noting that women play an important role in the Somali economy, and many large businesses are owned by women. Although no effort was made to bias the sample on the basis of gender, 30 percent of all respondents were female.

The fact that respondents were physically located in Eastleigh during this peak period of fighting simplified the issues related to security of both the participants and the research team. As a result, the survey technique employed may be viewed as simple random sampling of business owners in Eastleigh, a neighborhood that was the locus of the Mogadishu business community at the time. Because we were not able to formally measure the extent of exclusion bias arising from the choice of neighborhood, however, this technique should be regarded as a convenience sample of the larger business community of Mogadishu. Accordingly, not represented in the survey were those businesspeople who were too poor or vulnerable to leave as well as those few who were powerful enough to stay.

These exclusions do not, however, substantively undermine the goals and objectives of this study. On the one hand, businesspeople who were so poor that they could not change their own circumstances were also unlikely to be able to affect the level of political change this study addresses. These poorest businesspeople lack the ability to influence political outcomes in a civil war competition. While a survey of the urban poor in Mogadishu might reveal other interesting insights, this particular class of businesspeople is not the agent of social change with which this research is concerned.

On the other hand, members of the business community who were powerful enough to remain in Mogadishu during heavy fighting do have a profound ability to affect their political circumstances. These individuals often have their own private militias and strong clan networks, and are able to maintain their business operations amid the active conflict. Nonetheless, their exclusion from the survey does not undermine the research for two key reasons. First, the businesspeople in this class are but a small handful, so their inclusion in the survey would not have made a significant statistical difference. Second, the qualitative research involved in-depth interviews with these exact same elite businesspeople and included a review of the preliminary results of the survey with members of this class. The insights and political preferences of this class are therefore addressed through the interview work.[6] As a result, the survey provided a useful triangulation of the interview data collected on the Somali business class, which helped corroborate my findings.

The sampling method, questionnaire design, and ethical considerations of the survey were evaluated through a month-long pilot study that took place before the data collection began. The primary objectives of the pilot phase were to scrutinize the survey questions and protect the security of both respondents and the survey team. This involved extensive preliminary meetings with business owners, Somali academics, policy analysts, and peacebuilding practitioners. The participants in the pilot phase evaluated the survey method through three vetting processes: first, draft versions of the survey questions were presented to a select group of businesspeople for commentary; second, the field team and faculty members from the University of Nairobi and the

University of Mogadishu held meetings to discuss revised versions of the questions and sampling strategy; and third, the final survey text was reviewed by the Center for Research and Dialogue–Somalia, a Mogadishu-based research institution that has over a decade of experience conducting social scientific research in Somalia.

The primary concern raised during the pilot study was the security of both the research team and the survey respondents. Given the political climate in Somalia, direct questions about the business community's political activities would alarm respondents about the purpose of the study and put the survey team at risk. Moreover, because the Islamic Courts Union had become associated with the militant group, al-Shabaab, there were potentially serious legal consequences for those members of the business community who had financed the ICU. Members of the business community were acutely aware that al-Shabaab had been blacklisted by the United States as a terrorist organization and that being charged with financing the group could result in the freezing of assets and criminal charges.

The specific survey questions were therefore designed to collect political and social information about the business community without putting either the survey team or respondents at risk. The dependent variable of "Political Preference" in the survey asked business owners about their retrospective economic evaluations of the following four options: (1) the 2000–2004 Transitional National Government; (2) the 2004–2006 Transitional Federal Government; (3) the 2006 Islamic Courts Union; and (4) no government at all. By consulting with Somali business owners about the survey design during the pilot phase of the study, the team determined that this was the most ethical and safe method of capturing political preferences.

The two primary independent variables in the estimation are "warlord security costs" and "Islamist security costs." The survey asked respondents two questions: first, to estimate their total security costs under the reign of warlords from 2004 to 2006; and second, to estimate their costs under the Islamic courts in 2006. Both questions were measured on the same ascending five-point ordinal scale, ranging from none to very high. Three additional independent variables were also included in the estimation to test the role of identity on political preference: "clan trust," "Islamic trust," and "support for Islamic law." These variables are based on respondents' reactions to different statements about clan and Islam in business. Businesspeople were asked to respond on a five-point ordinal scale ranging from strongly disagree to strongly agree, and responses were then recoded into binary variables for the analysis.

For estimations, the quantitative analysis employs multinomial logistic regression analysis in STATA. Logit, rather than probit, was used so that the analysis could produce clear and interpretable coefficients, specifically risk ratios. The independence of irrelevant alternatives (IIA) problem was ruled out using the Hausman test, thereby making the utility of mlogit equal to that of mprobit. These quantitative results have been previously published in *International Security*; the journal article includes an extended discussion of the pilot study, sampling method, variables, and research design, and an alternative estimation.[7] The replication data, coding, and questionnaire text for the survey are all publicly available through the Harvard Dataverse System, alongside an online methodology appendix that accompanies the article.[8]

Observational Data

The narrative style of writing in this book draws on my experience in the field. Although I do not rely on any observational data to test my argument, my descriptive notes did help to build my narrative. That is, the observational work allowed me to add more colors, textures, and smells to the stories and characters in this book and hopefully connect the reader to these seemingly remote people and places. I recorded some of my observations in personal journals and occasionally through photography and video. Others I simply remembered. Indeed, the fact that my family hails from the trading elite in Peshawar made it easy for me to describe their opulent homes and secret businesses in intimate detail.

Even these descriptive elements of the narrative, however, do not rely wholly on my own memories and observations; rather, I engaged in extensive consultations to ensure that my portrayal of people and places remained objective and accurate.[9] As a result, all of my observational data have been corroborated and vetted through interviews, member checks, or expert review. For example, I first drafted my description of the 1980s arms bazaar in Darra Adam Khel from personal experiences in this place. To ensure that my representation was correct, however, I also shared my paragraphs with my networks from the region. I approached several people who hailed from this area and were deeply familiar with this arms bazaar during the Soviet-Afghan War and asked them to read my paragraphs and comment on my portrayal, with careful attention to the situations, sights, smells, and sounds. Each of them provided feedback that helped me to build an accurate visual description of this remote arms manufacturing town.

I used this consultative process to scrutinize all of the observational work so that my personal perspectives did not improperly bias the portrayal of different places and times. The overwhelming majority of the observational work for both the Afghan and Somali cases, such as descriptions of refugee camps, smugglers' bazaars, and battle-worn cities, are based on my personal observations and notes while living in and traveling through these troubled regions; all of my personal observations from the field were then vetted through this consultative review process.

A few of the stories from the Somali civil war, however, also draw from my experiences working on a documentary film project on small arms and light weapons proliferation with award-winning filmmaker Shelley Saywell. In 2007, I worked with this film team to create the feature *Devil's Bargain: A Journey into the Small Arms Trade*. The documentary was filmed in part on location in Kenya and Somalia, where I was hired to provide logistical support as the team recorded extensive interviews with militiamen, arms dealers, criminal gangs, aid workers, and refugees.

My role in this project was to help guide the film crew on how to safely and ethically collect raw footage on arms smuggling in East Africa. This involved working collaboratively with local news teams to film in the Somali border town of Bula Hawa. Because the local news teams were part of this community, the filmmaker acquired unique raw footage that offered an unadulterated view of the daily life of Somali militiamen, gangsters, and gun sellers. The local news crew ordinarily interacted with these respondents for its regular news broadcasts, so the film project did not disturb or offend anyone in the local community, and the authenticity and frankness of the recorded conversations were striking. Having actively participated in the acquisition of this footage, I judged it to be the most realistic observation of the everyday life of militiamen and gunrunners in Somalia on record.

To help my readers directly engage with the stories in this book, the filmmaker generously provided me with this previously unreleased raw documentary film footage, which was produced by and is a copyright of Bishari Films. Although these stories are not used to test the argument, I include some translated conversations from these previously unreleased recordings so that the reader may observe and experience the conflict at the ground level, as if through an unfettered window into this troubled and oft-forgotten part of the world. Through this unique lens, these actors are situated in their most natural element: at the checkpoint and the gun bazaar.

Finally, my narrative also draws on observations and insights gained from two years of near-daily communication and interaction with Somali humanitarian workers from the Dr. Hawa Abdi Foundation. For over twenty years, Dr. Hawa Abdi has provided emergency humanitarian assistance to tens of thousands of internally displaced persons across clan lines in the town of Lafoole, located in the strategic Afgooye corridor. From 2010 to 2013, I worked with Dr. Hawa's team in a pro bono capacity as a way to give back to the communities that I studied.

This work was not part of my research agenda, nor have I relied on these observations to evaluate my argument. My service did, however, involve countless hours of troubleshooting on how to safely and appropriately move emergency supplies through checkpoints in rebel-held territory, from the capital to the hospital. The Afgooye corridor is a key trade route connecting Mogadishu to other important cities, such as Baidoa, and control over this strategic region provides armed groups with an important source of revenue through taxation of business and smuggling activities. My humanitarian service with this team was a hands-on, practical education in ground-level civil war economics in Somalia, and my notes from this work reflect a participant observational lens. Indeed, although this book focuses on the power and opulence of the elite, these experiences made it possible for me to connect the stories of business interests and warlord politics to the tremendous human costs of the Somali civil war.

Ethical and Security Considerations

Given the vulnerability of human subjects in these conflict zones, there are always serious ethical and security considerations related to conducting fieldwork.[10] Scholars are responsible for managing the security of their respondents but also for ensuring the safety of all persons involved in the research, including local associates, assistants, and logistical workers that facilitate work on the ground.[11] Even after taking all of these precautions, it remains challenging and time-consuming for researchers to build and maintain trust-based relationships with their research subjects in these environments. This is especially true when these subjects are involved in violent or illicit activities and are thus naturally wary of outsiders.

Out of respect for these communities, I thus devoted considerable time and effort to building robust local networks before beginning my research.[12] I lived in the rowdy bazaars that I was studying long before my interview and survey work began. To assess the feasibility of this study, I spent several months in the street markets of Eastleigh in 2004 and 2007, and many more in the smugglers' bazaars of Peshawar in 2005 and 2006. This preparation involved adapting to local cultural, religious, and social norms, including a wide array of personal restrictions on mobility, dress, and free expression. In the more volatile areas, there was also the added stress of living amid nightly gun battles, suicide bombings, kidnappings, executions, riots, and sexual assaults. Working under these conditions for extended periods of time can be exhausting and lonely; however, while labor-intensive, this early toil made it possible to complete my research in an appropriate, efficient, and professional manner.[13]

Humility and patience are a necessity in these places. Throughout my research process, I forwent opportunities that could have increased the risk to any of my colleagues, associates, and research participants. I regularly declined meetings with individuals when an interview was deemed higher-risk, and opted not to travel unless my hosts assured me that there was no security risk associated with my visit. Over the years, this meant that the work was often delayed by unpredictable security situations well outside of my control. There were periods of boredom and bursts of activity, depending on conditions on the ground.

Arranging meetings with key players also required abundant patience. I made every effort to accommodate respondents so that we could meet under pleasant conditions, according to their needs for security, transparency, and comfort. Many of my Somali interviewees preferred for me to wait for them to come to Nairobi or Dubai. Some of my Pakistani and Afghan respondents would meet only in Peshawar. I made these accommodations to ensure that the interview experience was of minimal disruption. When an interview was deemed appropriate, I not only acquired the informed consent of my research subjects but also only proceeded with my work when I was able to provide credible guarantees that the research would not cause harm, both during and after the completion of the work.[14] If a respondent accidentally disclosed information that could be used against them, I discarded that material.

While time-consuming, affording my interviewees this courtesy improved the overall quality of the data. Honesty and respect are necessary for building and maintaining trust-based relationships with research subjects who are wary of outsiders. In Pakistan and Afghanistan, these relationships were easier to build because my personal networks provided me with special access. Maintaining the inherent trust in those relationships, however, required a truthful disclosure of my research purposes and goals, as well as a full discussion of the ethical considerations of my research, to all participants. It also demanded mindfulness about the magnitude of confessions that these respondents would be willing to make based on this trust, and thus I used restraint in my selection of research questions.

Because this study focuses on historical events, however, most of the smugglers I interviewed in Pakistan were past retirement age, and none of my questions to them focused on their current business activities. Rather, these interviews asked about their recollected experiences of doing business from the Soviet era to the early Taliban period. This older generation of business elites was therefore a much lower-risk study population, which made it easier to manage the ethical challenges of the research. Nonetheless, because of the high trust I enjoyed in these relationships, ensuring the anonymity of these respondents was particularly important. The names of all members of this business community have been kept anonymous. Even in cases where the individual is deceased or in the event that the individual has already been publicly identified, such as through a news report about an arrest or criminal conviction, names and other personal information is withheld wherever families could be inadvertently identified.

In Somalia and Kenya, having trust-based relationships also facilitated my fieldwork and gave me tremendous access to key players. My local colleagues and associates played an instrumental role in facilitating research meetings by drawing on their own intimate family and community networks to welcome me into otherwise closed circles. This transitive trust, however, also required that I be particularly conscientious of how the research affected these networks. In a transitive trust relationship, any breach on the part of the researcher affects the confidence of the entire network. Transparency throughout the research process was essential, as were guarantees of anonymity for the participants.

As a result, I offered all of my Somali business respondents the option of anonymity. Regardless of their choice, I made the decision to exclude all of their names from the book, as this was an elite group and to reveal some names could have inadvertently implicated others. Some high-level business owners, however, spoke exclusively about their own corporations; their comments therefore provide clues into their possible identities, even though I have excluded their names. As a result, in order to be mindful of their security, I made sure that none of the questions I posed to these business elites demanded anything that could have implicated them in any legal or security problems. Furthermore, I only referenced their companies when quoting them on their overall costs of doing business, a matter that is not controversial or legally problematic. Whenever a quote might have been considered contentious, I worked to anonymize the respondent and refer to the company in a general fashion, such as a "telecommunications firm" or a "sugar trader."

Working with local Somali researchers mitigated many of the practical challenges of this interview work but also presented other ethical concerns pertaining to delegating tasks.[15] For example, if the relationship between principal investigators and local field teams is distant, then delegation can reduce monitoring and oversight of the data collection process, undermining the quality of the results. Furthermore, because principal investigators are responsible for the security and well-being of both their field teams and their participants, delegation is not always consistent with the ethical requirements of the research. In those situations in which the delegation of fieldwork to research teams was necessary, such as in the completion of the large-scale survey research, I therefore remained on the ground throughout the study and held frequent meetings with these teams about their working conditions, as well as daily reviews of the questionnaire results to ensure quality control.

Importantly, the research assistants working on the survey were in paid positions, and it was therefore necessary to preemptively guard against the potential negative impact of the resulting power disparity within my teams.[16] Of course, research associates and assistants should be compensated appropriately for their labor, and foreign researchers should be diligent about ensuring fair wages and prompt payment. In poorer countries, however, relationships built between foreign principal investigators and their local partners are often fundamentally unequal in power, especially when local researchers depend on the work for their livelihood.

In addition to the ethical considerations, this inequality has important implications for the reliability and validity of the data. If local researchers fear that revealing negative information will jeopardize their jobs, then the data collection may become corrupted unbeknownst to the principal investigator. Being aware of these dynamics, I addressed these concerns with the survey team both before and during our field study. Regular meetings with the team were necessary not only to monitor and evaluate the data collection process but also to ensure that our channels of communication remained open. These conversations were essential for identifying any results that may have been questionable, so that potentially corrupted data could be excluded and discarded.

Working in "polite societies" also raised a unique set of ethical challenges; both Somalis and Pashtuns have strong honor codes regarding hospitality toward guests, which intrinsically meant they were more likely to extend themselves in support of my research, even when to do so might jeopardize their personal or financial welfare. Almost everyone is gracious and quick to say yes. Accordingly, I invested in building frank relationships with my local associates and colleagues so that pressing security matters could be addressed in a direct manner. But even in these close relationships, to get a candid response in a courteous culture I sometimes needed to explicitly state, "Please, do not be polite with me; I need you to tell me straight." All trained researchers working in hospitable societies, including those who are native to the places they study, must necessarily have these candid conversations lest unspoken signals, innuendo, and good manners blur the results.

Through these candid interactions, I also requested that my colleagues and associates review the written form of both the research design and interview questions before starting the research. This vetting process corrected mistakes in both language and approach and helped to ensure the work would not offend or alarm any of the research participants. These meetings also provided a space for us to work collaboratively and creatively on developing noninvasive strategies for data collection, which not only kept the project low-risk but also improved the quality and accuracy of the results.

Politeness was an important consideration with my research subjects as well, from the most powerful business tycoons to the humblest street merchants. The instinct to be gracious and hospitable is ubiquitous in these cultures and puts an added responsibility on the researcher. For example, everyone in Kabul will offer you a cup of tea, whether or not they have any to offer. To accept the tea in some circumstances would embarrass the host, whereas in other cases to decline would be an insult. Knowing the difference requires investing in cultural research before embarking on other forms of data collection. Security scholars are not ethnographers and should not be expected to conduct anthropological work in conflict zones. If researchers cannot navigate the simple challenge of tea, however, then they are at higher risk of unintentionally overextending their hosts in other important security matters.

The onus was therefore on me to navigate the unspoken cultural rules of these polite cultures before engaging in more targeted forms of data collection. In order to be a respectful guest, it was necessary to learn not only the art but also the spirit of these interactions. That meant knowing when and how to respectfully accept and decline invitations when appropriate, with the primary consideration always being the welfare of the host. I am tremendously indebted to my outstanding local colleagues for their guidance in learning these essential social graces.

Carrying out this work properly also required a reflective, intersectional evaluation of positionality in each field environment, a matter often dangerously overlooked by foreign security researchers.[17] From the perspective of my hosts, several aspects of my identity afforded me an "insider" position in these communities.[18] This was advantageous because most foreign academics are at risk of being suspected of espionage by states, armed groups, and local communities alike. These suspicions not only make the principal investigator a target but also jeopardize the security of any local members of the research team who have participated in the project. If respondents mistrust the research team, the resulting data may also be unreliable.

Given the specific security challenges of working with Islamists, my religio-cultural identity mitigated the extent to which my research was perceived as foreign, thus making it possible for me and my field teams to proceed with our work comfortably.[19] In many places, having this status resolved the unique challenges of conducting research on conflict in the Muslim world, allowing me to proceed safely and respectfully. My gender also made it easier for me to ask questions. Female researchers are widely seen as nonthreatening, both in the Muslim world and beyond. These gender dynamics made the fieldwork a respectful, peaceful, and calm process overall.[20]

Of course, many of my talented colleagues who are either male, non-Muslim, or otherwise foreign have conducted rigorous scholarly field research on jihadist groups. Their vantage point is different than mine but just as valuable. For example, if my colleagues and I were to interview the exact same Islamist supporter from Somalia, I might speak to him at the mosque during the day, and my male colleagues might chew khat with him at night. Both sides of our interview subject—the pious and the partygoer—are authentic. Only through trading notes can we get a genuine picture of our Islamist supporter. It is thus vital for all serious security scholars—male and female, insider and outsider—to take note of where they are standing.

Researchers of all backgrounds encounter unique challenges in the field. Indeed, although my particular positionality was advantageous in terms of access, it also put higher expectations on me to uphold local mores, which presented other serious difficulties. For example, although I benefited from having a male relative or patron with me, the fact that women cannot safely travel unaccompanied in these parts of the world was emotionally taxing and infringed on both my privacy and my freedom of mobility. There were also stressful interpersonal interactions, including with people who were genuinely supportive of my research. As a young researcher, one day I wore jeans, and one of my male colleagues threatened to slap me for dressing inappropriately. Managing these complex social challenges, while maintaining a healthy sense of self, required cultural awareness, personal discipline, and a robust support network.

Regardless of this personal stress, however, the fact remains that the foreign scholar has chosen to enter this environment and can also choose to leave it. Accordingly, it is worth noting that the relationship between researchers and their local host communities can often be exploitative and even predatory. Scholars are usually the primary professional and monetary beneficiaries of their own research, as their work advances their academic careers. Even highly policy-relevant work may take many years to yield results, if any, for the host communities.

For those of us who engage in field research, it is therefore a serious ethical responsibility to be mindful of what we take and what we invest back into the societies we study. Local communities often generously assist us with their time, access, and insights; in conflict-affected parts of the world, they do so under conditions of hardship. Considering this imbalance, there are many ways that foreign researchers can demonstrate appreciation and reciprocate this generosity.

Most basically, sharing data and results with local partners in the field makes the research more inclusive. To that end, I shared my published results with my colleagues overseas and ensured that my survey data and coding were publicly available online, so that scholars around the world could have equal access to my materials for replication. Although the ethical obligations of my research did not allow my qualitative field notes to be made public, I did work to present the overall results of my interview research to academic communities in my host societies whenever possible. I have also published my research in local journals and reviewed dissertations and papers from academics at the universities that hosted me during my field study.[21]

Working in parts of the world where there are serious humanitarian crises, I also made it a priority to invest my time, talent, and treasure in local initiatives in my host communities.[22] For example, whenever asked, I was happy to volunteer to provide grassroots aid organizations with proofreading and feedback on their grant proposals and reports. My two-year service with Dr. Hawa Abdi was another way that I worked to give back to the community in a pro bono capacity. Of course, not all humanitarian and aid organizations are created equal, and it took time for me to learn about and build relationships with local staff. Once these ties were developed, however, there were many simple, small interventions I could make to show respect for the communities that I studied, both during and after my research was complete, whenever asked. Although these service responsibilities at times felt heavy, by critically reflecting on the tremendous benefit I received from my research, it became clear that this level of commitment was entirely warranted.

Many scholars who conduct field research in poor or troubled areas are also in a position to offer this type of voluntary professional service. Some scholars, however, are understandably wary of these types of responsibilities. The need can appear infinite, and researchers may fear that if they show a willingness to help, they will be bombarded with requests. Academics are also under tremendous time pressures to publish their work, and the demands of additional voluntary service can seem burdensome. These fears, however, should not prevent researchers from carrying their own weight in their host communities, especially when asked. There are many creative solutions that the researcher can explore to share the burden of these responsibilities in a generous but sustainable manner. Maintaining a commitment to the principle of service necessarily requires strong and healthy boundaries that are self-protecting.

Researchers are especially well positioned to make valuable contributions to local universities and academic institutions. It is worth considering that many people living in conflict zones continue to attend schools and universities, and rarely do they enjoy the benefit of learning from guest lecturers and visiting scholars. Providing a well-planned lecture or seminar series can enrich the academic environment of these local institutions for both students and faculty alike. My experiences lecturing in Peshawar, Islamabad, Mogadishu, and Nairobi have been deeply rewarding, and I continue to enjoy being invited to speak at these universities. Mentoring junior students, giving guest lectures, and participating in local academic events in my host communities has made me a better scholar and a happier person. The young students at these institutions are exceptionally bright and thoughtful and a most encouraging source of hope for the future of these troubled regions.

As violence across the modern Muslim world surges, there is an urgent need for new scholarly research on contemporary jihadist groups in civil war–affected states. The challenges of conducting fieldwork in these regions are indeed significant; to succeed, this work requires preliminary assessments, in-field preparation, and robust research networks and partnerships with local teams. Developing appropriate and ethical methods for collecting data on these topics involves careful preparation at the design stage and humility throughout the research process. The challenges of this work are not, however, insurmountable, nor should they deter promising scholars from investing in focused, rigorous, and ethical fieldwork on these critical topics.

Contemporary international security crises are rapidly evolving. Fieldwork is essential for ensuring that our security research on jihadist groups is rigorous and that our policy interventions in these crisis zones are effective. As scholars, we are uniquely positioned to provide evidence-based analysis of the most pressing international security questions in the world today. In pursuing this work, we are guided not only by the existing literature on methods and ethics in civil war research but also by our own experiences. Indeed, our insights gleaned from the field add to this ongoing discussion about research methodology, which can help guide the next generations of scholars in search of truth in these dangerous places.

Notes

INTRODUCTION

1. Gun salesman 1 in Bula Hawa, Somalia. Unreleased film footage, copyright Shelley Saywell, *Devil's Bargain: A Journey into the Small Arms Trade*, DVD, documentary (Bishari Films, 2008). Quotes drawn from raw documentary film footage. I was engaged in the filmmaking process for this project as a fixer in East Africa and was responsible for providing access to the film crew to collect this footage. For a discussion of my involvement in this project, please see the Appendix on methodology.

2. Gun salesman 2 in Bula Hawa, Somalia, unreleased footage, Saywell, *Devil's Bargain*.

3. Interview with family member of Pakistani arms dealers, Toronto, Canada, July 2015.

4. Amnesty International, "Women in Afghanistan: A Human Rights Catastrophe" (Amnesty International, May 17, 1995), 5.

5. Female internally displaced person in Bula Hawa, Somalia, unreleased footage, Saywell, *Devil's Bargain*.

6. Hadith are authenticated and interpreted through the method of *Ijtihaad* (Islamic legal reasoning), wherein a chain of transmission needs to be established. This process confirms that the Hadith is both reliable and that the interpretation is consistent with legal opinions established in the historical precedent. *Ijtihaad* is performed by high-level Islamic scholars, such as ulema, muftis, and qadis, but the implications of their decisions are discussed widely within Islamic intellectual circles.

7. For a discussion of jihadist expansionism in the Levant, see Andrew Phillips, "The Islamic State's Challenge to International Order," *Australian Journal of International Affairs* 68, no. 5 (2014): 495–98; Aymenn Jawad al-Tamimi, "The Dawn of the Islamic State of Iraq and Ash-Sham," *Current Trends in Islamist Ideology* 16 (March 2014): 5–15.

8. Although state consolidation is a high bar for measuring political order, there is evidence that these Islamist groups did indeed achieve some measure of consolidation.

As the African politics literature suggests, an initial step toward state consolidation is establishing control over populations and borders. See Jeffrey Herbst, "Migration, the Politics of Protest, and State Consolidation in Africa," *African Affairs* 89, no. 355 (1990): 22; Jeffrey Herbst, "War and the State in Africa," *International Security* 14, no. 4 (1990): 118. Looking at consolidation as a spectrum, from strong states to failed ones, these Islamists show a much higher degree of political consolidation than their rivals.

9. For an extended discussion on the conceptual definition of modern jihadist proto-states, see Brynjar Lia, "Understanding Jihadi Proto-States," *Perspectives on Terrorism* 9, no. 4 (July 21, 2015): 31–44.

10. Olivier Roy, *Globalized Islam: The Search for a New Ummah* (New York: Columbia University Press, 2004); Cheryl Benard, *Civil Democratic Islam: Partners, Resources, and Strategies*, National Security Research Division (Santa Monica, CA: RAND Corporation, 2003); Nathan C. Funk, *Islam and Peacemaking in the Middle East* (Boulder, CO: Lynne Rienner, 2009).

11. While these are distinct approaches within the global Islamist community, there is also learning and evolution within each of these traditions. For example, Islamist groups that originated out of a Deobandi tradition in Pakistan and Afghanistan have evolved over the past decade to adopt Salafi and Takfiri ideas, fundamentally transforming their ideological orientation. While this variation is important, a complete analysis of the ideological variation within the global jihadi community is beyond the scope of this particular book. For a discussion, see Faisal Devji, *Landscapes of the Jihad: Militancy, Morality, Modernity* (Ithaca, NY: Cornell University Press, 2005); see also Thomas Hegghammer, "The Rise of Muslim Foreign Fighters: Islam and the Globalization of Jihad," *International Security* 35, no. 3 (December 1, 2010): 53–94.

12. Thomas Hegghammer, "The Ideological Hybridization of Jihadi Groups," *Current Trends in Islamist Ideology* 9 (July 2009): 26–45; Jacob N. Shapiro and C. Christine Fair, "Understanding Support for Islamist Militancy in Pakistan," *International Security* 34, no. 3 (January 1, 2010): 79–118.

13. Islamist groups and movements vary in both structure and ideology over time and space, and there is significant internal debate and difference of opinion on the goals, scope, and purpose of political Islam. Given the wide range of definitions in the existing literature, the term "Islamist" can include everything from a nonviolent student group to a terrorist network. For further explanation see Quintan Wiktorowicz, ed., *Islamic Activism: A Social Movement Theory Approach* (Bloomington: Indiana University Press, 2004); Martha Crenshaw, "The Debate over 'New' vs. 'Old' Terrorism," in *Values and Violence*, ed. Ibrahim A. Karawan, Wayne McCormack, and Stephen E. Reynolds (N.p.: Springer, 2008), 117–36.

14. Olivier Roy explains the phenomenon of globalized Islam as a "deterritorialisation" of Islamic culture. I build on Roy's detailed theoretical work to develop this concept. Roy, *Globalized Islam*; Benedict Anderson, *Imagined Communities: Reflections on*

the Origin and Spread of Nationalism (London: Verso, 2006); for a criticism of this characterization, see Salwa Ismail, *Rethinking Islamist Politics: Culture, the State and Islamism* (New York: I. B. Tauris, 2006).

15. The literal definition of jihad is "to struggle," and it is used to describe struggle against personal hardships as well as struggle against political or military repression. See Tibi Bassam, "War and Peace in Islam," in *The Ethics of War and Peace: Religious and Secular Perspectives*, ed. Terry Nardin (Princeton, NJ: Princeton University Press, 1996), 128–45; Sohail H. Hashmi, "Interpreting the Islamic Ethics of War and Peace," in *The Ethics of War and Peace: Religious and Secular Perspectives*, ed. Terry Nardin (Princeton, NJ: Princeton University Press, 1996), 146–66; Michael David Bonner, *Jihad in Islamic History: Doctrines and Practice* (Princeton, NJ: Princeton University Press, 2006); Bernard Lewis, *Islam: The Religion and the People* (Upper Saddle River, NJ: Wharton School Publishing, 2009); Ahmed Rashid, *Jihad: The Rise of Militant Islam in Central Asia* (New Haven, CT: Yale University Press, 2002); Sayed Abdul Ala Maudoodi, *Jihad in Islam*, 7th ed. (Lahore: Islamic Publications, 2001); Sayyid Quṭb, *Social Justice in Islam* (Oneonta, NY: Islamic Publications International, 2000); Mahmoud Ayoub, *Islam: Faith and History* (Oxford: Oneworld, 2004).

16. For a definition of contemporary jihadism and a characterization of jihadists as anti-Western "militant Sunni Muslim activists," which emerge out of anticolonial Islamism, see Firestone Reuven, " 'Jihadism' as a New Religious Movement," in *The Cambridge Companion to New Religious Movements*, ed. Olav Hammer and Mikael Rothstein (New York: Cambridge University Press, 2012), 263–85. For a detailed account of the rise and evolution of modern political Islam and jihadism, see Gilles Kepel, *Jihad: The Trail of Political Islam*, rev. ed. (London; New York: I. B. Tauris, 2009). For a comprehensive and detailed discussion of global anti-Western jihadist movements and their local and global supporters, see Farhad Khosrokhavar, *Inside Jihadism: Understanding Jihadi Movements Worldwide* (Boulder, CO: Paradigm, 2009).

17. Notably, clannism in Somalia is very multilayered. The Somali word for clan, *qabiil*, is an enormously complex and nested concept. All Somalis have multiple levels of clan identity, and the word *qabiil* can connote either major clan or subclan identity, depending on the context. For a discussion of clan dynamics, see Ioan M. Lewis, *Blood and Bone: The Call of Kinship in Somali Society* (Lawrenceville, NJ: Red Sea Press, 1994); Markus V. Hoehne, "Political Representation in Somalia: Citizenship, Clanism and Territoriality," in *Accord Issue 21: Whose Peace Is It Anyway? Connecting Somali and International Peacemaking*, ed. Mark Bradbury and Sally Healy (London: Conciliations Resources and Interpeace, 2010), 34–37; Florence Ssereo, "Clanpolitics, Clan-Democracy and Conflict Regulation in Africa: The Experience of Somalia," *Global Review of Ethnopolitics* 2, nos. 3–4 (March 2003): 25–40; Abdalla Omar Mansur, "The Nature of the Somali Clan System," in *The Invention of Somalia*, ed. Ali Jimale Ahmed (Lawrenceville, NJ: Red Sea

Press, 1995), 117–34; J. Abbink, *The Total Somali Clan Genealogy*, 2nd ed., African Studies Centre Working Paper 84 (Leiden: African Studies Centre, 2009).

18. Indeed, Gilligan explains that "[i]n the social sciences, in political discourse and in everyday conversation the English language meaning of the term ethnicity is closely related to the terms race, nation, a people, clan and tribe." Chris Gilligan, "Race and Ethnicity," in *Routledge Handbook of Ethnic Conflict*, ed. Karl Cordell and Stefan Wolff (New York: Routledge, 2011), 79–90, quotation on p. 79. Freeman argues that "Distinctions between tribes, ethnic groups and nations have rarely been made systematically or precisely in social science." Michael Freeman, "Theories of Ethnicity, Tribalism and Nationalism," in *Ethnic Conflict, Tribal Politics: A Global Perspective*, ed. Kenneth Christie (Richmond, Surrey, UK: Curzon, 1998), 15–33, quotation on p. 17. Fenton argues that the terms ethnic group, race, and nation share "a single centre—or 'core'. . . . Common to all three is an idea of descent or ancestry and very closely implicated in all three ways we find ideas about culture . . . [which] typically includes myths about the past, beliefs about the 'kind of people we are,' and the idea that 'culture' defines a group." Steve Fenton, *Ethnicity* (Malden, MA: Polity, 2003), 13. For a more extensive discussion of these concepts, see Walker Connor, "A Nation Is a Nation, Is a State, Is an Ethnic Group Is a . . . ," *Ethnic and Racial Studies* 1, no. 4 (October 1978): 379–88; Michael W. Hughey, *New Tribalisms: The Resurgence of Race and Ethnicity* (New York: New York University Press, 1998); Richard Jenkins, *Rethinking Ethnicity*, 2nd ed. (London: SAGE, 2008).

19. Crawford Young, *The Postcolonial State in Africa: Fifty Years of Independence, 1960–2010* (Madison: University of Wisconsin Press, 2012), 262; Guntram Henrik Herb and David H. Kaplan, eds., *Nested Identities: Nationalism, Territory, and Scale* (Oxford: Rowman & Littlefield, 1999).

20. For a critique of the use of the term "warlords" in the existing literature, see Roland Marchal, "Warlordism and Terrorism: How to Obscure an Already Confusing Crisis? The Case of Somalia," *International Affairs* 83, no. 6 (November 1, 2007): 1091–1106.

21. The term "warlord" is the subject of much controversy. Roland Marchal argues that the term "warlord" is not only poorly conceived but also overused (ibid.). Kimberly Marten defines the term as "individuals who control small pieces of territory using a combination of force and patronage." Kimberly Marten, *Warlords: Strong-Arm Brokers in Weak States* (Ithaca, NY: Cornell University Press, 2012), 3. Antonio Giustozzi proposes that a warlord "is a particular type of ruler, whose basic characteristics are his independence from any higher authority and his control of a 'private army,' which responds to him personally. A warlord who accepts subordination to another warlord becomes, in this definition, a vassal or a client warlord." Antonio Giustozzi, "Respectable Warlords? The Politics of State-Building in Post-Taleban Afghanistan," in *Working Papers Series*, Crisis States Programme–Development Research Centre (London: London School of Economics, 2003),

2. For a discussion on warlord politics in Africa, see William Reno, *Warlord Politics and African States* (Boulder, CO: Lynne Rienner, 1998). Scholars studying early twentieth-century Chinese warlords have employed alternate definitions; see Hsi-sheng Chi, *Warlord Politics in China, 1916–1928*, 1st ed. (Stanford, CA: Stanford University Press, 1976); Jerome Ch'en, "Defining Chinese Warlords and Their Factions," *Bulletin of the School of Oriental and African Studies, University of London* 31, no. 3 (1968): 563–600.

22. Note that some businesses hire private security to guard their consignments. For example, Le Sage makes the important observation that the distinction between a businessperson and a warlord is not perfectly neat; however, despite similarities, these are two conceptually distinct categories. See Andre Le Sage, "Somalia: Sovereign Disguise for a Mogadishu Mafia," *Review of African Political Economy* 29, no. 91 (March 1, 2002): 132–38.

23. Ibid.; Ahmed Rashid, *Taliban: Militant Islam, Oil and Fundamentalism in Central Asia* (New Haven, CT: Yale University Press, 2001); Jeanne K. Giraldo and Harold A. Trinkunas, *Terrorism Financing and State Responses: A Comparative Perspective* (Stanford, CA: Stanford University Press, 2007).

CHAPTER 1

1. The word *harash* loosely translates to "sale" but indicates that a vendor is willing to auction his or her goods wholesale. It signals that the goods in question have flooded the market, and supply exceeds demand. The pressure to offload these goods is therefore high.

2. Aisha Ahmad, "Agenda for Peace or Budget for War?," *International Journal* 67, no. 2 (2012): 313–31.

3. A tipping point model suggests that a rapid shift in social process happens if a sufficiently large enough number of actors are convinced of the existence of a better and viable alternative, and if these actors conceive of a mechanism through which they could coordinate their expectations. Gretchen Helmke and Steven Levitsky, "Informal Institutions and Comparative Politics: A Research Agenda," *Perspectives on Politics* 2, no. 4 (December 2004): 732. For an application of the tipping point model, see David D. Laitin, *Identity in Formation: The Russian-Speaking Populations in the New Abroad* (Ithaca, NY: Cornell University Press, 1998). Also see Thomas C. Schelling, *Micromotives and Macrobehavior* (New York: W. W. Norton, 1978); Thomas C. Schelling, *The Strategy of Conflict* (Cambridge, MA: Harvard University Press, 1960).

4. Within the literature on revolutions and social movements, threshold, bandwagon, and critical mass models explain how and why individual actions can precipitate rapid, unexpected levels of mass participation, with the idea that "relatively small movements can push above some critical level, triggering a process of positive feedback that leads to much more dramatic (nonlinear) change." Paul

Pierson, "Big, Slow-Moving, and . . . Invisible: Macrosocial Processes in the Study of Comparative Politics," in *Comparative Historical Analysis in the Social Sciences*, ed. James Mahoney and Dietrich Rueschemeyer (Cambridge: Cambridge University Press, 2003), 177–207, quotation on p. 184. See also: Mark Granovetter, "Threshold Models of Collective Behavior," *American Journal of Sociology* 83, no. 6 (1978): 1420–43; Michael W. Macy, "Chains of Cooperation: Threshold Effects in Collective Action," *American Sociological Review* 56, no. 6 (December 1, 1991): 730–47; Barbara Salert, "On the Concept of Threshold," in *Missing Elements in Political Inquiry: Logic and Levels of Analysis*, ed. J. A. Gillespie and D. A. Zinnes (Beverley Hills, CA: Sage, 1982), 61–80; Timur Kuran, "Sparks and Prairie Fires: A Theory of Unanticipated Political Revolution," *Public Choice* 61, no. 1 (April 1989): 41–74; Timur Kuran, "Now Out of Never: The Element of Surprise in the East European Revolution of 1989," *World Politics* 44, no. 1 (1991): 7–48; Gerald Marwell, *The Critical Mass in Collective Action: A Micro-Social Theory* (New York: Cambridge University Press, 1993); Anthony R. Oberschall, *Social Conflict and Social Movements* (Englewood Cliffs, NJ: Prentice-Hall, 1994).

5. Preliminary research in Syria has found that these criminal networks are related to Arab tribal structures in rebel-held areas. For further discussion, see Reinoud Leenders and Steven Heydemann, "Popular Mobilization in Syria: Opportunity and Threat, and the Social Networks of the Early Risers," *Mediterranean Politics* 17, no. 2 (July 1, 2012): 139–59.

6. Chris Dishman, "Terrorism, Crime, and Transformation," *Studies in Conflict & Terrorism* 24, no. 1 (2001): 43–58; Steven Hutchinson and Pat O'Malley, "A Crime–Terror Nexus? Thinking on Some of the Links between Terrorism and Criminality," *Studies in Conflict & Terrorism* 30, no. 12 (2007): 1095–1107. See also Vanda Felbab-Brown, *Shooting Up: Counterinsurgency and the War on Drugs* (Washington, DC: Brookings Institution Press, 2009); Daveed Gartensten-Ross et al., "The Crisis in North Africa: Implications for Europe and Options for EU Policymakers," *Clingendael Report* (The Hague: Netherlands Institute of International Relations, April 2015); Jonathan P. Caulkins, Mark A. Kleiman, and Jonathan D. Kulick, *Drug Production and Trafficking, Counterdrug Policies, and Security and Governance in Afghanistan* (New York University: Center on International Cooperation, April 10, 2011), 35; Antonio Giustozzi, "War and Peace Economies of Afghanistan's Strongmen," *International Peacekeeping* 14, no. 1 (January 1, 2007): 75–89; Seth G. Jones, *Counterinsurgency in Afghanistan* (Santa Monica, CA: RAND National Defense Research Institute, 2008).

7. Louise I. Shelley, *Dirty Entanglements: Corruption, Crime, and Terrorism* (New York: Cambridge University Press, 2014).

8. Peter Andreas, *Blue Helmets and Black Markets: The Business of Survival in the Siege of Sarajevo* (Ithaca, NY: Cornell University Press, 2011); Timothy Raeymaekers, *Violent Capitalism and Hybrid Identity in the Eastern Congo* (New York: Cambridge University Press, 2014).

9. Ahmed Rashid, *Taliban: Militant Islam, Oil and Fundamentalism in Central Asia* (New Haven, CT: Yale University Press, 2001); Barnett R. Rubin, "The Political Economy of War and Peace in Afghanistan," *World Development* 28, no. 10 (October 2000): 1789–1803; Cedric Barnes and Harun Hassan, "The Rise and Fall of Mogadishu's Islamic Courts," *Journal of Eastern African Studies* 1, no. 2 (July 1, 2007): 151–60; Roland Marchal, "Islamic Political Dynamics after the Somali Civil War: Before and After September 11," in *Islamism and Its Enemies in the Horn of Africa*, ed. Alexander De Waal (Bloomington: Indiana University Press, 2004), 114–45.

10. Paul Collier and Anke Hoeffler, "Greed and Grievance in Civil War," *Oxford Economic Papers* 56, no. 4 (2004): 563–95. Collier finds that the location of these resources affects rebel incentives with regard to violence and territorial control. See Paul Collier, "Doing Well out of War: An Economic Perspective," in *Greed and Grievance: Economic Agendas in Civil War*, ed. Mats Berdal and David M. Malone (Boulder, CO: Lynne Rienner, 2000). See also Paivi Lujala, "The Spoils of Nature: Armed Civil Conflict and Rebel Access to Natural Resources," *Journal of Peace Research* 47, no. 1 (2010): 15–28; Karen Ballentine and Jake Sherman, eds., *The Political Economy of Armed Conflict: Beyond Greed and Grievance* (Boulder, CO: Lynne Rienner, 2003); Paul Collier and Anke Hoeffler, "Resource Rents, Governance, and Conflict," *Journal of Conflict Resolution* 49, no. 4 (2005): 625–33; David Keen, *The Economic Functions of Violence in Civil Wars*, Adelphi Paper 320 (Oxford: Oxford University Press, 1998); Philippe Le Billon, "The Political Ecology of War: Natural Resources and Armed Conflicts," *Political Geography* 20, no. 5 (June 2001): 561–84; Michael Ross, "A Closer Look at Oil, Diamonds, and Civil War," *Domestic Political Violence and Civil War* 1, no. 1 (2013): 265–300; Indra De Soysa and Eric Neumayer, "Resource Wealth and the Risk of Civil War Onset: Results from a New Dataset of Natural Resource Rents, 1970–1999," *Conflict Management and Peace Science* 24, no. 3 (August 7, 2007): 201–18; Richard Snyder and Ravi Bhavnani, "Diamonds, Blood, and Taxes: A Revenue-Centered Framework for Explaining Political Order," *Journal of Conflict Resolution* 49, no. 4 (August 1, 2005): 563–97. By contrast, Humphreys argues that natural resources are associated with shorter wars, and that natural resource wars are more likely to end with military victory for one side than other wars. Macartan Humphreys, "Natural Resources, Conflict, and Conflict Resolution: Uncovering the Mechanisms," *Journal of Conflict Resolution* 49, no. 4 (August 1, 2005): 508–37.

11. Much of this literature focuses on non-lootable resources, such as petroleum. See, e.g., Hossein Mahdavy, "The Patterns and Problems of Economic Development in Rentier States: The Case of Iran," in *Studies in the Economic History of the Middle East, from the Rise of Islam to the Present Day*, ed. M. Cook (London: Oxford University Press, 1970), 428–67; Hazem Beblawi and Giacomo Luciani, eds., *The Rentier State: Nation, State, and the Integration of the Arab World*, vol. 2 (London: Croom Helm, 1987); Terry Lynn Karl, *The Paradox of Plenty: Oil*

Booms and Petro-States (Berkeley: University of California Press, 1997); Thad Dunning, *Crude Democracy: Natural Resource Wealth and Political Regimes* (Cambridge: Cambridge University Press, 2008). Whether or not petroleum should be considered a non-lootable resource is up for debate given that ISIS has produced vast amounts of revenue by smuggling crude oil. Regardless, petroleum is a commodity that requires huge capital investment by actors with a long-term horizon for investment, which makes it non-lootable unless the infrastructure is already in place. Nonetheless, there is also evidence that lootable resource abundance may affect state weakness. See, e.g., Paul Richards, *Fighting for the Rainforest: War, Youth and Resources in Sierra Leone* (Oxford: James Currey, 1996).

12. James D. Fearon and David D. Laitin, "Ethnicity, Insurgency, and Civil War," *American Political Science Review* 97, no. 1 (February 2003): 75–90; James D. Fearon, "Primary Commodity Exports and Civil War," *Journal of Conflict Resolution* 49, no. 4 (August 1, 2005): 483–507; Theda Skocpol, "Rentier State and Shi'a Islam in the Iranian Revolution," *Theory and Society* 11, no. 3 (1982): 265–83. Others have argued that rentier states are actually more durable against domestic uprisings, as regimes can use resource revenue to bolster their political and military positions against possible challengers. See, e.g., Beblawi and Luciani, *Rentier State*; Karl, *Paradox of Plenty*; Benjamin Smith, "Oil Wealth and Regime Survival in the Developing World, 1960–1999," *American Journal of Political Science* 48, no. 2 (April 1, 2004): 232–46. For a test of these two explanations, see Matthias Basedau and Jann Lay, "Resource Curse or Rentier Peace? The Ambiguous Effects of Oil Wealth and Oil Dependence on Violent Conflict," *Journal of Peace Research* 46, no. 6 (2009): 757–76.

13. William Reno, *Warlord Politics and African States* (Boulder, CO: Lynne Rienner, 1998).

14. Peter Andreas, *Blue Helmets and Black Markets: The Business of Survival in the Siege of Sarajevo* (Ithaca, NY: Cornell University Press, 2011).

15. The few scholars who have researched business actors in civil wars are: Andre Le Sage, "Somalia: Sovereign Disguise for a Mogadishu Mafia," *Review of African Political Economy* 29, no. 91 (March 1, 2002): 132–38; Stig Jarle Hansen, *Al-Shabaab in Somalia: The History and Ideology of a Militant Islamist Group, 2005–2012* (New York: Oxford University Press, 2013); Annette Idler, "Exploring Agreements of Convenience Made among Violent Non-State Actors," *Perspectives on Terrorism* 6, nos. 4–5 (September 10, 2012), 63–84; Annette Idler, María Belén Garrido, and Cécile Mouly, "Peace Territories in Colombia: Comparing Civil Resistance in Two War-Torn Communities," *Journal of Peacebuilding & Development* 10, no. 3 (September 2, 2015): 1–15; Andreas, *Blue Helmets and Black Markets*.

16. Adam Smith, *The Wealth of Nations* (New York: E. P. Dutton, 1910).

17. Simon Chesterman, Michael Ignatieff, and Ramesh Chandra Thakur, *Making States Work: State Failure and the Crisis of Governance* (Tokyo: United Nations University Press, 2005); John Paul Lederach, *Building Peace: Sustainable Reconciliation in*

Divided Societies (Washington, DC: United States Institute of Peace Press, 1997); Ashraf Ghani and Clare Lockhart, *Fixing Failed States: A Framework for Rebuilding a Fractured World* (New York: Oxford University Press, 2008); Robert I. Rotberg, ed., *When States Fail: Causes and Consequences* (Princeton, NJ: Princeton University Press, 2004); Stephen John Stedman, Donald S. Rothchild, and Elizabeth M. Cousens, eds., *Ending Civil Wars: The Implementation of Peace Agreements* (Boulder, CO: Lynne Rienner, 2002); Taisier Mohamed Ahmed Ali and Robert O. Matthews, eds., *Durable Peace: Challenges for Peacebuilding in Africa* (Toronto: University of Toronto Press, 2004).

18. Barnett R. Rubin, *The Fragmentation of Afghanistan: State Formation and Collapse in the International System*, 2nd ed. (New Haven, CT: Yale University Press, 2002).

19. Jeremy M. Weinstein, *Inside Rebellion: The Politics of Insurgent Violence* (Cambridge: Cambridge University Press, 2007).

20. My survey data and coding are available through the Harvard Dataverse System, published in conjunction with an article featuring this study. See Aisha Ahmad, "The Security Bazaar: Business Interests and Islamist Power in Civil War Somalia," *International Security* 39, no. 3 (January 1, 2015): 89–117. Supplementary Materials are available at https://dataverse.harvard.edu/dataverse/AhmadSomDat2015.

21. Aburahman M. Abdullahi (Baadiyow), "The Islah Movement: Islamic Moderation in War-Torn Somalia" (paper presented at Second Nordic Horn of Africa Conference, Oslo, Norway, 2008).

22. Bryan C. Price, "Targeting Top Terrorists: How Leadership Decapitation Contributes to Counterterrorism," *International Security* 36, no. 4 (2012): 9–46; Patrick B. Johnston, "Does Decapitation Work?: Assessing the Effectiveness of Leadership Targeting in Counterinsurgency Campaigns," *International Security* 36, no. 4 (2012): 47–79; Austin Long, "Whack-a-Mole or Coup de Grace? Institutionalization and Leadership Targeting in Iraq and Afghanistan," *Security Studies* 23, no. 3 (2014): 471–512; Keith Patrick Dear, "Beheading the Hydra? Does Killing Terrorist or Insurgent Leaders Work?," *Defence Studies* 13, no. 3 (2013): 293–337.

23. Charles Tilly, "War Making and State Making as Organized Crime," in *Bringing the State Back In*, ed. Peter B. Evans, Dietrich Rueschemeyer, and Theda Skocpol (Cambridge: Cambridge University Press, 1985), 169–91; Youssef Cohen, Brian R. Brown, and A. F. K. Organski, "The Paradoxical Nature of State Making: The Violent Creation of Order," *American Political Science Review* 75, no. 4 (December 1981): 901–10.

24. Charles Tilly, *Coercion, Capital, and European States, AD 990–1990* (Cambridge, MA: Wiley-Blackwell, 1990), 15.

25. Hendrik Spruyt, *The Sovereign State and Its Competitors: An Analysis of Systems Change* (Princeton, NJ: Princeton University Press, 1994). See also Hendrik Spruyt, "War, Trade and State Formation," in *The Oxford Handbook of Political Science*, ed. Robert E. Goodin (Oxford: Oxford University Press, 2009), 567–92.

26. Tilly, "War Making and State Making as Organized Crime," 170.

27. Even though Thies finds that modern civil wars do increase extractive capacity, this has not led to stronger states. Cameron G. Thies, "State Building, Interstate and Intrastate Rivalry: A Study of Post-Colonial Developing Country Extractive Efforts, 1975–2000," *International Studies Quarterly* 48, no. 1 (January 29, 2004): 53–72; Cameron G. Thies, "The Political Economy of State Building in Sub-Saharan Africa," *Journal of Politics* 69, no. 3 (August 2007): 716–31.

28. Reno, *Warlord Politics and African States*.

29. Robert H. Jackson and Carl G. Rosberg, "Why Africa's Weak States Persist: The Empirical and the Juridical in Statehood," *World Politics* 35, no. 1 (1982): 1–24; Boaz Atzili, "When Good Fences Make Bad Neighbors: Fixed Borders, State Weakness, and International Conflict," *International Security* 31, no. 3 (2006): 139–73; Mohammed Ayoob, *The Third World Security Predicament: State Making, Regional Conflict, and the International System* (Boulder, CO: Lynne Rienner, 1995); Michael C. Desch, "War and Strong States, Peace and Weak States?," *International Organization* 50, no. 2 (April 1996): 237–68; Jeffrey Ira Herbst, *States and Power in Africa: Comparative Lessons in Authority and Control* (Princeton, NJ: Princeton University Press, 2000); Robert H. Jackson, *Quasi-States: Sovereignty, International Relations and the Third World* (Cambridge: Cambridge University Press, 1993).

30. Jeffrey Herbst, "Responding to Civil War in Africa," *International Security* 21, no. 3 (Winter 1996): 120–44.

31. Collier and Hoeffler, "Greed and Grievance in Civil War"; James D. Fearon, "Why Do Some Civil Wars Last So Much Longer Than Others?," *Journal of Peace Research* 41, no. 3 (May 1, 2004): 275–301; Ted Robert Gurr, *Peoples versus States: Minorities at Risk in the New Century* (Washington, DC: United States Institute of Peace Press, 2000).

32. Wendy Pearlman and Kathleen Cunningham, "Nonstate Actors, Fragmentation, and Conflict Processes," *Journal of Conflict Resolution* 56, no. 1 (2012): 3–15; Kathleen Gallagher Cunningham, "Actor Fragmentation and Civil War Bargaining: How Internal Divisions Generate Civil Conflict," *American Journal of Political Science* 57, no. 3 (n.d.): 659–72; Kathleen Cunningham, Kristin Bakke, and Lee Seymour, "Shirts Today, Skins Tomorrow: Dual Contests and the Effects of Fragmentation in Self-Determination Disputes," *Journal of Conflict Resolution* 56, no. 1 (2012): 67–93; David E. Cunningham, Kristian Skrede Gleditsch, and Idean Salehyan, "It Takes Two: A Dyadic Analysis of Civil War Duration and Outcome," *Journal of Conflict Resolution* 53, no. 4 (2009): 570–97; Michael Findley and Peter Rudloff, "Combatant Fragmentation and the Dynamics of Civil Wars," *British Journal of Political Science* 42, no. 4 (October 2012): 879–901.

33. Stathis Kalyvas, "Ethnic Defection in Civil War," *Comparative Political Studies* 41, no. 8 (2008): 1043–68; Kathleen Gallagher Cunningham, "Divide and Conquer or Divide and Concede: How Do States Respond to Internally Divided Separatists?," *American Political Science Review* 105, no. 2 (2011): 275–97; Kelly M. Greenhill and

Solomon Major, "The Perils of Profiling Civil War Spoilers and the Collapse of Intrastate Peace Accords," *International Security* 31, no. 3 (2006): 7–40; Wendy Pearlman, "Spoiling Inside and Out: Internal Political Contestation and the Middle East Peace Process," *International Security* 33, no. 3 (2008): 79–109.

34. There is considerable debate about the causes of intragroup fragmentation and conflict. Key explanations highlight the role of ethnicity, clan, tribe, religion, ideology, socialization, micro-level organizational structure, and social capital or social networks in influencing cohesion. See Ashutosh Varshney, "Nationalism, Ethnic Conflict, and Rationality," *Perspective on Politics* 1, no. 1 (March 2003): 85–99; Henry E. Hale, *The Foundations of Ethnic Politics: Separatism of States and Nations in Eurasia and the World* (New York: Cambridge University Press, 2008); Scott Gates, "Recruitment and Allegiance: The Microfoundations of Rebellion," *Journal of Conflict Resolution* 46, no. 1 (2002): 111–30; Abdulkader H. Sinno, *Organizations at War in Afghanistan and beyond* (Ithaca, NY: Cornell University Press, 2008); Paul Staniland, "Organizing Insurgency: Networks, Resources, and Rebellion in South Asia," *International Security* 37, no. 1 (July 1, 2012): 142–77; Paul Staniland, "Between a Rock and a Hard Place: Insurgent Fratricide, Ethnic Defection, and the Rise of Pro-State Paramilitaries," *Journal of Conflict Resolution* 56, no. 1 (2012): 16–40; Paul Staniland, *Networks of Rebellion: Explaining Insurgent Cohesion and Collapse* (Ithaca, NY: Cornell University Press, 2014); Cunningham, Bakke, and Seymour, "Shirts Today, Skins Tomorrow"; Paul D. Kenny, "Structural Integrity and Cohesion in Insurgent Organizations: Evidence from Protracted Conflicts in Ireland and Burma," *International Studies Review* 12, no. 4 (December 1, 2010): 533–55; Victor Asal, Mitchell Brown, and Angela Dalton, "Why Split? Organizational Splits among Ethnopolitical Organizations in the Middle East," *Journal of Conflict Resolution* 56, no. 1 (2012): 94–117; Theodore McLauchlin and Wendy Pearlman, "Out-Group Conflict, In-Group Unity? Exploring the Effect of Repression on Intramovement Cooperation," *Journal of Conflict Resolution* 56, no. 1 (February 1, 2012): 41–66.

35. See, e.g., Ballentine and Sherman, *Political Economy of Armed Conflict*; Macartan Humphreys, "Natural Resources, Conflict, and Conflict Resolution Uncovering the Mechanisms," *Journal of Conflict Resolution* 49, no. 4 (August 1, 2005): 508–37; Mats R. Berdal and David Malone, eds., *Greed & Grievance: Economic Agendas in Civil Wars* (Ottawa: International Development Research Centre, 2000); Fearon, "Primary Commodity Exports and Civil War"; Ross, "A Closer Look at Oil, Diamonds, and Civil War"; Soysa and Neumayer, "Resource Wealth and the Risk of Civil War Onset"; Weinstein, *Inside Rebellion*.

CHAPTER 2

1. Many Islamic scholars have warned that the black flags prophecy in the opening epigraph of this chapter may have been a fabrication and ought be considered unreliable; however, its symbolic power in modern jihad remains striking.

2. The official flag of the Afghan Taliban is white with a black inscription of the Muslim declaration of faith. The black flag was flown with al-Qaeda during the mid- to late 1990s at training bases in Afghanistan and also in other parts of the world where they had bases. These were the first modern displays of this symbol. The use of the flag signaled an identity claim on the part of al-Qaeda that they are the prophesied army from Khorasan.

3. For a historical account of the rise of ISIS, see William Faizi McCants, *The ISIS Apocalypse: The History, Strategy, and Doomsday Vision of the Islamic State* (New York: St. Martin's Press, 2015).

4. There is very strong scholarly work on ideology and identity politics in these divided societies. See Kenneth Menkhaus, "There and Back Again in Somalia," *Middle East Research and Information Project*, February 11, 2007, which provides a clan explanation of the ICU in Somalia; Rasul Bakhsh Rais, *Recovering the Frontier State: War, Ethnicity, and the State in Afghanistan* (Karachi, Pakistan; New York: Lexington Books, 2009); Abdulkader Sinno, "Explaining the Taliban's Ability to Mobilize the Pashtuns," in *The Taliban and the Crisis of Afghanistan*, ed. Robert D. Crews and Amin Tarzi (Cambridge, MA: Harvard University Press, 2009), 59–98, which provides an ethnic explanation of the Taliban's success in Afghanistan; and Ahmed Rashid, *Taliban: Militant Islam, Oil and Fundamentalism in Central Asia* (New Haven, CT: Yale University Press, 2010). See also Roland Marchal, "Islamic Political Dynamics after the Somali Civil War: Before and after September 11," in *Islamism and Its Enemies in the Horn of Africa*, ed. Alexander De Waal (Bloomington: Indiana University Press, 2004), 114–45; Kenneth Menkhaus, "Political Islam in Somalia," *Middle East Policies*, 9, no. 1 (March 2002): 109–23; Kenneth Menkhaus, "Somalia and Somaliland: Terrorism, Political Islam, and State Collapse," in *Battling Terrorism in the Horn of Africa*, ed. Robert I. Rotberg (Washington, DC: Brookings Institution Press, 2005), 23–47; Farhad Khosrokhavar, *Inside Jihadism: Understanding Jihadi Movements Worldwide* (Boulder, CO: Paradigm Publishers, 2009); Angel Rabasa, *Radical Islam in East Africa* (Santa Monica, CA: RAND Corporation, 2009); Kathleen Collins, "Ideas, Networks, and Islamist Movements: Evidence from Central Asia and the Caucasus," *World Politics* 60, no. 1 (October 2007): 64–96.

5. Assaf Moghadam, *The Globalization of Martyrdom: Al Qaeda, Salafi Jihad, and the Diffusion of Suicide Attacks* (Baltimore: Johns Hopkins University Press, 2008); Assaf Moghadam, "Motives for Martyrdom: Al-Qaida, Salafi Jihad, and the Spread of Suicide Attacks," *International Security* 33, no. 3 (2008): 46–78; Peter L. Bergen, *Holy War, Inc.: Inside the Secret World of Osama Bin Laden* (New York: Free Press, 2001); Daniel Byman, "Fighting Salafi-Jihadist Insurgencies: How Much Does Religion Really Matter?," *Studies in Conflict & Terrorism* 36, no. 5 (2013): 353–71; Martha Crenshaw, "Explaining Suicide Terrorism: A Review Essay," *Security Studies* 16, no. 1 (2007): 133–62; Karen J. Greenberg, ed., *Al Qaeda Now: Understanding Today's Terrorists* (New York: Cambridge University Press, 2005); Kristopher K. Robison, Edward M. Crenshaw, and J. Craig Jenkins, "Ideologies of Violence:

The Social Origins of Islamist and Leftist Transnational Terrorism," *Social Forces* 84, no. 4 (June 2006): 2009–26; Robert Anthony Pape, *Dying to Win: The Strategic Logic of Suicide Terrorism* (New York: Random House, 2005); McCants, *The ISIS Apocalypse.*

6. David Kilcullen, *The Accidental Guerrilla: Fighting Small Wars in the Midst of a Big One* (New York: Oxford University Press, 2009).

7. Paul Staniland, *Networks of Rebellion: Explaining Insurgent Cohesion and Collapse*, Cornell Studies in Security Affairs (Ithaca, NY: Cornell University Press, 2014); Paul Staniland, "Organizing Insurgency: Networks, Resources, and Rebellion in South Asia," *International Security* 37, no. 1 (July 1, 2012): 142–77; Abdulkader Sinno, *Organizations at War in Afghanistan and Beyond* (Ithaca, NY: Cornell University Press, 2008).

8. Wendy Pearlman and Kathleen Cunningham, "Nonstate Actors, Fragmentation, and Conflict Processes," *Journal of Conflict Resolution* 56, no. 1 (2012): 3–15; Kathleen Gallagher Cunningham, "Actor Fragmentation and Civil War Bargaining: How Internal Divisions Generate Civil Conflict," *American Journal of Political Science* 57, no. 3 (March 2013): 659–72; Håvard Mokleiv Nygård and Michael Weintraub, "Bargaining between Rebel Groups and the Outside Option of Violence," *Terrorism and Political Violence* 27, no. 3 (May 27, 2015): 557–80; Hanne Fjelde and Desirée Nilsson, "Rebels against Rebels Explaining Violence between Rebel Groups," *Journal of Conflict Resolution* 56, no. 4 (August 1, 2012): 604–28; Seden Akcinaroglu, "Rebel Interdependencies and Civil War Outcomes," *Journal of Conflict Resolution* 56, no. 5 (October 1, 2012): 879–903.

9. The role of foreign support for jihadists is well established in the academic literature, especially with respect to the Taliban. See Frédéric Grare, *Pakistan and the Afghan Conflict, 1979–1985: With an Afterword Covering Events from 1985–2001* (Karachi: Oxford University Press, 2003); Ahmed Rashid, *Taliban: Militant Islam, Oil and Fundamentalism in Central Asia* (New Haven, CT: Yale University Press, 2001); Ahmed Rashid, *Descent into Chaos: The World's Most Unstable Region and the Threat to Global Security* (London: Penguin Books, 2009); Barnett R. Rubin and Ahmed Rashid, "From Great Game to Grand Bargain—Ending Chaos in Afghanistan and Pakistan," *Foreign Affairs* 87, no. 6 (2008): 30–44. Notably, much of this literature also presupposes the existence of an organized rebel group rather than examining the financial origins of initial formation. See, e.g., Idean Salehyan, Kristian Skrede Gleditsch, and David E. Cunningham, "Explaining External Support for Insurgent Groups," *International Organization* 65, no. 4 (October 2011): 709–44; Idean Salehyan, *Rebels without Borders: Transnational Insurgencies in World Politics* (Ithaca, NY: Cornell University Press, 2009).

10. For further reading on OFAC regulations, see Rudolph Lehrer, "Unbalancing the Terrorists' Checkbook: Analysis of U.S. Policy in Its Economic War on International Terrorism," *Tulane Journal of International and Comparative Law* 10 (2002): 333; Anne L. Clunan, "The Fight against Terrorist Financing," *Political*

Science Quarterly 121, no. 4 (December 1, 2006): 569–96; Matthew Levitt and Michael Jacobson, "The U.S. Campaign to Squeeze Terrorists' Financing the U.S. Campaign to Squeeze," *Journal of International Affairs* 62, no. 1 (2008): 67–85.

11. Byman suggests that al-Qaeda is actually so cash-strapped that it has since charged its affiliates for services and training. See Daniel Byman, "Buddies or Burdens? Understanding the Al Qaeda Relationship with Its Affiliate Organizations," *Security Studies* 23, no. 3 (July 3, 2014): 460. See also Greg Bruno, "Al-Qaeda's Financial Pressures," *Council on Foreign Relations*, February 1, 2010.

12. Gabriel Ardant, ed., *The Formation of National States in Western Europe* (Princeton, NJ: Princeton University Press, 1975); Charles Tilly, "War Making and State Making as Organized Crime," in *Bringing the State Back In*, ed. Peter B. Evans, Dietrich Rueschemeyer, and Theda Skocpol (Cambridge: Cambridge University Press, 1985), 169–91; Charles Tilly, *Coercion, Capital and European States, AD 990–1990* (Oxford: Wiley-Blackwell, 1990).

13. Tilly, "War Making and State Making as Organized Crime," 169.

14. John Stuart Mill, *Principles of Political Economy with Some of Their Applications to Social Philosophy* (London: Longman, Green, 1848), 69.

15. "Virtually every commercial transaction has within itself an element of trust, certainly any transaction conducted over a period of time." Kenneth J. Arrow, "Gifts and Exchanges," *Philosophy & Public Affairs* 1, no. 4 (1972): 343–62, quotation on 357.

16. Douglass North explains, "Trade does exist, even in *stateless* societies. Yet . . . the inability of societies to develop effective, low-cost enforcement of contracts is the most important source of both historical stagnation and contemporary underdevelopment in the Third World." Douglass C. North, *Institutions, Institutional Change and Economic Performance* (Cambridge: Cambridge University Press, 1990), 54 (emphasis in original).

17. World Bank, *World Development Report 2002: Building Institutions for Markets* (New York: Oxford University Press, 2002).

18. Jean-Philippe Platteau, "Institutional Obstacles to African Economic Development: State, Ethnicity, and Custom," *Journal of Economic Behavior & Organization* 71, no. 3 (September 1, 2009): 669–89; World Bank, *World Development Report 2002*.

19. Daniel Nettle, "Linguistic Fragmentation and the Wealth of Nations: The Fishman-Pool Hypothesis Reexamined," *Economic Development and Cultural Change* 48, no. 2 (2000): 335–48.

20. William Easterly and Ross Levine, "Africa's Growth Tragedy: Policies and Ethnic Divisions," *Quarterly Journal of Economics* 112, no. 4 (1997): 1203–50; Chaim Fershtman and Uri Gneezy, "Discrimination in a Segmented Society: An Experimental Approach," *Quarterly Journal of Economics* 116, no. 1 (2001): 351–77; Paul J. Zak and Stephen Knack, "Trust and Growth," *Economic Journal* 111, no. 470 (2001): 295–321; Edward L. Glaeser, David Laibson, Jose Scheinkman, and Christine L. Soutter, "Measuring Trust," *Quarterly Journal of Economics* 115, no. 3 (2000): 811–46.

21. Halvard Buhaug and Kristian Skrede Gleditsch, "Contagion or Confusion? Why Conflicts Cluster in Space," *International Studies Quarterly* 52, no. 2 (June 1, 2008): 215–33; Donald L. Horowitz, *Ethnic Groups in Conflict* (Berkeley: University of California Press, 1985); Timur Kuran, "Ethnic Dissimilation and International Diffusion," in *The International Spread of Ethnic Conflict: Fear, Diffusion, and Escalation*, ed. David A. Lake and Donald Rothchild (Princeton, NJ: Princeton University Press, 1998), 35–60; Nettle, "Linguistic Fragmentation and the Wealth of Nations."

22. James D. Fearon and David D. Laitin, "Violence and the Social Construction of Ethnic Identity," *International Organization* 54, no. 4 (2000): 845–77.

23. Deborah Brautigam, "Substituting for the State: Institutions and Industrial Development in Eastern Nigeria," *World Development* 25, no. 7 (1997): 1063–80.

24. This rationalist approach to identities does not discount the value and meaning of the identities themselves. Rather, it is precisely because images, symbols, and myths have persuasive power that individuals may strategically choose one identity over another. If an identity label lacks the ability to generate an emotional or cognitive response—fear, friendliness, trust—it is an identity without much social consequence. The value of an identity can be measured by the social power of its associated meaning: it matters to the extent that it is recognized. See David D. Laitin, *Language Repertoires and State Construction in Africa* (Cambridge: Cambridge University Press, 1992). See also, Günther Schlee, *How Enemies Are Made: Towards a Theory of Ethnic and Religious Conflict* (New York: Berghahn Books, 2008); David D. Laitin, *Identity in Formation: The Russian-Speaking Populations in the New Abroad* (Ithaca, NY: Cornell University Press, 1998); Randall Calvert, "Rationality, Identity, and Expression," in *Political Science: The State of the Discipline*, ed. Ira Katznelson and Helen V. Milner, 3rd ed. (Washington, DC: American Political Science Association, 2002); Russell Hardin, *One for All: The Logic of Group Conflict* (Princeton, NJ: Princeton University Press, 1995); Michael Hechter, *Principles Group Solidarity* (Berkeley: University of California Press, 1987); Ronald Rogowski, "Causes and Varieties of Nationalism: A Rationalist Account," in *New Nationalisms of the Developed West: Toward Explanation*, ed. Edward Tiryakian and Ronald Rogowski (Boston: Allen & Unwin, 1985); Stuart J. Kaufman, "Escaping the Symbolic Politics Trap: Reconciliation Initiatives and Conflict Resolution in Ethnic Wars," *Journal of Peace Research* 43, no. 2 (2006): 201–18. See also Lisa Wedeen, "Conceptualizing Culture: Possibilities for Political Science," *American Political Science Review* 96, no. 4 (2002): 713–28.

25. Fukuyama argues that trust among individuals and groups in a society impacts economic development as it affects transaction costs negatively. That is, higher trust among people results in informal and flexible business relations. On the contrary, lack of social capital in a society slows market activity and hinders economic development. Francis Fukuyama, *Trust: The Social Virtues and the Creation of Prosperity* (New York: Free Press, 1995). For social capital and transaction costs

also read Edward L. Glaeser, Rafael La Porta, Florencio Lopez-de-Silanes, and Andrei Shleifer "Do Institutions Cause Growth?," *Journal of Economic Growth* 9, no. 3 (2004): 271–303; Stephen Knack and Philip Keefer, "Does Social Capital Have an Economic Payoff? A Cross-Country Investigation," *Quarterly Journal of Economics* 112, no. 4 (1997): 1251–88; Zak and Knack, "Trust and Growth."

26. The Umayyad (660–749 AD) and the Abbasid (750–870 AD) Caliphates consolidated this new Islamic power. Maurice Lombard, *The Golden Age of Islam* (Princeton, NJ: Markus Wiener, 2003).

27. George F. Hourani and John Carswell, *Arab Seafaring: In the Indian Ocean in Ancient and Early Medieval Times*, expanded ed. (Princeton, NJ: Princeton University Press, 1995), 62. Over the course of several centuries, trade with Arab Muslims in East Africa and South Asia facilitated religious conversion to Islam. This conversion was not just a product of Arab proselytizing; adoption of Islam also provided clear material benefits. Those living under the caliphates could convert to avoid paying the *jizya* tax. The *jizya* tax was levied on the *dhimmi* population, that is, non-Muslim subjects living under Muslim rule. It is also referred to as the *dhimmi* tax.

28. For a discussion of the interaction between Buddhist and Islamic civilizations, particularly on their expanded trade relations throughout several Islamic Caliphates from the eighth to nineteenth centuries, see Johan Elverskog, *Buddhism and Islam on the Silk Road* (Philadelphia: University of Pennsylvania Press, 2010).

29. There are, of course, significant differences between the Shiite-dominated Iranian Revolution and contemporary Sunni extremist groups. Despite its distinctive attributes, the Iran case reveals important insights about the broader relationships between economic and religious interests. I use this comparison here for illustrative purposes to highlight broader processes.

30. Mehdi Mozaffari, "Why the Bazar Rebels," *Journal of Peace Research* 28, no. 4 (1991): 377–91.

31. Ibid., 381; Howard J. Rotblat, "Social Organization and Development in an Iranian Provincial Bazaar," *Economic Development and Cultural Change* 23, no. 2 (1975): 292–305.

32. Rotblat, "Social Organization and Development in an Iranian Provincial Bazaar."

33. Misagh Parsa, *Social Origins of Iranian Revolution* (New Brunswick, NJ: Rutgers University Press, 1989); Jeremy M. Weinstein, *Inside Rebellion: The Politics of Insurgent Violence* (Cambridge: Cambridge University Press, 2007).

34. Platteau, "Institutional Obstacles to African Economic Development," 39. For a discussion of how Pakistan has attempted to use Islamic identity to allay ethnic conflict, see Stephen P. Cohen, *The Idea of Pakistan*, 2nd ed. (Washington, DC: Brookings Institution Press, 2006). See also Seyyed Vali Reza Nasr, *Islamic Leviathan: Islam and the Making of State Power* (New York: Oxford University Press, 2001).

35. The utility of the business-Islamist alliance is well established in the literature on Iran. While there are significant differences between the Iranian Revolution

and the emergence of political Islamism in collapsed states, the Iran case provides useful insights on the role of economic factors in Islamic movements. See Ervand Abrahamian, "Structural Causes of the Iranian Revolution," *MERIP Reports*, no. 87 (1980): 21–26; Said Amir Arjomand, "Iran's Islamic Revolution in Comparative Perspective," *World Politics* 38, no. 3 (1986): 383–414; Mozaffari, "Why the Bazar Rebels."

36. Rotblat, "Social Organization and Development in an Iranian Provincial Bazaar."
37. Tilly, "War Making and State Making as Organized Crime."
38. Seminal works on civil war economies are: Peter Andreas, *Blue Helmets and Black Markets: The Business of Survival in the Siege of Sarajevo* (Ithaca, NY: Cornell University Press, 2008); Paul Collier and Anke Hoeffler, "Greed and Grievance in Civil War," *Oxford Economic Papers* 56, no. 4 (2004): 563–95; Paul Collier and Nicholas Sambanis, eds., *Understanding Civil War: Africa: Evidence and Analysis* (Washington, DC: World Bank, 2005).
39. Olson describes these types of actors as "stationary bandits." See Mancur Olson, *Power and Prosperity: Outgrowing Communist and Capitalist Dictatorships* (New York: Basic Books, 2000). For a discussion of how economic shocks created warlord politics in Africa, see William Reno, *Warlord Politics and African States* (Boulder, CO: Lynne Rienner, 1998).
40. If the rate of extortion in stateless societies is too high (so as to incite rebellion) or too low (causing warlords to engage in predatory behavior), then political order falls apart. For a game-theoretic model of this protection-extortion relationship between warlords and citizens, see Robert Bates, Avner Greif, and Smita Singh, "Organizing Violence," *Journal of Conflict Resolution* 46, no. 5 (2002): 599–628; the authors outline these consequences on 615.
41. Olson, *Power and Prosperity*, 8.
42. Robert Bates, *When Things Fell Apart: State Failure in Late-Century Africa* (New York: Cambridge University Press, 2008); Ted Gurr, *Why Men Rebel* (Princeton, NJ: Princeton University Press, 1970); James C. Scott, *The Moral Economy of the Peasant: Rebellion and Subsistence in Southeast Asia* (New Haven, CT: Yale University Press, 1976); Weinstein, *Inside Rebellion*, addresses this issue, arguing that those groups that have external sources of funding are more likely to abuse the civilian population than those that rely on the local population for resources.
43. Bates, *When Things Fell Apart*, 17.
44. Bates, Greif, and Singh, "Organizing Violence."
45. Jean-Paul Azam and Alice Mesnard, "Civil War and the Social Contract," *Public Choice* 115, nos. 3/4 (2003): 455–75; Bates, *When Things Fell Apart*; Bates, Greif, and Singh, "Organizing Violence"; Thomas Hobbes, *Leviathan* (New York: Oxford University Press, 2008); Beatriz Magaloni, *Voting for Autocracy: Hegemonic Party Survival and Its Demise in Mexico* (New York: Cambridge University Press, 2006); Bruce Bueno de Mesquita et al., *The Logic of Political Survival* (Cambridge, MA: MIT Press, 2003).

46. Theodore McLauchlin, "Loyalty Strategies and Military Defection in Rebellion," *Comparative Politics* 42, no. 3 (2010): 333–50. For discussion of kin ties in ethnic civil wars, see also Buhaug and Gleditsch, "Contagion or Confusion?"; David Lake and Donald Rothchild, eds., *The International Spread of Ethnic Conflict: Fear, Diffusion, and Escalation* (Princeton, NJ: Princeton University Press, 1998).

47. Rogowski, "Causes and Varieties of Nationalism: A Rationalist Account"; Fukuyama, *Trust*; Brautigam, "Substituting for the State"; Platteau, "Institutional Obstacles to African Economic Development."

48. In a competitive security market, the business class retains a degree of voice and exit power in these coercive relationships, but these options are always risky. On exit power, see Albert O. Hirschman, *Exit, Voice, and Loyalty: Responses to Decline in Firms, Organizations, and States* (Cambridge, MA: Harvard University Press, 1970). On Islamic movements, see Collins, "Ideas, Networks, and Islamist Movements"; Quintan Wiktorowicz, ed., *Islamic Activism: A Social Movement Theory Approach* (Bloomington: Indiana University Press, 2004).

49. The utilization of religious credentials by elites is a strategy for outbidding rival groups and generating a broader base of support. For a thorough discussion of religious outbidding, see Monica Duffy Toft, "Getting Religion? The Puzzling Case of Islam and Civil War," *International Security* 31, no. 4 (2007): 97–131.

CHAPTER 3

1. Robert Sampson and Momin Khan, *The Poetry of Rahman Baba: Poet of the Pukhtuns* (Peshawar: University Book Agency, 2005), 85.

2. In 1978, the heavily pro-Soviet communist Khalq faction of the PDPA then overthrew and killed the pro-communist president Daoud Khan in a violent coup, under the leadership of Nur Muhammad Taraki. In a subsequent coup, Taraki was killed in 1979 at his palace and was succeeded by Hafizullah Amin. Amin was then killed by Soviet commandos in 1979. His replacement, Babrak Karmal, was handpicked by the Soviet Union to rule Afghanistan throughout the occupation. For a history of the Saur rebellion and communist era in Afghanistan, see Thomas J. Barfield, *Afghanistan: A Cultural and Political History* (Princeton, NJ: Princeton University Press, 2012), 225–42; David B. Edwards, *Before Taliban: Genealogies of the Afghan Jihad* (Berkeley: University of California Press, 2002), 25–94.

3. Raja Anwar and Fred Halliday, *The Tragedy of Afghanistan: A First-Hand Account*, trans. Khalid Hasan (London: Verso Books, 1990), 186–93. While Soviet involvement is undisputed, the particular details of Amin's death still remain debated. Whether he was caught by random fire or deliberately targeted is unknown. One account alleges that he was shot dead by Sayed Mohammad Gulabzoi, former minister of communications who assumed the position of Minister of Internal Affairs a day after Amin was dead. See Rodric Braithwaite, *Afgantsy: The Russians in Afghanistan, 1979–1989* (New York: Oxford University Press, 2011), 96–102.

4. Partly because of the Islamic tradition of burying the body within twenty-four hours of death, there is no accurate and agreed-on number of civilian deaths from the decade-long Soviet-Afghan War, but estimates put the number of dead close to one million, including civilians, insurgents, and political prisoners. The communist era was known for its mass executions of political prisoners and dissidents, thus making the number of dead and disappeared even more difficult to determine. The precise numbers of internally displaced people and refugees is also undetermined but is in the several million. At the height of the Soviet invasion, the refugee camps at Peshawar were the largest in the world, and three million refugees were displaced in the Khyber Pakhtunkhwa province of Pakistan. For an account of the immediate impact of the invasion, see Louis Dupree, "Afghanistan in 1982: Still No Solution," *Asian Survey* 23, no. 2 (1983): 133–42.

5. Some witnesses claim that they and their agricultural lands suffered from chemical warfare, similar to Agent Orange. See Bo Huldt and Erland Jansson, *The Tragedy of Afghanistan: The Social, Cultural, and Political Impact of the Soviet Invasion* (London; New York: Croom Helm, 1988); Jeri Laber and Barnett R. Rubin, *"A Nation Is Dying": Afghanistan under the Soviets, 1979–87* (Evanston, IL: Northwestern University Press, 1988); Ralph H. Magnus, *Afghan Alternatives: Issues, Options, and Policies; [Papers from the Internat. Conference on Afghan Alternatives, . . . Held at the Monterey Inst. of Internat. Studies in Nov. 1983]* (New Brunswick, NJ: Transaction Publishers, 1985), 119. It is worth noting that 80 percent of the Afghan economy was traditionally agricultural.

6. These reforms sought to transform the feudal-capitalist Afghan agrarian economy directly into a communist system. Peasants had traditionally relied on their landlords for access to water, seeds, small loans, supplies, and connections to markets. Therefore, by eliminating the wealthy land-owning class, these new peasants-turned-small-landowners were unable to acquire the resources they needed to till their new plots, nor could they reach markets that would purchase their produce. The result was economic ruin for the rural poor. For a discussion of the reforms, see also Olivier Roy, *Islam and Resistance in Afghanistan* (New York: Cambridge University Press, 1990), 84–94. Furthermore, my interviews in Kandahar and Peshawar indicated that people who had temporarily fled would return to find their farmlands occupied by other people who also claimed historical ownership over the property. Confusion emerged over competing legal claims that have each had validity at various points in the history of the conflict. The communist land reform policy, the physical destruction of deeds and records through firefights and air raids, the increase in arbitrary confiscation by both the state and local strongmen, and the millions of people who were displaced over the past thirty years have made it incredibly difficult to untangle the legal issues surrounding property rights. See Liz Alden Wily, "Land Rights in Crisis: Restoring Tenure Security in Afghanistan," Issue Paper Series (Kabul: Afghanistan Research and Evaluation Unit, 2003), for a comprehensive discussion.

7. Ahmed Rashid, *Taliban: Militant Islam, Oil and Fundamentalism in Central Asia* (New Haven, CT: Yale University Press, 2001). The local khan is akin to the mayor of the village or community and has authority over secular political affairs. The mullah holds religious and spiritual authority in the community. Mullahs and khans traditionally worked side by side, offering complementary forms of leadership over their communities.

8. Quote from a *Harakat-ul-Islam* commander from Baraki-Rajan village. Almqvist Borje, "Eyewitnesses to the Afghan War," *World Affairs* 145, no. 3 (1982): 312.

9. At the time, Afghans made up over half of the world's total refugees and were the single largest displaced population in the world. The roughly six million refugees were divided almost equally between Pakistan and Iran. Most Pashtun refugees went to Pakistan, although Tajik and other ethnic groups also took up refuge in Pakistan. The Hazara population and other western Afghans opted for the closer Iranian border camps. The Iranian refugee camps were particularly attractive for Afghanistan's Shiite minorities. "Millions of Afghan Refugees in Exile after Soviet Pullout," *CNN*, February 14, 1999.

10. Despite efforts by the Pakistani government to assist both legal and illegal migrants, the living conditions at Jalozai were noticeably lower than those of UN-sponsored camps. But the refugees were permitted to work, and the government provided some education and health resources for Afghans living in camps. Much of this education, however, was provided for through the construction of new madrasas, financed by the Pakistani government with Saudi assistance. See C. Christine Fair, *The Madrassah Challenge: Militancy and Religious Education in Pakistan* (Washington, DC: United States Institute of Peace Press, 2008).

11. Pakistan not only supplied the mujahideen but also maintained the refugee camps at Peshawar and in other areas of Khyber Pakhtunkhwa at a hefty rate of USD$1–1.5 million per day. See Dupree, "Afghanistan in 1982." However, the Pakistani intelligence also utilized the refugee camps to further the military effort. The refugee camps also provided a useful cover to shuffle mujahideen forces across the border for rearmament and coordination purposes.

12. Vahid Brown and Don Rassler, *Fountainhead of Jihad: The Haqqani Nexus, 1973–2012* (New York: Oxford University Press, 2013).

13. Documentary Bonanza, "Soldiers of God: 1975–1988," *Cold War Series* (CNN, 1998).

14. According to Bergen, financial support began in 1980 with an estimated USD$20–30 million. The United States gradually increased its sponsorship of the mujahideen between 1983 and 1987. Peter L. Bergen, *Holy War, Inc.: Inside the Secret World of Osama Bin Laden* (New York: Free Press, 2001), 68.

15. The jihad adopted a very local character, and each ethnic and tribal community organized its own faction in support of the common effort. The mujahideen were symbolically united by their common anti-Soviet mission but had no central command structure. This flexible organizational structure allowed the rebellion to survive, even when one faction suffered an extreme blow.

16. Interviews with General Hamid Gul, Colonel Sultan Amir Tarar, Lieutenant General Ali Jan Aurakzai, Lieutenant General Asad Durrani, and Rostam Shah Momand in Peshawar, Rawalpindi, and Islamabad, Pakistan, June 2009.

17. Brigadier General Mohammad Yousaf directly oversaw the ISI's shipment of weapons from the Karachi Port to his weapon's storage facility in Rawalpindi and then to the mujahideen drop-off point in Peshawar. Mohammad Yousaf and Mark Adkin, *The Bear Trap: Afghanistan's Untold Story* (London: Leo Cooper, 1992), 158.

18. Brown and Rassler, *Fountainhead of Jihad*, 5.

19. During the Soviet-Afghan War, the Soviet-backed intelligence agency in Kabul underwent several transformations. In September 1979, Taraki's Intelligence agency, Organization for the Defense of the Interests of Afghanistan (Da Afghanistan da Gato da Satalo Aidara [AGSA]), was renamed by Amin to Workers' Intelligence Agency (Da Kargarano Amniyati Muassisa [KAM]). On January 11, 1980, the government announced the official replacement of Amin's KAM with the new Department of State Information Services (Riasat-i Khidmat-i Ettela'at-i Doulati [KHAD]). The director of the KHAD, Najibullah, reported directly to the KGB. Under Najibullah, in January 1986, KHAD became the Ministry of State Security (Wizarat-i Amaniyyat-i Dawlati [WAD]). According to Rubin, by 1987, WAD employed an estimated 15,000 to 30,000 professionals and had around 100,000 informants on its payroll; Rubin also charges that higher-level KHAD officials each had one or two KGB advisers. See Barnett R. Rubin, *The Fragmentation of Afghanistan: State Formation and Collapse in the International System*, 2nd ed. (New Haven, CT: Yale University Press, 2002), 132–34; Hafizullah Emadi, *Dynamics of Political Development in Afghanistan: The British, Russian, and American Invasions* (New York: Palgrave Macmillan, 2010), 113; Fred Halliday and Zahir Tanin, "The Communist Regime in Afghanistan 1978–1992: Institutions and Conflicts," *Europe-Asia Studies* 50, no. 8 (December 1, 1998): 1357–80. See also M. Hasan Kakar, *Afghanistan: The Soviet Invasion and the Afghan Response, 1979–1982* (Berkeley: University of California Press, 1995), chap. 9. on KHAD; and Arnold Anthony, *Afghanistan's Two-Party Communism: Parcham and Khalq* (Stanford, CA: Hoover Institution Press, 1983) on the communist parties in Afghanistan.

20. Kakar, *Afghanistan*, 166.

21. John F. Burns, "Kabul Journal; Now on the Beaten Path: A Jail with a Bloody Past," *New York Times*, December 2, 1989, sec. World.

22. Interview with Colonel Imam, June 2009.

23. Hekmatyar himself was born in the northern province of Kunduz and is among a more educated, urban class of Ghilzai Pashtuns. Pakistan continued to provide financial and military aid to these factions through the Peshawar channel during the civil war in Afghanistan and gave significant aid to HIG; HIG received the greatest share of these resources. Thomas H. Johnson, "Financing Afghan Terrorism: Thugs, Drugs and Creative Movements of Money," in *Terrorism Financing and State Responses: A Comparative Perspective*, ed. Jeanne K. Giraldo

and Harold A. Trinkunas (Stanford, CA: Stanford University Press, 2007), 93–114, quotation on p. 108.

24. Interview with General Hamid Gul, Islamabad, Pakistan, June 2009.

25. Interview with Colonel Imam, Rawalpindi, Pakistan, June 2009.

26. Two catalysts helped the expansion of modern opium poppy cultivation and production in Afghanistan. First, in the end of the 1970s major regional producers such as Iran, Pakistan, and India banned opium cultivation and production. Second, these bans came in tandem with the "governance vacuum" in Afghanistan and the rise of mujahideen groups that got involved in this illicit economy for financing their war efforts. For a discussion, see David Macdonald, *Drugs in Afghanistan: Opium, Outlaws and Scorpion Tales* (London: Pluto, 2007), 60–61. Furthermore, poppy cultivation is labor intensive (optimally employing a greater portion of population in agrarian societies) and Afghanistan's climate is very suitable for poppy crops; according to Clemens, Afghanistan produces 40–60 kg of opium per hectare of land compared to 8 kg in Laos and 9.5 kg in Myanmar, the leading producer of opium until 2003. Jeffrey Clemens, "Opium in Afghanistan: Prospects for the Success of Source Country Drug Control Policies," *Journal of Law & Economics* 51, no. 3 (2008): 407–32, quotation on p. 409. The tribal area, its business community, and its trucking industry played a vital role in boosting the dominance of opium poppy cultivation during the late 1970s. These factors were coupled with the decline in production in Laos, Myanmar, and Thailand. See Jonathan Goodhand, "Frontiers and Wars: The Opium Economy in Afghanistan," *Journal of Agrarian Change* 5, no. 2 (April 1, 2005): 191–216.

27. Interview with Colonel Imam, June 2009.

28. Ali Ahmad Jalali, *Afghan Guerrilla Warfare: In the Words of the Mujahideen Fighters* (St. Paul, MN: MBI Publishing Company, 2002).

29. Interview with Colonel Imam, June 2009.

30. The Soviets had considered removing Karmal before 1985. In March 1986, Karmal visited Moscow for a medical treatment and was persuaded to relinquish power. In May 1986, Najibullah took over the chairmanship of the PDPA Politburo from Karmal. In November 1986, the PDPA Politburo relieved Karmal from his post as chairman of the Revolutionary Council and called him back to Moscow, where he died in 1996. Artemy M. Kalinovsky, *A Long Goodbye: The Soviet Withdrawal from Afghanistan* (Cambridge, MA: Harvard University Press, 2011), 94–98.

31. Yousaf and Adkin, *The Bear Trap*, 159.

32. Stephen P. Cohen, *The Idea of Pakistan* (Washington, DC: Brookings Institution Press, 2004).

33. Interview with former Peshawar-based trader, January 2012.

34. The Federal Tax Ombudsman (FTO) claims that 75 percent of goods earmarked for Afghanistan are actually sold in Pakistani markets. Herald, "Herald Exclusive: The Billion Dollar Scam," *Dawn*, April 22, 2011.

35. Thomas Barfield, "The Durand Line: History, Consequences, and Future," Conference Report (Istanbul, Turkey: American Institute of Afghanistan Studies and the Hollings Center Conference, July 2007), 4.
36. Ibid. In 1893, the British demarcated the "Durand Line," named after the British foreign secretary of British India Henry Mortimer Durand. It ran directly through the mountains and legally divided Pashtun tribes and families across an unmarked divide.
37. Throughout history the tribes have not only fought invaders but also elites in Kabul who pushed too deeply into the countryside.
38. During the twentieth century, there were numerous failed attempts to modernize the Afghan state and bring the countryside under central government control. King Amanullah Khan (1919–1929) attempted a Western-type of reform of the Afghan state and society, which resulted in widespread mobilization and rebellion. King Mohammed Zahir Shah (1933–1973) also attempted some modest reforms before being ousted by his socialist cousin and brother-in-law Muhammad Daoud Khan in 1973.
39. Barfield, *Afghanistan*.
40. Ibid., 114. Also, as Rubin states, "Aid enabled the state to expand its organization and influence without attempting an economic or social transformation of the countryside." Rubin, *The Fragmentation of Afghanistan*, 20.
41. The three Anglo-Afghan wars took place in 1839–1842, 1878–1880, and 1919.
42. Barfield, *Afghanistan*.
43. In 1956, Pakistan became the first modern state to declare itself an Islamic Republic and construct a constitution on the basis of Islamic laws and principles. For a discussion of the role of Islam in the identity of the state, see Cohen, *The Idea of Pakistan*.
44. For this reason, Afghanistan was actually the only country in the world to vote against Pakistan's admission into the United Nations.
45. In a 1948 visit to Waziristan, Pakistani president Muhammad Ali Jinnah ordered the withdrawal of all armed forces from the tribal areas, declaring that there was no need for government troops because the tribal people were capable of defending the region themselves. This delegation of authority to tribal armies kept the relationship between the Pakistani government and its tribal population amiable for decades. This sixty-year-long status quo ended in the post-9/11 period when the redeployment of the Pakistan army in the tribal belt provoked a strong insurgent response among the restive tribes. As Hasnat notes, this deployment of Pakistani troops to the region has been highly contentious. See Syed Farooq Hasnat, "Pakistan & Afghanistan: Domestic Pressures and Regional Threats: Pakistan's Strategic Interests, Afghanistan and the Fluctuating U.S. Strategy," *Journal of International Affairs* 63, no. 1 (2009): 141–55.
46. In a 1947 prepartition referendum, the majority Pashtun populations in the North West Frontier Province (NWFP) voted overwhelmingly for inclusion in Pakistan.

Tribal leaders held a *Loya Jirga* to discuss the Indian partition and unanimously declared their preference for Pakistan. With a 50 percent voter participation rate within the Jirga system, there were 289,244 votes for Pakistan and 2,874 for India. Throughout the 1950s and 1960s, Pakistan also offered an increasing number of incentives to appease its tribal and Pashtun populations, including expanding economic, political, government, military, and employment opportunities. See Rizwan Hussain, *Pakistan and the Emergence of Islamic Militancy in Afghanistan* (Burlington, VT: Ashgate, 2005), 74.

47. Muhammad Khan and Ayaz Ahmed, "Foreign Aid-Blessing or Curse: Evidence from Pakistan," *Pakistan Development Review* 46, no. 3 (2007): 215–40.

48. Burki and Malik both argue that the threat of popular mobilization has prevented the Pakistani government from developing a more robust taxation system. Anas Malik, *Political Survival in Pakistan: Beyond Ideology* (New York: Routledge, 2011), 169; Shahid Javed Burki, *Changing Perceptions and Altered Reality: Emerging Economies in the 1990s* (Washington, DC: World Bank, 2000), 157. Other scholars have argued that Pakistan has the coercive power to tax its citizens but lacks the willingness to do so. They argue that government's unwillingness to levy taxes on property and agriculture is largely due to the power and interests of the landowning class, which has used its political influence to resist taxation. In fact, the Pakistani armed forces receive "a variety of benefits provided to retired personnel in the form of urban and rural land," thus creating a new class of landowners from within the military establishment. See Ayesha Siddiqa, *Military Inc.: Inside Pakistan's Military Economy* (London: Pluto, 2007), 19.

49. According to Fair et al., "The government relies on indirect taxes, primarily sales and excise taxes, for 70 percent of the revenues of the Central Bureau of Revenue. However, these taxes do not apply to the agricultural sector. . . . Since agriculture accounts for a fifth to a quarter of GDP, depending on the harvest, this is a large share of the economy to leave untapped. In addition, special exemptions are rife." Fair et al. further allege that "Pakistan's landed classes, both the traditional feudal families and retired military officers, who have become a new land-owning class, fiercely resist property taxes." Christine Fair et al., *Pakistan: Can the United States Secure an Insecure State?* (Santa Monica, CA: RAND, 2010), 124. Malik affirms this point, saying, "As is repeatedly stated, no Pakistani government has ever imposed an agricultural tax." Malik, *Political Survival in Pakistan*, 162.

50. Providing a safe and free transit route connecting landlocked countries to an ocean port is a courtesy that was traditionally extended by neighboring states. Such agreements were designed to facilitate mutually beneficial regional and international trade. This practice became mandatory in international law through the 1965 Convention on Transit Trade of Landlocked States, which made this provision a legal obligation.

51. *Ilm-o-khabar* is a transit permission.

52. The Afghan market was an important source of income for Pakistani-based transit traders. Transit traders profited from both the smuggling activities and the normal

trade to satisfy the Afghan markets. Especially because certain goods are time sensitive (Eid clothes, seasonal goods, fresh produce), these traders made their profit on the basis of facilitating the timely and secure arrival of these goods to the Afghan market.

53. Local police also charged a modest fee per truck to ensure that the shipment was not impeded on the roads, but these sums were fairly trivial.

54. Khurshid Hasan, "Pakistan-Afghanistan Relations," *Asian Survey* 2, no. 7 (September 1, 1962): 14–24; Vahid Brown and Don Rassler, *Fountainhead of Jihad: The Haqqani Nexus, 1973–2012* (New York: Oxford University Press, 2013), 35; Daveed Gartenstein-Ross and Tara Vassefi, "The Forgotten History of Afghanistan-Pakistan Relations," *Yale Journal of International Affairs* 7 (2012): 38; Peter R. Blood, "Daoud as Prime Minister, 1953–63," in *Afghanistan: A Country Study*, ed. Peter R. Blood (Washington, DC: GPO for the Library of Congress, 2001).

55. Both Khyber Agency and South Waziristan Agency are Pashtun tribal districts within the Federally Administered Tribal Areas of Pakistan, along the border of Afghanistan. Khyber Agency is closest to Peshawar and Jalalabad. South Waziristan is a rugged and remote mountainous region, south of Peshawar and north of Quetta, closest to Paktia province in Afghanistan.

56. By the 1990s, the smuggling industry consistently net well over a billion dollars in revenue annually. According to a 1999 World Bank Report, "unofficial re-exports of goods from Afghanistan into Pakistan [were] estimated at $1.96 billion (84% of the total trade) in 1997." Zareen Naqvi, "Afghanistan-Pakistan Trade Relations" (Islamabad, Pakistan: World Bank, 1999), 3. The statement that officials sponsored construction of the smugglers' bazaars is based on my interviews with prominent smugglers who insisted on giving tours of the bazaars in order to prove this point. I am unaware of any official government record of these construction projects, however.

57. Over the course of the war, the PDPA government accrued USD$10 billion of state debt from Moscow, which the regime was forced to use to purchase Soviet weapons. In 2007, Russia agreed to cancel 90 percent of the Afghan government's Soviet-era debt, the majority of which was forcibly accrued for purchase of weapons by the PDPA from the Soviet Union itself. "Russia Cancels Most Afghan Debt," *BBC*, August 6, 2007, sec. South Asia.

58. In addition to aid, a key "source of [PDPA] revenue came from export taxes levied on gas shipped to the Soviet Union. These taxes climbed from 17 percent of revenues in FY 1979 to an estimated 45 percent in FY 1983." J. Bruce Amstutz, *Afghanistan: The First Five Years of Soviet Occupation* (Washington, DC: National Defence University Press, 1986), 247.

59. Mohammad Yousaf and Mark Adkin, *Afghanistan: The Bear Trap; The Defeat of a Superpower*, 1st ed. (Havertown, PA: Casemate, 2001), 98–103.

60. A similar system currently exists for the shipment of NATO weapons and supplies to Afghanistan through Karachi. The difference is that NATO shipments are properly documented and are openly declared at Pakistan and Afghanistan borders,

whereas weapons shipments during the Soviet war were entirely covert using ficti-
tious paper work.

61. The maps of these Pakistani arms smuggling routes are based on my interviews with
   high-ranking ISI officers; I also cross-checked my interview data with the descriptions of these routes from Yousaf and Adkin, *Afghanistan*.

62. Interview with Colonel Imam, Rawalpindi, Pakistan, June 2009.

63. The Jamiat-i-Islami Party had a predominantly Tajik membership but was relatively
   more cosmopolitan than other ethnic parties, such as Uzbek commander Gen.
   Rashid Dostum's Junbesh-i-Milli Party. Jamiat had no single foreign supporter but
   received sporadic support from Pakistan, Saudi Arabia, Iran, Russia, India, and the
   United States.

64. Sayyaf developed a close relationship with al-Qaeda leader Osama bin Laden
   during the Afghan jihad. Ittehad received its main source of support through its
   pro-Saudi affiliation, which enabled it to raise huge amounts of private donations
   from Saudi Arabia and elsewhere in the Gulf. Both engaged in shocking acts of
   extremism: Sayyaf engaged in brutal cleansing campaigns against Shiite minorities,
   while Hekmatyar built a reputation for throwing acid on the faces of women who
   didn't wear a veil.

65. Interview with General Hamid Gul, Islamabad, Pakistan, June 2009.

66. See Rubin, *The Fragmentation of Afghanistan*, 198; and Yousaf and Adkin, *The Bear
   Trap*, for a more detailed discussion. This explains the flood of weapons in the
   Peshawar markets in the 1980s, which were far less expensive than in the Afghan
   markets.

67. Yousaf and Adkin, *The Bear Trap*, 105.

68. Interviews with leading smugglers who engaged in this activity, January 2012.

69. I personally witnessed both Hizb-i-Islami and Jamiat-i-Islami militias openly roam-
   ing the streets of Peshawar in the late 1980s and early 1990s, and the commanders of
   these groups regularly visited the leading members of the business community.

70. So direct was this coordination effort that these largest and most successful of the
   mujahideen groups were given the nickname "the Peshawar Seven." See Rubin, *The
   Fragmentation of Afghanistan*, chap. 9, for a discussion.

71. Soon after the Saur Revolution in April 1978, the PDPA issued a series of communist decrees between July and November of that year. As Ishiyama outlines, the
   first set of decrees mandated the abolishment of mortgages made before 1973 and
   forgave debts of landless peasants. Writing off mortgages and debts alienated the
   landed elites and disrupted the established systems. The second round of decrees
   ordered equality of genders, introduced a maximum limit for a bride dowry, and
   set age limits for marriage at eighteen for males and sixteen for females. It also
   outlawed forced marriages. The third batch of decrees introduced land reforms
   that redistributed arable land from the wealthy to the poorest. Since the communist revolutionaries came from an educated urban class, who constituted a secular minority, they soon found themselves pitted against the conservative rural

majority. Opposition from the ulema (clergy) was the fiercest, which led Taraki to pronounce them enemies of the regime. See John Ishiyama, "The Sickle and the Minaret: Communist Successor Parties in Yemen and Afghanistan after the Cold War," *Middle East Review of International Affairs* 9, no. 1 (2005): 7, 11–13; see also Peter Blood, *Afghanistan: A Country Study*, Area Handbook Series (Baton Rouge, LA: Claitor's Publication Division, 2001), and Halliday and Tanin, "The Communist Regime in Afghanistan 1978–1992," 1360.

72. Interview with Kabul-based schoolteacher, July 2015.

73. Islam was first introduced to the Afghanistan-Pakistan region in the seventh century through the Umayyad Caliphate, and by the end of the ninth century, Islam had become the dominant religion in the area. Over the course of the next thousand years, the region fell under at least seven different Islamic empires. However, while these imperial rulers primarily exerted control over large cities and urban industries, the majority of the countryside continued to rely predominantly on informal, local forms of governance.

74. The old Afghan kings utilized Islamic laws, norms, and institutions to legitimate their political authority, reduce the risk of uprisings, and smooth economic life. Islamic identity also served as a social lubricant for the business class to help establish trade agreements across local divisions. Islamic laws and institutions have long served as a common medium for facilitating economic and social relations across tribes, ethnicities, and empires. Barfield, *Afghanistan*, 5, 73–74. Both the eighteenth-century founder of the Afghan state Ahmad Shah Durrani and nineteenth-century ruler Amir Abdul Rahman Khan appealed to Islam to legitimate their rule over ethnic and tribal rivals. Rubin, *The Fragmentation of Afghanistan*, 46, 50. The Durrani Empire was an Islamic dynasty in its own right and was the second-largest Islamic empire in the world at that time, second only to the Ottoman Empire.

75. A jirga is a meeting of elders that includes representatives of parties to a dispute, which resolves the conflict through negotiated settlement. The jirga itself receives its legitimacy from its adherence to and primary purpose of upholding religious laws, norms, and institutions.

76. I use the masculine in the Afghan case because, unlike their Somali counterparts, Afghan and Pakistani women are largely excluded from this business activity. While Pashtun women do have a hidden economic power within the home and are important players in farming households, there simply isn't a class of Afghan women traders that I am aware of. Indeed, I have never met a single Pashtun woman who owned her own business in the transit trade.

77. This action is called *dhikr*, or remembrance of God, and it signifies that every time the person flips one of the beads on the chain, he or she has silently repeated a particular supplication. This religious practice is commonplace among devoted persons, who use dhikr throughout their day to establish a constant remembrance of God.

78. Hajj is the pilgrimage to Mecca, which Muslims are obligated to perform at least once in a lifetime. Those who are financially and physically able to perform the Hajj

more than once are expected to do so. Because of their greater material resources, members of the business community are expected to perform the pilgrimage to Mecca before they reach middle age.

79. The business class was dominated by elderly patriarchs who hold this religious distinction. Businesses are typically passed down to the patriarch's eldest son after he has acquired the requisite social status.

80. A *waqf is* a private endowment, which is earmarked for the creation and maintenance of an Islamic institution.

81. Tablighi-Jamaat is a conservative missionary revivalist group but boasts an apolitical, nonviolent, and purely spiritual mandate. The movement has a large following in the subcontinent.

82. The Shabi Jummah is a night of prayer held in the religious space of the Markaz from Thursday night until the Friday prayers. A Markaz is a Tablighi-Jamaat center or office that runs the missionary program. The Markaz is designed to accommodate overnight guests that are committed to prayers.

83. Interview with Peshawar-based trader, January 2012.

84. In villages in Khyber Pakhtunkhwa, the Imam or another respected community leader would approach landowners at harvest time and request '*ushr*, which is a charitable donation from the harvested crops. This collection was made during the Afghan jihad in support of the mujahideen.

85. Interview with Peshawar-based traders about experiences during the Soviet-Afghan War, January 2012.

86. One of their colleagues explained that "After the forty days, the drugs will have arrived at the expected destination, and then they will leave the Markaz and collect the profits of the consignment" (ibid.)

87. This businessman gave both *zakat* and *sadaqa*. Zakat is the mandatory 2.5 percent wealth tax on cash surplus, unoccupied property, and other evaluated assets that all Muslims are obligated to give to a needy person or a charity. Sadaqa is an optional charitable donation, the amount of which is discretionary.

88. Interviews with colleagues of this business tycoon, December 2011.

89. Author observations of conversations between Peshawar-based traders.

90. Interview with midsize Peshawar-based trader, December 2011.

91. Interview with General Asad Durrani, May 2009.

92. Quotes from interview with Kabul-based schoolteacher, July 2015. This curriculum was developed by the University of Nebraska at a cost of USD$51 million provided by the CIA. Ishtiaq Ahmed, "The Spectre of Islamic Fundamentalism over Pakistan (1947–2007)," in *Pakistan in Regional and Global Politics*, ed. Rajshree Jetly (London: Taylor & Francis, 2009), 150–80, quotation on p. 165. The curriculum was implemented by mujahideen in the schools and madrasas they ran in Pakistani refugee camps, and once the Peshawar Seven commanders took control of Afghanistan, they introduced this system to Afghan schools. These schools incorporated "struggle against the communists (jihad)" as part of their

education. Saif R. Samady, *Education and Afghan Society in the Twentieth Century* (Paris: UNESCO, 2001), 12. A new curriculum was introduced in 1994 with more peaceful content. Pia Karlsson and Amir Mansory, "Islamic and Modern Education in Afghanistan—Conflictual or Complementary?" (Stockholm University: Institute of International Education, 2004), 16.

93. Quotes from interview with Kabul-based schoolteacher, July 2015.

94. Virtually every Afghan faction claimed to be rooted in a political Islamic identity. Even Dostum's pro-communist ethnic Uzbek party rebranded itself as *Junbesh-i-Milli-Islami* (National Islamic Movement) after the Soviet withdrawal.

95. Each of these groups appealed to its ethnic and tribal base to consolidate its power. For a discussion of Pashtun ethnic politics within the Taliban, see Abdulkader Sinno, "Explaining the Taliban's Ability to Mobilize the Pashtuns," in *The Taliban and the Crisis of Afghanistan*, ed. Robert D. Crews and Amin Tarzi (Cambridge, MA: Harvard University Press, 2009), 58–89; and Rasul Bakhsh Rais, *Recovering the Frontier State: War, Ethnicity, and State in Afghanistan* (Lanham, MD: Lexington Books, 2008).

CHAPTER 4

1. Robert Sampson and Momin Khan, *The Poetry of Rahman Baba: Poet of the Pukhtuns* (Peshawar: University Book Agency, 2005), 573.

2. Barnett R. Rubin, *Afghanistan from the Cold War through the War on Terror* (New York: Oxford University Press, 2013).

3. Barnett R. Rubin, *The Fragmentation of Afghanistan: State Formation and Collapse in the International System*, 2nd ed. (New Haven, CT: Yale University Press, 2002); David B. Edwards, *Before Taliban: Genealogies of the Afghan Jihad* (Berkeley: University of California Press, 2002).

4. These descriptions are drawn from many conversations with many families from Kabul who lived through this time period. My visits to the old city still showed many of the scars from this era.

5. Interview with former Kabul resident who lived through the civil war, July 2015.

6. Ibid. This account is also recorded in a 1995 Amnesty International report. Amnesty International, "Women in Afghanistan: A Human Rights Catastrophe" (Amnesty International, May 17, 1995).

7. Interviews: Mazar-e-Sharif, Afghanistan (March 2005). Despite the predatory behavior of these commanders, the threat from rival ethnic or tribal groups was so severe that civilians were forced to rely on their own ethnic faction for protection. For example, several Uzbek women in Balkh province explained that the reason they politically supported General Rashid Dostum, a commander well known for perpetuating violent campaigns against women, was because they felt that he was the only commander strong enough to protect them from total genocide at the hands of other ethnic factions. This sentiment was broadly shared by members

of all ethnic groups across the country. In the center and south, ethnically and tribally motivated rape campaigns by militia were so systemic that entire villages were targeted by mujahideen factions. Aisha Ahmad, "Afghan Women: The State of Legal Rights and Security," *Policy Perspectives* 3, no. 1 (2006): 25–41. The Afghan civil war thus constituted an ethnic security dilemma in the classic sense. See Barry R. Posen, "The Security Dilemma and Ethnic Conflict," *Survival* 35, no. 1 (1993): 27–47; James D. Fearon, "Ethnic War as a Commitment Problem," Annual Meetings of the American Political Science Association, New York, Stanford University, 1994.

8. Interview with female doctor worker in rural Kandahar, March 2005.

9. Interview with humanitarian worker in rural Kandahar, March 2005.

10. Interview with Kabul resident who lived next door to the victim, July 2015.

11. There are several variations to this story, with minor differences in the details. Some say it was one girl, others two or three girls. Some versions say it was a young boy that was being sodomized, and others claim an entire family. I relay here the version of the story told to me by a colleague of Mullah Omar who was involved with the original Taliban movement in 1994. A similar account appears in Ahmed Rashid, *Taliban: Militant Islam, Oil and Fundamentalism in Central Asia* (New Haven, CT: Yale University Press, 2001), 25 which corroborates this version.

12. Matinuddin suggests that this could have been a local commander named Mansour. He also identifies Nadir Jan, Saleh Mohammad, and Doro Khan as prominent commanders in the region near Mullah Omar's village. Kamal Matinuddin, *The Taliban Phenomenon: Afghanistan 1994–1997* (Karachi: Oxford University Press, 1999), 23.

13. Interview with Mullah Abdul Salam Zaeef, August 2016.

14. Ahmed Rashid claims that there were thirty Taliban during the initial uprising. My colleague claimed that there were approximately forty. They agree on the number of rifles.

15. Interview with Mullah Abdul Salam Zaeef, August 2016.

16. Interview with former Taliban official, July 2016.

17. Ibid.

18. Ibid.

19. Rashid, *Taliban*, 31–33, 59.

20. Abdul Salam Zaeef, *My Life with the Taliban*, ed. Alex Strick van Linschoten and Felix Kuehn (London: Hurst, 2010), 62.

21. Ibid., 64. The "between forty and fifty" estimate comes from my interviews with the late Colonel Imam in June 2009.

22. Interview with former Taliban official, July 2016.

23. Ibid.

24. The twelve thousand figure is drawn from Rashid, *Taliban*, 29.

25. The most formidable Northern Alliance base was in Khwaja Bahauddin District in Takhar province. This was an ideal location for leaders and soldiers to operate from as it offered a safe passage across the Panj River into Tajikistan.

26. Sinno correctly points to the Taliban's ability to utilize Pashtun ethnic politics to gain political momentum in the south. The fact that the Taliban's *shura* (leadership council) was composed of mainly Pashtuns from the Ghilzai grouping of tribes adds credence to this argument. Abdulkader Sinno, "Explaining the Taliban's Ability to Mobilize the Pashtuns," in *The Taliban and the Crisis of Afghanistan*, ed. Robert D. Crews and Amin Tarzi (Cambridge, MA: Harvard University Press, 2009), 59–89. Moreover, anti-Taliban resistance was particularly fierce in the Hazara-dominated central region and the Tajik- and Uzbek-dominated western and northern regions, suggesting that the Taliban had limited support outside of the Pashtun belt. See Neamatollah Nojumi, *The Rise of the Taliban in Afghanistan: Mass Mobilization, Civil War, and the Future of the Region* (New York: Palgrave, 2002), chap. 15, for a discussion. For ethnic nationalist explanations, see Rasul Bakhsh Rais, *Recovering the Frontier State: War, Ethnicity, and State in Afghanistan* (Lanham, MD: Lexington Books, 2008). See Olivier Roy, *Islam and Resistance in Afghanistan* (New York: Cambridge University Press, 1990), and Edwards, *Before Taliban*. For Pakistani support explanations, see Rashid, *Taliban*; Larry P. Goodson, *Afghanistan's Endless War: State Failure, Regional Politics, and the Rise of the Taliban* (Seattle: University of Washington Press, 2001); and Davis Anthony, "How the Taliban Became a Military Force," in *Fundamentalism Reborn?: Afghanistan and the Taliban*, ed. William Maley (New York: New York University Press, 1998). Several chapters in Maley's edited volume address the role of foreign actors in the rise of the Taliban.

27. The Taliban got their name from the fact that many of them were students in Pakistani madrasas, from which their ultraconservative ideology originated. Rashid described these young madrasa students as surprisingly ignorant of their own culture and history. Rashid, *Taliban*, 31–33. For a discussion of how Islamic education in Pakistani madrasas affected the rise of the Taliban movement, see Thomas H. Johnson and M. Chris Mason, "Understanding the Taliban and Insurgency in Afghanistan," *Orbis* 51, no. 1 (2007): 71–89, and Christine Fair, *The Madrassah Challenge: Militancy and Religious Education in Pakistan* (Washington, DC: United States Institute of Peace Press, 2008). See also Peter Bergen and Swati Pandey, "The Madrassa Scapegoat," *Washington Quarterly* 29, no. 2 (March 1, 2006): 117–25, for a critical discussion of this argument.

28. Contributors to Maley's 1998 edited volume were among the first to investigate Pakistan's role in the conflict in Afghanistan; the authors charge that Islamabad used the Taliban as its proxy against India and other regional actors. William Maley, ed., *Fundamentalism Reborn?: Afghanistan and the Taliban* (New York: New York University Press, 1998).

29. Hizb-i-Islami–Gulbuddin (HIG), Hizb-i-Islami–Khalis (HIK), Ittehad, Harakat-i-Inqilab, Mahaz-i-Milli, and Jebhe-i-Nejat-i-Milli. Each of these groups espoused a comparable Islamist ideology to the Taliban movement, and HIK and Harakat-i-Inqilab in particular were rooted in a conservative Deobandi tradition that was very similar to the Taliban.

30. See Svante E. Cornell, "Taliban Afghanistan: A True Islamic State?," in *The Limits of Culture: Islam and Foreign Policy*, ed. Brenda. Shaffer (Cambridge, MA: MIT Press, 2006), 291–323, quotation on p. 269.

31. Interviews with General Hamid Gul, Colonel Sultan Amir Tarar, Lieutenant General Asad Durrani, Lieutenant General Ali Jan Aurakzai, Peshawar, Rawalpindi, and Islamabad, Pakistan, June 2009.

32. Some existing references to this process can be found in: Neamatollah Nojumi, "The Rise and Fall of the Taliban," in *The Taliban and the Crisis of Afghanistan*, ed. Robert D. Crews and Amin Tarzi (Cambridge, MA: Harvard University Press, 2008), 90–117; Ahmed Rashid, "Pakistan and the Taliban," in *Fundamentalism Reborn?: Afghanistan and the Taliban*, ed. William Maley (New York: New York University Press, 1998); Matinuddin, *The Taliban Phenomenon*; and Nojumi, *The Rise of the Taliban in Afghanistan*.

33. Several scholars make passing reference to the role of the business community in supporting the Taliban between 1994 and 1996, but none of the literature systematically investigates this phenomenon. The most rigorous field research on the relationship between the transit trade and the Taliban has been done by Pakistani journalist Ahmed Rashid, to whom virtually all other scholars refer when addressing the cross-border trade. See Ahmed Rashid, "Nothing to Declare," *Far Eastern Economic Review*, May 11, 1995; Ahmed Rashid, "Drug the Infidels," *Far Eastern Economic Review* 159, no. 20 (May 1997); and Rashid, "Pakistan and the Taliban." For an excellent analysis of the Afghan war economy, including a discussion of the transit trade, see Barnett R. Rubin, "The Political Economy of War and Peace in Afghanistan," *World Development* 28, no. 10 (October 2000): 1789–803.

34. Human Rights Watch, "Paying for the Taliban's Crimes: Abuses against Ethnic Pashtuns in Northern Afghanistan," Afghanistan, April 2002, 4.

35. The mujahideen divvied up the spoils of the fallen government, including political positions. For example, Ahmad Shah Massoud was appointed minister of defense, much to the discontent of his political rival Hekmatyar.

36. This story is based on an eyewitness account as told by the person involved in the dispute.

37. Interview with family of the PATTA president, January 2012.

38. "Aman New Afghan Trade Commissioner," *The Nation*, February 8, 1996.

39. If a checkpoint was particularly profitable, the commander could then ask for a higher percentage of the revenues for having provided such a lucrative business opportunity to the militiamen.

40. Nojumi, *The Rise of the Taliban in Afghanistan*, 117.

41. Interview with Mullah Abdul Salam Zaeef, August 2016.

42. Traders allege that truckers would share information with each other in order to corroborate their exaggerated stories of the rate of extortion on the roads, so that they could collectively overcharge the traders.

43. Interview with trader, January 2012.

44. Interview with a midsize Peshawar-based trader, January 2012.

45. This account is based on author observations, and interviews with relatives of the PATTA president's family and the participants of this business deal, January 2012.

46. This account is based on interviews with the participants of this botched deal, January 2012.

47. Rashid, "Pakistan and the Taliban," 77. Rashid goes on to say that even these figures are likely grossly understated, and the real amount of lost customs duty revenues is much higher.

48. Ibid., 78.

49. Interview with Peshawar-based trader, January 2012.

50. Interview with Mullah Abdul Salam Zaeef, August 2016.

51. Interview with former Taliban official, July 2016.

52. Interview with Mullah Abdul Salam Zeef, August 2016.

53. Ibid.

54. The tradition on Eid-ul-Adha is to sacrifice a lamb, sheep, goat, or cow and share the food with family, neighbors, and the poor. This tradition is practiced by virtually every household in the community that can afford meat and is shared with all of those who cannot.

55. Interview with leading fundraiser for Taliban, Peshawar, Pakistan, June 2009.

56. Interview with Mullah Abdul Salam Zaeef, August 2016.

57. The hundi system is synonymous with the hawala system in Somalia. A hawala is a private money transfer company, which takes the place of banks.

58. Interview with Taliban fundraiser, Peshawar, Pakistan, June 2009. Rahim Afridi passed away some time ago, which is why his name is disclosed here. After September 11, 2001, certain Karachi-based Islamic charitable organizations, such as al-Rashid Trust and al-Akhtar, were blacklisted by the US State Department for financing terrorist organizations. These trusts, like many others in Pakistan, were set up during the Taliban period to channel charitable donations to the Taliban government. The sponsorship of the Taliban by charitable donations allowed extremist actors from the Gulf States, such as bin Laden, the opportunity to exert significant political influence over the cash-strapped Taliban leadership.

59. During the civil war period, there were shocking levels of inflation, massive counterfeit operations, and even competing currencies created by different factions. By the late 1990s, the Afghani was practically worthless and most Afghans relied on Pakistani rupees or American dollars. There is therefore no truly reliable currency conversion or measurement of the purchasing power of the Afghani to evaluate this sum. It is therefore a value that should be read as a qualitative statement from the Taliban's perspective.

60. Zaeef, *My Life with the Taliban*, 67.

61. Interview with Peshawar-based trader, Peshawar, Pakistan, June 2009.

62. Ibid.

63. Interview with Mullah Abdul Salam Zaeef, August 2016. '*Ushr* is a 10 percent tax on agricultural produce, half of which is given to the poor and the other half of which goes to the political leadership. The Taliban asked for zakat from their constituents right away, and began to charge '*ushr* after consolidating their political power.

64. Barnett Rubin, "U.S. Policy in Afghanistan," *Muslim Politics Report* 11 (February 1997): 6.

65. Interview with General Hamid Gul, Islamabad, Pakistan, June 2009.

66. Interview with Colonel Imam, Rawalpindi, Pakistan, June 2009.

67. Interview with Mullah Abdul Salam Zaeef, August 2016.

68. Interview with Colonel Imam, Rawalpindi, Pakistan, June 2009.

69. In September 1994, Taliban representative Mullah Mohammad Rabbani was welcomed in Kabul by Jamiat-i-Islami President Rabbani. Rashid, *Taliban*, 26.

70. One lakh is equal to 100,000 Pakistani rupees. Based on available currency conversion estimates, in the mid-1990s, USD$1 was worth 20–30 Pakistani rupees, which made this contribution equal to approximately USD$10,000 to USD$15,000.

71. Interview with Colonel Imam, Rawalpindi, Pakistan, June 2009.

72. Quoted from Rashid, *Taliban*, 27.

73. Roy Gutman, *How We Missed the Story: Osama Bin Laden, the Taliban, and the Hijacking of Afghanistan* (Washington, DC: US Institute of Peace Press, 2008), 65.

74. Interview with Colonel Imam, Rawalpindi, Pakistan, June 2009.

75. Nojumi, *The Rise of the Taliban in Afghanistan*, 118, and Rashid, *Taliban*, 27, agree that it was approximately two hundred foot soldiers.

76. Gutman, *How We Missed the Story*, 65; Rashid, *Taliban*, 27; Nojumi, "The Rise and Fall of the Taliban," 104.

77. Interview with leading fundraiser and financial manager for the Taliban shura, Peshawar, Pakistan, June 2009.

78. Interview with Colonel Imam, Rawalpindi, Pakistan, June 2009.

79. The Peshawar–Kabul route would have been preferable. However, the magnitude of insecurity on the northern Peshawar-Jalalabad-Kabul road at this time forced Pakistan to pursue the less profitable but more secure southern Quetta-Chaman-Kandahar route. See Rashid, *Taliban*, 26–28, for a description of these events. See also Nojumi, "The Rise and Fall of the Taliban." Neamatollah Nojumi differs with Rashid on the dates, arguing that these events began in August 1994. However, the general story is agreed on by the authors and corroborated by my field interviews with Pakistani officials and members of the transit trade community.

80. Steve Coll, *Ghost Wars: The Secret History of the CIA, Afghanistan, and Bin Laden, from the Soviet Invasion to September 10, 2001*, reprint ed. (New York: Penguin Books, 2004), 282–97.

81. For example, Ambassador Peter Tomsen, former US special envoy to Afghanistan from 1989 to 1992, argued that "a secret April 22, 1994 telegram cable by the American Embassy in Islamabad to Washington, citing that 'an extremely well informed and reliable source' reported that the Taliban's Spin Boldak attack 'was

preceded by artillery shelling of the base from Pakistani Frontier Corps positions' inside Pakistan." However, the cable predates the October 12 assault on Spin Boldak by several months, long before the Taliban shura even considered moving against HIG forces. Peter Tomsen, *The Wars of Afghanistan: Messianic Terrorism, Tribal Conflicts, and the Failures of Great Powers* (New York: Public Affairs, 2011), 535.

82. US embassy (Islamabad) cable, "1995ISLAMA01792: Finally, a Talkative Talib: Origins and Membership of the Religious Students Movement," February 20, 1995, 6.

83. This currency conversion is in the original cable.

84. The fact that there were no foreign observers in Spin Boldak at the time of the Taliban takeover makes it difficult to ascertain whether the Pakistani intelligence was involved in the operation. But this cable, as well as my candid interviews with the ISI, does provide some insight into the incident. US embassy (Islamabad) cable, "1995ISLAMA01792: Finally, a Talkative Talib: Origins and Membership of the Religious Students Movement," 6.

85. Ibid.

86. Rashid, *Taliban*, 28; Nojumi, *The Rise of the Taliban in Afghanistan*, 118.

87. Interview with Colonel Imam, Rawalpindi, Pakistan, June 2009.

88. Quote from Rashid, *Taliban*, 28.

89. Interview Mullah Abdul Salam Zaeef, August 2016.

90. Rashid, *Taliban*, 28–29; interview with Colonel Imam, Rawalpindi, Pakistan, June 2009.

91. Interview with General Aurakzai, June 2009.

92. This refrain was oft-repeated by members of the transit trade community.

93. Author observations; interview with relatives of the PATTA president, January 2012.

CHAPTER 5

1. See Ken Menkhaus, "Governance without Government in Somalia Spoilers, State Building, and the Politics of Coping," *International Security* 31, no. 3 (2006): 74–106; Terrence Lyons, *Somalia: State Collapse, Multilateral Intervention, and Strategies for Political Reconstruction* (Washington, DC: Brookings Institution, 1995); Jamil A. Mubarak, "The 'Hidden Hand' behind the Resilience of the Stateless Economy of Somalia," *World Development* 25, no. 12 (1997): 2027–41.

2. Interview with a former Mogadishu resident from the Darod-Marehan clan, September 2009.

3. This interview was conducted in Dadaab camp for the production of a documentary film on small arms and light weapons trafficking, produced by Shelley Saywell. I worked alongside Shelley on her film, which was filmed on location in multiple parts of both Kenya and Somalia. Shelley Saywell, *Devil's Bargain: A Journey into the Small Arms Trade*, DVD, documentary (Bishari Films, 2008).

4. Helen Fogarassy, *Mission Improbable: The World Community on a UN Compound in Somalia* (Lanham, MD: Lexington Books, 1999); Grant Dawson, *"Here Is Hell": Canada's Engagement in Somalia* (Vancouver: UBC Press, 2007); John L. Hirsch, *Somalia and Operation Restore Hope: Reflections on Peacemaking and Peacekeeping* (Washington, DC: United States Institute of Peace Press, 1995); Ken Rutherford, *Humanitarianism under Fire: The US and UN Intervention in Somalia* (Sterling, VA: Kumarian Press, 2008).

5. Aisha Ahmad, "Agenda for Peace or Budget for War?," *International Journal* 67, no. 2 (2012): 313–31.

6. Sherene Razack, *Dark Threats and White Knights: The Somalia Affair, Peacekeeping, and the New Imperialism* (Buffalo, NY: University of Toronto Press, 2004); *Dishonoured Legacy: The Lessons of the Somalia Affair: Report of the Commission of Inquiry into the Deployment of Canadian Forces to Somalia* (Ottawa: Minister of Public Works and Government Services Canada: Available from Canadian Govt. Pub., 1997). See also Gérard Prunier, "Somalia: Civil War, Intervention and Withdrawal (1990–1995)," *Refugee Survey Quarterly* 15, no. 1 (January 1, 1996): 35–85.

7. Rutherford, *Humanitarianism under Fire*.

8. For a discussion of the lessons of the failed intervention, see Walter Clarke and Jeffrey Herbst, eds., *Learning from Somalia: The Lessons of Armed Humanitarian Intervention* (Boulder, CO: Westview Press, 1997).

9. Ismail I. Ahmed, "The Heritage of War and State Collapse in Somalia and Somaliland: Local-Level Effects, External Interventions and Reconstruction," *Third World Quarterly* 20, no. 1 (1999): 113–27; Kenneth D. Bush, "When Two Anarchies Meet: International Intervention in Somalia," *Journal of Conflict Studies* 17, no. 1 (June 1, 1997): 55–78; Scott Peterson, *Me against My Brother: At War in Somalia, Sudan and Rwanda* (New York: Routledge, 2001).

10. Interview conducted by Bula Hawa field team. Saywell, *Devil's Bargain*.

11. With the possible exceptions of the Adal and Ajuuraan sultanates, the precolonial Somalia was politically decentralized. "They were a nation, not a state, although they possessed all the prerequisites for effective statehood," says Ioan M. Lewis, *Understanding Somalia: Guide to Culture, History and Social Institutions* (London: HAAN, 1993), 25. Also see David D. Laitin and Said S. Samatar, *Somalia: Nation in Search of a State* (London: Gower, 1987), 10–17. For a history of the Ajuuraan, see Lee V. Cassanelli, *The Shaping of Somali Society: Reconstructing the History of a Pastoral People, 1600–1900* (Philadelphia: University of Pennsylvania Press, 1982), chap. 3. Though the Ajuuraan sultanate extracted taxes from farming communities, taxation of nomadic populations is much more difficult logistically. Herbst's thesis that precolonial African states developed with an entirely different relationship between power, territory, and population is particularly useful here. Jeffrey Herbst, *States and Power in Africa: Comparative Lessons in Authority and Control*, 1st ed. (Princeton, NJ: Princeton University Press, 2000).

12. According to Connah, the hinterland exported ivory, rhinoceros horn, tortoise-shell, ambergris, gold, copper, iron, rock crystal, frankincense, myrrh, mangrove poles, ebony and other timbers, sandalwood, and slaves to the coastal cities, which then traded them for imported goods that were needed in both the urban and rural regions. Textiles were imported for the hinterland, whereas luxury goods were imported for the wealthy urban elite in coastal cities. "The East African coastal settlements were acting as entrepôts," argues Connah, "that is to say commercial centres of import, export, collection and distribution, at a more complex level than might be expected in a simple coastal trading town." Graham Connah, *African Civilizations: An Archaeological Perspective*, 2nd ed. (New York: Cambridge University Press, 2001), 219.

13. Exposure to Arab Islam began as early as the eighth century, and religious conversion in Somalia took place between the eleventh and fifteenth centuries; see Laitin and Samatar, *Somalia*, 8, 44.

14. Connah, *African Civilizations*, 216–17.

15. See Michael van Notten, *The Laws of the Somalis: A Stable Foundation for Economic Development in the Horn of Africa* (Trenton, NJ: Red Sea Press, 2005); Lewis, *Understanding Somalia* for a survey of Somali clan, religion, and culture.

16. When the Suez Canal opened in 1839, European powers increased their interest in the Horn of Africa as an important connection to trade in the Far East. The increased interest of Europe in the Horn also provided an opportunity for Ethiopia to manipulate great power rivalries to acquire a steady supply of arms and expand their influence into the Somali Ogaden region. Laitin and Samatar, *Somalia*, 48, 52.

17. "A series of large-scale development projects designed to lay the foundations of a prosperous colony were initiated," explain Laitin and Samatar. "These included a system of plantation farming in which banana, cotton, sugar, and numerous citrus fruits were raised ... the construction of roads to facilitate trade, the digging of scores of wells to improve the pastoral section of the economy, and the introduction of basic health and education services" (ibid., 59).

18. The British ignobly named Sayyid Muhammad the "Mad Mullah" for leading a resistance against colonial domination. This racial epithet is indicative of the prevailing British and European white supremacist attitudes toward African liberation throughout the colonial period.

19. Abdi Ismail Samatar, *The State and Rural Transformation in Northern Somalia, 1884–1986* (Madison: University of Wisconsin Press, 1989), 86. Medani argues that this policy of indirect taxation "would continue throughout modern Somali history," as the state lacked the ability to directly tax its population in the postcolonial period. Khalid Mustafa Medani, "Globalization, Informal Markets and Collective Action: The Development of Islamic and Ethnic Politics in Egypt, Sudan and Somalia" (PhD diss., University of California, Berkeley, 2003), 200.

20. Peter T. Leeson, "Better off Stateless: Somalia before and after Government Collapse," *Journal of Comparative Economics* 35, no. 4 (2007): 689–710.

21. Interviews with Mogadishu-based businesspeople, October 2009.

22. William Reno, "'Somalia and Survival in the Shadow of the Global Economy," Queen Elizabeth House Working Paper Series, Working Paper 100 (Northwestern University, 2003), 20; William Reno, "Somalia: State Failure and Self-Determination in the Shadow of the Global Economy," in *Globalization, Violent Conflict and Self-Determination*, ed. Valpy FitzGerald, Frances Stewart, and Rajesh Venugopal, St. Antony's Series (London: Palgrave Macmillan UK, 2006), 161–63.

23. Reno, "Somalia and Survival in The Shadow of the Global Economy," Queen Elizabeth House Working Paper Series, Working Paper 100, 21.

24. Mubarak, "The 'Hidden Hand' behind the Resilience of the Stateless Economy of Somalia," 2028.

25. Leeson, "Better off Stateless," 694.

26. Benjamin Powell, Ryan Ford, and Alex Nowrasteh, "Somalia after State Collapse: Chaos or Improvement?," *Journal of Economic Behavior & Organization* 67, nos. 3–4 (2008): 657–70.

27. Cold War interference in the Horn of Africa not only hindered the development of the Somali state but also encouraged the growth of the informal economy. Medani states, "The colonial legacy thus set a pattern in which foreign aid would continue to be more significant than domestic production." Medani, "Globalization, Informal Markets and Collective Action," 200.

28. Interview with Mogadishu-based businessman, 2009.

29. Interview with leading Somali warlord, 2009.

30. This information was uncovered through several interviews with members of the Mogadishu business community who gained their fortunes during this tumultuous period using these methods.

31. Ahmad, "Agenda for Peace or Budget for War?," 323–24.

32. Some of the wealthiest businesspeople I interviewed had originally made their fortunes through aid contracts, and then later expanded into other industries.

33. See Peter Andreas, *Blue Helmets and Black Markets: The Business of Survival in the Siege of Sarajevo* (Ithaca, NY: Cornell University Press, 2008), for a detailed explanation of the relationship between international humanitarian intervention and aid and local criminal activity.

34. Interview with Somali trader from Suuq Ba'ad market, November 2009.

35. Interview with Dr. Deqo Mohamed, January 2012.

36. Interview with businessman working in water distribution, November 2009.

37. Interview with CEO of large Somali trading corporation, November 2009.

38. Some of this analysis on pillaging of aid in Somalia has been published in Aisha Ahmad, "Agenda for Peace or Budget for War?," 313–31.

39. Interview with Dr. Hawa Abdi Dibwaale, 2012.

40. Ibid.

41. Allegations of toxic waste dumping by European companies, with the consent of Somali warlords, are widely believed to be true across the country. After the 2004 tsunami, several toxic tankards were washed from Somali waters onto the beaches, confirming the magnitude of the problem. Foreign journalists attempting to research this issue have been shot for trying to track the European companies responsible for these crimes. Having interviewed a Somali warlord who is widely believed to have made such a deal, I can attest that this particular area of research is a most perilous line of inquiry.

42. Material asceticism is highly valued in both Salafi and Sufi variants of Islam, as practicing Muslims are expected not to revere worldly possessions. While there is no prohibition against wealth accumulation per se, there are abundant Islamic teachings against greed and materialism.

43. Interview with dean of Mogadishu-based business school, Nairobi, Kenya, November 2009. This individual's quote was corroborated by several other interviewees, and it is considered common knowledge among the Mogadishu business community.

44. Interview with ICU chief legal counsel, Nairobi, Kenya, November 2009.

45. Interview with professor from Mogadishu University, Nairobi, Kenya, November 2009.

46. Interview with chair of business association, Nairobi, Kenya, November 2009.

47. Somali hawalas are the lifeblood of all Somali business. There are no formal banks in Somalia, and hawalas are used for all money transfers. Exacting a small fee, these companies guarantee safe transfer of money between individuals, businesses, and diaspora communities within seconds. Hawalas make money flow possible in the absence of any formal banking institutions, and they have become so efficient that they are often more competitive than using international banks. See Khalid Mustafa Medani, "Financing Terrorism or Survival? Informal Finance and State Collapse in Somalia, and the US War on Terrorism," *MERIP Middle East Report* 32, no. 2 (2002): 2–9.

48. For example, until its assets were frozen in 2001 on controversial antiterrorism charges, Barakat was the largest hawala in Somalia. However, the current Somali telecom giant Hormud is essentially run by the entire Barakat enterprise and is widely seen to be the same company, only operating under a different, less controversial name. Other hawalas are also known to be part of larger enterprises that include telecom companies.

49. Interview with dean of Mogadishu-based business school, Nairobi, Kenya, November 2009.

50. Roland Marchal, "Islamic Political Dynamics after the Somali Civil War: Before and after September 11," in *Islamism and Its Enemies in the Horn of Africa*, ed. Alexander De Waal (Bloomington: Indiana University Press, 2004), 115.

51. Interview with ICU chief legal counsel, Nairobi, Kenya, October 2009. "Wahhabi" is a term commonly used for Salafi Islam. Wahhabism is considered a highly conservative version of Salafism, which originated in eighteenth-century Saudi Arabia.

Wahhabism has spread to other regions through Saudi funding of religious schools. In the Somali context, the terms "Salafi" and "Wahhabi" can be used interchangeably without serious conceptual problems; however, "Salafi" is a more accurate term for the belief system.

52. Roland Marchal, "A Survey of Mogadishu's Economy" (European Commission/Somali Unit [Nairobi]), August 2002.

53. Kenneth Menkhaus, "Somalia and Somaliland: Terrorism, Political Islam, and State Collapse," in *Battling Terrorism in the Horn of Africa*, ed. Robert I. Rotberg (Washington, DC: Brookings Institution Press, 2005), 23–47.

54. Andre Le Sage, "Somalia: Sovereign Disguise for a Mogadishu Mafia," *Review of African Political Economy* 29, no. 91 (March 1, 2002): 132–38; Kenneth Menkhaus, *Somalia: State Collapse and the Threat of Terrorism* (New York: Oxford University Press for the International Institute for Strategic Studies, 2004).

55. Aisha Ahmad, "The Security Bazaar: Business Interests and Islamist Power in Civil War Somalia," *International Security* 39, no. 3 (2015): 89–117.

56. The TNG was also formed during a time of global economic prosperity, before the crackdown on Somali remittances after the September 11, 2001, terrorist attacks.

57. The SRRC declared the TNG to be illegitimate and sympathetic to Islamic fundamentalism. This claim allowed members of the SRRC to plead for external economic and military resources to undermine the TNG.

58. I was a guest at the presidential inauguration of Abdullahi Yusuf, and the audience was replete with the most powerful warlords in Somalia, each of whom had been given a new parliamentary title.

CHAPTER 6

1. Interview with CEO of El Ma'an Port Authority, November 2009.

2. Ibid. This quote refers to the experience of the Adani family before it created the port and amassed their own private security forces.

3. This exchange was recorded by a trained Somali film crew in Bula Hawa, Somalia. Shelley Saywell, *Devil's Bargain: A Journey into the Small Arms Trade*, DVD, documentary (Bishari Films, 2008).

4. These interviews were conducted by the film crew in Dadaab camp, May 2007. Saywell, *Devil's Bargain*.

5. This exchange was recorded by a trained Somali film crew in Bula Hawa, Somalia. Saywell, *Devil's Bargain*.

6. "Somalia's Moderate Islamist Leader," *BBC*, January 22, 2007, sec. Africa.

7. Cedric Barnes and Harun Hassan, "The Rise and Fall of Mogadishu's Islamic Courts," *Journal of Eastern African Studies* 1, no. 2 (July 1, 2007): 151–60.

8. The ICU is also referred to in the literature as the Union of Islamic Courts (UIC) and the Supreme Council of Islamic Courts (SCIC).

9. Kenneth Menkhaus, "The Crisis in Somalia: Tragedy in Five Acts," *African Affairs* 106, no. 424 (2007): 357–90; Stig Jarle Hansen, *Al-Shabaab in Somalia: The History and Ideology of a Militant Islamist Group, 2005–2012* (New York: Columbia University Press, 2013); Harry Verhoeven, "The Self-Fulfilling Prophecy of Failed States: Somalia, State Collapse and the Global War on Terror," *Journal of Eastern African Studies* 3, no. 3 (November 1, 2009): 405–25.

10. Khat is a popular narcotic drug that is consumed widely in the Horn of Africa region. Khat is chewed almost ubiquitously in Somalia, and soccer is one of the most popular social activities in the country. Banning these were wildly unpopular moves. Notably, in Somalia, the khat industry is dominated by women.

11. Kenneth Menkhaus, "There and Back Again in Somalia," *Middle East Research and Information Project*, February 11, 2007.

12. Barnes and Hassan, "The Rise and Fall of Mogadishu's Islamic Courts," 151–60; Shaul Shay, *Somalia between Jihad and Restoration* (New Brunswick, NJ: Transaction Publishers, 2008); and Jon Abbink, "The Islamic Courts Union: The Ebb and Flow of a Somali Islamist Movement," in Stephen Ellis and Ineke van Kessel, *Movers and Shakers: Social Movements in Africa* (Boston: Brill, 2009), 87–113.

13. Menkhaus, "There and Back Again in Somalia," and author interview with Matt Bryden, Nairobi, Kenya, 2009.

14. Interview with Darod business supporter of the ICU, 2009.

15. Mohamed Abdi Farah, "Islamists Welcome Defected Government Militia in the Capital," *SomaliNet News*, December 15, 2006.

16. Ibid.

17. See Alexander De Waal, *Islamism and Its Enemies in the Horn of Africa* (Bloomington: Indiana University Press, 2004); Barnes and Hassan, "The Rise and Fall of Mogadishu's Islamic Courts"; Shay, *Somalia between Jihad and Restoration*; and Verhoeven, "The Self-Fulfilling Prophecy of Failed States," for a critique of the allegations that the ICU was a terrorist organization.

18. Stig Hansen's pioneering field research showed that the Mogadishu business community provided the Islamic Courts with essential monetary support. Hansen's research on the ICU points to the importance of both the ideological and material reasons that the business community provided financial support to the ICU. The empirical record shows that the business community shifted its resources toward the ICU and against Mogadishu's warlords, but the literature does not clearly explain why. See Stig Jarle Hansen, Atle Mesøy and Tuncay Kardas, eds. *The Borders of Islam: Exploring Huntington's Faultlines, from Al-Andalus to the Virtual Ummah*, (New York: Columbia University Press, 2009), 127–38; Kenneth Menkhaus, "Political Islam in Somalia," *Middle East Policies* 9, no. 1 (March 2002): 109–23; Kenneth Menkhaus, "Governance without Government in Somalia Spoilers, State Building, and the Politics of Coping," *International Security* 31, no. 3 (2006): 74–106; Christian Webersik, "Mogadishu: An Economy without a State," *Third World*

Quarterly 27, no. 8 (2006): 1463–80; Roland Marchal, "A Survey of Mogadishu's Economy" (European Commission/Somali Unit [Nairobi]) (August 2002); Andre Le Sage, "Somalia: Sovereign Disguise for a Mogadishu Mafia," *Review of African Political Economy* 29, no. 91 (March 1, 2002): 132–38; Andre Le Sage, "Stateless Justice in Somalia," Report (The Centre for Humanitarian Dialogue, July 2005); Stig Jarle Hansen, "Civil War Economies, the Hunt for Profit and the Incentives for Peace (The Case of Somalia)," in *AE Working Paper* (2007).

19. This estimate is drawn from interviews with leaders of the Mogadishu business community between October and November 2009. Hansen's 2007 survey found that 69 percent of the business community admitted to voluntarily contributing to the Islamic Courts. See Hansen, "Civil War Economies, the Hunt for Profit and the Incentives for Peace (The Case of Somalia)"; Webersik, "Mogadishu."

20. Interview with executive of large Somali trading corporation, November 2009.

21. Interview with one of the largest traders in Somalia, November 2009.

22. The departure of UNOSOM also resulted in the closure of both the main seaport and airport in Mogadishu, as control over these lucrative trading ports was a point of great contention between rival clans. Instead, the business community was forced to use smaller airstrips and a natural seaport fifteen kilometers away from Mogadishu at El Ma'an for import and export. The El Ma'an port became the primary entry point for goods entering markets in the Horn of Africa, and its owners became some of the richest in Somalia. However, transporting goods from these airstrips and seaports to the main trade markets in downtown Mogadishu meant that additional transportation costs had to be paid at the checkpoints along the roads. These additional transportation and security fees were added to the sale price in the market, thus inflating the cost of goods.

23. Interview with Mogadishu-based trader, November 2009.

24. Ibid.

25. Interview with head of the Suuq Ba'ad market, November 2009.

26. Interview with Mogadishu-based trader, November 2009.

27. Interview with economics professor from Mogadishu University, 2009.

28. Interview with Mogadishu-based businesswoman, 2009.

29. Although the size of the demand for sugar made it impossible for her to dominate the sugar market in Baidoa, this businesswoman and those privileged few like her profited enormously from the low transportation costs.

30. Interview with Mogadishu-based businesswoman, 2009.

31. Interview with frustrated Mogadishu-based trader, 2009.

32. See Mancur Olson, *Power and Prosperity: Outgrowing Communist and Capitalist Dictatorships* (New York: Basic Books, 2000) for a discussion on the different behaviors and interests of stationary versus roving bandits.

33. Interview with Mogadishu-based import-exporter, 2009.

34. Interview with Mogadishu-based trader, November 2009.

35. Interview with head of Coca-Cola Company in Mogadishu, November 2009.

36. Interview with Mogadishu-based trader, November 2009.
37. Interview with Mogadishu-based businesswoman, 2009.
38. Interview with El Ma'an associate executive, October 2009.
39. Interview with CEO of El Ma'an Port Authority, November 2009.
40. Menkhaus, "Governance without Government in Somalia Spoilers, State Building, and the Politics of Coping," 85–86.
41. Interview with leading business sponsor of the ICU, November 2009.
42. Menkhaus, "Governance without Government in Somalia Spoilers, State Building, and the Politics of Coping," 88.
43. Barnes and Hassan, "The Rise and Fall of Mogadishu's Islamic Courts," 153.
44. Interview with leading business sponsor of the ICU, 2009.
45. Roland Marchal, "Islamic Political Dynamics after the Somali Civil War: Before and after September 11," in *Islamism and Its Enemies in the Horn of Africa*, ed. Alexander De Waal (Bloomington: Indiana University Press, 2004), 137.
46. Interview with leading business sponsor of the ICU, 2009.
47. Interviews with early members of the ICU movement and civil society actors suggest that the diaspora and other non-Somali Islamist actors were actually late players, supporting the Islamists after the latter had already purged the clan warlords. There continues to be a dearth of academic research on the impact of Somali diaspora support on the civil war, however. For an assessment of money transfer agencies and diaspora politics in Somalia, see Khalid Mustafa Medani, "Financing Terrorism or Survival? Informal Finance and State Collapse in Somalia, and the US War on Terrorism," *MERIP Middle East Report* 32, no. 2 (2002): 2–9.
48. Interview with leading business sponsor of the ICU, 2009.
49. Interview with head of Coca-Cola Company in Mogadishu, November 2009.
50. Muse Sudi Yalahow is a Hawiye-Abdgal warlord from another subclan.
51. The executive argued that Rage, who owned Esaley airstrip, was landing CIA planes and acquiring material support from the Americans: "When the US gave money to Rage, the Adani family supported [Sheikh] Sharif because he brought stability. Then Bashir captured our technicals and positions and he was moving to capture El Ma'an port. He said, 'It's not me who has the authority to give back technicals and positions; the authority is with the Americans. I met with the officers from the CIA and InterPol to get back our technicals. The US said Rage is their friend." Interview with CEO of El Ma'an Port Authority, November 2009.
52. Ibid.
53. The 70 percent figure was corroborated in many interviews with the business community. Stig Hansen's 2007 survey work in Mogadishu argues that 69 percent supported the ICU. Hansen, "Civil War Economies, the Hunt for Profit and the Incentives for Peace (The Case of Somalia)."
54. This figure is reported by John Prendergast of the International Crisis Group in an interview with *The Guardian*. He is quoted as saying: "This was counter-terrorism on the cheap. This is a backwater place that nobody really wants to get involved in,

so [they] thought, let's just do this and maybe we'll get lucky." Rory Carroll, Xan Rice, and Oliver Burkeman, "Fall of Mogadishu Leaves US Policy in Ruins," *The Guardian*, June 10, 2006, sec. World news.

55. Interview with head of Mogadishu market, 2009.

56. Interview with professor from Mogadishu University, 2009.

57. Interview with Mogadishu-based trader, November 2009.

58. Interview with Mogadishu-based businesswoman, 2009.

59. The results of this study are published in Aisha Ahmad, "The Security Bazaar: Business Interests and Islamist Power in Civil War Somalia," *International Security* 39, no. 3 (January 1, 2015): 89–117; and the survey text, replication data, and a detailed methodological appendix for this study are available online. Please also see the Appendix in this manuscript.

60. The TNG was used as the residual category in the analysis. The two primary independent variables in the estimation are "warlord security costs" and "Islamist security costs." The analysis used multinomial logit analysis in STATA. Logit, rather than probit, was used so that the analysis could produce clear and interpretable coefficients, specifically risk ratios. Negative relationships are therefore indicated by values lower than 1. The independence of irrelevant alternatives (IIA) problem was ruled out using the Hausman test, thereby making the utility of mlogit equal to that of mprobit. Several diagnostic tests were conducted to rule out problems of multicollinearity with all independent variables in the model.

61. Table 6.1 shows the complete results of the estimation, with risk ratios and the standard error in parentheses, using the TNG as the residual category. Figure 6.1 builds on these results, and shows only statistically significant coefficients; this figure is designed for the lay reader to understand these results. Note that these exact results have already been published in the article cited in n. 59, along with replication data, coding, and the methodological appendix.

62. This is in spite of the fact that 79 percent of all respondents stated that general insecurity was the greatest challenge facing their business and that 97 percent said they would be willing to pay higher taxes in order to have a central government.

63. This finding suggests that future research needs to explore the possibility of a curvilinear relationship between income and political activism in civil war competition.

64. Businesspeople were asked to respond on a five-point ordinal scale ranging from strongly disagree to strongly agree, which were then recoded into binary variables for the analysis.

65. Interview with female owners of large khat-trading corporation, Nairobi, Kenya, November 2009.

66. It is possible that respondents who indicated they had university-level education include those who pursued Islamic studies at a university level. Islamic universities across the Middle East are a popular destination for wealthier Somalis seeking advanced education. However, it is not possible to decipher this nuance from these

survey results, and further investigation is needed in order to ascertain the relationship between education type and political preference.

67. Interview with CEO of El Ma'an Port Authority, November 2009.
68. Ibid.
69. Ibid.
70. Interview with Mogadishu-based trader, November 2009.
71. Interview with businessman who opposed the ICU, November 2009.
72. Interview with the owner of the largest cigarette business in Somalia, May 2007.
73. Ibid.

CHAPTER 7

1. Interview with General Aurakzai, Islamabad, May 2009.
2. Author interviews, June 2009, January 2012.
3. Interview with villagers, Balkh province, Afghanistan, May 2005.
4. Barbara Crossette, "Taliban's Ban on Poppy a Success, U.S. Aides Say," *New York Times*, May 20, 2001, sec. World.
5. The motives behind the ban are disputed, and some scholars argue that the ban was actually a strategic move to manipulate global heroin prices. For a discussion, see Chris J. Dolan, "United States' Narco-Terrorism Policy: A Contingency Approach to the Convergence of the Wars on Drugs and against Terrorism," *Review of Policy Research* 22, no. 4 (2005): 451–71; Jeffrey Clemens, "Opium in Afghanistan: Prospects for the Success of Source Country Drug Control Policies," *Journal of Law & Economics* 51, no. 3 (2008): 407–32; Hermann Kreutzmann, "Afghanistan and the Opium World Market: Poppy Production and Trade," *Iranian Studies* 40, no. 5 (2007): 605–21.
6. For a discussion of the opium industry in Afghanistan, see Jonathan Goodhand, "Frontiers and Wars: The Opium Economy in Afghanistan," *Journal of Agrarian Change* 5, no. 2 (April 1, 2005): 191–216; David Macdonald, *Drugs in Afghanistan: Opium, Outlaws and Scorpion Tales* (London: Pluto, 2007).
7. Interview with prominent cigarette trader from Mogadishu, November 2009.
8. Interview with CEO of El Ma'an Port Authority, November 2009.
9. David Kilcullen, *The Accidental Guerrilla: Fighting Small Wars in the Midst of a Big One* (New York: Oxford University Press, 2009).
10. For a discussion of how terrorists use attacks to provoke a reaction, see David A. Lake, "Rational Extremism: Understanding Terrorism in the Twenty-First Century," *Dialogue IO* 1, no. 1 (2002): 15–29; See also Andrew H. Kydd and Barbara F. Walter, "The Strategies of Terrorism," *International Security* 31, no. 1 (2006): 49–80.
11. In fact, the Taliban even officially thanked the Americans for "the help that the US provided during the struggle against the Soviets." US Department of State (Washington, DC) cable, "SECRET ISLAMABAD 008803 Osama bin

Laden: Taliban Spokesperson seeks New Proposal for Resolving bin Laden Problem," National Security Archive, November 28, 1998, <http://www.gwu.edu/~nsarchiv/ NSAEBB/NSAEBB134/Document%204%20-%20STATE%20220495.pdf>.

12. US embassy (Islamabad) cable," 1995ISLAMA01792 Finally, a Talkative Talib: Origins and Membership of the Religious Students Movement," National Security Archive, February 20, 1995, <http://www.gwu.edu/~nsarchiv/NSAEBB/ NSAEBB97/tal8.pdf>.

13. US embassy (Islamabad) cable, "1995ISLAMA01686 Meeting with the Taliban in Kandahar: More Questions than Answers," National Security Archive, February 15, 1995, <http://www.gwu.edu/~nsarchiv/NSAEBB/NSAEBB97/tal7.pdf>.

14. Fawaz A. Gerges, *The Far Enemy: Why Jihad Went Global* (Cambridge: Cambridge University Press, 2005), 76.

15. Lawrence Wright, *The Looming Tower: Al Qaeda and the Road to 9/11*, reprint ed. (New York: Vintage, 2007), 164–56.

16. Peter L. Bergen, *Holy War, Inc.: Inside the Secret World of Osama Bin Laden* (New York: Free Press, 2001), 88–89; Gerges, *The Far Enemy*, 145–49.

17. Gerges, *The Far Enemy*, 235.

18. Ibid., 236; Najwa Bin Laden, Jean P. Sasson, and Omar Bin Laden, *Growing up Bin Laden: Osama's Wife and Son Take Us Inside Their Secret World* (New York: St. Martin's Press, 2009), 135.

19. Mullah Nourallah is believed to be Haji Saz Nur of the Ittehad group led by Sayyaf. See Kevin Bell, "Usama Bin Ladin's 'Father Sheikh': Yunus Khalis and the Return of Al-Qa'ida's Leadership to Afghanistan" (West Point: Combating Terrorism Center—West Point, May 14, 2013), n. 267. There are several conflicting accounts of bin Laden leaving Sudan and getting to Afghanistan. See Bin Laden, Sasson, and Bin Laden, *Growing up Bin Laden*, 142–44; Steve Coll, *Ghost Wars: The Secret History of the CIA, Afghanistan, and Bin Laden, from the Soviet Invasion to September 10, 2001*, reprint ed. (New York: Penguin Books, 2004), 325–26; Bergen, *Holy War, Inc.*, 92–93.

20. Gerges, *The Far Enemy*, 141–42.

21. See Abdul Salam Zaeef, *My Life with the Taliban*, ed. Alex Strick van Linschoten and Felix Kuehn (London: Hurst, 2010), 131–39; Gerges, *The Far Enemy*, 192–99.

22. US embassy (Islamabad) cable, "2000ISLAMA 00567 A/S Inderfurth and S/ CT Sheehan Meet Taliban Representatives," National Security Archive, February 1, 2000, <http://www.gwu.edu/~nsarchiv/NSAEBB/NSAEBB134/Doc%2015. pdf>.

23. US embassy (Islamabad) cable, "1998ISLAMA09488 Usama Bin Ladin: Charge Underscores U.S. Concerns on Interviews; Taliban Envoy Says Bin Ladin Hoodwinked Them and It Will Not Happen Again," National Security Archive, December 30, 1998, <http://www.gwu.edu/~nsarchiv/NSAEBB/NSAEBB134/ Doc%2014.pdf>.

24. Zaeef, *My Life with the Taliban*, 138.

25. US Department of State (Washington, DC) cable, "SECRET STATE 220495 Osama bin Laden: Taliban Spokesperson Seeks New Proposal for Resolving bin Laden Problem," National Security Archive, November 28, 1998, 4, http://www.gwu.edu/~nsarchiv/NSAEBB/NSAEBB134/Document%204%20-%20STATE%20220495.pdf.

26. US embassy (Islamabad) cable, "1998ISLAMA06863 Demarche to Taliban on New bin Laden Threat," National Security Archive, September 14, 1998, http://www.gwu.edu/~nsarchiv/NSAEBB/NSAEBB134/Doc%206.pdf.

27. US Department of State (Washington, DC) cable, "1998STATE177309 Afghanistan: Taliban Convene Ulema, Iran and Bin Ladin on the Agenda," National Security Archive, September 25, 1998, 4, <http://www.gwu.edu/~nsarchiv/NSAEBB/NSAEBB97/tal26.pdf>.

28. US embassy (Islamabad) cable, "1998ISLAMA09488 Usama Bin Ladin: Charge Underscores U.S. Concerns on Interviews; Taliban Envoy Says Bin Ladin Hoodwinked Them and It Will Not Happen Again," National Security Archive, December 30, 1998, <http://www.gwu.edu/~nsarchiv/NSAEBB/NSAEBB134/Doc%2014.pdf>

29. US embassy (Islamabad) cable, "1998ISLAMA06863 Demarche to Taliban on New bin Laden Threat," National Security Archive, September 14, 1998, 2, <http://www.gwu.edu/~nsarchiv/NSAEBB/NSAEBB134/Doc%206.pdf>.

30. Interview with Mullah Abdul Salam Zaeef, August 2016. I note that Zaeef personally visited Mutawakkil in July 2016 on my behalf, because he was ill and unable to speak with me directly. During this meeting, Zaeef explicitly asked Mutawakkil about reports that alleged that he had attempted to warn the Americans of bin Laden's plot in 2001. In response, Mutawakkil stated that these reports were categorically false. I thank both Zaeef and Mutawakkil for going out of their way to address this point of confusion.

31. Only Hekmatyar stubbornly rejected the US operation, choosing to fight against both the Taliban and the Americans at once.

32. Azam Ahmed, "Penetrating Every Stage of Afghan Opium Chain, Taliban Become a Cartel," *New York Times*, February 16, 2016.

33. Quote translated from film footage by Jamie Doran, *Afghan Massacre: The Convoy of Death*, documentary (2002), segment found at 13:14–15:20 minute mark.

34. For one of many incidents of gang rape by Northern Alliance militiamen, see Aryn Baker, "Warlords Toughen US Task in Afghanistan," *Time*, December 9, 2008.

35. Interview with female parliamentarian in Afghan National Assembly, who was seated next to Sayyaf's men in parliamentary sessions, October 2006.

36. US embassy (Kabul) cable, "09KABUL3890_a Kandahar Politics Complicate US Objectives in Afghanistan," Wikileaks, December 6, 2009, <https://wikileaks.org/plusd/cables/09KABUL3890_a.html>.

37. United Nations Office on Drugs and Crime, "Corruption in Afghanistan: Bribery as Reported by the Victims" (UNODC, 2010), 3.

38. Roland Paris, "Is Corruption the Cost of Saving Afghanistan?," *Globe and Mail*, July 11, 2012. *New York Times* foreign correspondents Matthew Rosenberg and Graham Bowley made an equally scathing assessment of graft in Afghanistan: "The United States is leaving behind a problem it underwrote over the past decade with tens of billions of dollars of aid and logistical support: a narrow business and political elite defined by its corruption, and despised by most Afghans for it." Matthew Rosenberg and Graham Bowley, "Intractable Afghan Graft Hampering U.S. Strategy," *New York Times*, March 7, 2012.

39. Timothy Clack and Robert Johnson, eds., *At the End of Military Intervention: Historical, Theoretical, and Applied Approaches to Transition, Handover, and Withdrawal* (Oxford: Oxford University Press, 2015), 371–72.

40. Integrity Watch Afghanistan, "Afghan Perceptions and Experiences of Corruption: A National Survey 2010" (Integrity Watch Afghanistan, July 8, 2010).

41. This popular proverb tells the story of a man who took his revenge after one hundred years and then fretted that he had acted hastily. It is meant to signify the importance of patience in seeking vengeance over one's enemies.

42. As the older warriors passed on, the younger generation of Taliban fighters had more familiarity and experience with al-Qaeda's Salafi Islamist ideology than their own religious traditions. Over time, a number of Takfiri, or "excommunication" splinter groups, emerged in the volatile border region with Pakistan, which labeled anyone who opposed them an apostate and then brutally murdered them. The ideological shift of certain parts of the Taliban insurgency to a more extremist Salafi and Takfiri orientation is evident from the evolution of both the content and publication methods of their jihadi media operations over the course of the past ten years. For a detailed analysis, see Alex Strick van Linschoten and Felix Keuhn, *An Enemy We Created: The Myth of the Taliban-Al-Qaeda Merger in Afghanistan* (New York: Oxford University Press, 2012).

43. Peter L. Bergen, *Manhunt: The Ten-Year Search for Bin Laden from 9/11 to Abbottabad* (New York: Crown Publishers, 2012).

44. "Somalia Unrest Worries Bush," *Al Jazeera English*, June 3, 2006.

45. Ibid.

46. Matt Bryden interview in Saywell, *Devil's Bargain: A Journey into the Small Arms Trade*, DVD, documentary (Bishari Films, 2008). See also Harry Verhoeven, "The Self-Fulfilling Prophecy of Failed States: Somalia, State Collapse and the Global War on Terror," *Journal of Eastern African Studies* 3, no. 3 (2009): 405–25.

47. For a discussion on the successes and failures of al-Qaeda in Somalia in the pre-ICU period, see Kenneth Menkhaus, "Somalia and Somaliland: Terrorism, political Islam, and State Collapse," in *Battling Terrorism in the Horn of Africa, ed. Robert I. Rotberg* (Washington, DC: Brookings Institution Press, 2005), 38–44.

48. Hiiraan Online, "The Union of Islamic Courts in Mogadishu Break the Silence (Press Release)," accessed June 17, 2016, https://www.hiiraan.com/news/2006/

jun/somali_news6_7.aspx; Rory Carroll, "Mogadishu's New Rulers Reassure West," *The Guardian*, June 14, 2006, sec. World news.

49. "Somali Islamists Deny Terror Role," *BBC*, June 7, 2006, sec. Africa.

50. Hiiraan Online, "The Union of Islamic Courts in Mogadishu Break the Silence (Press Release)." Emphasis in original.

51. Carroll, "Mogadishu's New Rulers Reassure West."

52. At the peak of its activity, AIAI had received funds from Osama bin Laden's emerging al-Qaeda network. While AIAI operated exclusively in the Somali theater, Aweys' group cooperated with the perpetrators of the 1998 bombings of the US embassies in Kenya and Tanzania. In fact, the 1998 embassy attacks first brought bin Laden and his organization into the spotlight and raised concerns about Somalia's connection to transnational terrorist organizations. Although AIAI had formally dissolved before the rise of the ICU, many of the supporters of the Islamic courts had a history of involvement with the early movement.

53. "Profile: Somalia's Islamic Courts," *BBC*, June 6, 2006, sec. Africa.

54. Menkhaus, *Battling Terrorism in the Horn of Africa*.

55. Robert F. Worth, "U.N. Says Somalis Helped Hezbollah Fighters," *New York Times*, November 15, 2006.

56. This botched 2006 report was produced by the UN Monitoring Group team led by Bruno Schiemsky and Mel Holt. In 2008, leadership of the UN Monitoring Group was handed to Matt Bryden, an expert on Somali politics who has traveled extensively across Somalia and speaks Somali.

57. US embassy (Addis Ababa) cable, "05ADDISABABA3984 Ethiopia: PM Meles Welcomes USG Engagement on Somalia, Calls It Greatest Long-term Security Threat," Wikileaks, November 11, 2005, http://wikileaks.cabledrum.net/cable/2005/11/05ADDISABABA3984.html.

58. See Ken Menkhaus, "There and Back Again in Somalia" *Middle East Research and Information Project*, February 11, 2007.

59. After multiple border wars, an unresolved territorial dispute, and accusations of political interference, the majority of Somalis consider Ethiopia to be their most dangerous regional rival. For a greater understanding of the historic rivalry between Somalia and Ethiopia, see Peter Schwab, "Cold War on the Horn of Africa," *African Affairs* 77, no. 306 (1978): 6–20.

60. Despite having tacit connections to transnational networks as early as 2006, al-Shabaab began as a principally domestic Islamist movement. In 2007, the group's key goal was the expulsion of foreign forces from Somali territory.

61. On al-Shabaab's early popularity, see Stig Jarle Hansen, *Al-Shabaab in Somalia: The History and Ideology of a Militant Islamist Group, 2005–2012* (New York: Columbia University Press, 2013). I also draw on interviews with community leaders from the Darod-dominant Gedo region in October 2009 and Hawiye-dominant Middle Shabelle region in September 2011, February 2012, and February 2013.

62. Interview with the leader of the Mogadishu-based civil society organization, Toronto, Canada, 2008.
63. Ibid.
64. Somalia's first known suicide bombing occurred in September 2006 in Baidoa, targeting the TFG's president at the time, Abdullahi Yusuf. See "Somali Leader Escapes Attack—Africa & Middle East—International Herald Tribune," *New York Times*, September 18, 2006.
65. Matt Bryden, "The Reinvention of Al-Shabaab: A Strategic Choice or Necessity?" *Center for Strategic International Studies* (February 2014).
66. Aisha Ahmad, "Going Global: Islamist Competition in Contemporary Civil Wars," *Security Studies* 25, no. 2 (2016): 353–84.
67. Quote from video, "Labayk Ya Usama" (We hear your call, Osama), Al-Kitaib Media Foundation, 2009.
68. Interviews with Dr. Hawa Abdi's staff, February 2012.
69. Although the children were returned, fears of child soldier abductions skyrocketed. The staff closed the school and organized the evacuation of tens of thousands of IDPs from Afgooye to Mogadishu. This account is based on field reports and author interviews, February 2012.
70. For details, see "Letter dated 12 July 2013 from the Chair of the Security Council Committee pursuant to resolutions 751 (1992) and 1907 (2009) concerning Somalia and Eritrea addressed to the President of the Security Council," 439–84.
71. UN Monitoring Group, "Letter dated 27 June 2012 from the members of the Monitoring Group on Somalia and Eritrea addressed to the Chairman of the Security Council Committee pursuant to resolutions 751 (1992) and 1907 (2009) concerning Somalia and Eritrea."
72. This exchange is based on the author's observations, February 2013.
73. "Can Somalia's Cheap Peacekeeping Defeat Al-Shabab?," *BBC News*, accessed June 17, 2016, http://www.bbc.com/news/world-africa-18392212.
74. Interviews with members of Somali Chamber of Commerce, Mogadishu, Somalia, February 2013.
75. Christopher Anzalone, "The Life and Death of Al-Shabab Leader Ahmed Godane," *CTC Sentinel* 7, no. 9 (September 2014): 19–23.
76. Kilcullen, *The Accidental Guerrilla*.
77. Verhoeven, "The Self-Fulfilling Prophecy of Failed States."
78. For a discussion of global al-Qaeda networks, see Jean-Pierre Filiu, "The Local and Global Jihad of Al-Qa'ida in the Islamic Maghrib," *Middle East Journal* 63, no. 2 (2009): 213–26; David Kilcullen, *Counterinsurgency* (Oxford: Oxford University Press, 2010); Daniel Byman, "Buddies or Burdens? Understanding the Al Qaeda Relationship with Its Affiliate Organizations," *Security Studies* 23, no. 3 (2014): 431–70.
79. For a discussion of the relationship between local and global Islamists, see Kilcullen, *The Accidental Guerrilla*.

CHAPTER 8

1. For a full translation of the quote in the opening epigraph and the details of its origins and usage, please see the guest post by Aymenn Jawad al-Tamimi in Aaron Y. Zelin, "Famous Anasheed: 'Madin Kas-Sayf' by Abu Ali," *JIHADOLOGY: A Clearinghouse for Jihādī Primary Source Material, Original Analysis, and Translation Service*, March 3, 2013, http://jihadology.net/2013/03/03/guest-post-famous-anasheed-madin-kas-sayf-by-abu-ali/.

2. Brynjar Lia, "Understanding Jihadi Proto-States," *Perspectives on Terrorism* 9, no. 4 (July 21, 2015): 31–41; Stathis Kalyvas, "Is ISIS a Revolutionary Group and If Yes, What Are the Implications?," *Perspectives on Terrorism* 9, no. 4 (July 21, 2015): 42–47; Thomas Hegghammer and Petter Nesser, "Assessing the Islamic State's Commitment to Attacking the West," *Perspectives on Terrorism* 9, no. 4 (July 21, 2015): 14–30; David Kilcullen, *The Accidental Guerrilla: Fighting Small Wars in the Midst of a Big One* (New York: Oxford University Press, 2009).

3. This account is based on author observations, Beirut, Lebanon, July 2016.

4. Author observations, Beirut, Lebanon, July 2016.

5. Interview with Dr. Amine Lebbos, Beirut, Lebanon, July 2016.

6. Daniel Byman, *Al Qaeda, the Islamic State, and the Global Jihadist Movement: What Everyone Needs to Know* (New York: Oxford University Press, 2015); Michael Weiss and Hassan Hassan, *ISIS: Inside the Army of Terror* (New York: Regan Arts, 2015).

7. Interview with Dr. Amine Lebbos, Beirut, Lebanon, July 2016.

8. John Turner, "Strategic Differences: Al Qaeda's Split with the Islamic State of Iraq and Al-Sham," *Small Wars & Insurgencies* 26, no. 2 (March 2015): 208–25.

9. There many competing militant factions mobilized against both the Syrian government and the Daesh threat, including the nationalist Free Syrian Army (FSA) and a large number of smaller factions that have coalesced into an umbrella network called the Islamic Front (IF).

10. Daesh not only espoused a violent global Islamist ideology and recruited thousands of foreign fighters to fill its ranks but also drew support from existing tribal communities. Reinoud Leenders and Steven Heydemann, "Popular Mobilization in Syria: Opportunity and Threat, and the Social Networks of the Early Risers," *Mediterranean Politics* 17, no. 2 (Summer 2012): 139–59.

11. Matt Bradley, "ISIS Declares New Islamist Caliphate," *Wall Street Journal*, June 29, 2014.

12. Quote from Daesh video, *The End of Sykes-Picot*, June 29, 2014.

13. Over the course of the conflict, the Sunni tribes on both sides of the Iraqi-Syrian border mobilized support behind different Islamist groups at various stages of the conflict, switching sides when the tide of battle has shifted in any group's favor. For a discussion of tribal politics in Iraq, see Nour Malas and Ghassan Adnan, "Sunni Tribes in Iraq Divided over Battle against Islamic State," *Wall Street Journal*, May 22, 2015.

14. Aisha Ahmad, "Going Global: Islamist Competition in Contemporary Civil Wars," *Security Studies* 25, no. 2 (April 2016): 353–84.

15. Martin Chulov, "Isis to Mint Own Islamic Dinar Coins in Gold, Silver and Copper," *The Guardian*, November 14, 2014. Note, however, that in practice, the US dollar continues to be the gold standard for Daesh: Joshua Keating and Christina Cauterucci, "The Official Currency of ISIS's Caliphate: The U.S. Dollar," *Slate*, February 16, 2016.

16. Jose Pagliery, "Inside the $2 Billion ISIS War Machine," *CNNMoney*, December 6, 2015, http://money.cnn.com/2015/12/06/news/isis-funding/index.html.

17. Sarah Almukhtar, "ISIS Finances Are Strong," *New York Times*, May 19, 2015

18. Patrick B. Johnston and Benjamin Bahney, "Hitting ISIS Where It Hurts: Disrupt ISIS's Cash Flow in Iraq," *New York Times*, August 13, 2014. See also Matthew Levitt, "Show Me the Money: Targeting the Islamic State's Bottom Line," *The Washington Institute*, October 1, 2014; Raheem Salman and Yara Bayoumy, "Insight—Islamic State's Financial Independence Poses Quandary for Its Foes," *Reuters India*, September 2014.

19. Bilal A. Wahab, "How Iraqi Oil Smuggling Greases Violence," *Middle East Quarterly* 13, no. 4 (Fall 2006): 53–59; Peter Andreas, "Criminalizing Consequences of Sanctions: Embargo Busting and Its Legacy," *International Studies Quarterly* 49, no. 2 (June 1, 2005): 335–60.

20. Interview with Dr. Renad Mansour, Beirut, Lebanon, July 2016.

21. Ibid. Emphasis was in original.

22. Ibid.

23. Damien McElroy, "Iraq Oil Bonanza Reaps $1 Million a Day for Islamic State," July 11, 2014; Valérie Marcel, "ISIS and the Dangers of Black Market Oil," *Chatham House*, accessed August 5, 2015, https://www.chathamhouse.org/expert/comment/15203; Borzou Daragahi and Erika Solomon, "Fuelling Isis Inc," *Financial Times*, September 21, 2014; Bilal A. Wahab, "How Iraqi Oil Smuggling Greases Violence," *Middle East Quarterly* 13, no. 4 (Fall 2006): 53–59.

24. Louise Shelley, "Blood Money: How ISIS Makes Bank," *Foreign Affairs*, The Anthology, November 30, 2014, https://www.foreignaffairs.com/articles/iraq/2014-11-30/blood-money.

25. Interview with Dr. George Masse, Chair of International Affairs Department, American University of Science and Technology, Beirut, Lebanon, July 2016.

26. Ibid.

27. Interview with Dr. George Labaki, Notre Dame University, Beirut, Lebanon, July 2016.

28. Interview with Dr. Renad Mansour, Beirut, Lebanon, July 2016.

29. Interview with Dr. Yezid Sayigh, Beirut, Lebanon, July 2016.

30. Ibid.

31. Margaret Coker, "How Islamic State's Secret Banking Network Prospers," *Wall Street Journal*, February 24, 2016.

32. "How ISIS Governs Its Caliphate," *Newsweek*, February 12, 2014; Salman and Bayoumy, "Insight—Islamic State's Financial Independence Poses Quandary for Its Foes."

33. Joseph Thorndike, "How ISIS Is Using Taxes to Build a Terrorist State," *Forbes*, August 18, 2014; Salman and Bayoumy, "Insight—Islamic State's Financial Independence Poses Quandary for Its Foes."

34. David Francis and Dan De Luce, "Hitting the Islamic State's Oil Isn't Enough," *Foreign Policy,* November 17, 2015; Mara Revkin, "ISIS' Social Contract: What the Islamic State Offers Civilians," *Foreign Affairs*, January 10, 2016.

35. Revkin, "ISIS' Social Contract: What the Islamic State Offers Civilians,"

36. Ben Hubbard, "Life in a Jihadist Capital: Order with a Darker Side—In a Syrian City, ISIS Puts Its Vision into Practice," *New York Times*, July 23, 2014.

37. Francis and De Luce, "Hitting the Islamic State's Oil Isn't Enough."

38. Salman and Bayoumy, "Insight—Islamic State's Financial Independence Poses Quandary for Its Foes."

39. Interview with Dr. Renad Mansour, Beirut, Lebanon, July 2016.

40. Revkin, "ISIS' Social Contract: What the Islamic State Offers Civilians."

41. Jean-Charles Brisard and Damien Martinez, "Islamic State: The Economy-Based Terrorist Funding," *Thomson Reuters*, October 2014, 5.

42. Joanna Paraszczuk, "The ISIS Economy: Crushing Taxes and High Unemployment," *The Atlantic*, September 2, 2015.

43. Revkin, "ISIS' Social Contract: What the Islamic State Offers Civilians."

44. Hubbard, "Life in a Jihadist Capital: Order with a Darker Side."

45. Interview with peace researcher, Bamako, Mali, July 2016.

46. Interview with political analyst, Bamako, Mali, July 2016.

47. Ibid.

48. Interview with peace researcher, Bamako, Mali, July 2016.

49. Ibid.

50. Ibid.

51. Ibid.

52. In January 2007, an Algerian Salafi jihadist group announced that it was rebranding itself as AQIM. The new group primarily aimed at overthrowing the Algerian government and establishing a new regime based on sharia. On the relationship between al-Qaeda and regional affiliates, see Jean-Pierre Filiu, "The Local and Global Jihad of Al-Qa'ida in the Islamic Maghrib," *Middle East Journal* 63, no. 2 (April 1, 2009): 213–26. See also Karen J. Greenberg, *Al-Qaeda Now: Understanding Today's Terrorists* (New York: Cambridge University Press, 2005); Christina Hellmich, *Al-Qaeda: From Global Network to Local Franchise* (Halifax: Fernwood, 2011); Michael W. S. Ryan, *Decoding Al-Qaeda's Strategy: The Deep Battle against America* (New York: Columbia University Press, 2013); Assaf Moghadam, *The Globalization of Martyrdom: Al-Qaeda, Salafi Jihad, and the*

Diffusion of Suicide Attacks (Baltimore: Johns Hopkins University Press, 2008); Fawaz A. Gerges, *The Rise and Fall of Al-Qaeda* (New York: Oxford University Press, 2011); Bruce O. Riedel, *The Search for Al-Qaeda: Its Leadership, Ideology, and Future* (Washington, DC: Brookings Institution Press, 2008); Jean-Luc Marret, "Al-Qaeda in Islamic Maghreb: A 'Glocal' Organization," *Studies in Conflict & Terrorism* 31, no. 6 (June 2008): 541–52. See also David A. Lake, "Rational Extremism: Understanding Terrorism in the Twenty-First Century," *Dialogue IO* 1, no. 1 (2002): 15–29.

53. Wolfram Lacher, "Organized Crime and Conflict in the Sahel-Sahara Region," *Carnegie Endowment for International Peace*, September 13, 2012, accessed April 4, 2017, http://carnegieendowment.org/2012/09/13/organized-crime-and-conflict-in-sahel-sahara-region-pub-49360.

54. Zachary Laub and Jonathan Masters, "Al-Qaeda in the Islamic Maghreb," *CFR Backgrounders*, updated March 27, 2015. David Lewis, "Al Qaeda's Richest Faction Dominant in North Mali," *Reuters*, July 26, 2012.

55. Interview with peace researcher, Bamako, Mali, July 2016.

56. Lacher, "Organized Crime and Conflict in the Sahel-Sahara Region."

57. Daveed Gartenstein-Ross, Nathaniel Barr, George Willcoxon, and Norhan Basuni, "The Crisis in North Africa: Implications for Europe and Options for EU Policymakers," Clingendael Report (The Hague, Netherlands: Netherlands Institute of International Relations, April 2015), 4.

58. Interview with peace researcher, Bamako, Mali, July 2016.

59. Interview with civil society organization from northern Kidal region, Bamako, Mali, July 2016.

60. ECOWAS, "The Political Economy of Conflicts in Northern Mali," *ECOWAS Peace and Security Report* 2 (Dakar, Senegal: ECOWAS and ISS, April 2013).

61. Interview with Malian scholar, Bamako, Mali, July 2016.

62. Laub and Masters, "Al-Qaeda in the Islamic Maghreb".

63. Louise I. Shelley, *Dirty Entanglements: Corruption, Crime, and Terrorism* (Cambridge: Cambridge University Press, 2014), 235; see also, Jean-Pierre Filiu, "Could Al-Qaeda Turn African in the Sahel?" Carnegie Middle East Program, Paper 112, June 2010, 4.

64. Morten Bøås cited in Jamie Doward, "How Cigarette Smuggling Fuels Africa's Islamist Violence," *The Guardian*, January 27, 2013.

65. Interview with civil society organization from northern Kidal region, Bamako, Mali, July 2016.

66. Interview with Malian legal scholar, Bamako, Mali, July 2016.

67. Lacher draws these figures from a 2009 UNODC report. See Lacher, "Organized Crime and Conflict in the Sahel-Sahara Region."

68. Baz Lecocq and Georg Klute, "Tuareg Separatism in Mali," *International Journal: Canada's Journal of Global Policy Analysis* 68, no. 3 (September 1, 2013): 424–34.

69. "Mali: Des Membres d'Ansar Dine Font Sécession et Créent Leur Propre Mouvement," *RFI*, January 24, 2013.

70. Interview with Malian legal scholar, Bamako, Mali, July 2016.

71. In December 2012, Belmokhtar announced his departure from AQIM and the creation of his own al-Qaeda faction, called the Masked Brigade, which would later merge with MUJWA into al-Murabitoun.

72. "Belmokhtar's Militants Merge with Mali's Mujao," *BBC News,* August 22, 2013.

73. Doward, "How Cigarette Smuggling Fuels Africa's Islamist Violence."

74. Ibid.

75. Shelley, *Dirty Entanglements*, 235; Laub and Masters, "Al-Qaeda in the Islamic Maghreb."

76. Shelley, *Dirty Entanglements*, 235; Dario Cristiani and Riccardo Fabiani, "Al Qaeda in the Islamic Maghreb (AQIM): Implications for Algeria's Regional and International Relations," Instituto Affari Internazaionali, April 2011, 7; Laub and Masters, "Al-Qaeda in the Islamic Maghreb"; J. L. Marret, "Al-Qaeda in Islamic Maghreb: A 'Global' Organization," *Studies in Conflict and Terrorism* 31, no. 6 (2008): 541–52; Jean-Pierre Filiu, "Al-Qaeda in the Islamic Maghreb: Algerian Challenge or Global Threat?" Carnegie Middle East Program, Paper 104, October 2009, 7.

77. Interview with civil society activists from northern Kidal region, Bamako, Mali, July 2016.

78. UNODC, *The Transatlantic Cocaine Market* (Dakar, Senegal: UNODC, 2011); UNODC, *Transnational Organized Crime in West Africa: A Threat Assessment* (Dakar, Senegal: UNODC, 2013); UNODC, *Cocaine Trafficking in West Africa: The Threat to Stability and Development* (Dakar, Senegal: United Nations Office on Drugs and Crime, 2007); Walid Ramzi, "North Africa: AQIM Partners with Colombian Drug Cartel," All Africa, December 5, 2014; "Drug Seizures in West Africa Prompt Fears of Terrorist Links," *The Observer*, November 29, 2009; Juan Miguel del Cid Gómez, "A Financial Profile of the Terrorism of Al-Qaeda and Its Affiliates," *Perspectives on Terrorism* 4, no.4 (2010): 3–27.

79. Interview with civil society activists from northern Kidal region, Bamako, Mali, July 2016.

80. ECOWAS, "The Political Economy of Conflicts in Northern Mali," 3.

81. David Edward Brown, "The Challenge of Drug Trafficking to Democratic Governance and Human Security in West Africa," *The Letort Papers* (Carlisle, PA: Strategic Studies Institute, US Army War College (May 2013), 20–21.

82. Interview with local journalist, Bamako, Mali, July 2016.

83. Interview with civil society activists from northern Kidal region, Bamako, Mali, July 2016.

84. International Crisis Group, "Tunisia's Borders: Jihadism and Contraband," Middle East and North Africa Report No. 148 (Brussels: International Crisis Group, November 2013), i.

85. Interview with local resident, Peshawar, Pakistan, June 2009.

86. Zaffar Abbas, "Pakistan's Undeclared War," *BBC News*, September 10, 2004.

87. C. Christine Fair, "The Militant Challenge in Pakistan," *Asia Policy* 11, no. 1 (2011): 124–25.

88. Hassan Abbas, "A Profile of Tehrik-I-Taliban Pakistan," *CTC Sentinel*, Combating Terrorism Center at West Point, 1, no. 2 (January 2008): 1–4.

89. For a discussion on these insurgencies, see Paul Staniland, *Networks of Rebellion: Explaining Insurgent Cohesion and Collapse*, Cornell Studies in Security Affairs (Ithaca, NY: Cornell University Press, 2014); Jacob N. Shapiro and C. Christine Fair, "Understanding Support for Islamist Militancy in Pakistan," *International Security* 34, no. 3 (January 1, 2010): 79–118; Rasul Bakhsh Rais, *Recovering the Frontier State: War, Ethnicity, and the State in Afghanistan* (Karachi, Pakistan; New York: Lexington Books, 2009).

90. Interview with leading members of the ISI, Rawalpindi and Islamabad, Pakistan, June 2009.

91. Barnett R. Rubin and Ahmed Rashid, "From Great Game to Grand Bargain—Ending Chaos in Afghanistan and Pakistan," *Foreign Affairs* 87, no. 6 (2008): 30–44; Stephen D. Krasner, "Talking Tough to Pakistan: How to End Islamabad's Defiance," *Foreign Affairs* 91 (2012): 87.

92. Catherine Collins, "Financing the Taliban: Tracing the Dollars behind the Insurgencies in Afghanistan and Pakistan," Counterterrorism Strategy Initiative Policy Paper (New America Foundation, 2010).

93. Ibid., 11.

94. Greg Smith, "The Tangled Web of Taliban and Associated Movements," *Journal of Strategic Security* 2, no. 4 (December 2009): 31–38.

95. Haqqani was originally from Paktia province in Afghanistan and developed his powerful insurgent network over the course of the anti-Soviet jihad and Taliban era. Haqqani focused his operations on Afghanistan, while Mehsud led the charge against Pakistani forces.

96. Anand Gopal, Mansur Khan Mahsud, and Brian Fishman, "Inside the Haqqani Network," *Foreign Policy*, June 3, 2010.

97. Mark Mazzetti, Scott Shane, and Alissa J. Rubin, "Brutal Haqqani Clan Bedevils U.S. in Afghanistan," *New York Times*, September 24, 2011.

98. Matthew DuPee, "Afghanistan's Conflict Minerals: The Crime-State-Insurgent Nexus | Combating Terrorism Center at West Point," accessed October 2, 2016, https://www.ctc.usma.edu/posts/afghanistans-conflict-minerals-the-crime-state-insurgent-nexus.

99. Arabinda Acharya, Syed Adnan Ali Shah Bukhari, and Sadia Sulaiman, "Making Money in the Mayhem: Funding Taliban Insurrection in the Tribal Areas of Pakistan," *Studies in Conflict & Terrorism* 32, no. 2 (January 26, 2009): 102; Alexandra Evans, "Taliban Cheers Reopening of NATO Supply Routes," *Foreign Policy*, July 31, 2012.

100. Aram Roston, "How the US Army Protects Its Trucks—by Paying the Taliban," *The Guardian*, November 13, 2009; Douglas A. Wissing, *Funding the Enemy: How U.S. Taxpayers Bankroll the Taliban,* 1st ed. (Amherst, NY: Prometheus Books, 2012).

101. See Gretchen Peters, "Crime and Insurgency in the Tribal Areas of Afghanistan and Pakistan," ed. Dan Rassler (West Point, NY: Combating Terrorism Center at West Point, October 2010).

102. Tim Craig and Haq Nawaz Khan, "Pakistani Taliban Splits into Two Major Groups amid Infighting," *Washington Post*, May 28, 2014.

103. Katharine Houreld and Jibran Ahmad, "Crime Spree Helps Pakistani Taliban Squirrel Away Cash before Raids Begin," *Reuters*, July 10, 2014.

104. Tim Craig and Haq Nawaz Khan, "Pakistani Taliban Leaders Pledge Allegiance to Islamic State," *Washington Post*, October 14, 2014; Saud Mehsud and Mubasher Bukhari, "Pakistan Taliban Splinter Group Vows Allegiance to Islamic State," *Reuters*, November 18, 2014.

105. See the opening vignette and introduction in chapter 2 for details on this prophecy.

106. "ISIL and the Taliban," *Al Jazeera: Special Series,* November 1, 2015.

107. Zia-U-Rahman Hasrat, "IS Runs Timber Smuggling Business in Afghanistan, Officials Say," *VOA*, February 8, 2016; "Islamic State Smuggling Timber into Pakistan, Say Afghan Officials," *Express Tribune*, February 10, 2016.

108. Shamsul Islam, "Active Recruitment: Law Minister Confirms Da'ish Footprint in Punjab," *Express Tribune*, January 5, 2016.

109. Riazul Haq, "In Rare Admission, Pakistan Recognises Growing Presence of Islamic State," *Express Tribune*, February 10, 2016.

110. "Isis Actively Recruiting in Afghanistan, Says US General," *The Guardian*, May 23, 2015.

CHAPTER 9

1. This narrative is based on author interviews and observations, Beqaa Valley, Lebanon, July 2016.

2. Vahid Brown and Don Rassler, *Fountainhead of Jihad: The Haqqani Nexus, 1973–2012* (New York: Oxford University Press, 2013); Anand Gopal, Mansur Khan Mahsud, and Brian Fishman, "Inside the Haqqani Network," *Foreign Policy*, accessed August 15, 2015, http://foreignpolicy.com/2010/06/03/inside-the-haqqani-network/; Michael Semple, "How the Haqqani Network Is Expanding from Waziristan," *Foreign Affairs*, September 26, 2011; Georg Klute, "From Friends to Enemies: Negotiating Nationalism, Tribal Identities, and Kinship in the Fratricidal War of the Malian Tuareg," *L'Année du Maghreb*, no. 7 (December 20, 2011): 163–75; Baz Lecocq and Georg Klute, "Tuareg Separatism in Mali," *International Journal: Canada's Journal of Global Policy Analysis* 68, no. 3 (September 1, 2013): 424–34; Amatzia Baram, "Neo-Tribalism in Iraq: Saddam Hussein's Tribal Policies 1991–96," *International Journal of Middle East Studies* 29, no. 1 (February 1997): 1–31.

3. Farhad Khosrokhavar, *Inside Jihadism: Understanding Jihadi Movements Worldwide* (Boulder, CO: Paradigm Publishers, 2009); Thomas Hegghammer, "The Ideological Hybridization of Jihadi Groups," *Current Trends in Islamist Ideology* 9 (2009): 26–45, 158; Robert Brenton Betts, *The Sunni-Shi'a Divide: Islam's Internal Divisions and Their Global Consequences* (Washington, DC: Potomac Books,

2013); John Turner, "Strategic Differences: Al Qaeda's Split with the Islamic State of Iraq and Al-Sham," *Small Wars & Insurgencies* 26, no. 2 (March 4, 2015): 208–25; Aisha Ahmad, "Going Global: Islamist Competition in Contemporary Civil Wars," *Security Studies* 25, no. 2 (April 2, 2016): 353–84.

4. I credit this particular phrase to Barnett Rubin, who so often reminds his audiences that outside of Afghanistan people talk about religion or ideology, whereas inside of Afghanistan people talk about money.

5. Boaz Atzili, "When Good Fences Make Bad Neighbors." *International Security* (2006/2007): 139–73; Mohammed Ayoob, *The Third World Security Predicament: State Making, Regional Conflict, and the International System* (Boulder, CO: Lynne Rienner, 1995); Michael C. Desch, "War and Strong States, Peace and Weak States?" *International Organization* 50, no. 5 (Spring 1996): 237–68; Jeffrey Herbst, *States and Power in Africa: Comparative Lessons in Authority and Control*, 1st ed. (Princeton, NJ: Princeton University Press, 2000); Robert Jackson, *Quasi-States: Sovereignty, International Relations, and the Third World* (New York: Cambridge University Press, 1993); Cameron G. Thies, "State-Building, Interstate, and Intrastate Rivalry: A Study of Post-Colonial Developing Country Extractive Efforts, 1975–2000," *International Studies Quarterly* 48 (2004): 53–72; Cameron G. Thies, "The Political Economy of State Building in Sub-Saharan Africa," *Journal of Politics* 69, no. 3 (2007): 716–31. Jackson and Rosberg argue that new international laws and norms preserved these failed states, even when there was no empirical justification of their sovereignty. Robert H. Jackson and Carl G. Rosberg, "Why Africa's Weak States Persist: The Empirical and the Juridical in Statehood," *World Politics* (1982): 1–24.

6. Bijan Omrani, "The Durand Line: History and Problems of the Afghan-Pakistan Border," *Asian Affairs* 40, no. 2 (July 1, 2009): 177–95; Amin Saikal, "Securing Afghanistan's Border," *Survival* 48, no. 1 (March 1, 2006): 129–42.

7. Baz Lecocq, "This Country Is Your Country: Territory, Borders, and Decentralisation in Tuareg Politics," *Itinerario* 27, no. 1 (March 2003): 59–78; Markus Virgil Hoehne and Dereje Feyissa, "Centering Borders and Borderlands: The Evidence from Africa," in *Violence on the Margins*, ed. Benedikt Korf and Timothy Raeymaekers, Palgrave Series in African Borderlands Studies (New York: Palgrave Macmillan, 2013), 55–84. In her classic work, Touval argued that these borders would necessarily lead to conflict, a position that evidence now confirms. Saadia Touval, *The Boundary Politics of Independent Africa* (Cambridge, MA: Harvard University Press, 1972).

8. John Gee, "The Ottoman Empire and World War I: It Could All Have Been Very Different . . .," *Washington Report on Middle East Affairs* 33, no. 7 (October 2014): 24, 26; Toby Dodge, "Can Iraq Be Saved?," *Survival* 56, no. 5 (September 3, 2014): 7–20.

9. Youssef Cohen, Brian R. Brown, and A. F. K. Organski, "The Paradoxical Nature of State-Making: The Violent Creation of Order," *American Political Science Review* 75, no. 4 (1981): 901.

10. Charles Tilly, *The Formation of National States in Western Europe* (Princeton, NJ: Princeton University Press, 1975), 42.

11. Ibid.; Charles Tilly, "War Making and State Making as Organized Crime," in *Bringing the State Back In*, ed. Peter Evans, Dietrich Rueschemeyer, and Theda Skocpol (Cambridge: Cambridge University Press, 1985), 169–91.

12. Charles Tilly, *Coercion, Capital, and European States: AD 990–1992* (Oxford: Blackwell, 1992).

13. For a discussion on the challenges and successes of these measures, see Anne L. Clunan, "The Fight against Terrorist Financing," *Political Science Quarterly* 121, no. 4 (December 1, 2006): 569–96; Aimen Dean, Edwina Thompson, and Tom Keatinge, "Draining the Ocean to Catch One Type of Fish: Evaluating the Effectiveness of the Global Counter-Terrorism Financing Regime," *Perspectives on Terrorism* 7, no. 4 (August 27, 2013): 62–78. See also Marieke de Goede, *Speculative Security: The Politics of Pursuing Terrorist Monies* (Minneapolis: University of Minnesota Press, 2012); Nicholas Ryder, *The Financial War on Terrorism: A Review of Counter-Terrorist Financing Strategies since 2001* (New York: Routledge, 2015); Thomas J. Biersteker and Sue E. Eckert, *Countering the Financing of Terrorism* (New York: Routledge, 2007).

14. Guy Ben-Porat, "Between Power and Hegemony: Business Communities in Peace Processes," *Review of International Studies* 31, no. 2 (April 2005): 325–48; Nissim Cohen and Guy Ben-Porat, "Business Communities and Peace: The Cost-Benefit Calculations of Political Involvement," *Peace & Change* 33, no. 3 (July 1, 2008): 426–46; Timothy L. Fort and Cindy A. Schipani, *The Role of Business in Fostering Peaceful Societies*, reissue ed. (Cambridge: Cambridge University Press, 2011).

15. Robert F. Worth, "U.N. Says Somalis Helped Hezbollah Fighters," *New York Times*, November 15, 2006.

16. Harry Verhoeven, "The Self-Fulfilling Prophecy of Failed States: Somalia, State Collapse and the Global War on Terror," *Journal of Eastern African Studies* 3, no. 3 (2009): 405–25.

17. Muhammad Qasim Zaman, *Modern Islamic Thought in a Radical Age: Religious Authority and Internal Criticism* (New York: Cambridge University Press, 2012); Alvi Hayat, "The Diffusion of Intra-Islamic Violence and Terrorism: The Impact of the Proliferation of Salafi/Wahhabi Ideologies," *Middle East Review of International Affairs* 18, no. 2 (2014): 38–50.

18. For a detailed discussion of the differences between Salafist and Wahhabist traditions, and the diversity within them, see Joas Wagemakers, "The Enduring Legacy of the Second Saudi State: Quietist and Radical Wahhabi Contestations of Al-Wala' Wa-l-Bara'," *International Journal of Middle East Studies* 44, no. 1 (February 2012): 93–110; Joas Wagemakers, *A Quietist Jihadi: The Ideology and Influence of Abu Muhammad Al-Maqdisi* (New York: Cambridge University Press, 2012); Frederic Wehrey, "Saudi Arabia's Anxious Autocrats," *Journal of Democracy* 26, no. 2 (2015): 71–85.

19. Mohamed Nawab Bin Mohamed Osman, "Hizb Ut-Tahrir," in Shahram Akbarzadeh, ed., *Routledge Handbook of Political Islam* (New York: Routledge, 2012), Chapter 8.

20. Bob Woodward, *Bush at War* (New York: Simon & Schuster, 2002), 153.

21. Michael R. Gordon, "Fateful Choice on Iraq Army Bypassed Debate," *New York Times*, March 17, 2008; Davide Mastracci, "How the 'Catastrophic' American Decision to Disband Saddam's Military Helped Fuel the Rise of ISIL," *National Post*, May 23, 2015.

22. "Libya UN Resolution 1973: Text Analysed," *BBC News*, March 18, 2011; Justin Morris, "Libya and Syria: R2P and the Spectre of the Swinging Pendulum," *International Affairs* 89, no. 5 (September 1, 2013): 1265–83.

23. Ernesto Londoño and Greg Miller, "CIA Begins Weapons Delivery to Syrian Rebels," *Washington Post*, September 11, 2013.

24. For the debate on the R2P doctrine, see Robert A. Pape, "When Duty Calls: A Pragmatic Standard of Humanitarian Intervention," *International Security* 37, no. 1 (July 1, 2012): 41–80; Gareth Evans, Ramesh Thakur, and Robert A. Pape, "Correspondence: Humanitarian Intervention and the Responsibility to Protect," *International Security* 37, no. 4 (2013): 199–214; Roland Paris, "The 'Responsibility to Protect' and the Structural Problems of Preventive Humanitarian Intervention," *International Peacekeeping* 21, no. 5 (October 20, 2014): 569–603; Robert A. Pape, "Response to Roland Paris Article," *International Peacekeeping* 22, no. 1 (January 1, 2015): 9–10.

25. Koran, Surah al-Furqan, verse 25:63.

APPENDIX

1. See, e.g., Carolyn Nordstrom and Antonius C. G. M. Robben, eds., *Fieldwork under Fire: Contemporary Studies of Violence and Survival* (Berkeley: University of California Press, 1995); Carolyn Nordstrom, *A Different Kind of War Story* (Philadelphia: University of Pennsylvania Press, 1997); Susan Thomson, An Ansoms, and Jude Murison, eds., *Emotional and Ethical Challenges for Field Research in Africa: The Story behind the Findings* (New York: Palgrave Macmillan, 2013); N. Patrick Peritore, "Reflections on Dangerous fieldwork," *American Sociologist* 21, no. 1 (1990): 359–72; Marie Smyth and Gillian Robinson, eds., *Researching Violently Divided Societies: Ethical and Methodological Issues* (London: UN University Press and Pluto Press, 2001); Julie Van Damme, "From Scientific Research to Action in Southern Kivu: Ethical Dilemmas and Practical Challenges," in Susan Thomson, An Ansoms, and Jude Murison, eds., *Emotional and Ethical Challenges for Field Research in Africa* (London: Palgrave Macmillan, 2013), 84–95; Elizabeth Jean Wood, *Insurgent Collective Action and Civil War in El Salvador* (New York: Cambridge University Press, 2003), chaps. 2 and 3; Elizabeth Jean Wood, "The Ethical Challenges of Field Research in Conflict Zones," *Qualitative Sociology* 29 (2006): 373–86.

2. On ethnography in Political Science, see Lisa Wedeen, "Reflections on Ethnographic Work in Political Science," *Annual Review of Political Science* 13, no. 1 (2010): 255–72; G. Baiocchi and B. T. Connor, "The *Ethnos* in the *Polis*: Political Ethnography as a Mode of Inquiry." *Sociology Compass* 2 (2008): 139–55; L. Bayard de Volo, "Participant Observation, Politics, and Power Relations: Nicaraguan Mothers and U.S. Casino Waitresses," in *Political Ethnography: What Immersion Contributes to the Study of Power*, ed. Edward Schatz (Chicago: University of Chicago Press, 2009), 217–36; Edward Schatz, ed., *Political Ethnography: What Immersion Contributes to the Study of Power* (Chicago: University of Chicago Press, 2009); Charles Tilly, "Afterword: Political Ethnography as Art and Science," *Qualitative Sociology* 29 (2006): 409–12.

3. Intra-Hawiye clan competition defines much of the political landscape in Mogadishu and considerable effort was made to include respondents from a range of Hawiye sub- and sub-subclan groups. I also interviewed leading CEOs from non-Hawiye clans, including the Darod and Isaaq.

4. This survey is the first and largest of its kind; two previous studies have presented simple statistical data based on smaller samples of the Mogadishu business community, but these researches provide descriptive statistics rather than regression analyses. See Stig Jarle Hansen, "Civil War Economies, the Hunt for Profit and the Incentives for Peace (The Case of Somalia)," in *AE Working Paper*, 2007; and Roland Marchal, "A Survey of Mogadishu's Economy" (European Commission/Somali Unit [Nairobi]), (August 2002).

5. A number of scholars have successfully managed to conduct surveys in failed states. See, e.g., Jason Lyall, Kosuke Imai, and Graeme Blair, "Explaining Support for Combatants during Wartime: A Survey Experiment in Afghanistan," *American Political Science Review* 107, no. 4 (2013): 679–705.

6. With respect to investigating the role of clan politics in business, it would be ideal to collect exhaustive survey data on the clan identities of all the major shareholders from all of the large countrywide corporations across Somalia, rather than relying on self-reporting by the CEOs of these corporations. Unfortunately, such an investigation would have raised a number of ethical and security concerns, as these businesses do not readily disclose the details of their internal organizational structures.

7. Aisha Ahmad, "The Security Bazaar: Business Interests and Islamist Power in Civil War Somalia," *International Security* 39, no. 3 (January 1, 2015): 89–117.

8. Supplementary Materials for Aisha Ahmad, "The Security Bazaar: Business Interests and Islamist Power in Civil War Somalia," *International Security* 39, no. 3 (Winter 2014/15): 89–117, are available at https://dataverse.harvard.edu/dataverse/AhmadSomDat2015.

9. On ethnography as data, see Lee Ann Fujii, "Five Stories of Accidental Ethnography: Turning Unplanned Moments in the Field into Data," *Qualitative Research* 15, no. 4 (2015): 525–39. See also Luca Jourdan, "From Humanitarian to Anthropologist: Writing at the Margins of Ethnographic Research in the Democratic Republic of

Congo," in Susan Thomson, An Ansoms, and Jude Murison, eds., *Emotional and Ethical Challenges for Field Research in Africa* (London: Palgrave Macmillan, 2013), 12–26.

10. Sarah M. Brooks, "The Ethical Treatment of Human Subjects and the Institutional Review Board Process," in *Interview Research in Political Science*, ed. Layna Mosley (New York: Cornell University Press, 2013), 45–66; Lee Ann Fujii, "Research Ethics 101: Dilemmas and Responsibilities," *PS: Political Science and Politics* 45 (2012): 717–23; Wood, "Ethical Challenges of Field Research in Conflict Zones"; and the essays of Susan Thomson, An Ansoms, and Jude Murison, eds., *Emotional and Ethical Challenges for Field Research in Africa* (London: Palgrave Macmillan, 2013),

11. See Lino Owor Ogora, "The Contested Fruits of Research in War-Torn Countries: My Insider Experiences in Northern Uganda," in Susan Thomson, An Ansoms, and Jude Murison, eds., *Emotional and Ethical Challenges for Field Research in Africa* (London: Palgrave Macmillan, 2013), 27–41.

12. On ethnography in social science, see Peregrine Schwartz-Shea and Dvora Yanow, eds., *Interpretive Research Design Concepts and Processes* (New York: Routledge, 2012).

13. Wood, "Ethical Challenges of Field Research in Conflict Zones"; and Thomson, Ansoms, and Murison, *Emotional and Ethical Challenges for Field Research in Africa.*

14. On consent of informants, see Lauren MacLean, "The Power of the Interviewer," in Layna Mosley ed., *Interview Research in Political Science* (Ithaca, NY: Cornell University Press, 2013), 67–83, see in particular 73–76; Susan Thomson, "Academic Integrity and Ethical Responsibilities in Post-Genocide Rwanda: Working with Research Ethics Boards to Prepare for Fieldwork with 'Human Subjects,'" in Thomson, Ansoms, and Murison, *Emotional and Ethical Challenges for Field Research in Africa*, 139–54; Wood, "Ethical Challenges of Field Research in Conflict Zones," 379–81.

15. See Melani Cammett, "Using Proxy Interviewing to Address Sensitive Topics," in *Interview Research in Political Science*, ed. Layna Mosley (New York: Cornell University Press, 2013), 124–43.

16. See, e.g., MacLean, "Power of the Interviewer"; Smyth and Robinson, *Researching Violently Divided Societies*; Suruchi Thapar-Björkert and Marsha Henry, "Reassessing the Research Relationship: Location, Position and Power in Fieldwork Accounts," *International Journal of Social Research Methodology* 7, no. 5 (2004): 363–81.

17. See, e.g., Tey Meadow, "Studying Each Other: On Agency, Constraint and Positionality in the Field," *Journal of Contemporary Ethnography* 42, no. 4 (2013): 466–81; Candice D. Ortbals and Meg E. Rincker, eds., "Symposium: Fieldwork, Identities, and Intersectionality: Negotiating Gender, Race, Class, Religion, Nationality, and Age in the Research Field Abroad," *PS: Political Science and Politics* 42, no. 2 (2009): 287–328; Shahnaz Khan,

"Reconfiguring the Native Informant: Positionality in the Global Age," *Journal of Women in Culture and Society* 30, no. 4 (Summer 2005): 2017–35; Lauren MacLean, "The Power of the Interviewer," in Layna Mosley, ed., *Interview Research in Political Science* (Ithaca, NY: Cornell University Press, 2013), 67–84; Jill McCorkel and Kristen Myers, "What Difference Does Difference Make? Position and Privilege in the Field," *Qualitative Sociology* 26, no. 2 (June 2003): 199–231.

18. On the value of both insider and outsider perspectives in research, see, e.g., Heike Becker, Emile Boonzaier, and Joy Owen, "Fieldwork in Shared Spaces: Positionality, Power and Ethics of Citizen Anthropologists in Southern Africa," *Anthropology Southern Africa* 28, nos. 3–4, (2005): 123–32; Hale C. Bolak, "Studying One's Own in the Middle East: Negotiating Gender and Self-Other Dynamics in the Field," *Qualitative Sociology* 19, no. 1 (1996): 107–31; Robyn Dowling, "Power, Subjectivity and Ethics in Qualitative Research," in *Qualitative Research Methods in Human Geography*, ed. I. Hay (Melbourne: Oxford University Press, 2000), 19–29; Sharan B. Merriam, Juanita Johnson-Bailey, Ming-Yeh Lee, Youngwha Kee, Gabo Ntseane, and Mazanah Muhamad, "Power and Postionality: Negotiating Insider/Outsider Status within and across Culture," *International Journal of Lifelong Education* 20, no. 5 (2001): 405–16; Patricia O'Connor, "The Conditionality of Status: Experience-Based Reflections on the Insider/Outsider Issue," *Australian Geographer* 35, no. 2 (2004): 169–76.

19. For a continued discussion on positionality, see MacLean, "Power of the Interviewer"; Lorna Gold, "Positionality, Worldview and Geographical Research: A Personal Account of a Researcher Journey," *Ethics, Place and Environment* 5, no. 3 (2002): 223–37; Richa Nagar with Farah Ali and the Sangatin Women's Collective, "Collaboration across Borders: Moving beyond Positionality," *Singapore Journal of Tropical Geography* 24, no. 3 (2003): 356–72.

20. On gender in fieldwork, see, e.g., T. Arendell, "Reflections on the Researcher-Researched Relationship: A Woman Interviewing Men," *Qualitative Sociology* 20, no. 3 (1997): 341–68; Sandra Meike Bucerius, "Becoming a 'Trusted Outsider': Gender, Ethnicity, and Inequality in Ethno-Graphic Research," *Journal of Contemporary Ethnography* 42, no. 6 (September 2013): 690–721.

21. Some examples of my publications for a local audience include: Ahmad, "Islamic Movements in Afghanistan and Somalia: A Comparison," *Policy Perspectives* (Institute for Policy Studies—Pakistan), August 2009; Ahmad, "Talking to the Enemy: Strategies for Initiating Peace Negotiations in Afghanistan," *Policy Perspectives* (Institute of Policy Studies—Pakistan); Special Edition on Afghanistan, March 2007; I. Farah, A. Ahmad, and D. Omar, "Cross Border Weapons Proliferation in the Horn of Africa: The Case of Mandera, Kenya, Melkasufta, Ethiopia, and Bula Hawa, Somalia," in *Controlling Small Arms in the Horn of Africa and the Great Lakes Region* (Waterloo: Project Ploughshares, 2006); Ahmad, "Disarmament, Demobilisation, and Reintegration in Afghanistan: The ANBP, Post-Conflict Peacebuilding, and Warlords," *Journal of Afghanistan Studies* (December 2004).

22. On the challenges of reciprocity, see, e.g., Christina R. Clark-Kazak, "Research as 'Social Work' in Kampala? Managing Expectations, Compensation and Relationships in Research with Unassisted, Urban Refugees from the Democratic Republic of the Congo," in Thomson, Ansoms, and Murison, *Emotional and Ethical Challenges for Field Research in Africa*, 96–106; Lauren MacLean, "The Power of the Interviewer," in Layna Mosley ed., *Interview Research in Political Science* (Ithaca, NY: Cornell University Press, 2013), 75–76; Marie D. Price, "The Kindness of Strangers," *Geographical Review* 91, nos. 1–2 (January–April 2001): 143–50.

Index

Page numbers in *italics* indicate images and maps. Numbers followed by *t* or *f* indicate tables or figures, respectively.

support for Jamiat-i Islami, 246n63

support for mujahideen, 32–38, 46, 240n14

support for Somalia, 103, 145, 263n51

Universal Declaration of Human Rights, 194

university education, 135–138, 137t, 138f, 139

UNOCAL-Delta oil pipeline, 86

USC. *See* United Somali Congress

'ushr, 71, 86, 89–90, 248n84, 254n63

USSR. *See* Union of Soviet Socialist Republics

Uzbek faction, 62, 66, 74, 149, 249n94

violence, 194

ethnic, 65–66, 149

extremist, 145, 147

genocidal, 65, 166, 246n64

jihadist, 145–159

resurgence of, 150

sexual, 66–67, 166

against women, 65–67, 121, 246n64, 249–250n7, 267n34

voluntary taxes, 140, 189

Wahhabis. *See* Islam

waqf (charitable trust), 55, 248n80

war economy, xv–xvi, 1, 119–120, 196, 242n26

warfare

drone strikes, 158, 179, 181

effects on agriculture, 31

guerrilla, 37, 149

warlord-parliamentarians, 117–118, 260n58

warlords. *See also specific individuals*

definition of, xxi–xxii, 224nn20–21

economic interests, 7, 25–26, 107, 188, 259n41

foreign support for, 150

local, 65

political alliances, 10–11, 237n39

Somalia Reconstruction and Restoration Council (SRRC), 116

warlord taxes, 128–132, 135–138, 137t, 138f, 225n22

protection fees, 131–132

security costs, 5–6, 23–26, 264n60

weapons trade. *See* arms trade

Weinstein, Jeremy, 8

West Africa, 161

WFP. *See* World Food Programme

women

in khat industry, 261n10

in research, 207, 217, 283n20

treatment of, 71, 121, 144, 149–150, 166, 246n64, 247n76, 249–250n7, 267n35

violence against, 65–67, 121, 249–250n7, 267n34

World Food Programme (WFP), 105–106

xeer (Somali customary legal code), 101

xenophobia, 21

Yazidis, 166

The Year of Unity 1433, 156

Yousaf, Mohammad, 33, 38, 49, 241n17

Yusuf, Abdullahi, 116–117, 124, 154, 260n58, 270n64

Zadran, Maulavi Sardar, 180–181

Zaeef, Abdul Salam, ix, 67–69, 76, 81–84, 87, 91, 147–148, 267n30

zakat, 71, 86, 89–90, 135, 169–170, 248n87, 254n63

Zaman, Haji, 75

Zangawat, Afghanistan, 69

al-Zawahiri, Ayman, 165

Zhawara, Afghanistan, 33–34